Skira Dictionary of Modern Decorative Arts. 1851–1942

Valerio Terraroli

Skira Dictionary of Modern Decorative Arts 1851–1942

Graphic Concept
Marcello Francone

Editing
Emanuela Di Lallo

Layout
Monica Temporiti

Translation
Susan Wise

Iconographic Research
Massimo Zanella

First published in Italy in 2001 by
Skira Editore S.p.A.
Palazzo Casati Stampa
via Torino 61
20123 Milano
Italy

Printed and bound in Italy.
First edition

ISBN 88-8491-025-0

Distributed in North America and
Latin America by Rizzoli International
Publications, Inc. through St. Martin's
Press, 175 Fifth Avenue, New York,
NY 10010.
Distributed elsewhere in the world by
Thames and Hudson Ltd., 181a High
Holborn, London WC1V 7QX,
United Kingdom.

Introduction

On May 1st, 1851, back in the London of Queen Victoria's youth, at the opening of the World Fair, an event the Prince consort Albert and Henry Cole had energetically implemented, contemporaries immediately realised they were witnessing a crucial moment of the nineteenth century. For the first time, the technical means of the entire industrialised world were placed beside the so-called "fine arts", on the one hand, and articles of decorative art, embodying an everlasting tradition of craftsmanship, on the other. Indeed the situation is even more striking if we are aware that Joseph Paxton's Crystal Palace erected in Hyde Park, a paean to the most advanced technologies of iron and glass, presented strictly Romantic-style paintings and sculpture alongside furnishing and decoration items featuring the most daring, spectacular eclectic and historicist imagination, ranging from neo-gothic to neo-medieval, from neo-rococo to neo-Renaissance, next to utterly modern creations, such as curved steel furniture produced by the Viennese firm Thonet, clearing the way to the forthcoming alliance between artisanal design and industrial mass-production.

It was not until the advent of the late-symbolist mood, with the development of modernist stylistic trends, but above all with the concept of art as a model and an instrument of change in society, of art for everyone, art as life, that the decorative arts recovered their role, on the theoretic level, as a product possessing an intrinsic artistic value. The peremptory claim, although in open contradiction with cultural and market realities, was that the new style, modernism — in Italy called liberty, in France and Belgium art nouveau, in Germany Jugendstil, in Mitteleuropa Secession — would lead to modernity and to the overall evolution of society through architecture and the decorative arts viewed as reproducible, connected with everyday life and housing, detached from the figure of the creator-artist, beautiful but no longer unique, exclusive and inimitable. In France the two world fairs, on the occasion of the centennial of the Revolution (Paris, 1889) and of the dawning of the twentieth century (Paris, 1900), openly sanctioned forms, models and finalities belonging to international modernism, whereas in Italy the 1902 International Exhibition of Turin represented the acme of the Italian and European decorative and industrial arts, fully acknowledging the notion of dignity and artistic value of the industrial arts, yet illustrating all the while the decline of the creative phase and of the inventive and most ideological blossoming of theoretic modernism, and of liberty in particular. The outbreak of the First World War, the collapse of the *belle époque* illusions, the hard-won economic-industrial recovery converged with a profound transformation in the decorative arts, with the use of precious, unique forms and materials, while experimenting mass-production of aesthetically valid items on the industrial level. "Faced with the new school's iconoclastic rationalism, that sentences us to live surrounded by relentless expressions of usefulness without the least ornamental embellishments, we plead for the gift of a touch of beauty, to soften, enhance, and ennoble the harshness of everyday life with the smile of the divine, the one and only indispensable superfluity" (Margherita Sarfatti in the introduction to the Italian pavilion at the 1925 Paris expo). In Europe and the United States, the 1920s and 1930s were the years of the rise and decline of the Arts Déco, and Novecento style. Actually deco was not a style, since it did not present an ideology justifying it on a theoretic level, nor feature socially useful aims, nor intend to alter productive structures. Instead it was the dispassionate, elegant expression of a middle- and upper-middle class that wished to erase the memory of the tragedy of the First World War along with the political-social clashes of the 1910s. Yet deco taste was not a return to the past, or at least not in an imitative sense, but was bred on meaningful cultural references: its genetic code, for a large part, passed down the modernist legacy, but in its strictest, sparest Central-European version, that is, of the Vienna or Munich Secessions, revisited in light of the ironic, playful spirit of futurist creations and cubist graphics. Simultaneously, the deco manner blended the lively taste for exoticism typical of European culture since the eighteenth century, and therefore a fondness for *chinoiseries* and *japonaiseries*, with a revival of the extreme refinement, we might even say gratuitousness in its preciousness, of "Louis-Quinze" style. Deco culture equally bore influences and inspirations drawn from important archaeological finds: Tutankhamen's tomb, Aegean civilisations (Cretan and Cycladic), and for the United States in particular, the unearthing in the Yucatán of Mayan sites and the Aztec pyramids of Teotihuacán.

Technological acceleration, the demands of the international market, the use of new materials, the theoretic, experimental attitudes of laboratories like the Bauhaus of Dessau, decisively directed the decorative arts toward industrial production, as evidenced also by the exhibitions of the Monza Biennales (1923, 1925, 1927, 1930), that in 1930 precisely became the Milan Triennales devoted to the decorative and industrial arts. The colossal E42 project in Rome, that fascism wished to bring about for its worldwide promotion and that was never carried out, marked to a certain extent the close of a historic phase of Western civilisation, where architecture and the decorative and/or industrial arts combined the aesthetic formal values of supreme craftsmanship, of the most rigorous artistic sensibility, with the operational means of industry. Following the Second World War, industrial design would put an end to the century-old dispute between art and industry, between art and everyday life, as well as to the organisation and justification of world fairs, at least in their self-referential and celebrative modalities arisen from 1851 London, with its magnificent opportunities and promises of progress for humanity owed to new technologies and their applications to everyday life.

The *Skira Dictionary of Modern Decorative Arts* takes stock of over a century of artistic creations in the field of modern age decorative arts, in Europe and the United States, in connection with changes of taste and style: beginning with the first World Fair held in London in 1851 up to the definitive trend of the market and production toward industrial design after the Second World War and especially since the early 1950s.

Under nearly one thousand concise headings, the *Dictionary* offers readers and scholars, but also collectors and anyone interested in the arts, precise data, technical indications, stylistic and individual traits of artists and manufactories, of decorative arts forms and models, from Biedermeier up to the production of industrial design. The headings, arranged in alphabetical order, survey a multiple series of typologies, including glass and stained-glass, majolica, porcelain, furnishings, fabrics, silverware, jewellery, metals, plastics, crystals, enamels, classified by executive techniques and materials, manufactories and laboratories, artists, craftsmen and designers, typologies of style and taste.

An appendix contributes to a more thorough coverage and especially to a more effective use of the *Dictionary*: the graphic reproduction of potteries' and porcelain manufactories' trademarks, signatures and trademarks of artists and laboratories, active in Europe and the United States, and a bibliography *raisonné* of references, classified by issues and typologies.

My heartfelt gratitude goes to the publishing firm Skira and to Massimo Vitta Zelman who believed in and backed this project, to Emanuela Di Lallo who edited it with the utmost care, with Doriana Comerlati and Alessandra Montini, to Massimo Zanella, who enthusiastically helped in the iconographic research, and to the photographer Marco Rapuzzi.

My affectionate thanks to all my colleagues and friends who with their discerning comments and precious advice contributed to enhance the quality of the work, and in particular to Luciano Colantonio, Paola Franceschini, Paola Venturelli, Marco Arosio, Giorgio Servadei.

Special, fond thoughts go to Andreina and Lorenzo whose patience and commitment sustained and assisted in this exacting yet gratifying task, the eventual omissions and errors of which should be attributed exclusively to myself.

Valerio Terraroli
Milan, June 2001

Acid cutback glassware. Technique referring to glass processing with acid and belonging to glassworks art production; thus named in the United States, where Frederick → Carder developed it at the → Steuben Glass Works in 1932. The technique uses etching processes, transferring by printing (or etching) a drawing onto the surface of a vase or a glass article, using a wax-base ink; after the reserved surface has been protected with wax, the piece is soaked in acid. The result recalls cameo-glass, being two layers of contrasting coloured glass material or else a single layer with a hand- or transfer-etching on the outer, usually lighter coloured, surface.

Acid etching. Technique allowing to obtain decorations on the surface of glass by the use of hydrofluoric acid, and that can range from the shallowest incision to deep hollowing. The item is coated with resin or wax or a linseed oil impasto, then proceeding with the etching using a metal stylus until the glass surface is reached; it is then soaked in a mixture of water, acid and potassium fluoride; the depth of the incision is directly proportional to the time the item is exposed to corrosion. The technique, invented in 1771, was not commonly practiced until the middle of the nineteenth century, but it was in France, with Emile → Gallé, that it would be widely applied, in order to obtain relief etching, and in Bavaria, at Zweisel, for producing the "iced" effect on the surfaces. In Bohemia at the turn of the century experiments were made to produce a type of decoration by applying a thin layer of coloured glass on a colourless glass article so as to give, with etching, a greater relief to the design. In 1871, in the United States, Benjamin Tilgham of Philadelphia patented the → sandblasting method for executing outlined designs.

Adams, English potters. The name identifies three different family branches working in Anglo-Saxon pottery production during the nineteenth century. The first refers to William Adams (1748–1831), a native son of Brick House, whose production is not known to be particularly significant, whereas a second strain relates to William Adams (1772–1829), born in Stoke, who produced flow-blue ware for the United States market, a series pursued by his son William (1798–1865). Another William Adams belongs to the third group: born in Greengates, after being a disciple of → Wedgwood, he specialised in the production of creamware and particularly in groups of household pottery imitating Wedgwood dark blue jasper models; his activity was sustained by his son Benjamin (who died in 1820). The headquarters of the William Adams and Sons company is at Tunstall and Stoke (Staffordshire), where it is documented since 1769 and still active today, after having been taken over by Wedgwood in 1966. Renowned for the high quality of its products, especially the blue and white pottery inspired from porcelain imported from China, during the twentieth century it produced mostly toilet articles and tableware, with printed motifs drawn either from eighteenth-century models or historical subjects (the 1913 *Shakespearian Series* or the *Cries of London* ones are famous), but equally juvenile tableware with Victorian-style themes and country scenes, flower or fruit compositions on a cream-coloured base, and lustre-glaze items.

Adams & Company. United States glassworks active in Pittsburgh by 1851 and up until 1889, it replaced the Stourbridge Flint Glass Works, a laboratory John Robinson founded in 1823. Specialising in crystal glassware and moulded glass tableware, over the years the company diversified its production, offering etched glass and cut glass, and later on → *opaline* (milk glass) furnishings and household items.

Adderley. English pottery opened at Longton (Staffordshire) in 1906, then become Joined Ridgway Potteries in 1947, and today still active within the Royal Doulton Group. It produces pottery and porcelain sets for hotels and restaurants (known as *Steelite China*) adorned with printed floral subjects, but equally items for children like the 1939 *Zoo Alphabet*.

Pietro Maccaferri, railing on a design by Giuseppe De Col (for Aemilia Ars), iron, 1902. Bologna, Museo Davia Bargellini

Adularia. Semi-precious stone also called "moon-stone", with pale, transparent hues, used in → art nouveau style jewellery.

Aemilia Ars. Artisanal firm founded in Bologna in 1898, it was backed by a group of shareholders headed by count Francesco Cavazza and artists connected with the eclectic architect Alfonso Rubbiani (1848–1913), including Alfredo Sezanne, Gigi Bonfiglioli, Achille Casanova and Giuseppe De Col, to establish a centre promoting the principal crafts of Emilia and offering designs and projects, not just by the founding artists but also by the craftsmen themselves, selected in a yearly contest (the first was issued in March 1899). In 1900 the company became a joint-stock cooperative, opened its own store, but failed to take part in the Paris fair that year, whereas its presence at the 1902 Turin fair was significant, and highly successful. During that period it merged with the embroidery and lace firm founded in 1901 by countess Lina Bianconcini Cavazza and Carmelita Zucchini, who had anonymous local workers reproduce antique laces from their collections; with the merger new items appeared also, by the artists Pasquinelli, Alfredo Tar-

tarini and Rubbiani himself. Despite the Turin success, owed to the variety of items displayed and the quality of the creations (including Sezanne's glass vases and Dudovich's posters), in 1903 the company decided to limit production to antique handmade embroidery and lace, and in 1904 in Florence proceeded to sell all the other items it had produced. The models, drawn also from sixteenth- and seventeenth-century embroidery books, were quite famous all over the world (exhibited at Saint Louis in 1904 — on that occasion Mrs. Vanderbilt ordered a magnificent tablecloth embroidered with peacocks — at Liege in 1905, Milan in 1906 and Brussels in 1910) and were reproduced in decorative arts reviews (for instance in *The Studio* in 1914).

Agate. Glass technique developed by Louis Comfort → Tiffany around 1895 whereby the artist sought to reproduce in glass the natural streaks of the agate stone. The method consists of melting in the melting-pot various opaque-coloured glasses, and stirring them to obtain streaks; then, withdrawn from the fire to prevent the colours from blending, the glass is glazed. In case the surface turns black, the glass paste is cut and glazed from the inside so as to enhance the effect of the streaks; when it takes on a typical brown-red colour the glass paste is called "metal glass". In 1887 for the → New England Glass Company Joseph → Locke patented *agate glass*, that is, the item is completely or partly coated with a metal-base colour, then sprayed with a liquid which on evaporating leaves shiny spots on the surface, then definitively made fast by annealing.

Air-locks / Air-traps. Glass technique Benjamin → Richardson patented in 1857 that consists of introducing in the glass paste air bubbles arranged so as to form a decorative motif, usually with a criss-cross, lozenge, diamond or else round (called *obnail* motif) pattern. The glass is blown into a mould with spikes arranged in the desired pattern, then a second layer of blown glass traps the remaining air in the locks; sometimes the piece can be further enhanced with a third layer of opaque white or coloured glass, → glossed by being soaked in acid, with etched decorations.

Alabaster. A material used since antiquity either for making sculptures and decorative elements, or for furnishings. In modern times it had a particularly important phase in Volterra (Italy), because of the presence of a number of laboratories and the local Art Institute, beginning in the mid-eighteenth cen-

Umberto Borgna workshop, potiche vase, alabaster with gold highlighting, 1930. Volterra, Istituto Statale d'Arte

tury and especially between 1791 and 1799 with the Inghirami workshop. During the nineteenth century, especially in connection with the eclectic taste and the revival of period styles, alabaster production increased, mainly for export. At that time the elaborate candelabras carved by the Viti e Tangassi laboratories were produced, in 1865 for Maximilian of Hapsburg, emperor of Mexico (they can be seen today at Volterra in Palazzo Viti), and the countless series of boxes and tables imitating sixteenth-century Florentine inlays, or yet again neo-gothic clocks and souvenirs of the principal monuments of Florence. Giuseppe Bessi and his laboratory introduced, within the traditional production of decorative alabasters, floral and explicitly → liberty elements both in busts of maidens or groups of *putti* or mothers and children and in → art nouveau vases. Ruggero Martini, in the mid-1920s, was the author of exotic or broadly orientalising echoes featured in monumental table lamps supported by figures of odalisques, followed by the *Dancers* from the Rossi e Castellucci firm, the Bessi laboratory and especially Umberto Borgna. It was precisely Umberto Borgna, but Ottorino Aloisio, Mario Urbani and architect Bruno La Padula as well, who produced the finest, most popular → art deco creations of the Volterra alabaster firms, that may be seen in the vases, ribbed, perforated and etched, in the little animals, the groups of *pulcinella* and jazz musicians and classical theatre masks, often enhanced by gilding and with explicit references to pottery (in particular the forms created by Gio → Ponti for → Richard-Ginori), to decorative stuccoes (especially Alfredo → Biagini) and to glass (including Guido → Balsamo Stella's etchings and Carlo → Scarpa's models for → Venini).

Alba Docilia. Italian pottery that takes its name from the Latin designation for Albisola; founded in 1919 by the turner Adolfo Rossello on returning from an apprenticeship in Naples, it became a co-operative in 1923 and in 1924 the property of the Rossello family. Run by the painter Mario Gambetta, the company endeavoured to revive classical → Albisola majolica ware by using models from the eighteenth- and nineteenth-century Chiodo and Levantino laboratories, but revisited with an → art deco stylisation: by 1923 the decorations *a mézzero* (imitating woven woolen shawls with large flowers) and orientalising motifs insured Alba Docilia's success at the Monza Triennales. *(Pl. 1)*

Albini, Franco (1905–77). Italian architect and designer. He opened his own studio in Milan in

1930, ran "Casabella" (1945–46), taught architecture in Venice and Turin (1949–63). In furnishings he offered highly modern solutions for his day, from the transparent portable radio in 1938 (never produced) to the *Room for a man* (1936, for the VI Triennale), and the tensile-structure bookshelf/divider (1939).

Albisola. Name of a group of Italian manufactories working in the Savona area by the seventeenth century; of particular interest, the laboratories of the Grossi family (from 1641 to 1698), with the lantern trademark, and of Bernardo Corradi, and between the eighteenth and the early nineteenth centuries the Levantinos' production, mainly tableware with sketch-like decorations drawn from subjects found in Alessandro Magnasco's paintings. In modern times, the Albisola factories underwent a fundamental revival in the early twentieth century, with the opening and conversion of several furnaces for making art pottery. In 1903 Giuseppe Mazzotti's laboratory opened, then in 1919 → Alba Docilia, created by the turner Adolfo Rossello, in 1920 the firm M.A.S. (Maioliche Artistiche Savonesi) run by Dario Ravano (to which the painter Ivos Pacetti and the decorator Roggiapane contributed); again in 1920 → La Casa dell'Arte was formed by Guido Barile, Giuseppe Agnino and the painter Manlio Trucco, just back from Paris and who in 1922 opened La → Fenice, later taken up by Ernesto Daglio. In the Mazzotti factory Giuseppe's sons, Tullio and Torido, combined Albisola pottery with Marinetti's conceptions; this connection with futurism led to a production, newer in decoration than in form, presented at the 1925 Paris fair. Tullio d'Albisola, in particular, in 1927 contacted Filippo Tommaso Marinetti, with Bruno Munari and Nino Strada, for precise — even theoretic — instructions on how to transform pottery along futurist lines. The results of this collaboration were publicised in 1929 at the exhibition *Thirty-three Futurists* in the Milanese Galleria Pesaro; their association went on for a decade, involving the presence of about forty artists in twenty official futurist exhibitions. Later on, in 1938, the theoretic manifesto *Ceramics and Aeroceramics*, signed by Marinetti and Tullio d'Albisola, was published in Turin on the *Gazzetta del Popolo*. *(Pl. 4)*

Alcock Henry Pottery. English pottery, established at Cobridge (Staffordshire) in 1910 and closed in 1935, producing tableware either in white paste or with → *cloisonné* decoration on a coloured background, that in the 1920s revived Pratt's multicoloured prints created after 1840.

Allerton. English pottery active at Longton (Staffordshire) between 1859 and 1942, specialising in the creation of tableware and children's toys, among which the famous *Noah's Ark*, produced in 1926.

Aller Vale Art Pottery. English pottery active at Torquay (Devon) from 1887 and closed down in 1962, producing decorative items and tableware with floral motifs and pastoral scenes; in 1904, the *Crocus* model was the first of a series of vases, containers and *cache-pots* drawn from typically → art nouveau themes and styles: flowered stalks, crocus corollas and polychrome tulips were executed on extremely refined blue or black grounds. In 1934 several groups of mosaic pottery with bright blue hues and overlaid lighter patterns were created.

Aller Vale Art Pottery, vase of the Crocus *series, polychrome pottery, ca. 1910*

Altare. Italian glassworks located in the Savona hinterland, active since the tenth century owing to the presence of French or Belgian glass masters. Their peak occurred in the fifteenth and sixteenth centuries (the statutes of the Altare Glass Corporation date from 1495 to 1793), a period in which they greatly benefitted by the freedom to export — even their techniques — totally unknown in Murano factories. Altare glassmaking families (Protti, Dagna, Saroldi and → Bormioli) spread their products and processing techniques worldwide, but in their homeland their decline by the early nineteenth century was such that only five furnaces were still running; however, the creation of the → S.A.V. (Società Artistico-Vetraria) revived production in tune with the international modern style and, later on, with that of the 1920s and 1930s. The local Glass Museum, connected with the Institute for the Study of Glass and the Art of Glass, conserves a collection documenting exclusively nineteenth- and twentieth-century productions, since for the earlier centuries it is impossible to certify the provenance, whether from Altare furnaces or from potteries "in the style of". Activity goes on today on both the industrial and the artisanal level, in which Savona designers take part.

Guido Andlovitz (for Società Ceramica Italiana di Laveno), potiche vase, pottery decorated with chinoiseries, 1925–26

Amberg. German pottery, founded in 1759 in Bavaria by Simon Hetzendörfer, specialising in the production of white majolica household tableware, occasionally with polychrome decorations. In 1790 the factory began producing cream-yellow majolicas, and during the nineteenth century reproducing models of Ludwigsburg porcelain; it closed down in 1910. The trademark consists of the coupling of two letters of the name: "AB".

Amberg, Adolf (1874–1913). German sculptor and designer trained in Berlin and Paris, who from 1894 to 1904 designed ornamental objects and silverware for the Bruckmann & Sohn factory of Heilbronn: the monumental silvered fountain dubbed *German Music*, realised with architect Otto Rieth for the 1900 Paris World Fair, dates from that period. Between 1904 and 1905, for the → Berlin porcelain factory, Amberg modelled countless figures — male and female — drawn from exotic themes, for a monumental centrepiece called *Wedding Procession. (Pl. 18)*

Amberina. A type of American glass, used between 1883 and 1920, that when blown or poured into a mould takes on the colour of amber, but during reheating becomes bright red owing to the gold specks in the glass paste; if heating continues, the colour turns to purple. It is a glass that has various shades, ranging from amber at the bottom to bright ruby at the top.

Amourette. Exotic wood used in marquetry because of its very hard texture.

Amstelhoek. Dutch pottery founded in Amsterdam in 1897 by Willem Christiaan Hoeker, extended in 1900 with a division for producing furniture and a workshop for metal items, all conceived for an inexpensive market. In pottery the firm offered dark-coloured vases and bowls with white inlays, brown vases with blue decorations and small animal-shaped vases with white inlays on dark grounds. In 1903 it went bankrupt, although still producing earthenware under the trademark Voorheen Amstelhoek until 1907, when it was taken over by the majolica firm Haga, which then in 1910 merged with the larger De Distel plant.

Andlovitz, Guido (1900–65). Italian potter trained in Venice and devotee of the antique classical pottery conserved in the museums of Grado and Aquileia, he joined the Società Ceramica di → Laveno with which he began collaborating in 1923, giving its pottery and earthenware production a new artistic bent and design marked by his Central European tradition, where ties with the Viennese Secession and French influences blended with reminiscences of rococo and Eastern hints, owed to his Venetian experience, and later on with late-futurist accents as well. Receptive to the most varied novelties from the Italian and French artistic spheres, he drew from them a personal, rather original inspiration that he applied to limited series of pottery and porcelain, as well as to household ware produced at Laveno. His favourite themes were neo-eighteenth-century and French traditional forms, featuring a subtle, elegant graphism in the floral motifs, and cubo-futurist geometric forms. White or ivory pottery with polychrome figures and vases decorated with pastoral scenes or relief geometric elements are typical of his production during the 1930s. With the Società Ceramica Italiana he took part in all the Monza Biennales and the Milan Triennales. *(Pls 5 and 60)*

Andolfato, Francesco (b. 1924). Italian glass-etching master who gave his name to a workshop opened in 1953 in Venice, specialising in the etching of eighteenth-century-style mirrors and decorative items; he attended several Venice Biennales (1962 and 1968) with glass articles which were executed on designs by the painter Mirko Casaril. In 1990 the firm closed down its traditionally classical-style activity.

André, Alfred (1839–1919). French goldsmith, employed by a number of collectors, such as the Rothschilds, restoring damaged Renaissance jewellery and enamelled items; he introduced countless fakes on the market, designed and executed in his workshop, considered for a long time to be original Renaissance or Limoges school articles. André was also associated with F. Spitzer, engaged in producing and selling period items acquired even by the Victoria and Albert Museum of London (where collections of drawings from André's workshop were also conserved).

André, Emile (1871–1933). French architect and designer, active in Nancy, where he returned after a series of trips to Egypt, Tunisia and Italy, first as architect associated with Eugène Vallin, then as professor of applied arts and architecture, with Emile → Gallé, at the → Nancy School, and furniture designer with a marked → art nouveau style.

Angell, Joseph II (ca. 1816 – ca. 1891). English silversmith who in 1849 inherited a leading London silverware workshop; he is known especially for the precious silver casket adorned with medallions featuring the portraits of Anthony and Cleopatra (London, Victoria and Albert Museum) and the rich series of silver items including trays, centrepieces and vases decorated with chiseling, reliefs and enamels, admired at the 1851 London fair.

Angyal, Béla (1847–1928). Hungarian designer trained in Vienna and active in landscape painting, he is known for the outstanding series of designs for pottery items, but equally for his lace creations, for which he renewed the traditional Magyar pillow lace repertory, creating with his sister Emma the Professional Lace School of Körmöcbánya, producing by 1880 items successfully shown in international events.

Antimacassar. Term first referring to an oil used in the production of hair brillantine, and that defined, in the late nineteenth century, a crocheted white cotton cover used to protect the arms and back of armchairs from direct contact with the seated person's arms and head.

Antonelli, Elia (1887–1951). Italian potter, he taught from 1922 until the Second World War in the professional school of Cascina, and in the first three Monza Biennales, directed by → Cambellotti, exhibited small animals and decorative items in painted and glazed terra cotta, obtaining a fair success.

Apátfalva. Hungarian pottery, formed in 1836 to produce bricks, but in the early twentieth century, under the name "Zsigmond Nagy earthenware factory", created earthenware decorative vases with folklore motifs and multicoloured majolica flowers, using for the first time the trademark "Made in Hungary". The firm was active until 1928.

Apati, Abt Sandor (1870–1916). Hungarian pottery designer, trained in Budapest and Munich, from 1898 to 1908 he worked for the → Zsolnay pottery of Pécs, designing decorative items, statuettes, plates, pottery for architecture and also one-offs, like the very handsome → glossed vase with the female nude appearing at the mouth, shown in Turin in 1902.

Apt. French pottery founded in the city of the same name by César Moulin and kept in the family until 1852. The most well-known tableware of the various factories in Apt is a brown and yellow marbled type of pottery, as well as figurines, single or in groups, and household items. The most renowned plants in the nineteenth century were those of La Veuve Arnoux and Elzéar Bennet.

Arabia O.Y. Finnish pottery founded in 1874 right outside Helsinki as a branch of the Swedish firm → Rörstrand, that held majority control over the factory up to 1916, although it had already operated independently since 1884. Beginning in 1895, with the stock of models and designs by Thure Oberg (1871–1935) and Alfred William → Finch (1854–1930), Arabia produced a noteworthy series of → art nouveau vases that were exemplary in the Finnish artistic tradition. In 1922 the factory underwent a radical transformation, specialising during the 1930s in the production of household tableware with utterly modern forms. In 1946 Kaj Frank became head designer, opening the way to the collaboration of many art potters like Toini Muona, Ulla Procopé and Kyllikki Salmenhaara. The factory is still active today. (Pl. 2)

Aretini, Zulimo. Italian potter, belonging to a family of potters from Monte San Savino, first working for → Richard-Ginori and the → Fornaci di San Lorenzo, then on his own at Arezzo and Perugia (here as art director of the Fontivegge factory). Aretini remained faithful to the Umbria-Arezzo pottery tradition, reviving executive techniques of the past with modern décors: graffito, relief, scratched and perforated, successfully exhibiting in the Monza Biennales and the Milan Triennales.

Argental. Term used by the Compagnie de Verrerie et Cristallerie de → Saint-Louis, working in the Alsace-Lorraine region (German territory from 1871 to 1918) to sign certain items either as "Saint-Louis-Munzthal" or as "D'Argental" (the French placename for "Munzthal").

Argy-Rousseau, Gabriel (1885–1953). French glassmaker known for having created a clear vitreous paste as resonant as crystal, precisely called → pâte de cristal, used for making lamps, lampshades, pendants and brooches, incense burners and vases decorated with → art nouveau style floral motifs, that in the mid-1920s were reduced to elegantly rhythmed and stylised forms. In 1914 for the first time he took part in an exhibition, in 1919 created a series of enamelled perfume bottles, in 1921 with Gustave-Gaston Moser-Millot opened the shop *Les Pâtes de Verre d'Argy Rousseau* employing dozens of workers. In 1928 he made a series of glass paste sculptures designed by Marcel Bourraine, but the crash of 1929 led to a decline in production and the glassworks closed down; the artist then began working on his own, making commissioned plaques on religious subjects and angular vases with striped, bright, jewel-like coloured surfaces. *(Pl. 3)*

Ariel. Ornamental glass processing technique used by Edvin Öhrström at the → Orrefors Glasbruk by 1936. It is a variant of → *eglomisé* glass, in which air bubbles forming figurative or abstract motifs are introduced.

Arkinstall & Sons. English pottery active at Stoke (Staffordshire), between 1903 and 1925, known mainly for its production of souvenirs.

Arneudo, Eugenio (active between 1881 and 1930). Italian cabinet-maker and renowned upholsterer from Turin, inventor of a couch-bed and period "Louis-Quinze" and "Louis-Seize" furniture acclaimed at the 1898 Turin fair. In 1902, still in Turin, he presented along with mechanical couch-beds a dining-room in modernist style. From 1905 to 1924 he ran the Turin professional school for upholsterers.

Arpels, Julien (1884–1951). French jeweller, co-founder with his brother Charles (1880–1951) and his cousin Alfred → Van Cleef (1873–1938) of the Maison Van Cleef & Arpels in Paris in 1906, first for cutting and selling precious stones, then with the arrival in 1921 of his younger brother Louis (1886–1976), for the creation of jewellery that was highly successful at the 1925 fair. In 1926 the artistic direction was taken over by René Van Cleef Puissant (1897–1942) who hired René-Sim Lacaze as designer, active between 1922 and 1939 (famous for his Egyptian-style ribbon bracelets). In 1935 the new trademark bore the column of Place Vendôme and the mark "V.C.A."; in the same year a new shop in Montecarlo was opened, in 1939 in New York. The firm is still active.

Arrasene. Typical nineteenth-century silk, wool or chenille thread for embroidery.

Art deco. Definition of a taste, rather than a style, that received its worldwide consecration at the 1925 Paris *Exposition des Arts Décoratifs et Industriels*. The expression refers to the type of products presented in that exhibition (furnishings, furniture, art items) as well as the taste they expressed. Also called "1925 style", it appears to have its roots in the international Modern Movement, sprung from the floral stock of the Franco-Belgian

Deco-style auditorium of the Wiltern Theater, Los Angeles, 1930

Gustavo Pulitzer, deco-style jewel-box, walnut wood, zebra-wood and rosewood with maple inlays, 1927

Mauboussin, deco-style pendent watch, platinum, crystal, baguette diamonds and cabochon lapis-lazuli, 1925

→ art nouveau and Italian → liberty styles, but especially recognisable by the linearity and graphism derived from the Austrian and Munich Secession, yet in a more opulent version and with the use of precious materials, eliminating the typically modernist dynamic aspects, preference for asymmetry and wavy lines. It appeared with its special features right after the First World War throughout Europe, but particularly in France, with the founding of the Compagnie des Arts Français Süe et Mare, and the activity of outstanding cabinet-makers and decorators such as → Ruhlmann and → Rateau, and in Austria with the Viennese workshops' evolution (→ Wiener Werkstätte) toward deco style under the manager Josef → Hoffmann. In Italy deco taste was especially asserted during the four Monza exhibitions (1923, 1925, 1927, 1930), owing to the presence of significant personalities like Gio → Ponti, the designer for porcelain and pottery for → Richard-Ginori, Emilio → Lancia and Tomaso → Buzzi for furnishings, Alfredo → Ravasco for jewellery, Duilio → Cambellotti, Guido → Balsamo Stella and the → Venini glassworks. The rise of rationalism and the crash of 1929 led to the swift decline of an openly ornamental, refined, precious and hedonistic taste. In the United States deco taste became quite popular both in architecture (the Chrysler Building in New York) and in interior

decorating, especially for film-theatres and theatres, also subject to the influence of far-eastern, Hispanic, occasionally neo-eighteenth-century, but Egyptian, Central American, Russian and African elements as well. Distinctive features of the deco repertory include abstraction, distorsion and formal simplification drawn from the experiments of the artistic avant-gardes (cubism, Russian constructivism, futurism), along with the favourite themes of stiffened, schematised floral elements, youthful figures of modern women, zig-zag, snake and arrow movements, spiral and shell-shaped elements, triangles, small squares, groups of stars, wavy lines, borrowed from the secessionist tradition, and a great display of gold, silver, precious marbles. The Arts Déco movement strived for the preservation of the handsome, refined, important and exclusive item and the defence of a rich, exuberant standard of decoration as opposed to the strict, bare notions of the various rational-functional schools. *(Pls 6 and 81)*

Art Furniture Company. English laboratory that made furnishings on designs by E.W. → Godwin between 1860 and 1870. The definition also includes a whole series of furniture, based on architects' designs, where the reaction against eclectic furniture, a sort of neo-rococo taste in dark, massive woods, was explicit; instead simple, austere forms were sought, enhanced by the use of oak and walnut with their unvarnished veins used as decoration. The presence of ornament reveals a first connection with neo-medieval, and then Japanese tradition, authentic forerunners of → Arts & Crafts furnishings.

Art nouveau. Definition, generally speaking, concerning the set of historical-artistic features that, between the last decade of the nineteenth century and the very first years of the twentieth, characterised architecture, decorative arts, fashion and part of the figurative production in Europe and the United States. Reviews, exhibitions and especially the big world fairs contributed to spreading this style that coincided with the middle-class demand for novelty at the time of its spectacular economic and political promotion, expressing it in a common idiom — notwithstanding national variations — immediately recognisable despite its different names: art nouveau, precisely, in the French-speaking countries, modernism in Spain, → liberty or floral style in Italy, → Jugendstil in Germany, Sezessionstil in Austria and the Hapsburg

Victor Horta, art nouveau interior of Solvay house in Brussels, 1894

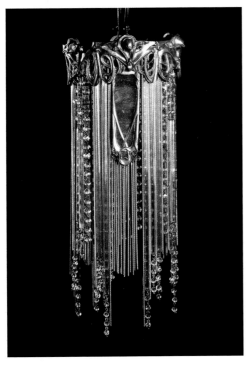

Hector Guimard, art nouveau pendant, gilt bronze, glass and brass, ca. 1909. Paris, Musée d'Orsay

empire, the modernist style presented itself as a controversial reaction to academic tradition and to nineteenth-century eclectic, imitative taste, choosing for its inspiration not history, but nature reinvented with an emphasised linearity, highly metamorphic and having an explicit decorative intention. Essential to the aesthetic theorising of international modernism was the concept of design unity, which in architecture concerned the flowing, interchangeable relationship between inside and outside spaces and a substantial design-stylistic consistency between structure, decoration and furnishing. In the decorative arts it was expressed by the renovated quality of any designed item, harmony between function and chosen form, the possibility of serial reproduction with the ideal aim of making art for everyone, and therefore a radical change in housing and taste. The alliance between art and industry became an essential factor of the movement, particularly in Germany owing to the experience of the crafts schools and multi-functional workshops in Munich and Dresden (the Vereinigte Werkstätte für Kunst im Handwerk, created in 1897–98, and the Deutscher Werkbund, founded in 1907), and in Vienna (the → Wiener Werkstätte, opened in 1903), setting the theoretic and applied basis for industrial design. *(Pls 7 and 8)*

Arte della Ceramica. Italian pottery opened in Florence by Galileo → Chini (art director), Giovanni Vannuzzi, Giovanni Montelatici (potters) and Vittorio Giunti (technical director) in 1896, producing utterly modern pieces, inspired by → art nouveau models and that met with immediate success at the 1898 Turin fair. The arrival of Galileo's cousin, Chino Chini, in 1897, and later on of the sculptor Domenico Trentacoste, explains the additional production of small pottery sculptures for furnishings. The trademark, first two tiny hands, in 1898 (and up to 1909) became a pomegranate, appearing on the more traditional pieces, or on the pottery with drippings or articles in gres in a special grey colour with cobalt blue decorations.

Artel. Association of Bohemian artists active between 1908 and 1934 with the aim to counter serial industrial production, encouraging quality and style in everyday items. Not having its own laboratories, the association ran a store where it sold other factories' productions, and took part in the 1923 exhibition in Monza, in Prague in 1924 and, with painted glass, in the Paris exposition of 1925.

Galileo Chini (for Arte della Ceramica), vase with trees and butterflies, glazed polychrome majolica, 1903–04

Artigas José (b. 1892). Potter of Spanish origin working from 1924 in Paris, where he was known for some particularly refined, unadorned ceramics. It was not until the 1930s that he began to work with several painters to decorate his ceramics, in particular with Raoul Dufy and Joan Miró.

Arts & Crafts. A store opened in The Hague in 1898 for the sale of furnishings and decorative items of either Dutch or foreign make, but all strictly modernist in style; in 1900 Chris Wegerif became art director, and immediately concentrated on furniture made by the firm, hiring Dutch cabinet-makers and producing its own batik fabrics, created by his wife Agatha Gravestein. The factory-store closed down in 1904.

Arts & Crafts Movement. Group of artists and craftsmen formed around 1880, based on the conceptions William → Morris and John Ruskin ex-

pressed about the equality of the different arts, the aim to connect art with life and idea with deed; notions that materialised in the furnishing of the Morris house at Upton, the so-called "Red House" designed by Philip → Webb in 1859, where each detail was studied in its morphological and functional aspects. In 1860 Morris opened the Morris, Marshall, Faulkner & Co. shop in London to produce and sell everyday items, interior furnishings and furniture designed and made by artists, whereas in 1888 he began to organise applied art exhibitions conceived and produced by the Arts & Crafts Movement: worth mentioning is the elegant cabinet-writing desk designed in 1893 by George → Jack, in walnut with inlaid paler wood figuring thistle flowers and leaves, oak foliage and acorns, rendered not just in a naturalistic style but with a marked care for the decorative value of the enveloping, soft lines. *(Pl. 9)*

Ashbee, Charles Robert (1863–1942). English architect, pupil of G.F. Bodley, he became the main organiser of the → Arts & Crafts Movement, embodying one of the most significant moments of the clash with Victorian tradition: an admirer of Frank Lloyd → Wright, whom he met in 1901, he told about it in the introduction to a monographic study devoted to the American architect published in Berlin by 1911. In 1915 he left England for Cairo, as English lecteur at the university. Designer, creating furnishings and works in silver, as well as the author of numerous publications, in 1888 he founded the Guild and School of Handicraft at Toynbee Hall, in the London East End, for which he designed a group of modern furniture, barer than the ones → Morris designed for Glasgow. During the same period he was engaged in making items in metal and silver, in thoroughly → art nouveau style but without giving in to the slightest decorative naturalism; such items, produced by his school as well, met with noteworthy success in exhibitions in Paris, Dusseldorf, Vienna and Munich. In 1891 the school moved to Essex House, in the Mile End of London, and in 1902 to Chipping Campden, where it changed its name to School of Arts and Crafts, remaining active from 1904 to 1914: during that period Ashbee strived to revive the English tradition of craftsmanship and agriculture. His most well-known book appeared in 1909, *Modern English Silverwork*.

Ashby Potter's Guild. English pottery, opened at Woodville (Derbyshire) in 1909 and closed in 1922, active in the production of earthenware and

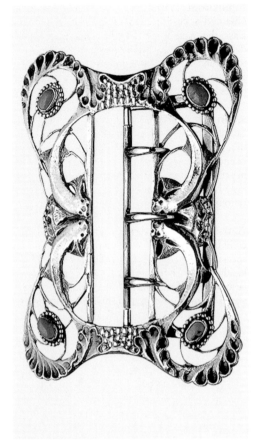

Charles Robert Ashbee (for Guild and School of Handicraft), belt buckle with fish, silver and turquoises, 1897. Cheltenham, Cheltenham Art Gallery and Museum

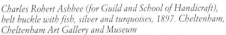

Ashby Potter's Guild, vase, pottery and coloured enamels, ca. 1912

art pottery objects. Associated with the designer Thomas Camm and using the glazed colours produced by Pascoe Tunnicliffe, under the brand "Vasco Ware" the pottery won prizes in Brussels (1910) and Turin (1911). Vases, bowls, biscuit dishes, tobacco boxes, cakestands, inkstands, candelabras and liturgical articles were made in dark blue and dark green pottery, with an Eastern flavour, using → *aventurine* and as of 1913 a *flambé* decoration.

Ashtead Potters. English pottery, active at Ashtead (Surrey) between 1923 and 1935, producing furnishing items, tableware and figurines, backed by leading designers such as Allan Wyon and Joan Pyman. Inspired by either more explicitly → art deco forms or more architectural ones in the

→ Wedgwood Group. Specialising in the creation of table sets and household tableware, it stands out by the special influence of Eastern subjects: mostly floral themes, printed in blue or red on a white ground.

Atterbury & Company. United States glassworks founded in Pittsburgh in 1859, mainly producing blown and printed tableware.

Aubusson. Term encompassing a group of tapestry laboratories, developed between Clermont-Ferrand and Limoges in the early sixteenth century, characterised by the fact that their production did not come from organised factories but household workshops. The finest and most famous tapestry products were the furniture upholstering decorated with illustrations drawn from La Fontaine's fables, from drawings after contemporary etchings and from *Seascapes* from the school of Vernet. During the nineteenth century production of the series executed in the seventeenth and eighteenth centuries was resumed; in 1939 a new production unit opened, based on cartoons provided by contemporary artists like Jean → Lurçat, Lucien Coutaud, Raoul Dufy, Graham Sutherland and Marc Saint-Saëns: the colour range was greatly simplified, and inspired by medieval tapestries and Central American traditional ethnic fabrics.

Auger, Georges (1864–1935). French goldsmith who after restoring in 1900 the firm his father Alphonse had founded in 1862 (La Maison Auger), began to produce some of the most famous jewellery of the → art nouveau era, besides book bindings, bowls and decorative swords.

Ault Faïence / Ault Potteries. English pottery of Derbyshire, founded in 1887 and closed down in 1974, renowned for the production of kitchen and table ware, toilet articles, mantelpieces and furnishings, including vases, boxes and *cache-pots*; at first inspired by → Arts & Crafts and later by naturalistic → art nouveau style, it met with a great success at the 1896 Chicago world's fair.

Aurene. Type of → iridescent glass used by Frederick → Carder for the → Steuben firm by 1904, very similar to → Tiffany's → *favrile* glass: the colour is obtained by combining metal and non metal glasses, onto which a solution of stannous chloride is sprayed, giving a velvety sheen to the brown, red, gold, blue and green colours.

A.VE.M. Glass works opened in 1932 at Murano by Antonio Luigi Ferro under the name Arte Vetraria Muranese, that produced refined processings of Venetian glass updated to twentieth-century taste, like the blown glass designed by Vittorio ⋅ Zecchin and the sculptures conceived by the master glassmaker Emilio Nason. In 1939, under the art direction of Giulio Radi, the production of polychrome items with cased silver and gold leaf was introduced. From 1952 to 1955, the director being Giorgio Ferro, the painter Luigi Scarpa Croce worked with the factory, making the series of *Morbidi sommersi*, as well as Anzolo Fuga, who designed large abstract compositions in → milk glass and → *murrines*. The firm is still operating.

Aventurine. Amber-coloured, gold-mottled glass, obtained by casting copper specks into the molten glass; the name is owed to the randomness of the discovery, that occurred at Murano between the sixteenth and seventeenth centuries; it was remarkably popular during the nineteenth and twentieth centuries.

Avon Art Pottery. English pottery, opened at Longton in 1930 and closed down in the early sixties, that produced furnishings, knick-knacks, vases and containers, teapots, fruitstands, dessert sets in one or more colours, aligned on the "thirties'" taste both in the forms and geometric-style decorations.

Aynsley John & Sons. English pottery, founded in Longton in 1864 and independent until 1970, specialising in the production of celebrative objects, handpainted figurines and animals, table sets; for the latter during the 1930s the decoration was mainly abstract, inspired by the German Secession style.

B

Baccarat. One of the best-known French glass and crystalware trademarks, created in 1764 by Monseigneur de Montmorency-Laval, bishop of Metz, who, under the protection of Louis XV, set up a glassworks at Baccarat, a small town close to Lunéville, so as to be able to use the vast resources of the nearby woods for its furnaces. The works was first run by Antoine Renault, under the name Verreries Renault et Cie, then after 1768 Verreries de Baccarat and from 1773 Verreries de Sainte-Anne, owed to the small chapel raised inside the sheds dedicated to the glassmakers' patron saint. At first it produced English-style soda glass for household use and industry; in 1802 the factory was handed down to the Renault heirs and in 1806 to Lippmann-Lippmann. In 1816 the firm was taken over by the Belgian industrialist Aimé-Gabriel D'Artigues (1778–1848) who, transferring his Voneche factory from Namur there, and with permission of Louis XVIII, erected a building for producing crystal glass and a second one for decoration of the new firm Verreries de Voneche à Baccarat. In 1823 the firm, taken over by other owners, assumed the present name of Compagnie des Cristalleries de Baccarat and began producing → *agate* glass, → *opalines* and alabastrine glass. In 1846 one of its most celebrated productions took off: → *millefiori* glass and → paperweights. Baccarat signed its own pieces more frequently than other firms (with the initial "B", in reference to the two craftsmen, both named Battestine, followed by the year — this occurring particularly between 1846 and 1849), and produced bright-coloured items with flowers, fruit, reptiles and butterflies, sometimes on a rocky background, or else the "saturation" type, with close-set glass canes containing corollas and stylised animal profiles. The creation of *sulfures* (opaque glass used for etching medals and cameos and then placed inside transparent glass) goes back to 1848. From 1851 to 1858 under the art direction of Jean-Baptiste Toussaint it began producing coloured glass, and from 1867 to 1883 under Paul Michaut using wheel-etching. Baccarat's leading products were the drinking services created for Louis XVIII (1823), Charles X

(1828), Louis-Philippe (1839–40) and the *Empire* set (gold-trimmed) from the *Harcourt* series (six ovate sides on a hexagonal foot and stem and facetted knob). Present from 1855 at the great world fairs, Baccarat showed pieces in wheel-etched glass, imitating sixteenth-century Milanese crystal, and by 1867 → acid etched glass. Beginning in the 1920s the factory produced, mostly on Georges Chevallier's designs, extremely thin crystals with an exceptional resonance, paying more attention to form than to the traditional nineteenth-century elaborate decoration. Moulded blown glass bottles adorned with portraits (from 1824) were executed at the Trélon branch. *(Pl. 10)*

Baccarini, Domenico (1883–1907). Italian potter active at Faenza, he founded a coterie of art devotees, with Rambelli, → Melandri, → Nonni, Guerrini and Testi. After studying in Florence, in 1902 he returned to Faenza and began making pottery for the Fabbriche Riunite. He spent some time in Rome in 1903, then resuming his activity in Faenza with the → Minardi brothers factory, making works featuring late-romantic, pre-Raphaelite themes, then switching to → liberty style in small domestic scenes and groups with children.

Bacchus George & Sons. English glassworks in Birmingham, specialising in coating objects in coloured glass; it was one of the first to practice decals onto glass (as of 1809).

Bachmetov. Russian glassworks founded in 1763 at Nikol'skoe, near Saint Petersburg, and specialising in coloured glass; in 1790 it was divided in three workshops that by 1802 mass-produced sheet glass, household items and dishware. In 1808 the factory was successful enough to compete with European imports, producing in turn opaque, opalescent and coloured glass with inserted medallions, and crystal items. After 1861 the factory went into a slump; in 1884 it was taken over by prince Obolensky, who gave it a fresh start, launching the industrial production of elegant perfume bottles.

Baillie, Scott (1865–1945). English architect and designer; on his own by 1893 he received a number of commissions from Poland, Russia, Switzerland, the United States, England and Germany. His masterpiece was the furnishing of the palace built at Darmstadt for the grand duke Ernst Ludwig von Hessen (1898), executed by the Guild of Handicrafts, with solid, "streamlined" furniture, adorned with a combination of → art nouveau naturalistic inspiration and Secession geometric lines.

Bakalovitz E. & Söhne. Austrian glassworks, active since the early twentieth century, known for its production of → iridescent glass items designed by R. Bakalovitz Graz (owner of the labortory), the architect Josef → Hoffmann and the designer Koloman → Moser, in keeping with → art nouveau models but in a plainer, stricter version; as well as small furniture like its black wood, nickel and glass tea table, designed by Gisela Falke von Lilienstein and shown at the 1902 Turin exhibition.

Bakalovitz E. Söhne. A store for the sale of glass items opened in Vienna in 1845 and which in 1891, owing to the founder's son Wilhelm, initiated a close collaboration with the glassworks, collaborating in particular from 1899 to 1904 with a large group of artists, including → Hoffmann, Koloman → Moser, Jutta Sika, Leopold Bauer, and after 1906 Joseph Maria → Olbrich and Otto → Prutscher, offering graphic designs for the most part executed by the Mery's Neffe and → Lötz Witwe manufactories (the latter in 1900 began also producing for Bakalovitz metal supports for lamps and chandeliers). Between 1904 and the outbreak of the First World War the store turned to → iridescent glass and etched glass.

Bakewell's Glass Work. United States glassworks founded in 1808 at Pittsburgh by Benjamin and Edward Ensell; in 1813 it joined up with another factory called Pittsburgh Flint Glass Manufactory. If the first production dealt mainly in bottles, pitchers and flasks, alongside with flint glassware, in 1810 it also began producing etched, then coloured and ground glass. It became known for the creation of a table set for the White House during Monroe's presidency (1817) and a group of historical flasks with cameo portraits of famous citizens placed on the base. Active until 1882.

Ball, Tompkins & Black. Important silverware firm opened in New York in 1839, after having taken over Marquand & Co. in 1801, specialised in tableware and gift items very similar to → Tiffany's; after Erastus Tompkins retired in 1851, by 1876 the factory, still active, took the name Black, Starr and Frost. Among the designers who worked for the New York firm John Chandler Moore deserves mention, for a magnificent neo-rococo silver teapot (New York, The Metropolitan Museum of Art).

Ballin, Mogens (1871–1914). Danish designer, painter and ironwork master; initially strongly influenced by the Nabis and Paul Gauguin, he subsequently decided to give up painting for ironwork. In 1899 he founded an important workshop in Copenhagen, where two of the most famous modern Danish sculptors, Rhode and → Jensen, worked; here a series of silver items, jewellery, vases and lamps in silver and → pewter based on French → art nouveau models was produced.

Balsamo Stella, Guido (1812–1941). Italian glass etcher and designer, from Murano, from the start he devoted himself to the decorative arts, soon beginning to take part in the Brera Biennales in Milan (1902) and Venice. As of 1905 he studied in Munich, where he was in touch with Secession artists, and by 1914, in Sweden, began etching on glass and crystal following the example of the → Orrefors manufactory, with techniques he was to introduce in Italy, where he returned right after the war. Trained in the Prague and the → Wiener Werkstätte modernist style, during his stay in Florence (1918–22) he made drawings for blown glass produced by the Vetreria Artistica → Barovier, then, in collaboration with the Bohemian etcher Franz Pelzel, created at Colle Val d'Elsa the Laboratorio Balsamo di Firenze for producing thick-walled crystal and etched Venetian blown glass with classical themes revisited in → art deco style. In 1925 he opened his own workshop on Giudecca, that lasted just a few months; then, still with Pelzel, he entered → S.A.L.I.R., the Venetian factory that adopted Balsamo Stella's style throughout the 1930s, during which, in 1926, the two became its art and technical directors (for Balsamo Stella up to 1931). In 1930 at Monza he displayed a series of works illustrating modernism (jazz musicians, divers, masked figures, mermaids), but as of 1929 he ran there the Istituto Superiore Industriale e Artistico (I.S.I.A.), remaining until 1932: at that time he created a series of furniture in which motifs belonging to the glass tradition can be found, applied in relief onto the flat surfaces, with profiled edges or coloured wood inlays. *(Pl. 11)*

Baratti, Bruno (b. 1911). Italian potter, in 1926 he joined the workshop of the Pesaro potter Pietro Ciccoli, who followed the classicising, traditional trend of the → Molaroni factory, and up to 1938 he also produced there subjects drawn from Novecento painting, such as the 1937 *Risveglio* dish.

Barbe, Jules. French designer specialising in enamel decoration and gilding glass items; after the 1878 Paris fair he was hired in London by Webb & Sons for the Dennis Glasswork, where he worked, around 1880, on decorating sets in → *burmese* glass for the court of Queen Victoria.

Barbedienne, Ferdinand (1810–92). French furniture-maker, but also very famous bronze-caster in the Paris of Napoleon III and friend of sculptors like Barye. After forming a company with Achille Collas in 1839, he opened in 1847 his own casting workshop in Paris, employing up to three hundred associates and artists, including → Carrier-Belleuse, producing bronze copies of sculpture, original sculptures, silverware and items, eclectic and especially neo-Renaissance and "Louis-Seize" period furniture. In 1850 he won the commission to decorate the formal halls in the Paris Hôtel de Ville with furniture copied after the Italian Renaissance. By the eighties, inspired by the vogue of Chinese and Japanese curios, he marketed bronze imitations of far-eastern items, such as the bronze and → *champlevé* enamel vase with lion heads shown in 1862 (London, Victoria and Albert Museum). He became world famous in 1851, when at the London fair he showed an ebony and bronze bookcase with posts carved by Clesinger imitating sculptures by Ghiberti and Michelangelo. *(Pl. 12)*

Barbetti. Italian cabinet-makers working in Florence and inventors of Italian neo-Renaissance furniture. The founder of the laboratory was Angiolo (1805–73), originally from Siena, who in 1841 opened the workshop in Florence, producing sculpture and cabinet-work, for which he was one of the first craftsmen to use machines. He took part in the first world fairs (London, 1851; Paris, 1861; Vienna, 1873) and made the monumental organ at Villa Demidoff and the furnishings for Villa Favard in Florence (around 1860). His son Rinaldo (1830–1904) began his own career as a goldsmith to later enter his father's workshop, making a fabulous library for the Rothschild Palace in London and the furnishings for the President's cabinet at the Chamber of Deputies of Montecitorio (1882). Fol-

lowers of the Barbetti's workshop artisanal tradition were Francesco Morini, Egisto Gaiani, Luigi and Angiolo Faloni.

Barbini, Alfredo (b. 1912). Italian master glassmaker, after his apprenticeship with the → S.A.I.A.R. Ferro Toso firm and the Società Anonima Vetrerie e Cristallerie of Murano, he met the sculptor Napoleone → Martinuzzi of the → Zechin Martinuzzi factory who urged him to work with solid glass and produce sculptures. Promoted to master in the → V.A.M.S.A. factory in 1937, he stayed on until 1944; in 1946 he became art director of Gino → Cenedese & C. and took part in the 1948 Venice Biennale with several large → corroded glass sculptures. In 1950 he opened a glassworks in his own name where, along with his son, he is still active.

Barker Bros. English pottery, active in Longton from 1876 to 1981, known for the production of kitchenware and juvenile tableware (the ware inspired by the *Daily Mail* comics, made in 1919, is especially well-known), usually on a white ground.

Barlows. English pottery, active in Longton between 1920 and 1952, creating furnishing items in semi-porcelain and polychrome pottery with Victorian-style themes and shapes.

Barovier. Murano glassworks founded in 1884 by Giovanni Barovier (1839–1908) and his nephews Benedetto (1857–1930), Giuseppe (1863–1942) and Benvenuto (1855–1932), all masters working in the → Salviati firm. Named Artisti Barovier only in 1890 (at Antonio Salviati's death), it executed neo-Renaissance items (shown in London in 1891 and in Paris in 1889), and initiated at the same time an interesting production of floristic glass and → *murrine* items, the latter often designed by artists (such as Wolf Ferrari and Vittorio → Zecchin). In 1919 Benvenuto's sons, Ercole (1889–1974) and Nicolò, and Giuseppe's son, Napoleone, joined the firm, creating the Vetreria Artistica Barovier, that was remarkable for its blown glass animals, *murrine* vases and, by 1929, the *Primavera* series (elegant vases in white glass with black handles clearly → art deco in style, designed by Ercole, working in the factory until 1972), as well as for the invention of colour hot-processing without melting, used for instance in the *Marina Gemmata*, *Laguna Gemmata* and *Autunno Gemmato* series (1935–36); the latter is a superb amber-coloured vase with side handles in moulded crystal. In 1936, after parting with his

Umberto Bellotto (for Vetreria Artistica Barovier), bowl, mosaic glass with polychrome tesseras and wrought iron, 1920–24

brother Nicolò, Ercole joined up with the → S.A.I.A.R. Ferro Toso factory, that in 1939 became Barovier Toso & C. and in 1942 Barovier & Toso. If pre-war production was mainly heavy, colourless or monochrome glass, that of the 1950s featured polychrome tesseras and the use of rough surfaces, as in the *Barbarian* series (vases covered with blue dots) and *Euganei*, inspired by primitive culture, and the *Sidone* glass (1957), with special decorative effects produced by the introduction of small polychome squares. *(Pls 13–15 and 119)*

Basile, Ernesto (1857–1932). Italian architect and designer, working mainly in Sicily or Rome, one of the leading representatives of Italian → liberty style. The son of a teacher at the Faculty of Architecture in Palermo, he began his career in the ambit of the eclectic tradition, but at the turn of the century developed his own style inspired from French → art nouveau models, like at the Grand Hotel Villa Igiea in Palermo (1898–1900), where he was assisted by the painter Ettore De Maria Bergler, for essentially floristic decorations, and by → Ducrot-Golia for the furnishings. In 1898 Basile began collaborating with the latter firm, sprung from the company of Vittorio Ducrot (1867–1942, furniture-maker on an industrial scale) and Carlo Golia (Palermo representative of a Turin wallpaper company), offering a series of bare, elegant furniture styles, suited for mass-production. The furnishing of the café Ferraglia in Rome (1901) and the great success obtained at the Turin fair (1902) sanctioned the revival Basile suggested, even obvious in the maple office (1902), no longer seen in terms of decoration but favouring elegant and rhythmic forms, and distinguished by transparent frames produced by solid wood dap-joints; later hundreds of copies, dubbed "Turin style", were produced by Ducrot-Golia. On the other hand he expressed a more monumental concept in a series of furniture made with inlays of different or precious materials: for instance the 1903 mahogany *secrétaire* with its architectural structure drawn from the Renaissance, yet lightened in → liberty style by bronzes modelled by the sculptor Antonio Ugo and paintings, on the insides of the doors, executed by Ettore De Maria Bergler.

Bassanelli, Renato (1896–1973). Italian potter, in 1919 he started up in Rome the factory Keramos Ceramiche d'Arte, that became one of the most important furnaces of the capital, exporting items to Egypt and the Americas. Concerned by the renovations in the Campidoglio area, the furnace closed down in 1928 and Bassanelli moved to Biella, where, in 1929, he founded the S.A.C.B. (Società Anonima Ceramiche Biellesi). Then returning to

Ernesto Basile (for Ducrot-Golia), furnishings for an office, maple, 1902

Rome, he again opened a furnace, where he produced spectacular glazed terra cotta one-offs, several on Tomaso → Buzzi's designs, others inspired by Etruscan art and Renaissance pottery. Polychrome items were produced only the first year, being nearly exclusively monochrome after 1930. Usually the artist would fully sign his own works or mark them with his initials and a rose.

Bates, Kenneth F. (1904–94). United States enamel decorator, the author of *Enameling: Principles and Practice*, that appeared in 1951, an essential text for the popularising of traditional and modern enamel techniques and used as a handbook, also in the Cleveland Art Institute where he taught for forty years. He was a prolific graphic artist, especially of botanical motifs, that he frequently expressed in enamel, and whose pieces can be found in a large number of private collections throughout the United States.

Baudouine, Charles (b. 1808). Furniture-maker, of French birth but working in New York, where around 1830 he opened a laboratory that was active until 1856, with at least seventy cabinet-makers producing laminated-rosewood furniture similar to → Belter's, but with a few variations in the mounting of the parts, nearly always in neo-rococo style, with rich, pompous plant-shaped carvings and fretwork.

Bauer J.A. Pottery Company. United States pottery, active in Los Angeles from 1909 to 1962, producing household dishware and flower containers, with elegantly streamlined forms, particularly jars featuring a horizontal bead-work decoration, in vivid, single colours.

Baugrand, Gustave (1826–70). French designer of jewellery and tea sets and caskets, to which he often applied the technique of → *cloisonné* and → *champlevé* enamel, working with many enamel artists including Lefournier, the Solier brothers and Alfred Meyer. The firm his father Victor (1803–72) opened in Paris won fame at the 1867 Paris fair with superb Egyptian-style enamelled jewellery, but also produced items in Renaissance and "Japanese" styles.

Bauhaus. Name of the state school of architecture and applied arts established in Weimar in 1919 by the architect Walter Gropius, backed by the grand duke of Saxony, and active until 1933 when the rise of Nazism forced it to close down. The purpose of

the school was to counter the invasion and dangers of the industrial civilisation by a new type of teaching — inspired by both the experiments of the English → Arts & Crafts Movement, and the German Deutscher Werkbund school — cancelling the separation between artist and craftsman in order to create total, consistent works. Gropius called many artists to teach at Weimar, including G. Marks for

Ludwig Mies van der Rohe, round table and armchair, nickel-plated steel, black lacquered wood and woven straw, 1927. Darmstadt, Bauhaus Archive

pottery, A. Meyer for architecture, G. Muche for textiles, P. Klee for art glass, Wasily Kandinsky for mural painting, L. Moholy-Nagy for metal. However, industry's lack of collaboration put the school in serious difficulty, so in 1925, invited by the town council, it moved to Dessau in a new building designed by Gropius himself, that became an international focal point. In 1928 political pressures forced Gropius to resign, replaced by Meyer, in turn replaced in 1930 by Ludwig → Mies van der Rohe, who in 1931 left the school along with Klee. *(Pl. 16)*

Baumgarten. United States tapestry company founded in New York in 1893 by William Baumgarten, with the essential assistance of a master weaver come from the English Windsor Tapestry Manufactory. Transferred to Williamsbridge (New York), the firm closed down in 1912 after having produced blankets, upholstery fabrics and imitations of eighteenth-century tapestry panels.

Bay State Glass. United States glassworks opened in 1853 at Cambridge (Massachusetts) and closed around 1877, specialised in producing mirrors and plain leaded glass, modelled and etched.

Beatty & Sons. Unites States glassworks active at Steubenville (Ohio), known for its production of blown and pressed glassware, especially goblets.

Bega, Melchiorre (1898–1978). Italian architect and designer, after graduating in 1922, he specialised in interior design, furnishing steamers, theatres, clinics, hotels and private homes. His father Vittorio owned a joinery in Bologna with many employees, that was transferred to the new premises designed by Melchiorre in 1923, where he also became a designer of countless series of furnishings in the ruling → deco style and that were diffused in nearly every Italian city; between 1933 and 1938 he renovated many Perugina and Motta shops and Banco di Roma premises. He was director of the review *Domus* from 1940 to 1944.

Begger C.J. Belgian silver factory founded in Utrecht in 1857 and active under that name since 1868, being the leading Belgian firm producing medals; in 1889 it was promoted to the rank of royal factory (for having created, commissioned by William III, a "Louis-Quinze" table set), enjoying that title up to 1919 ("Koninklijke Utrechtse Fabriek Van Zilverwerk NV C.J. Begger"), and producing neo-eighteenth-century style articles until 1895, when a strongly → art nouveau trend was introduced, with the presence of elegant floral motifs. In 1919 the factory was taken over by its competitor Van Kempen.

Behrens, Peter (1868–1940). German architect and designer who started off as a painter, graphic artist and designer of glass, jewellery, furniture and porcelain in tune with the wavy, elegant → art nouveau style. By 1898 he undertook to make prototypes of glass flasks, with simple, linear profiles, for industrial production; in 1899 he joined the Die Sieben group in Darmstadt, the artists' colony founded by the grand duke Ernst Ludwig von Hessen on the model of the English → Arts & Crafts Movement, with the purpose of merging all the arts. Around 1900–04 Behrens designed for himself a house in Darmstadt: characterised by a system of ribs, diagonals and rising curves, faceted like crystal, it illustrated the ideal of total art, excluding the slightest reference to art nouveau decoration. In his conception of furniture, the architect came to identify the items with the persons who were to use them: chairs with curved arms and softer lines for women, chairs with upright backs for men, use of birchwood enhanced by frames in ebonied wood

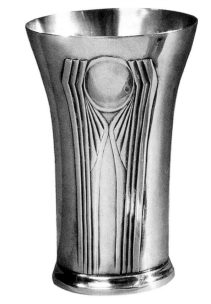

Peter Behrens, chalice, embossed silver, ca. 1902

recalling Biedermeier and announcing → art deco: furnishings that met with success in Turin in 1902. In 1907 he began working for A.E.G., a company for which he designed extremely modern industrial structures of great simplicity and series of prototypes, including electric radiators, street lamps, boilers, industrial equipment, household items, all characterised by utterly plain forms and proportions; he also worked in advertising graphics. In 1922 he began teaching at the Faculty of Architecture of Vienna, and then of Berlin.

Bel Geddes, Norman (1893–1958). United States designer, one of the 1920s and 1930s best known and qualified, between 1927 and 1932 he produced household items. He created prototypes for many companies, like I.B.M. and General Motors, and was one of the leading figures of United States → art deco, also as polemicist: in his book *Horizons* (1932), he expressed the need for a modern dynamism and suggested a series of futurist designs for buildings and transportation means. His *Skyscraper Cocktail Service and Manhattan Tray* dated 1937 is very famous: a set of metal glasses with strictly geometric, highly elegant lines.

Bell J. & M.P. & Co. Scottish pottery, opened in Glasgow in 1842 and closed in 1928, specialised in tableware on a white ground with navy and blue decorations inspired by a neo-eighteenth-century period décor with cartouches containing landscapes: the decorative forms and themes nearly all (at least between 1840 and 1890) derived from the *Warwick Vase Pattern.*

Belleek Pottery. Porcelain factory founded in 1863 in Northern Ireland, specialised in feldspathic porcelain, translucid and light with a pearly glaze, shown for the first time in Dublin in 1865. The Dublin architect W.R. Armstrong designed groups of plates and small shell-shaped vases, successfully shown in the United States at the Centennial Exhibition (1876), so that in 1872 the United States → Ott & Brewer firm of Trenton already began producing similar tableware, precisely named *Belleek*. During the 1880s and 1890s production of porcelain with a like design was launched — but far more refined in the models and the decoration — by various companies, including the → Lenox Company and → Knowles (that called the item *Lotus Ware*). The best known productions of the factory include tea sets in white paste with pearly reflections imitating shells and coral, and sweets and bread baskets made with woven porcelain strips imitating wicker baskets. *(Pl. 17)*

Bellezza, Giovanni (1807–76). Italian silversmith, active in Milan, with a classicist style that in time turned into a romantic type of verism; his fame was mainly owed to the execution of a silver amphora and basin, designed by Ferdinando Albertolli, offered in 1842 by the city of Milan to Victor Emmanuel II on the occasion of his nuptials with Adelaide of Austria, and of two reliquaries of the Very Precious Blood (Mantua, Basilica of Sant'Andrea) executed in gold on the model of the ones made in the past by the goldsmith Nicola da Milano on Benvenuto Cellini's design and confiscated by the Austrians in 1848. A bronze caster, celebrated for a monumental clock executed for Charles Albert with friezes, allegorical figures and portraits of famous astronomers, his production of profane silverware and jewellery is not well documented; his name is connected with the altar for the chapel of the Madonna dell'Albero in the Milan Cathedral, begun in 1854 and completed in 1860.

Bellosio, Eugenio (1847–1927). Italian silversmith pupil of Giovanni → Bellezza, he was active in Milan where he specialised in producing neo-Renaissance items in the style of Benvenuto Cellini: his formal plate of 1884 (Milan, Castello Sforzesco), in embossed and lightly gilt silver, represents the head of Medusa surrounded by a Centauromachia, and the 1887 silver and jasper fruit dish (Milan, Castello Sforzesco) was an authentic revival of the Lombard mannerist tradition. He presented with noteworthy success astounding chiselled items, again in that style, at the 1898 Turin fair, and made in silver the altar of the parish church of Santa Marta at Magreglio, in Brianza. The creator also of important pieces of sacred goldwork, he continued to follow the eclectic, neo-gothic taste, as for the pastoral for Cardinal Ferrari in 1894 and the chalice for canon Casati in 1915 (both in Milan, Cathedral treasure). Not unaware of French cultural influences in the *pompier* style, in 1887 the silversmith executed, commissioned by doctor Giovanni Rizzi, a gorgeous table set with cast female nudes and etchings with *ramages* and painted glass (Milan, Castello Sforzesco). A fine chiseller but also a good setter of precious stones, he was Alfredo → Ravasco's master.

Bellotto, Umberto (1882–1940). Italian ironwork master he became known in 1903 for executing the railings of the café-restaurant of the Venice Biennale, copied on the ones of the Verona Arche Scaligere, and from 1905 to 1907 he collaborated with Cesare Laurenti in furnishing the restaurant *Lo Storione* of Padua, where he combined traditional ironwork with explicitly → liberty rhythms. Yet his real consecration came at the Venice Biennale of 1914, where he had a one-man show of eclectic, quotationist pieces, featuring the imaginative use of various materials combined with iron (leather, wood, pottery and especially glass). He was a leading figure at the Monza Biennales from 1923 to 1927, and during the 1920s and the 1930s his work was characterised by a personal, highly elegant interpretation of → art deco and → Jugendstil models, with hammered iron in organic forms that grip and contain blown glass bulbs with changing colours.

Belter, John Henry (1804–1963). United States furniture-maker, born in Stuttgart, he emigrated to the United States in 1844 and began working in Duncan Phyfe's (1768–1854) workshop, but the technical know-how acquired in Germany, the taste borrowed from Biedermeier and the German rococo revival led him to give his own name to a New York type of furniture: "Belter furniture" is upholstered and distinguished by intricately carved and fretted friezes. Having already tried out in Germany the method for curving wood with heat, Belter took out a patent for the technique using his favourite wood, rosewood: between 1847 and 1858 he experimented with layers of rosewood (from six to eight) forming a panel 2,5 cm thick, then steam-profiled and carved; likewise he invented single-piece profiled backs for chairs and armchairs. Using English and American samples, he opened a first workshop on Broadway, and in 1858 a big factory on Third Avenue that went bankrupt however in less than a decade. His furniture characterised the United States housing tradition since the mid-nineteenth century, with a substantial decorative and monumental excess of eighteenth-century German models and a proliferation of fruit, flowers, leaves, carved cartouches and virtuoso fretwork, a taste followed by the manufactories of George Henkels in Philadelphia, Prudent→Mallard in New Orleans and Léon → Marcotte and Gustav → Herter in New York.

Beltrami G. & Co. Italian glassworks, active in Milan by 1901 with cartoons by Giovanni Buffa. After 1906 the firm was given important commissions, including the glass windows for the Grand Hotel of San Pellegrino Terme, *La Fonte* and the monumental velarium with *La Primavera* (1907), the ensemble of stained-glass windows for the Villa Beyerlé in Cairo (1909), the one for the Villa of Queen Margherita in Bordighera (1915) and the huge velarium over the hall of Montecitorio (1908–18), all works featuring an explicit floral style. At the death of Giovanni Beltrami, in 1926, the art laboratory was run by Buffa.

Bennett. Unites States pottery created in Baltimore in 1846 by the English brothers Edwin and William Bennett; among the first to execute *biscuit* porcelain jugs with a sage green or blue ground and white decorative reliefs, by 1853 it began mass-producing majolica; its catalogue presents numerous types of household tableware along with interesting ornamental items. In 1856 William Bennett retired from the firm.

Bennington. United States pottery created in the town of the same name in Vermont in 1793, that began producing items in gres by 1815. Passed down in 1823 to the son of the founder, John Norton, it kept up its activity until 1894. Between 1842 and 1843, his nephew (same name), associated with Christopher Webber Fenton, founded a factory named United States Pottery that produced finer quality and artistically more ambitious pieces and where, as of 1846, the English potter John Harri-

Beltrami G. & Co., stained-glass window with peacocks, "monaco" glass, white glass and enamel, 1902

son worked, initiating a production in *biscuit* porcelain with white decorations on a coloured ground of figurines and buds. In 1849 Fenton patented flint enamel: a glaze speckled with yellow, brown, navy blue and orange, used either for ornamental items or for everyday tableware (the tankards with a whippet-shaped handle were famous). Active until 1858, the factory produced on English models specifically American decorations, like reliefs with waterfalls (*Niagara Falls*) and tankards with portraits of famous Americans (*Toby-Jugs*).

Benson, William Arthur Smith (1854–1924). English architect and designer, friend of William → Morris, he designed furniture and tapestries for the firm Morris & Co. In 1880 he opened his own workshop for producing polished metal items, an activity that grew until 1887, the year a factory was founded in Hammersmith that kept up production even after Benson retired in 1920. The Morris-style articles were sold in the shop opened in Bond Street in 1894.

Berg, Elis (1881–1954). Swedish glass designer, celebrated draughtsman and creator of models for the → Kosta factory from 1927 to 1954, particularly famous for his drawings etched on glass.

Bergé, Henri (1870–1937). French glass and porcelain decorator, who was responsible for the decorations of the → *pâte de verre* vases made between 1897 and 1914 by the → Daum Frères glassworks of Nancy, of which he became director in 1900. The creator of graphic works and posters, by 1908 he concentrated on producing prints for works in glass executed by the Daum factory and Alméric → Walter.

Berlage, Hendrik Petrus (1856–1934). Dutch architect and designer, he was one of the first to give a radically new direction to architectural and furnishing design in an anti-academic and revival style, using a vocabulary that specifically borrowed from → art nouveau freedom of invention, the ethical values of art, the ideal of art for everyone and the rational bareness of forms and decorations. His well-known oak sideboard (The Hague, Gemeentemuseum), executed in 1900–01, was entirely without decoration, held to be superfluous, to the benefit of proportions and a precise balance of its various components; like most of the furniture Berlage designed, it too was assembled in the → 't Binnenhuis laboratory of Amsterdam. He also cre-

ated designs for strict, pure glass items for the → Baccarat and the → Pantin glassworks.

Berlin. Porcelain factory founded in 1752 under the name Königliche Porzellan-Manufaktur (K.P.M.), that had a remarkable production throughout the eighteenth century. Beginning in 1786, and up to the 1820s, under the patronage of Frederick William II, it produced porcelain featuring a cold-white hue owed to the use of a different kind of kaolin in the china clay, with classicist styles and influenced by Empire models from the → Sèvres factory. In the years 1827–50 production of → lithophanes began, porcelain plates with intaglio designs — some of the most interesting of the period — that reproduced pictures of famous works visible against the light, and series of tableware and ornamental items in Victorian style. In 1878 Hermann Seger became director, being the inventor of the process enabling to execute vases with simple profiles copied after Chinese porcelains, featuring *flambé* glazes in the colour of oxblood, and yellow, purple and green (*Seger-Porzellan*), and that led to a rebirth of the factory. In the early twentieth century there was an increase in models provided by sculptors: Josef → Wackerle, Paul → Scheurich and, especially, Adolf → Amberg, the author of many compositions called *Wedding Procession*. As of 1903 the presence is documented, in the factory, of Hermann Hugo Hubatsch (1878–1940), who presented the theme of the female figure in contemporary garb and environment (*Fashionable lady sitting in a rococo armchair*). Between 1908 and 1926 the art director of the firm was Theodor Hermann Schmuz-Baudiss (1859–1942) who introduced a serial, but elegant, production of tableware with → art nouveau décors; but it was only in 1929 that they began producing plain, highly elegant tea sets designed by Trude Petri-Raben (b. 1906): prototypes of many sets made later in Europe and the United States. *(Pls 18 and 21)*

Berlin. Metal factory active from 1800 to 1840 under the name Prussian Royal Iron Foundry that produced, based on drawings by leading artists such as K. Friedrich Schinkel, decorative items, jewellery, knick-knack statuettes, but also household utensils for smoking, sewing or writing, ranging from neoclassical to neo-gothic to neo-rococo styles. There were three foundries involved in this kind of processing: Gleiwitz, outside of Berlin, established in 1796, that produced architectural adornments and small relief panels, began to decline around 1830, closing down entirely in 1845; the Berlin foundry, closed in 1848, and the Sayn plant, that went on producing until 1865 and was then taken over by Krupp. Many nineteenth-century furnishing items were imitated and borrowed in → deco style in the 1930s by the renovated Berlin metal production.

Berlin. Embroidery factory active since 1804, date at which appeared various collections of drawings printed on a checquer coinciding with the mesh of the canvas, so as to be reproduced with accuracy. These were usually panels embroidered by non-professional craftswomen in polychrome woolen yarn, died in Berlin, on square canvases and with floral or figurative motifs, the latter referring to religious subjects; today the designs are printed directly on the canvas and the embroidered panels are used for upholstery or framed individually like paintings.

Bertoia, Harry (b. 1915). United States sculptor and designer of Italian birth, he settled in the United States in 1930. He is especially known for the small shell-shaped armchair, executed in 1952 for Knoll Associated Inc. and later called *Bertoia*, where the seat is hung between the arms and can be adjusted depending on the position of the person sitting in it, while the shell is a profiled net of chromium-plated steel wire. Bertoia was able to exploit to the utmost the plastic possibilities offered by foam rubber and iron rods, using them in the overall designing of architecture as well as in furnishings.

Beswick John. English pottery, active at Longton since 1894 and still working within the Royal Doulton Group (since 1969), producing furnishings, household tableware, small animals and decorative figurines.

Beurdeley, French furniture-makers. Louis-Auguste-Alfred (1808–82) worked in Paris, where he greatly extended his activity during the Second Empire, specialising in period furniture and bronzes, occasionally cleverly interpreted. His son, Alfred-Emmanuel-Louis (1847–1919) gave a further boost to the family firm by concentrating on the production of copies and reproduction of eighteenth-century furnishings. The factory closed down in 1895. *(Pl. 19)*

Biagini, Alfredo (1896–1952). Italian sculptor and potter, son of a Roman goldsmith, after studying in Paris, he joined a group of young artists belonging to the Roman Secession, and along with the creation of sculptures in bronze (mainly animals on marble bases) or in plaster, he began modelling high-fired majolicas, presented successfully at the first Roman Biennale in 1921 and at Monza in 1923. His extremely refined stucco decorations for the Quirinetta theatre of Rome (1927) were clearly → deco in spirit.

Bianconi, Fulvio (b. 1915). Italian glass designer, born in Padua, he began designing glass in 1946, creating a series of perfume bottles for the GI.VI. Emme firm, and soon after got in touch with the → Venini factory, for which he made the vase *Fazzoletto* (Handkerchief): the symbol of the firm in postwar days, thanks to the elegant naturalness of the glass folded toward the top like an open, starched fabric. In 1948 he attended the Biennale with the series of → milk glass and polychrome paste figures of the *Commedia dell'Arte*, and in 1951 at the Milan Triennale with the "cased" vases and the famous *Pezzati*. Working for other furnaces too, the artist remained attached to Venini, for which he produced in 1965 the series of *Informali* vases. *(Pl. 20)*

Bigot, Alexandre (1862–1927). French potter, minerology scholar, at the turn of the century he became an expert in pottery with cristalline and *flambé* glazes. In 1894 he initiated a production of refined speckled and spotted vases and gres amphoras, then in 1897 series of terra cottas intended as architectural elements, that climaxed in the preparation of animal friezes, on a model by R.Jouve, for the main entrance of the 1900 Paris fair. During the 1910's and 1920's he kept up the line of production in connection with the new style in architecture with concrete and pottery ornament, like in the façade of Saint-Jean in Montmartre.

Bijouterie. Costume jewellery in plastic, especially bakelite, in vogue at the end of the First World War. Drawn from a variety of geometric motifs, made of celluloid and strass, from Egyptian themes and the entire → deco trend typical of the 1920s: including palm fronds and exotic animals, stylised figurines and wavy motifs. Heavy, solid bracelets in fake ivory, jet and imitation jade came into fashion in 1929, when the American heiress Nancy Cunard came back from an African safari loaded down with ivory bracelets of every style imaginable. The crash of 1929 multiplied the production of low-price jewellery, made of modest materials, but Coco Chanel would be the one to definitively launch the fashion of explicitly imitation jewellery to show off on her clothes: from bakelite bracelets with huge mounted coloured

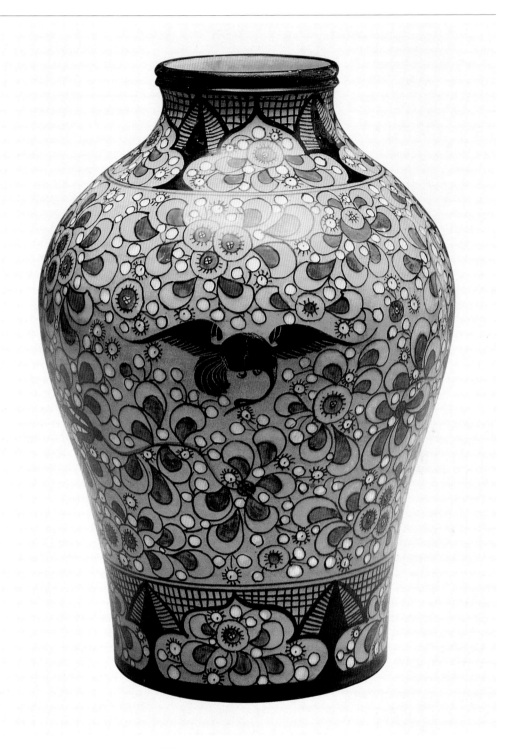

1. Alba Docilia, vase, polychrome majolica, 1924

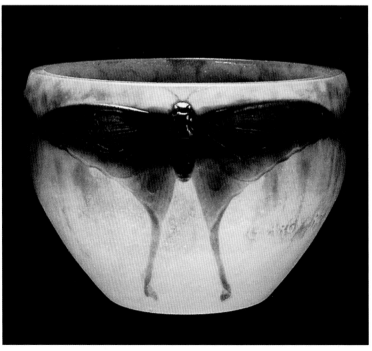

4. Tullio d'Albisola (for M.G.A., Albisola) vase, polychrome majolica, 1930–31

5. Guido Andlovitz (for Società Ceramica Italiana di Laveno), potiche vase, earthenware coated with red glaze, ca. 1928

6. William van Alen, deco-style lift doors, several types of wood and brass, 1929. New York, Chrysler Building

7. Galileo Chini, art nouveau vase, polychrome majolica, ca. 1900

8. Otto Eckmann, waterlily art nouveau vase, soft paste porcelain, eggshell glaze and coloured enamels, gilt bronze mount, 1900

9. May Morris (for William Morris & Co., Arts & Crafts), screen, carved mahogany and embroidered silk, ca. 1889

10. Baccarat, perfume bottles, crystal, 1925.
Paris, Musée des Arts Décoratifs

11. Guido Balsamo Stella (for S.A.L.I.R.), Venus and dolphin *and* Tight-rope walker *vases, etched crystal, 1928–30*

12. Ferdinand Barbedienne, tripod vase, gilt bronze and enamels, 1862. London, Victoria and Albert Museum

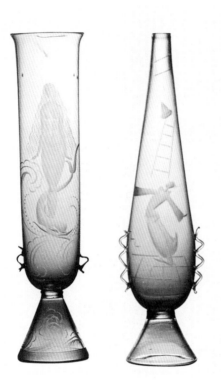

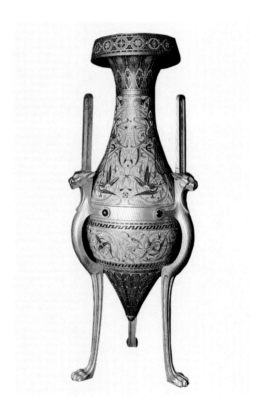

13. Ercole Barovier, Primavera *glass vase with handles and finishings in black glass paste, 1929–30*

14. Artisti Barovier, vase with murrine glass body, stylised decorations in navy, red and yellow tones, 1918–19

15. *Artisti Barovier, murrine glass vase, 1914*

16. *G. Stolzl (Bauhaus), tapestry, wool on linen weft, 1927–28.*
Darmstadt, Bauhaus Archive

17. *William Henshall
(for Belleek Pottery),
porcelain basket
of the* Shamrock *series,
ca. 1900*

18. *Adolf Amberg
(for Berlin Royal Porcelain
Manufactory),* Europa
on the bull, *porcelain, 1912.
Berlin, Bröhan-Museum*

19. Alfred Beurdeley, piano, mahogany, marqueteries in several essences, 1881

20. *Fulvio Bianconi (for Venini),* Harlequin, *flecked glass and glass paste, 1948*

stones to clips and buttons, created by Elsa Schiaparelli, in the most unexpected forms. The typologies found on the market are: geometric, intaglio, transparent and engraved (with floral and "fish" motifs), and bijoux with figures. *(Pls 24 and 81)*

Bill, Max (b. 1908). Swiss architect and designer, trained at the → Bauhaus and leading theorist in the formation of modern design. The author, in 1949, of the *Die Gute Form* programme for the Schweizerische Werkbund*,* in 1950 he published *Form*, a study devoted to his master Henry → van de Velde and, from 1951 to 1956, ran the Hochschule fur Gestaltung on the model of the Bauhaus. As regards design, he produced prototypes for the Braun firm, the typewriting fount *Patria*, triangular three-legged coffee-tables and heart-shaped armchairs (1949–50), chairs with flat parts, therefore stackable (1950–51), a solar-rays lamp (1951) and electric wall-fixtures with superb finishings (1958).

Bilston. English metal factories, founded in Staffordshire in the last decade of the seventeenth century; active in the eighteenth century, they underwent a remarkable revival during the nineteenth century, specialising in tin-plated iron items, snuffboxes, trays, small boxes, decorated with the *japanning* technique, that is, the imitation of Oriental lacquer obtained by spreading on a thin iron-plate a layer of black pitch glaze, heat-dried and subsequently decorated in colour or gold.

Biltons. English pottery, active at Stoke from 1901 to 1998, producing resistant kitchen and table ware, especially tea sets with floral patterns on a white ground and coffee cups with animals and other nature themes.

Bimann, Dominik (1800–57). Bohemian glass etcher, among the most renowned Biedermeier creators, he performed his apprenticeship at the → Harrachov glassworks while attending the Academy of Fine Arts of Prague. Working in Prague and during the summer at the spa of Frantiskovy-Lazne (formerly Franzenbad), he is known for his etched glass medallions, but also for tableware and various items, nearly all made by the Harrachov firm, onto which he etched in clear outlines landscapes, allegories, little genre scenes and reproductions of famous paintings.

Bindensboll, Thorvald (1846–1908). Danish pottery designer, working at the → Copenhagen earthenware factory, he is known for having developed a personal style in pottery decoration, consisting of abstract ornaments, obtained by combining graffiti and enamel techniques with dashes of colour and uneven, apparently random, circular movements. A far cry from the most familiar → art nouveau styles, his items stem from naturalist inspirations, becoming a non-figurative language akin to the expressionist avant-gardes.

Bing, Samuel (1838–1905 or 1919). Dealer and promoter of → art nouveau, he began at Hamburg as an antique and art dealer, then moving to Paris in 1871. In 1875, after a long trip in the East, he founded the review *Le Japon artistique*, opened the Parisian shop *La Porte Chinoise* for selling far-eastern items, mainly Japanese, and later a branch in New York. He went to the United States in 1893 on a French government mission, to study architecture and design, and was struck by the constructive novelty of Richardson and Sullivan. Back in Europe in 1895 he opened in Paris, in rue de Provence, the gallery *L'Art Nouveau*, where he presented and sold, along with paintings by Bonnard, Munch, Vuillard and Toulouse-Lautrec, also furnishings, glass, metal, jewellery by craftsmen following the modernist trend, that in fact owes its name to Bing's store. Promoter and backer of → Van de Velde and → Tiffany, he found a compeer in the German art critic Julius Meier-Graefe, who opened in Paris the *Maison Moderne* in 1896–97.

Bing & Grondhal. Danish porcelain factory opened in Copenhagen in 1853, it produced few pieces of great interest up to 1885, when P. Krohn (1840–1905) became art director for a decade, introducing in production styles and decorations that were already forerunners of → art nouveau taste (*Heron* dinner set, 1888). The factory kept up its activity during the 1920s, commercialising statuettes of children and women in contemporary attire based on designs by Ingeborg Plockross-Irminger (b. 1872), and in the 1930s with tableware (chocolate set by Kaj Bojesen, 1930–31). Among the many artists who gave their designs to this manufacturer (and to the Royal Danish manufactury) there was also Jean Gauguin (1881–1961), Paul's son.

't Binnenhuis. A joint-stock company founded in 1900 in Amsterdam by Jacob van den → Bosch, W.C. Hoeker and Hendrik Petrus → Berlage, with the aim of designing, producing and marketing furnishing items for the home, especially streamlined furniture with very restrained decorations. In 1913 a fire destroyed the laboratory and Berlage left the company; despite Van den Bosch's attempt to re-launch the firm, it closed down in 1929 and was permanently dissolved in 1936.

Binns, Charles Fergus (1857–1934). English potter, author of high-fired gres dishware imitating old Chinese pottery, he is especially known for introducing in the United States the formula of the "Studio Potter", meaning the crafts workshop for producing pottery instead of mass- or at least large-scale production and with many employees, and for publishing in 1922 the essential *The Potter's Craft*, outlining the precepts of the revival of crafts and the creation of one-offs. In 1900 he became the first director of the New York School of Clay Working, later named New York College of Ceramics.

Birk, Rawlins & Co. English pottery, founded at Stoke in 1900 and closed down in 1933, known for creating knick-knacks with birds perched on bases shaped like tree-trunks and small models of cottages, cathedrals and historic colleges.

Black Starr & Frost. United States jewellery firm, founded in New York in 1810 and transferred to Fifth Avenue in 1912; after producing throughout the nineteenth century traditional and eclectic style celebrative items, during the 1920s it began creating highly imaginative and top quality jewellery.

Blancher, R. Ernest (1855–1935). French enamel decorator active in the circles of the Limoges revival school, a pupil of Louis → Dalpayrat. During the 1860s, Lord Arundel commissioned from him fourteen panels illustrating the *Via Crucis* for the All Saints' church of Wardour (Hampshire), executed with a light impasto enamel and delicate shading in the flesh tones, the figures being outlined and modelled by whitish-pink glazing. Blancher also made brooches, book bindings and candelabras, all items signed in the front "E. Blancher, Limoges".

Blaschka, Leopold (1822–95). Bohemian glass designer and expert naturalist, with his son Rudolph (1857–1939) he is the most renowned representative of the naturalistic trend in German glass production; working in Dresden, he invented floristic compositions called "Harvard flowers" and executed countless glass reproductions of sea fauna and flora exhibited in the Museum of Natural History of Dresden and in many collections all over the

world, among which we should mention the Kreismünster naturalistic collection, with its group of medusas reproduced in glass.

Blenko Glass Co. United States glassworks founded in 1922 at Milton (Virginia) and still active, known for its initial production of leaded stained glass windows for religious buildings and prestigious private residences and, as of 1929, also of coloured plate glass for building and a group of decorative and household items.

B.M.C. Italian pottery founded at Sesto Fiorentino in the early 1930s by Messeri and Barraud, producing tableware and coffee and tea sets in explicitly twentieth-century style, presenting stylised decorations on white ground and bright colours, reflecting the influences of Guido → Andlovitz and the cubo-rationalists.

Boch Frères. Belgian pottery, founded in 1767 at Sept Fontaines (Saarland), but that only took up the above trademark toward the middle of the nineteenth century for the production of household tableware and candle-sticks. Between the 1920s and 1940s, the factory was one of the leading representatives of → deco style in Belgium by the forms given to the vases, drawn from either Cretan and archaic Greek pottery or from models suggested by the cubo-secessionist tradition, usually with a white ground and floral adornments with trailing blossoms. Among the decorators mention should be made of Charles Catteu, active until 1930, and in particular his large black-and-white amphora on a pedestal with painted elephants and *ramage* relief decoration on the base. The trademark is usually "Keramis Made in Belgium" along with the series number, or else printed "Boch F[es] / La Louvière / made in Belgium / Fabrication Belgique".

Böck Josef. Austrian porcelain factory active in Vienna as of 1898 under the name Wiener Porzellan-Manufaktur J. Böck, employing famous names also working for the → Wiener Werkstätte, such as Koloman → Moser, Otto → Prutscher and Dagobert → Peche: the same artists created, besides the series in secessionist style, show-windows and advertising posters.

Boda. Swedish glassworks founded in 1864 by the glassmakers Widlund and Scheutz from the → Kosta glassworks, which in 1970 took over the factory, known for the production of glass items with unconventional shapes and backed by an ample group of innovatory designers.

Böhm, August (1812–90). Bohemian glass etcher, in Biedermeier style and active in numerous workshops (aside from Bohemia, Hamburg, → Stourbridge, London and the United States), he is renowned for portraits, battle scenes, little genre scenes and horses etched on plateglass and goblets.

Bois durci. Cabinet-making term patented in 1855 by F.C. Lepage and used in France and England between 1850 and 1900. It is an artificial material used to imitate ebony and consisting of a mixture of sawdust, water and blood that, heated and then cold-moulded, gave rise to medallions, rosettes and decorative friezes for furnishings.

Bonazzi, Emma (1881–1959). Italian designer, she graduated from the Fine Arts Academy of Bologna, and in 1913 joined the Roman Secession and then took part in the Venice Biennales of 1920 and 1922. In the field of decorative arts she very tastefully combined various materials like wool, silk, cloth, paint, for figures and moods inspired by Klimt; she worked for a number of years for Perugina, designing clever wrappings and boxes for sweets in → deco style.

Bontemps, Georges (1799–1884). French glassmaker, known for having published in 1868 the *Guide du Verrier*, an authentic glass-processing handbook. Director, from 1823 to 1848, of the → Choisy-le-Roi factory, where he studied the various processes for obtaining quality coloured glass in industrial quantities, in 1827 he began producing → *opalines* and in 1839 filigree glass items imitating Venetian articles. He emigrated to Great Britain in 1848, joining the Chance Bros firm in Smethwick, near Birmingham.

Boote T. & R. English potters, owners of an earthenware factory that opened in 1842 in Staffordshire and specialised in the production of → *parian ware*, the so-called "parian porcelain", white, with slightly rough surfaces and therefore similar to statuary marble, used mainly for making busts and figures (more rarely vases and decorative platters), and with which inlaid earthenware, tiles and tableware with iron mineral are produced. At the 1851 London fair they showed a number of pieces, among which a copy of the *Portland* vase.

Booz bottle. Special kind of flask made in the United States around 1860 by the Whitney glassworks for the Philadelphia whisky producer E.G. Booz, distinguished by the schematised shape of a two-storey house, with etched windows, sloped roof and a chimney (the neck of the bottle); around 1931 production of coloured glass bottles began.

Bormioli. Family-run Italian glassworks active at → Altare since the thirteenth century and gradually in many European regions: members of the Bormioli family are documented in Picardy in the seventeenth century. The activity went on during the eighteenth century, and special mention goes to the brothers Costantino (1876–1934) and Cimbro (1879–1961) for their production of → art nouveau vases and items of particular refinement whose composition they never disclosed. In the twentieth century part of the business moved to Parma with Rocco Bormioli for the mass-production of drinking services and household articles.

Borsani. Italian cabinet-makers, active at Varedo (Milan) since the early 1920s. Gaetano Borsani (1886–1955) began taking part in the Monza Biennales in 1925, winning quite a success for his graphite-grey painted furniture that highlighted geometric, streamlined forms and etched arabesque decors; the colouring in delicate hues (grey, yellow, green) made up for the chromatic monotony of the woods used, usually durmast or walnut. While in 1927 the factory offered furnishings in French → deco style with etched decors set in square frames in the centre of smooth surfaces, in 1928 the first walnut-root furniture appeared, distinguished by the skillful combination of the natural root designs and the elegant fluting that lightened the massive dimension of the pieces. The success obtained by the participation in the Milan Triennales and trade fairs incited the factory to equally introduce the use of precious woods, including palm, pear, box, ebony, elm, *madrone* (a light-coloured essence from Madras), and refined facings in typical twentieth-century style (leather, zebra and cow hide, vellum). In 1933, with the design *La casa minima*, presented at the Triennale of that same year, his son Osvaldo (1911–85) came into play, designing in 1933 the new premises of the firm at Varedo and opening the Arredamenti Borsani store in Milan, with permanent exhibitions of his creations. The factory is still active.

Bosch, Jacob van den (1868–1948). Dutch designer, trained at the Amsterdam decorative arts school

(1885–90), he was one of the founding members, with the architect → Berlage, of the → 't Binnenhuis, for which he created simple, elegant furniture; besides he designed tiles for the Holland pottery firm and made frescoes and wall decorations.

Boston and Sandwich Glass Company. United States glassworks founded in 1823 at Sandwich (Massachusetts) by Deming Jarves, who in 1828 specialised, advised by Hiram Dillaway, in making pressed moulded glass for creating bowls, tableware and dishes and in → lacy glass, but also Venetian and English style glass, → paperweights and etched coloured glass oil lamps; in 1830 production of → *opaline* glass began. In 1858, when Jarves left, the competition of other factories took over, and the factory closed down in 1888.

Boston Silver Glass Co. United States glassworks founded at Cambridge in 1857 by A. Young, specialised in silvered glass items; it closed down in 1871.

Bott, Thomas (1829–70). English porcelain painter, after training at the → Stourbridge glassworks, he became a portraitist and pottery painter at Birmingham. In 1852 he was hired by the → Worcester porcelain factory, where he developed a personal pictorial technique distinguished by white glazed enamel decorations on a dark blue ground: that method was called "Limoges dishware" owing to the close colour likenesses with medieval enamels from Limoges, although it was used on vases with shapes recalling Greek pottery and subjects connected with Victorian classicism. His son Thomas John (1854–1932), a porcelain painter as well, after initiating at Worcester became art director in → Coalport from 1890 to 1932.

Bottazzi, Umberto (1865–1932). Italian potter, one of the founders, with → Cambellotti, Grassi, Marcucci and Menasci, of the *La Casa* group, engaged in restoring the relationship between everyday life and art. After attending the 1912 Venice Biennale with an earthenware group figuring fish made for → Richard-Ginori, Bottazzi began taking part in important exhibitions either with majolicas or stained-glass windows (1912 opalescent velarium for the Old England Hotel in Rome).

Osvaldo Borsani, bar, maple and parchment, 1935

Bottoni, Piero (1903–73). Architect and designer, in 1928 he founded with others the Italian Movement for Rational Architecture and in 1929 designed an armchair in steel tubing with double springs, a leather seat and twisted hemp string back, later purchased by the → Thonet firm. For the 1930 Monza Triennale he executed the *Casa elettrica* for the Edison company. The furnishings designed during the 1930s were varied, all characterised by their multi-functional aspect and the modernism of the materials used, particularly steel, maple and pear wood, lacquers, sandstone and foam rubber.

Boucheron, Frédéric (1830–1902). French jeweller, founder of the Paris firm in 1858, that moved to the Palais Royal in 1866, when it began to attend international fairs (Paris, 1867; Philadelphia, 1876; Paris, 1889), meeting with staggering success. The premises were moved to Place Vendôme, where it became a favourite with celebrities: from Sarah Bernhardt to the Rothschilds. It was awarded great acknowledgement during the Paris 1925 fair, where it offered distinctly → deco-style or Oriental-type jewellery. Among the leading designers for the

Louis Boucheron, brooch, coral, onyx and brilliants, 1925

firm, Lucien Hirtz (1864–1928) deserves mention for his *Aigle*, *Valkyrie*, and *Lionne* brooches. After his son Louis (1874–1959) joined the firm, it opened branches in London and New York, became a trust company of the Shah of Persia (1931), and in the late 1930s went back to figuration in jewellery, unlike the strictly geometric and decorative options characterising it up to then.

Bourain, Marcel. French sculptor, known for the small furnishing bronzes executed in the 1920s and widely imitated, their subjects being dancing female figures, nude or costumed, and imitating Hellenistic-tradition chryselephantine statuary. The subjects, connected with antiquity (Amazons, goddesses such as Diana huntress) or with European tradition (Pierrots, Spanish dancers), were executed in bronze with gilt or silver patina and inlays of ivory (for the faces and hands), glass, silver, copper and other metals, nearly always mounted on precious marble bases. His pieces were always distributed by the → Etling firm of Paris that usually marked the sculptures.

Bourdery, Louis (1859–1901). French enamel decorator, one of the leading figures of the revival Limoges school, he decorated large urns with either classical or contemporary motifs; among the smaller pieces figured book bindings, candelabras, plates, settings for stones, usually signed in the front with the initials "L.B." He also worked in polychromy and the *grisaille* technique, drawing a black line on the copper surface, which he then coated with a base upon which he spread transparent enamels, finishing it off by highlighting the outlines and the creases of the draperies with liquid gold.

Bourne & Son. English pottery active from 1812 to 1834 at Belper and then Derby, where it is still active, known for the production of brown gres jugs adorned with relief hunting scenes with whippet-shaped handles.

Bracquemond, Joseph-Auguste, called Félix (1833–1914). French painter and etcher who, after learning the enamel painting technique from J.T. → Deck, began decorating pottery items, drawing his inspiration from Japanese art as early as the 1850s. Dating from this period was a majolica table set from the → Creil factory with painted insects, flowers, animals and leaves in asymmetrical patterns that was a great success in Paris (1867) and in Vienna (1873). In 1870 he began working with the Manufacture de → Sèvres, and for ten years ran the ornament workshop in the → Haviland factory at Auteuil; he also prepared designs for jewellery, book bindings, fabrics and silverware, all featuring a clarity of inspiration and a soberness of form that set them clearly apart from the repetitive contemporary *japonaiseries*. In 1902 he took part in the execution of the furnishings for Villa Sapinière at Evian for baron Vitta (shown at the Paris Salon that same year).

Bragg. English factory active in Birmingham in the second half of the nineteenth century, producing items in gold, silver and plated copper with enamel applications, but also creating enamelled signs and nameplates commissioned by London trades. The trademark displays a triple triangle with the initials of the firm ("T. & J. Bragg").

Brain E. & Co. English pottery, opened in 1885 at Fenton (Staffordshire) and closed in 1992, always using the trademark "Foley China", for the tableware production, including the memorable *Art for the Table* set, made in 1934 for an exhibition in the London Harrods department store, characterised by decorative themes still in → deco style.

Brampton. English pottery active since the eighteenth century in Derbyshire and up to the early twentieth century. The production was brown household tableware, but during the nineteenth century more precious series of cocoa-colour dishware, with relief decorations and the inside glazed green, were turned out, and in particular jugs representing allegorical and grotesque characters (*Toby-Jugs*).

Brandt, Edgar (1880–1960). French metal designer, active from an early age in iron processing and the execution of jewellery and items in other metals as well; in 1919 he opened a workshop in Paris where on his own designs he made articles that would be acclaimed at the 1925 Paris fair, for which he created the famous *Door of Honour* with five iron and brass panels in a thoroughly → deco style. Being the most renowned metalwork artist of the 1920s both in Europe and in the United States, he opened in New York the Ferrobrandt Inc. firm, offering interior furnishings for public and private buildings. Widely imitated by other workshops, Brandt achieved fame for his ability to transfer the deco ornamental idiom (spirals, scrolls, stylised animals) onto iron and bronze, with highly refined *martelé* finishing. His firm produced in huge quantities radiator shields, fire-screens, chimney accessories, umbrella stands and centrepieces, but equally jewellery, trays, vases and silver paperknives. *(Pl. 22)*

Brandt, Marianne (b. 1893). German designer, one of the most famous metalwork designers at the → Bauhaus, where she came to teach in 1923, after studying at the Weimar Kunsthochschule and traveling in France and Scandinavia. Her prototypes proposed the use of pure, geometric forms (cylinders, hemispheres, cones) for tea pots, cups and ashtrays, later mostly made in → nickel silver.

Brandt, Paul Emile. Swiss jeweller, active in the 1920s and 1930s and known for the execution of bracelets, clip brooches, watches, boxes, cigarette-holders in lacquer on silver or else gold and platinum with mounted precious stones; his particularly luxurious articles were always distinguished by geometric patterns arranged symmetrically, zig-zags and a wide use of black lacquer and black onyx.

Brangwyn, Frank (1867–1956). English painter and designer, he achieved great fame as a designer of rugs, furniture and furnishing fabrics. After initiating with William → Morris and taking up the modernist idiom, he worked for Samuel → Bing's Paris firm; with the decline of floral-type → liberty, he turned to a plain, popular design, presenting at Ghent in 1913 a series of inexpensive furniture.

Brannam C.H. English pottery, opened at Barnstaple (Devon) in 1879 and still active today, known for a series of vases with graffiti decorations and vitrified glazes on blue or green grounds executed around 1890. *(Pl. 23)*

Brateau, Jules-Paul (1844–1923). French metal designer, trained with the sculptor Nadau and the goldsmith Bourdoncle, he presented at the Parisian 1874 and 1878 *Salons* tableware inspired by Italian Renaissance models, but made of tin, using special casting and chiselling techniques that emphasised, by the use of virtuoso processings, the qualities of fluidity and simple opacity of tin. In later exhibitions he practiced the so-called "Clodion style", making pitchers with decorations drawn from Dürer (1886 and 1887), and began working for jewellers like → Boucheron, → Falize, → Vever, creating outstanding pieces in the eclectic, historicist vein, such as his masterpiece, the *Pandora* casket, executed in 1893 with the enamelist Paul Grandhomme (Paris, Musée des Arts Décoratifs). In the Paris 1900 fair, he exploited the decorative features of tin to their utmost, presenting a series of extremely refined jewels made of that humble material, while concurrently beginning to work with glass paste, with which he was to produce during nearly a decade delicate transparent glassware. Brateau drew a great deal of his inspiration from antiquity (for instance the silver treasure of Boscoreale unearthed in 1895), from Byzantine culture and the Italian Renaissance, but he also created pieces featuring elegant, wavy, consistently → art nouveau lines.

Bretby Art Pottery. English pottery, opened in 1883 at Woodville (Derbyshire) and closed in 1997, well known for the execution of decorative and furnishing items, and especially, in the 1920s, of vases, amphoras and bowls with forms which were drawn from Greek and Italic pottery, and monochromes (cobalt blue, orange, grey, violet) in → deco style.

Breuer, Marcel (1902–81). United States architect and designer of Hungarian descent, student at the → Bauhaus from 1920 to 1925, he became director of the wood-work department in 1925; in 1935 he left Germany for England and in 1937 arrived in the United States to work with Gropius (until 1941) and later on his own. He introduced into homes and offices chromium-plated metal tubing and modular furniture, definitively turning his back on hand-craftsmanship and initiating standardised industrial production. In 1921–22 he executed several chairs on the model of Rietveld's, with a softer back and seat and presenting different features; the first steel-tubing chair dated from 1925: called *Wasily*, it featured a steel frame on which strips of leather or cloth were stretched; the model, immediately taken up by the Bauhaus, is still under production. In 1928 he thought up a chair made in metal tubing segments onto which Viennese straw panels were attached; in 1933 adjustable furniture in strips of aluminium; in 1936 there appeared the moulded balsa *chaise longue* and in 1935–37 one in curved → plywood.

Marcel Breuer, dining-room, chromium-plated metal, black and white lacquered wood, 1926

Brinckmann, Carlotta (1876–1965). German textile designer, she often worked with her sister Ida (1872–1947) making tapestries and medieval-style textiles, restoring tapestries and fabrics from Berlin museums (as of 1901); in 1919 she founded a studio at Bergedorf, that then transferred to Celle in 1920, remaining active until 1961.

Britannia Pottery Co. Pottery opened in Glasgow in 1920 and closed down in 1935, active in producing tableware decorated with polychrome geometric patterns on blue-grey or white grounds inspired by abstract and rayonnist art.

Britzin, Ivan Savelievitch (active between 1860 and 1917). Russian jeweller, working for the → Fabergé firm, in 1860 he opened in Saint Petersburg his own business where he produced small items featuring inlaid geometric decorations in precious metals and enhanced by translucid colours cast with gold and silver, especially photograph frames and cigarette holders adorned in pale blues and greens, occasionally whites. Britzin also produced filigree enamels with opaque colours, known on the international market as *émail russe*, that were exported to Great Britain and the United States between 1900 and 1917. Because of the Bolshevik revolution, he transferred his activity to Stockholm, later opening a branch in Los Angeles.

Brocard, Philippe (active between 1867 and 1890). French glassmaker known for reviving the enamelling technique previously used in Syria in the Middle Ages and making copies of mosque lamps; equally the inventor of original Islamic-style items, he presented a selection of them in the 1867 Paris fair that were a great success, also with Emile → Gallé.

Broncit. Glass-processing technique patented by the → Wiener Werkstätte and used by → Lobmeyr, around the year 1910, on Josef → Hoffmann's designs, featuring opaque black geometric decorations on glass.

Brozzi, Renato (1885–1963). Italian sculptor and jeweller, born in Parma, he acquired a certain fame at the Esposizione del Sempione in Milan (1906) with a series of embossed silver platters decorated with extremely elegant floristic motifs. He moved to Rome, became a master of medallistics and the chisel, specialising in small sculptures, bronze and silver, representing animals depicted with a vi-brant verism and in a lively, brilliant style. In 1919 he initiated his prolific relationship with Gabriele D'Annunzio, that would last until the poet's death in 1938; for D'Annunzio he executed medals, epaulettes for his uniforms, bowls, friezes, small and big animals in various metals, among which *Cheli*, a bronze turtle in a real shell, placed in the dining-room of Vittoriale degli Italiani at Gardone Riviera on lake Garda, and sets of silver plates embossed with the motif of the Franciscan girdle.

Brunelli, Luigi Maria (1878–1966). Italian cabinet-maker, active in Milan, where in 1906, in collaboration with Carlo → Zen, he designed a series of furnishings for the Fabbrica Italiana di Mobili in tune with the modernist trend; in 1923 at the first Monza Biennale he exhibited furniture and sketches for costumes.

Buccellati, Mario (1891–1965). Italian jeweller, after working for the Milan jeweller Beltrami-Besnati, he took it over in 1919; the instant international success of his articles led him to open a second shop in Rome in 1925 and one in Florence in 1929. In 1922 he had met Gabriele D'Annunzio, who ordered from him an endless series of bracelets, pectorals, cigarette holders, little boxes, cuff links, silver furnishings, tie pins, rings. His style, at first thoroughly → art nouveau, in the early 1920s developed into a special, highly elegant interpretation of → deco taste, inspired by barbarian and Byzantine jewels and using enamels, → *cabochon* stones, seed-pearls and semi-precious stones along with traditional precious stones, mounted in non-precious metals like brass. In the 1930s came the neo-Renaissance period, featuring the use of yellow gold and meshwork for mounting stones. *(Pl. 25)*

Buffa, Paolo (1903–70). Architect and designer, the son of Giovanni (painter and executor of stained-glass windows, for which he founded with → Beltrami, Cantinotti and Zuccaro an important Milanese workshop), he began working in 1928 at Gio → Ponti and Emilio → Lancia's studio, from whom he drew his inspiration in creating furniture that also reflected Tomaso → Buzzi's exquisite, soaring elegance. First a strict "neo-classic" and then a convinced twentieth-century adept, Buffa skillfully used briar-root in openly → deco forms, occasionally with a vaguely Eastern bent; his designs were carried out by the faithful furniture-makers Turri, Lietti, and especially, → Quarti.

21. Ernst Böhrn (for Berlin Royal Porcelain Manufactory), lamp-holder vase, porcelain, 1928. Berlin, Bröhan-Museum

23. C.H. Brannam, vases of the Barum *series, polychrome majolica, 1904*

24. Necklace and compact, bakelite and strass, France, 1928–30

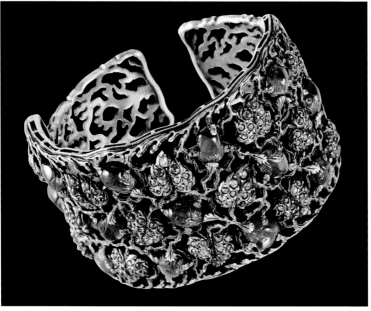

25. Mario Buccellati, rigid bracelet, silver, gold, rubies and sapphires, 1924

26. Tomaso Buzzi (for Venini), twin-neck vase, blue laguna glass with gold leaf and milk glass, 1930–31

27. Tomaso Buzzi (for Venini), bowl, red laguna glass with gold leaf, 1930–31

28. Duilio Cambellotti, Zodiac vase, bucchero pottery, 1924

29. Frederick Carder, vases, phial, dish and glass, favrile glass,
1930–33

30. Carlton Ware, vase with chinoiseries, soft paste porcelain, 1920

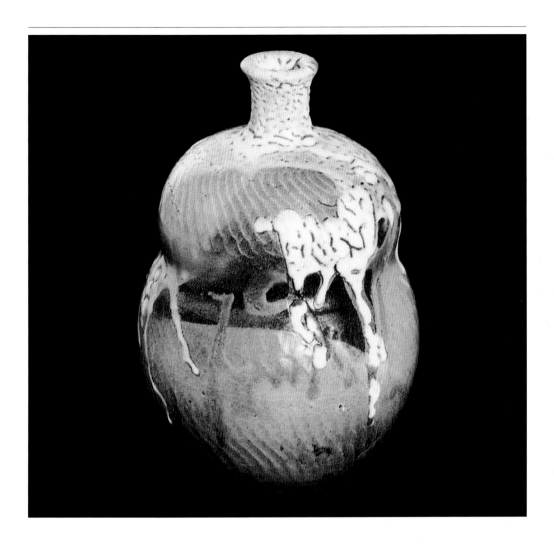

31. *Giacomo Cappellin, vase, blue blown glass, 1920–21*

32. *Jean-Joseph-Marie Carriès, vase, earthenware with reliefs, ca. 1890*

33. C.A.S., vase, majolica terra cotta with air-brushed paint, 1930

34. Cauldon Potteries, Rose Bowl, *soft paste porcelain, ca. 1905*

35. Pietro Chiesa, alabastrine stained-glass window, opalescent glass, 1926–27. Gardone Riviera, Il Vittoriale

37. Galileo Chini, ovate vase, glazed polychrome majolica, ca. 1925

38. Galileo Chini, vase, polychrome majolica, ca. 1900

Buffalo Pottery Company. United States pottery, founded at Buffalo in 1901 and still active. Having initiated with a production of semi-porcelain articles called *Blue Willow* (that is, sets of tableware inspired from the Anglo-Saxon *Blue China* models, with Chinese landscapes and decorations on a white ground), between 1905 and 1909 the factory turned to the reproduction, either painted or printed, of floral decorations drawn from Japanese Imari vases and European-style → art nouveau, but also figures of United States history (George Washington) or fairy tales (Cinderella). In 1908 it initiated the famous *Delaware* series, continued until 1925, that was inspired by colonial themes in an overall revival of the American colonial epic, featuring compositions by Ralph Stuart, according to → Arts & Crafts' stylistic precepts, usually painted on a yellow ochre ground. In the 1910s the factory continued to offer sets of kitchenware and tableware with red and black geometric decorations on a white ground, inspired by the Secession, for a small Arts & Crafts-style colony called Roycrofters of East Aurora (active in New York), of which the trademark is an "R" in a circle topped by a two-armed cross.

Bugatti, Carlo (1855–1940). Italian cabinet-maker, a student at Brera, architecture graduate, active in the workshop of the cabinet-maker Mentasti, he opened his own shop in Milan in 1888 and sent a Turkish smoking room and a Japanese-style screen to the Italian fair in London, where he was awarded a prize and began to receive orders from the firm → Liberty & Co. In the following years he developed a highly original, often imitated style that blended an utterly modernist conception with styles drawn from far- and middle-Eastern cultures, but also from romanesque art, with a fluent use of vellum, also painted, ivory, brass and copper inlays, braided rope, mother-of-pearl and pyrographed decorations. Some of his furniture, with paintings by Riccardo Pellegrini and Alphonse → Mucha, was presented at important fairs: Turin (1898), Paris (1900) and especially Turin (1902); it was precisely that show that marked his triumph, owed to an outstanding series of curved pieces, authentic forerunners of mid-twentieth-century design, a sideboard in the shape of a monumental snail, a table resting on a spiral, chairs with G-shaped modelled supports. His success was such that in 1900 he was commissioned for the furnishings of the Khedive palace in Istanbul. In 1907, out of the blue, he sold his business in Milan and moved to Pierrefonds, in France, and began a collaboration with the Hebrand foundry, where his sculptor son

Buffalo Pottery Company, table set of the Delaware *series, polychrome majolica, 1908–25*

Carlo Bugatti, chair and dressing-table, wood faced with painted parchment and brass, 1902

Rembrandt, a specialist in small animal bronzes, had been working for some time, with designs for silver tableware, small decorative bronzes and ivories mounted in metal.

Bullers. English pottery, active at Milton (Staffordshire) from 1932 to 1952, producing artistic and furnishing items in high-fired porcelain, imitating Oriental porcelains: the vases and articles, made in *céladon*, → *aventurine*, → *craquelure* or eggshell and *flambé*, display forms having the simplicity of Japanese containers and vases.

Bunzlau. German potteries active in Silesia since the late Middle Ages, known for the production of gres reddish-grey tableware coated with ferruginous dust, thus having a coffee-coloured glaze. During the eighteenth and nineteenth centuries they specialised in the creation of gres coffee pots and decanters, while a series of neo-classical vases produced by Johann Gottlieb Altmann, again in gres, dates to around 1810; toward mid-century the decorative production focused on a series of neo-gothic articles. Around the end of the nineteenth century the factories were converted to industrial standards.

Burges, William (1827–81). English architect and designer particularly skilled in neo-medieval period furnishings, among which should be mentioned the ones executed for his own London home in Melbury Road, and for his historicist-style remodeling of several ancient manor houses, such as Cardiff Castle for the marquess of Bute, in 1865, and Coch Castle in 1875. Gifted with a great imagination and a fine sense of colour, he created furniture decorated with paintings by the pre-Raphaelite painters Burne-Jones and Poynter and modern use items with excessively fussy and medieval-style features (washbasin of 1880 at the Victoria and Albert Museum). He also designed neo-gothic tapestries for the Jeffrey & Co. firm, and iron furnishing items covered with precious and semiprecious stones.

Burgess & Leigh. English pottery, active at Burslem (Staffordshire) since 1862, for the execution of household tableware. After a nineteenth-century tradition relating to *chinoiserie* (*Blue Willow*), English cottage and countryside themes, in 1921 the factory began also producing toilet articles and tableware decorated with two-coloured motifs on a grey ground and with white stylised floral themes on a blue ground.

Burgun Schverer & Co. Lorraine glassworks founded at Meisenthal, taken over by Germany in 1871 and given back to France in modern times, taking the name Verrerie de Meisenthal. Between 1867 and 1870 Emile → Gallé performed his apprenticeship there, also signing several pieces, and it was the only German factory producing cameo glass with themes drawn from the Venetian tradition and having a naturalistic inspiration. Typical features of the factory were casing metal sheets in the vitreous paste, → acid etchings, gildings, along with fire-glazing of the pieces and → hammered surfaces. The trademark appearing on the pieces is an etched thistle, the Lorraine cross and the inscription "Verrerie d'Art de Lorraine BS & Co".

Burmese Glass. Type of glass produced in the United States, distinguished by a colour that shades from yellow to green to pink, and made for the first time in 1885 by the → Mount Washigton Glass Company of New Bedford (Massachusetts), with either shiny or dull finishings. Also produced in Great Britain at → Stourbridge by the Thomas → Webb & Sons firm by 1886; in its salmon pink and lemon yellow versions it is called *Queen's Burmese*.

Burnham Signs. English manufactory active in London as of 1877 and now merged with the Garniers firm, known for its production of ornamental signs in enamelled glass and, later on, of enamelled and framed earthenware signs. In 1899 they began producing single letters of the alphabet in enamelled metal for forming inscriptions and in 1902 all kinds of plates and inscriptions.

Buthaud, René (1886–1986). French potter, initially a decorator of silver items, he later turned to pottery, exhibiting his creations for the first time in 1920: his vases and bottles are distinguished by plain, archaic forms, usually graffito-decorated and hand-painted and then glazed, nearly always in brownish and ochre tones and with either geometric (rectangles, spirals, waves, circles) or figurative motifs, in particular female nudes inspired by the *fauve* style and by Henri Matisse, but with → deco-style geometric and somewhat African art accents.

Buzzi, Tomaso (1900–81). Italian architect and designer, claimed to be one of the most significant trendsetters in Italy from the 1920s up to the 1960s. After graduating in 1923 from the Politecnico of Milan, he started off designing theatre sets and costumes, opened his own studio in Milan in 1924 and in 1927, with his friends → Ponti, → Marelli, → Lancia, → Chiesa and → Venini, formed the *Il Labirinto* group for which he designed furniture, stained-glass windows, pottery, embroidery, silverware, lamps, rugs, wrought iron. In 1932 he replaced Napoleone Martinuzzi as art director for the Venini glassworks, for which he created the series of *corrosi*, *sommersi*, *laguna* and *alga* glass. He collaborated with the review *Domus* and other monthlies devoted to furnishings and the decorative arts. His obsessive care for detail and artisanal execution classified his furnishings as unrepeatable one-offs, distinguished by their light, wavy outlines, the preciousness of the inlays and the use of chiselled bronze decorations. *(Pls 26 and 27)*

C

Cabochon. Processing method that gives an oval, dome-like shape to precious and semi-precious stones, emphasising their smooth, unfaceted surfaces, resembling the type of gemstones used for mountings in barbarian, Byzantine and medieval jewellery, later revived in → liberty, Viennese Secession and especially → art deco styles.

Cacciapuoti. Italian pottery founded in Naples by Cesare, descendant of a dynasty of Campanian majolica producers, where the sculptors Vincenzo Gemito and Ciffariello Dorsi worked as well. In 1927 the two sons, Mario (b. 1890) and Guido (b. 1892) moved to Milan, where, in partnership with Angelo Bignami, they opened the factory Grès d'Arte Cacciapuoti Bignami & C., meeting with immediate, lasting success owed to the variety and con-

Guido Cacciapuoti, Fox, majolica terra cotta, 1928–32

stant updating of the available models. Typical items of this workshop are the three-dimensional groups representing animals modelled and painted by Guido Cacciapuoti in keeping with naturalist canons.

Cadinen. German pottery created at the instigation of William II in the town of Elbing, near a clay deposit he owned, that at first reproduced Greek

vases and fifteenth- and sixteenth-century Italian pottery (in the style of Della Robbia), later also executing reliefs and figures in glazed pottery on designs and projects by German sculptors such as Emil Pottner, Ludwig Manzel and Adolf → Amberg. During the 1910s and 1920s production aimed at architectural decoration (like for instance the facing of the Cadinen Saal in neo-rococo style in the Weinhaus Kempinski, now torn down, and the Kaiser Friedrich Bad at Wiesbaden, executed in 1913) as well as gres tableware. The factory closed down in 1945.

Cadorin. A family of Venetian artists. Vincenzo (1854–1925), a cabinet-maker and decorator, attended the world fairs of Paris (1900), Turin (1902), Saint Louis (1904) and the Venice Biennales (after

Guido Cadorin (for Vetreria Artistica Barovier), bottle, blown glass and navy glass paste, 1922

1914) with furniture and furnishing items in an elegant version of → liberty, reflecting French taste in the exuberance of the plant motifs and the use of small heads and supple female bodies as well as Viennese geometric rigour. His son Guido (1892–1976), mostly known as a painter belonging to the Ca'Pesaro group, in the 1920s turned to the decorative arts, etching on linoleum and stone, creating lacquered articles and stained-glass windows, designing glass for the Vetreria Artistica → Barovier (shown at the 1922 Venice Biennale), pottery (exhibited at Monza in 1923 and 1925), fabrics and wall decorations in exquisitely → deco style.

Calcite glass. Technique invented around 1915 by Frederick → Carder for the → Steuben Glass factory. It consists of a translucid, cream-white glass, obtained with the addition of bone powder (phosphate of calcium) similar to calcite, hence its name; three layers of vitreous paste are molten together, while the outer layer, in order to create iridescent effects, is sprayed with lead chloride. This variety of glass is used for decorative items and especially for lighting, owing to the diffused softness of light shining through the translucid material. Occasionally the surfaces can be decorated with → acid etchings or hand-etched drawings highlighted by a brown oxide.

Caldwell & Co.. American silversmith laboratory working in Philadelphia since 1839 and still active, known for having made, toward the mid-nineteenth century, formal dishes rather similar to those made in New York by → Tiffany.

Cambellotti, Duilio (1876–1960). Italian potter and painter, after training and being admired as a painter and illustrator, he became interested in pottery around 1907: after visiting the manufactory → Fornaci di San Lorenzo di Chino and Galileo → Chini, he began purchasing bowls and dishes from the popular furnaces in Trastevere and decorating them with motifs drawn from the Roman countryside, and juvenile and archaeological themes. He started up a collaboration with the review *La Casa* (founded in 1908), presenting pottery, sculptures and furniture, inspired by rustic and archaic life, at the Agro Romano exhibition in 1911. From 1912 to 1917 he held courses on the applied arts in girls' professional schools, and in 1912, in collaboration with → Bottazzi, Grassi and the master glassmaker Cesare Picchiarini, he organised the first stained-glass exhibition, renovating the traditional nineteenth-century

style with coloured vitreous pastes and lovely, utterly modern forms. From 1919 to 1928 he executed an important series of pottery vases and useful ware for the laboratory of the Regio Istituto Nazionale per l'Istruzione Professionale (R.I.N.I.P.), which was associated with the Museo Artistico Industriale of Rome, and backed by Fernando Frigiotti (an expert in the bucchero technique), Romeo Berardi, Virgilio Retrosi and Roberto → Rosati. In 1921 he presented a very abundant selection of bronzes and pottery in a one-man show at the Società d'Arte Moderna Italiana in Rome, an exhibition that travelled to Holland as well and that made Cambellotti famous beyond Roman circles. He attended the Monza Biennales in 1923 and 1925, with a rich production of furnishings again inspired by rustic tradition, potteries, especially bucchero, and stained-glass. During the 1930s he worked on the decoration of important public buildings at Bari, Latina and Ragusa, and around 1935 executed an outstanding series of painted and glazed terra-cotta vases (Faenza, Museo Internazionale della Ceramica), in emulation of the Etruscan tradition from Vetralla and sparsely decorated (with abstract figures). *(Pl. 28)*

Canonsburgh Pottery Company. United States porcelain factory, active in Pennsylvania from 1901 to 1976, producing furnishings for bathrooms, table- and useful ware for hotels and restaurants, the latter featuring a crème impasto and relief decorations in neo-eighteenth-century style.

Cantagalli, Ulisse (1839–1902). Italian potter, by 1872 in Florence he ran a furnace that belonged to his family and had produced tableware since the eighteenth century; in 1878 he undertook to reproduce Renaissance Italian glazed majolicas and Persian and Hispano-Moresque ware. The factory Figli di Giuseppe Cantagalli in Florence (that is, Ulisse and his brother Romeo) won international admiration during the 1880s and 1890s for the production of art majolicas that also became decorations in the style of Della Robbia for the Cassa di Risparmio di Pistoia building and the majolica paving for the Borgia apartments in the Vatican Palaces. After Ulisse died in Cairo, in 1902 the firm passed down to his children, who combined with their period production the creation of modern, up-to-date forms in international style, winning a wide success in exhibitions, particularly the Paris fair in 1925. A number of artists collaborated with the firm during the 1920s and 1930s: Guido → Balsamo Stella (in 1921), Romano Dazzi, Antonio Maraini (in

1919), Carlo Guerrini, Gianni Vagnetti (in 1930) and Amerigo Menegatti, mainly in the representation of rustic, peasant themes.

Cappellin Venini & C. Italian glassworks founded in 1921 by Giacomo Cappellin (1887–1968), Paolo → Venini, Luigi Ceresa and Emilio Ochs, who took over Andrea Rioda's furnace. Under the art direction of Vittorio → Zecchin, the glassworks executed extremely thin blown glass items with delicate colours or transparent glass imitating objects figuring in sixteenth-century Italian paintings (*Veronese Vase, Tintoretto Vase*). After a conspicuous success in the first two Monza events, in the 1924 Venice Biennale and the 1925 Paris fair, the company broke up in May of that same year, separating into Vetri Soffiati Venini & C. (V.S.M.), run by Paolo Venini and Emilio Ochs, and Giacomo Cappellin's Maestri Vetrai Muranesi Cappellin & C. (M.V.M.), with the master glassmakers and Vittorio Zecchin. At the end of 1926 the latter handed over the management to the young architect Carlo Scarpa, who created light blown glass usually in geometric forms with a trunco-conical base, then introducing a series of glass in bright-coloured, light paste or else adorned with festoons (*Phoenician glass*), and later → milk glass items with gold and silver leaf that, along with the "vertical-canes" glass and the *Millefiori Vases*, were highly successful at the first Milanese Triennale (Monza, 1930). The factory was dissolved in 1932. Cappellin moved permanently to Paris, where he opened a laboratory to produce perfume bottles. (*Pls 31 and 90*)

Carabin, François (1862–1932). French cabinetmaker, from Alsace, he began his career as an etcher, and then moved to Paris where he worked executing intaglios for a furniture-maker in Faubourg Saint-Antoine. In 1884 he founded the Société des Artistes Indépendants, with the painters Signac and Seurat, and in the midst of the symbolist era became famous for the creation of either purely decorative carved articles, or chairs and tables, adorned with full female figures, like the 1893 chair and the 1890 bookstand shaped like a book upheld by four figures (Strasbourg, Musée des Beaux-Arts).

Caranza, Amédée de. French glass designer, from 1890 to 1918 he was a partner in the H.A. Copillet & Cie factory of Noyon (destroyed in 1918), who created a plentiful series of vases and articles in → art nouveau style endowed with delicately → iridescent surfaces.

Cardeilhac, Ernest (1851–1904). French jeweller and silversmith, after his success at the 1898 Paris fair, he became director of the laboratory his grandfather Antoine Vital had founded in 1802 and, in collaboration with Lucien Bonvallet, executed → art nouveau articles for the Maison Samuel → Bing, with themes drawn from nature and often made in different materials, such as ivory, exotic woods and offering various patinas. In 1951 the firm merged with → Christofle & Cie.

Carder, Frederick (1864–1963). English glass designer. Born at Stourbridge, he studied with Emile → Gallé, and in the years 1880–1903 designed for the English firm → Stevens and Williams Ltd., then moving permanently to the United States, where he opened his own studio, producing plain glass for the Thomas Haweks & Co. of Corning, New York. Focusing on experimenting with coloured glass in keeping with the → art nouveau manner, he founded with that same Haweks and other partners the → Steuben Glass Works, then sold in 1918 to Corning Glass Co., of which Carder became art director, a position he

François Carabin, Montandon *bookshelf, 1890. Paris, Musée d'Orsay*

held until 1933. His outstanding creativity led to an incredible number of highly effective pieces in the most varied colours, such as *Acqua Marine, Cyprian, Florentia, Grotesque, Verre de Soie* and *Jade*, in completely → liberty style. While he was director he used the "lost wax" (cire perdue) technique on various items, that he then personally signed and dated, while a great many pieces Steuben produced during the 1950s and 1960s bear his name in reference to the prototype he had created. Several modernist pieces dating from 1932 were subsequently etched. *(Pl. 29)*

Cardew, Michael (b. 1901). English potter, he trained at Saint Ives under B. → Leach between 1923 and 1926, then opening a studio in Winchcombe. Drawing his inspiration from English tradition, he specialised in producing household tableware, especially big carafes for cider, in semi-liquid clay coated with leaded enamel. In 1942 he moved to South Africa, becoming director of the pottery school of Achimota College; after getting married at Vumé, he began executing items in gres, always with decorations in geometric and ethnic patterns.

Carlton Ware. English pottery, active at Stoke from 1890 up to 1987, known for a very diversified production of tableware and table and kitchen furnishings and, in the 1920s, for series of large vases adorned with polychrome *chinoiseries* on cobalt blue grounds and displaying an interesting use of glaze techniques. *(Pl. 30)*

Carraresi e Lucchesi. Italian pottery active in Florence since the early 1930s, producing tableware and furnishings, such as vases with geometric shapes and bright-coloured air-brush decorations.

Carrickmacross. Lace produced in Ireland, composed of pieces of cambric applied by needlework onto a net-like background, using the cut-stitch technique; beginning around the mid-nineteenth century the pieces that were joined with the tulle stitch were called "Carrickmacross guipure".

Carrier-Belleuse, Albert-Ernest (1824–87). French sculptor, a major figure in the decorative arts during the Second Empire. Having fled to England after taking part in the uprisings of 1848–1849, he worked at the → Minton pottery, where he acquired processing and decoration techniques for both glazed majolica and porcelain. On his return to Paris in 1855, he soon asserted himself as a portraitist and decorator in pottery and bronze, especially for furnishings in which the female figure as supporting element prevailed, rendered in opulent forms and in classical attire (onyx and gilt metal centrepiece, executed by the firm Alphonse Pallu & Cie., circa 1862, London, Victoria and Albert Museum, or else monumental bronze torch-holders, highly appreciated by Napoleon III). In 1864 young Auguste Rodin began working in his studio, for the execution of reliefs and figures in unglazed pottery and porcelain (*Titan's Vase*, London, Victoria and Albert Museum). Art director of the → Sèvres porcelain manufactory from 1875 to 1887, the artist also designed pieces of silver tableware for the → Christofle firm and various furnishing items.

Carriès, Jean-Joseph-Marie (1855–94). French sculptor and potter, known for his production of bronze busts; in the period between 1880 and 1890, in the midst of the fad for *japonaiseries*, he worked on making art pottery near some clay de-

Cartier, brooch, platinum, brilliants, rock crystal and black enamel, 1925

Cartier, brooch figuring a scarab with an intaglioed fumé quartz body, cabochon emerald eyes, antique faïence blue wings adorned with cabochon emeralds and brilliants, 1924

Albert-Ernest Carrier-Belleuse, centrepiece, porphyry, silver and porcelain, 1886. Paris, Musée d'Orsay

posits in the Nièvre (Saint-Amand-en-Puisaye, where in 1890 an artists' community was formed, Château Montriveau and Cosne), processing dishes and vases with extremely simplified forms (emulating *Raku* pottery) and decorated with opaque, speckled, *flambé*, shaded enamels, introducing a fashion that would become widely popular in turn-of-the-century France. He also tried out creating figurative sculpture in gres, but with less significant results. *(Pl. 32)*

Cartier. French jewellery workshop, founded in Paris in 1847 by Louis-François Cartier (1819–1904), that after various transfers settled in its present premises on the Rue de la Paix in 1899, sustained by a remarkable popularity for the creation of "Napoleon-Trois" style jewellery, as well as the revival of neo-eighteenth-century and neo-Renaissance mountings and forms. In 1874 his son Alfred (1841–1925) joined in the management of the business, in turn followed by his own son Louis in 1908; but it was not until 1910 that the firm achieved worldwide fame under the combined direction of the three brothers, Louis in Paris, Pierre in New York and Jacques in London, always producing spectacular, luxurious jewellery, heightened by a conspicuous use of precious stones and, above all, diamonds mounted in classical forms and models, but also inspired by ancient Egypt and the Far East.

C.A.S. Italian pottery founded in 1919 at Savona by Bartomoleo Rossi under the name Ceramiche Artistiche Savonesi: one of the most interesting laboratories of Albisola majolica, known for its production of items in the classical → Albisola style, beholden to the floral tradition, as well as for the adoption of new forms and decorations, especially linked up with futurism (crested spheres, faceted polyhedrons and stylised figurines). The collaboration of Giovanni Acquaviva, a futurist artist, was of significance. *(Pl. 33)*

Casalini. Italian cabinet-making factory, active in Faenza between 1836 and 1950 under the name Società Anonima Cooperativa, known for the production of luxury and period furniture; around 1890 it began introducing pottery tiles in furniture and attending international events. In 1896 the potter Francesco → Nonni was engaged, working there until 1926, and contributing, with the designer Giovanni Guerrini, to the transition from → liberty furnishings in the style exemplified by the Bologna firm → Aemilia Ars to thoroughly → deco forms.

Cascella, Basilio (1860–1951). Italian painter and potter, who was responsible for reviving art pottery in the Abruzzo. In 1917 he learned his craft at the Bozzelli furnace at Irpino (Chieti) and was soon producing large polychrome majolica panels with female figure subjects, inspired by nymphs and naiads, centaurs and archaic-rustic themes in a naturalist style. In 1926 he presented a series of interesting panels in → deco taste for the buildings of the Montecatini spas, and between 1929 and 1931 executed the series of painted tiles that form the five monumental lunettes with views of Italian cities in the passengers' hall of the Central Station of Milan.

Cassina Amedeo. Italian furniture factory active at Meda since 1927 in the production of ladies' needle-work tables made of maple and of mahogany, lined in fabric. Since the early 1930s the firm made furniture for La Rinascente department stores, especially armchairs and upholstered couches with plain lines, made in walnut, mahogany and rosewood, using steam-curved beech that characterised the well-known 1930s armchairs designed by Paolo → Buffa.

Castellani, Pio Fortunato (1794–1865). Italian goldsmith active in Rome, renowned for having discovered the techniques the Etruscans used for processing filigree with tiny gold grains. Specialised in the reproduction of Etruscan and Magna Graecian jewellery, in 1853 he left the management of the workshop to his two sons Alessandro (1823–83) and Augusto (1829–1914), who presented their father's works in many international exhibitions and extended their sources for new creations to include Byzantine and Carolingian jewellery.

Cauldon Potteries. English pottery, opened in 1904 at Shelton (Staffordshire) and known for several series, produced in the early twentieth century, of hand-painted porcelain with floristic patterns — especially roses — on white grounds and gildings reflecting the decorative manner of the Victorian era. *(Pl. 34)*

Ceccaroni Rodolfo. Italian pottery active at Recanati since 1917, producing pieces in glazed terra cotta decorated with merely a few plain colours, in particular dishes and bowls with devotional subjects rendered in a stylised form and with a folk spirit.

Cellini, Renzo (1898–1934). Italian potter active in Rome, he became technical director of the pottery laboratories of the Scuola di San Michele in 1922, then in 1924 opened his own furnace at Pratica del Mare and founded a firm called Igne collucent; at the end of the 1920s he created the review *Keramos*.

Cenedese, Gino (1907–73). Italian master glass-maker; in 1946 he founded the Gino Cenedese & C., associating with, among others, Alfredo → Barbini, and presenting a selection of his works at the 1948 Biennale. During the 1950s, having broken off his connection with Barbini, he turned to other designers such as Napoleone → Martinuzzi, Fulvio → Bianconi, the painter Luigi Scarpa Croce and Riccardo Licata; after 1959 the art direction of the firm was taken over by Antonio Da Ros, the creator of magnificent pictorial *sommersi* (cased glass).

Ceragioli, Giorgio (1861–1947). Italian painter and decorator, active in Turin as furnishings designer as well: in 1892 he created a centrepiece for the nuptials of Umberto I and Margherita, and for the Turin fair of 1902 executed pavilions, furnishings and tableware, extremely elegant → liberty style pottery vases and silver bindings for the Società Ceramica Fiorentina, and silver tableware; the same year he was co-founder of the review *L'Arte Decorativa Moderna*. While providing drawings for book bindings, insignias, diplomas, plates, medals, silverware and jewellery, Ceragioli also sent a number of executive designs for tapestries and textiles to the silk manufactory of San Leucio whose art director was his friend Giovanni Tesorone.

Chalcedony. Opaque glass imitating semi-precious stones, such as onyx, agate, jasper and precisely chalcedony, obtained by blending molten glass of two or more colours and modelling the paste in the desired forms.

Champlevé. A decorative technique whereby the enamel paste is poured into the hollows etched on the surface of the item, usually silver, copper, bronze or another metal alloy.

Chaplet, Ernest (1835–1909). French potter, trained at the → Sèvres manufactory, he started off imitating Renaissance, Oriental and Hispano-Moresque ware, but around 1880 became acquainted with Gauguin, firing all of his pottery pieces; then with the Nabis group he discovered rustic Normandy pottery, launching a production of gres pieces with simple forms enhanced with bright colours. In 1885 he opened a laboratory in

Paris for the → Haviland firm and in 1887 a porcelain factory at → Choisy-le-Roi, where he fired vases in traditional Chinese style, glazed with the *flambé* technique.

Chareau, Pierre (1883–1950). French architect and designer, whose production was midway between → deco and 1920s rationalism; having grown up in a family of shipbuilders, he deemed it essential in designing furnishings to consider expense and functional outcome, giving up the use of precious materials, typical of deco, and producing designs for kitchens, children's rooms, wicker furniture (including round tables with a spiral support and chairs with a flared base, 1928). Yet at the 1925 Paris fair he set aside those principles, displaying a famous design for the furnishing of a library-den conceived for a hypothetical French embassy: palm-wood shelves, running along circular walls, and sliding in order to shield the skylight, defined the space around at centre a *table gigogne* (a table with triangular sliding planes), an ebony armchair upholstered in orange leather and a Macassar ebony desk (Paris, Musée des Arts Décoratifs), equipped with slanted, sliding shelves conceived according to precise functional intentions influenced by cubist aesthetics, previously used in 1919 in a design for a desk by the Bo-

Pierre Chareau, bookshelf and writing-desk, palm wood, veneered in rosewood and lacquered beech, 1925. Paris, Musée des Arts Décoratifs

hemian Antonin Prochàzka. In 1930 he launched the production of an ingenious chair made of unbroken steel tubular, derived from Marcel → Breuer's renowned armchair.

Charpentier, Alexandre (1856–1909). French sculptor and designer, he began by designing strictly streamlined furnishings in keeping with → Arts & Crafts precepts, but at the turn of the century adhered to floristic modernism, adopting wavy, enveloping lines executed in carved light-coloured woods, like for instance the well-known bookstand of 1901 (Paris, Musée des Arts Décoratifs).

Chelsea Keramic Art Works. United States pottery founded in 1886 at Chelsea (Massachusetts) by Alexander Robertson for making useful ware. In 1872 his brother Hugh (1845–1908) joined the company, introducing the production of art pottery, for instance copies of Greek vases, several samples of which, executed in 1876, are conserved in the Museum of Fine Arts of Boston. Again in 1876 production of a special type of tableware was launched, akin to items from the Limoges manufactory, with underglaze decorations and the addition, next to the commercial trademark, of the inscription "Bourg-la-Reine". While the influence of Chinese majolica can also be observed, since by 1884 they produced vases with monochrome or blue-green, reddish-green, yellow-green, oxblood red and *flambé* glazes, they worked with contemporary artists as well: in fact they made medallions and vases with decorations executed on designs by Gustave Doré and Hans Makart. The factory closed in 1888, and was taken over in 1891 by a Boston industrial group; at that time they began production of tableware with a crackled glass surface that became widely popular. In 1896 the laboratories moved to Dedham (Massachusetts), hence the change of name to → Dedham Pottery, meeting with considerable success in several United States fairs (Saint Louis, 1904). At the death of Hugh Robertson, his son William became director, limiting production to household ware. The factory closed down permanently in 1943.

Chéret, Gustave-Joseph (1838–1894). French sculptor and potter, brother of the etcher and lithographer Jules Chéret, a pupil of → Carrier-Belleuse, he started working in a porcelain factory at Boulogne-sur-Mer, then shifting to the → Christofle firm and to other French companies, finally becoming director of the Pallemberg at Cologne. Art director at the → Sèvres manufactory in 1886–87,

that same year he executed designs for the → Baccarat glassworks; a versatile modeller in the eclectic manner, in his later production he offered thoroughly → art nouveau works, such as in the well-known gres dish of 1904, figuring a female nude barely surfacing from the material and two dragonflies (Berlin, Kunstgewerbemuseum).

Chessa, Gigi (1898–1935). Italian painter and designer active in Turin, a pupil of Felice Casorati, he was one of the most loyal collaborators of the → Lenci pottery, opened in the Piemontese city in 1919: up to 1922 as designer of furniture and rugs, and later on of pottery and the staging of the factory's displays at the exhibitions of Monza (1923, 1927) and Paris (1925). His furnishings, hats, dolls, textiles and potteries were aligned on → deco taste, then lightened and simplified in the 1930s, as can be seen in the furnishings of the café Fiorina in Turin, made in aluminium and crystal.

Chiardoly (or Chairdola), Secondo. Italian potter, active in Rome in the 1920s and 1930s, in 1923 he offered vases inspired by the Austrian Secession, decorated with black stripes and small squares on a white ground, plant themes and stylised birds with two-dimensional painting again on a white ground. He usually signed his pieces with a triangle surrounded by the letters "CBR".

Chiesa, Pietro (1892–1948). Italian glassmaker active in Milan. After a short apprenticeship in the laboratory of the cabinet-maker Giovanni Battista → Gianotti, in 1921 he opened *La Bottega di Pietro Chiesa*, where he produced mainly artistic stained glass in a highly elegant → deco style, in which he revived medieval tradition and → art nouveau art glass experiments. Chiesa worked either on his own designs or on cartoons by prominent designers and artists, such as the series produced between 1924 and 1935 for D'Annunzio's Vittoriale degli Italiani, works by Guido → Cadorin, Guido → Marussig, Gio → Ponti, or the ones executed on ideas by Campigli, Carpi, Fini, Sironi and Oppi, or else, in collaboration with the naval architect Gustavo Pulitzer, stained-glass for the most elegant Italian cruise ships. Co-founder in 1927 of the group *Il Labirinto* (with → Venini, → Marelli, → Buzzi, → Lancia, → Ponti), he also began producing lamps and furnishings in glass, crystal, wood and metal. In 1933 with Ponti he founded → Fontana Arte (part of the Luigi Fontana glassworks), its production being outstanding not only because of the modern spirit of

Galileo Chini, stained-glass window, painted glass coated with lead, ca. 1908

the forms adopted but also by the quality and refinement of the materials employed: wood associated with mirror or glass surfaces, curved crystal, glass and crystal combined with steel. *(Pl. 35)*

Chini, Galileo (1873–1956). Italian painter and potter, after training in decorative arts in his father's restoration business and Florentine art schools, from 1897 to 1904 he was art director of the pottery and porcelain factory → Arte della Ceramica of Florence, founded in 1896 and that between 1902 and 1904 changed its name to Arte della Ceramica Fontebuoni. When in 1907 the firm was taken over by Chini & Co., run by one of his relatives under the name "Manifattura → Fornaci di San Lorenzo, Mugello", he became its art director up to 1927, while the firm kept on producing his models until 1944. Inclined to Anglo-Saxon graphism, from William → Morris to Beardsley, and to → Jugendstil and the floral motifs → art nouveau had diffused, Chini altered traditional fashions and patterns in an utterly modern spirit, also using glazing and gres techniques, the items thus produced winning him wide acclaim in Turin (1898) and Paris (1900); during the 1910s he was inclined to go beyond the naturalist lesson, adopting geometric and stylised decorations recalling Klimt. He regularly attended the Venice Biennales from 1901 to 1936, and between 1911 and 1914 travelled to Thailand, coming back laden with exotic inspirations that enabled him to renew his style: shifting from the worn-out → liberty stylistic elements of vases with flowers and wavy decorations to classical and archaic models enhanced with explicitly → deco motifs. *(Pls 7 and 36–38)*

Choisy-le-Roi. French pottery founded in 1814, yet that only achieved a certain fame in 1863 when, under the art direction of Hippolyte Boulanger, it launched a well-organised production in the field of industrial wares, architectural and sheerly ornamental decoration. Present at all the nineteenth-century world fairs, beginning with the Great London Fair of 1851, it marketed the most varied styles, some in the historicist vein, and even experimented with all sorts of materials, from traditional to marbled majolica. In 1878 the firm changed management, concentrating its production exclusively on industrial and sanitary ware, closing down permanently in 1934.

Christian, Désiré (b. 1846). French glass designer, up until 1896 he was head-designer for the firm → Burgun Schverer & Co., later founding, with his brother François and son Armand, a new glassworks

Hans Christiansen, drinking service, glass and gildings, ca. 1903. Darmstadt, Künstlerkolonie Museum

Hans Christiansen (for Villeroy & Boch), vase with poppies, chromolithographed and painted earthenware, ca. 1898. Darmstadt, Künstlerkolonie Museum

called "Christian Frères et Fils", that produced abundant series of → art nouveau decorative pieces featuring layers of different colours, acid-processed, enhanced with intaglios, enamel decorations and applications of drops of glass. The items can display the inscription "Désiré Christian" or the initials "D.Ch."

Christiansen, Hans (1866–1945). German designer, after training as a painter and decorator in Munich, he began experimenting with a two-dimensional style in the decorative arts, spurred by his fascination for the Japanese woodcuts he collected. Struck by the opalescent beauty of → Tiffany glass he had seen in Chicago in 1893, he decided to study the techniques of opalescent glass with the glassmaker Karl Engelbrecht; in 1897 he began collaborating with the Munich review *Jugend*, and in 1899 was one of the founding members of the → Darmstadt artists' colony. Conspicuous among his works that were closest to international → art nouveau are his textiles and wallpapers (with a rhythmic repetition of wavy lines), silver jewellery, polychrome stained glass and household glass items.

Christofle, Charles (1805–63). French silversmith, founder of the greatest firm in France producing silverware and electroplated silverware articles, still active today. Although he started off as a jeweller, around 1840 he became interested in silver items and silverware, and in 1842 acquired the exclusive rights to exploit → Elkington's patent for electroplating. Selecting an openly eclectic style, from "Louis-Quinze" to "Louis-Seize", he enjoyed the protection of Napoleon III, who commissioned him in 1853 to make an important table service (Paris, Musée des Arts Décoratifs). Alongside tableware, the firm also executed bronze furnishing items, designed by Carrier-Belleuse, and supports, again in bronze, for Second Empire furniture imitating "Louis-Quinze" style. In 1863 the firm passed down to his son Paul (1838–1907) and nephew Henri Bouilhet (1830–1910), who was in charge of organisation at the headquarters at Saint-Denis as well as in the Brussels, Vienna and Karlsruhe branches. They presented at the 1900 Paris fair a new type of metal glass dubbed *Gallia* (heavier than electroplated ware), with which in the 1910s and 1920s they executed superb pieces in → art nouveau and → deco style, up to 1935, when they produced the tableware for the steamer *Normandie*. Leading foreign designers also worked for the firm, among whom Tapio Wirkkala and Gio → Ponti (his table candlesticks shaped like stylised cornucopias and arrows were outstanding).

Cintra. Glass processing technique invented by Frederick → Carder in 1917 for the → Steuben Glass Works: the mass of heated glass is rolled over a marble or metal surface onto which a light dust of coloured glass has been previously scattered; once modelled, the piece is overlaid with a layer of clear glass. Decoration can consist of vertical different-coloured stripes, the rim being black glass paste.

Clemente Fratelli. Italian cabinet-making factory, active at Sassari between 1870 and 1951, renowned for carved, refined furnishings displayed in several national and international events. The true renewal of its production was owed to Gavino Clemente (1861–1947), a scholar of Sardinian folklore who, on the occasion of the 1902 Turin fair, launched a series of furnishings inspired by the rustic and peasant tradition of Sardinia, that won him wide acclaim throughout the 1920s.

Clichy. French glassworks founded in 1837 by M. Rouyer and G. Maes at Billancourt, then transferred to Clichy-la-Garenne in 1839, known for its production of → paperweights and furnishing items with → *millefiori* decorations from 1846 to 1857. In 1885, after being taken over by the Lander family, who began producing coloured glass, it was renamed Cristalleries de Sèvres et Clichy.

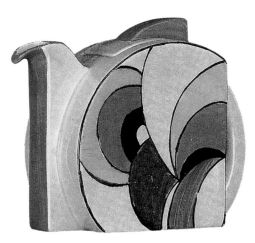

Clarice Cliff, teapot, ca. 1932

Cliff, Clarice (1899–1972). English pottery decorator, she was one of the most famous interpreters of → deco taste in painted decoration of pottery articles and tableware, adornments that during the 1930s featured on the one hand the use of *fauve* expressive styles and pictorial techniques (*Monsoon* series of round wall plates, 1930) along with French art deco models, and on the other utterly abstract designs (*Biarritz dinner service*, 1934) borrowed from the Central European Secessions and the → Bauhaus, such as the distinguished *Geometric Service* (1935), where the purity of form was heightened by the use of black and red.

Clifton Art Pottery. United States pottery, active at Newark (New Jersey) between 1906 and 1914, specialising in the production of vases and furnishing articles with archaic forms, in red earthenware with black or brown decors in emulation of the figurative models of the American Indians.

Cloisonné. Decorative technique whereby the enamel paste is poured into partitions (*cloisons*) formed by a grid of metal laminas soldered on the surface of the article: these create the design and, despite their being extremely thin, remain visible.

Clough Alfred. English pottery, whose trademark was "Royal Art Pottery", active in Staffordshire from 1913 to 1978, known for its production of large *cache-pots* on supporting pillars, petrol lamps and mantelpiece clocks, vases with lids and flower vases, drawn from French *belle époque* models, with an excess of polychrome decorations.

Clutha. Glass processing technique patented by James Cooper & Sons of Glasgow, a kind of forerunner of a certain type of → liberty glassware. The glass material is greenish or yellow, turquoise, brown-green or fumé with cased air bubbles, white and pink stripes, spots of → *aventurine*: the name comes from the Gaelic translation of the River Claid. The most interesting items produced with this technique were the glassware designed by Christopher → Dresser and George → Walton, inspired by Japanese decorative themes.

Coalport and Coalbrookdale. English porcelain factory, active since 1795 in Staffordshire and still working within the → Wedgwood plant, known for extremely refined series of tea sets, mantelpiece vases and flower vases with neo-eighteenth-century forms, as well as for the elegant floristic decorations on green, white and navy grounds with a generous use of gilding.

Colclough & Co. English pottery, founded in 1887 at Longton and closed down in 1931, known for its production of small heads and female figurines with typically 1920s and 1930s hairstyles and attire: a significant contribution to the spreading of → deco fashion and taste in Great Britain.

Cole, Henry (1808–82). English designer and critic, between 1847 and 1850 he founded Summerly's Art Manufactures that, intent on attracting artists to industrial production (especially pottery) with the aim of improving the quality of household items and the public taste, called upon painters and sculptors such as John Linnel, Richard Redgrave and John Bell. One of the main organisers of the universal exhibition of 1851, Cole was then named director of the new-born South Kensington Museum of London, which would become the Victoria and Albert Museum.

Coleman, William Stephen (1830–1904). English potter active by 1870 at the Copeland factory and then at → Minton, where he designed a well-known tableware service with transfer-printed decorations

James Cooper & Sons, bowl designed by Archibald Knox (for Liberty & Co.), clutha glass and pewter, 1904

Coalport and Coalbrookdale, two-handled bowl dubbed Incoronation Chalice, *polychrome porcelain, 1902*

with lenticular drawings of vegetables and flowers. He is known for having drawn one-off medallions and formal dishes with figured subjects in the manner of William Crane. In 1871 he become director of the Art Pottery Studio, a firm created by Minton in the Kensington district, gathering dilettantes devoted to painted decoration of pottery.

Colenbrander, Theodorus (1841–1930). Dutch potter, dedicated to the designing of textiles and to painting, in the last decade of the nineteenth century he turned to abstract compositions, vaguely plant-like, in emulation of *batik* fabrics from the Javanese tradition. From 1884 to 1888 he ran the pottery of → Rozenburg in The Hague, and from 1895 to 1901 the Amersfoort factory producing wallpaper and textiles.

Collcutt, Thomas Edward (1840–1924). English architect and designer, mainly known for his designs of furnishings that at first displayed simple forms in neo-gothic style and were made of oak, then turning in the 1870s to a neo-Renaissance manner, like in the famous ivory-intaglioed cabinet, with carved and painted panels, processed glass panes, shaped supports and countless compartments, assembled by the Collinson & Lock firm and acclaimed at the 1871 London exhibition. For the same company he had previously conceived the chair with shaped legs and back with bars held by a cross bar, that would become a symbol of Victorian taste. He anonymously designed entire productions, like the catalogue for Collinson & Lock (1870) and for other London factories, like → Gillow and Maple & Co.

Collinot, Eugène-Victor (d. 1882). French potter, known for having published in 1859, with Adalbert de Beaumont, a collection of 217 etchings titled *Recueil de dessins pour l'art et l'industrie*, an authentic repertory for the decorative arts, especially pottery. As a matter of fact in 1862 Collinot opened at Boulogne-sur-Seine a factory for producing tableware inspired by Iznik Ottoman and Persian ware, featuring the theme of stylised flowers and a generous use of navy and blue. One of the outstanding collaborators of the plant was Léon Parvillé (d. 1885), famous for his skill in imitating the styles of Near-Eastern pottery and his enamel-painting technique.

Colonna, Edward (1862–1936). United States architect and designer, born in Cologne and resident in Brussels during his studies, he went to New York in 1882 to work at the studio of → Tiffany and Associated Artists, but after a few years he moved to Dayton (Ohio), designing sleeping-cars and lounge cars for the Barney & Smith Manufacturing Co. In 1887 he published *Essay on Broom-Corn*, a text that classified the stylistic features and the artistic merits of modernism with a certain advance on the assertion of → art nouveau in Belgium. He practiced his activity as designer between 1898 and 1903 in Paris, in conceiving consistently → liberty jewellery, furnishings and household utensils for Samuel → Bing's firm. In 1905 he returned permanently to the United States.

Colonnese. Neapolitan pottery founded in the early nineteenth century by Salvatore Colonnese, a modeller who had learned his craft in the → Giustiniani factory. When he left the firm to his sons Francesco and Gaetano sometime between 1834 and 1836, production, along with the common useful ware, turned to artistic items imitating English ware and the forms and decorations of classical Roman pottery. The trademark is the name of the factory.

Combing. A glass-processing technique that produces a decoration of parallel wavy lines or imitating feathers on the hot glass filaments by means of a stylet or a comb-shaped tool.

Cometti, Giacomo (1863–1938). Italian furniture-maker, one of the most renowned furnishing designers in Italian → liberty style, a collaborator of the sculptor Leonardo Bistolfi for the execution of floral decorations on funeral monuments, toward the end of the nineteenth century he turned to the decorative arts and arts applied to industry, executing his own drawings and designs that were highly successful at the Turin fair of 1902, in keeping with the most exuberant Italian floral taste. Fascinated nonetheless by the experiments of the Austrian Secession and the multi-functional aims of the Glasgow School, he founded a workshop for making textiles, metals and furnishings available at low prices. Again in 1902 he collaborated with Galileo → Chini for the decoration and furnishing of Villa Falcioni at Domodossola. In the 1890s his familiarity with the futurist and secessionist movements enabled him to adhere enthusiastically to → deco taste, making furniture, like the writing-desk painted in green aniline (1920) and the dressing-table in ebonied wood on a design by the painter Felice Casorati, where the futurist conception was obvious. During the 1930s he attended all the decorative arts exhibitions in Turin.

Giacomo Cometti, sideboard, oak, brass and marble, 1902. Miami, Wolfsonian Foundation

Conradsminde. Danish glassworks opened in 1834 in Jutland that produced, besides colourless glass, articles presenting a singular, vivid and particularly rare cobalt blue tone. It discontinued its activity in 1857.

Cooper, Susie (1902–95). English pottery decorator, fascinated by cubist and abstract art, she produced between 1928 and 1929 several pitchers adorned in pure colours arranged in fitted geometric forms; then won over by → deco trends she discovered at the 1925 Paris World Fair, she developed her own idiom, characterised by the use of naturalist and plant themes in a geometric, purely decorative style on the crème grounds of dishes, teapots and kitchen ware. *(Pl. 39)*

Cooperativa Ceramica Imola. Italian pottery founded at Imola in 1874 by Giuseppe Bucci for the serial production of tableware and tiles; toward the 1930s the art direction called upon Walter Martelli, Marino Bandoni, Umberto Marfisi and Mino Monducci. Some of the most renowned creations are the ovate vases, with handles shaped like bunches of grapes, adorned with polychrome female figures at play or at work, in the spirit of Ponti's models.

Copenhagen. Danish pottery founded in 1779, specialising in the production of refined tableware and elegant navy and white services, as well as the series of statuettes figuring Norwegian peasants and miners. After going through a slump in the early nineteenth century, the plant was revived in the years 1828–57 under the management of Gustav Friedrick Hetsch, who in 1835 began reproducing in miniature all the works of the most famous Danish sculptor: Bertel Thorvaldsen. Sold by the Royal family in 1868, the pottery merged with the Alumina factory in 1882, and in 1885, under the art direction of the painter and architect Emile Arnold Krog (1856– 1931), it regained fame by putting on the market high-quality artistic items, often designed by important artists and executed with the technique of underglaze colours in shades of slightly misted grey and navy, a formula that can still be found in today's production. The articles designed between the 1890s and 1930s featured the use of decorations inspired by Japanese art and re-elaborated in keeping with the → art nouveau figurative genre: Chinese-style vases with abstract decorations obtained with transparent glazes, and figures of peasants, designed by Christian Themsen (1860–1921), birds, fish and various animals, by K.T. Kyhn (b. 1880) and T.C. Madsen (1880–1965). The trademark is still the original one: three underglazed navy waves.

Copier, Adries Dirk (b. 1901). Dutch glass designer, he was hired by the → Leerdam Royal glassworks in 1917 and in time became its art director, notably stepping up its fame and the quality of its products. The two series made on his designs are *Serica*, limited series of severe, streamlined glassware, and *Unica*, consisting of one-offs.

Cornelius & Co. United States factory founded in Philadelphia in 1812 and specialising in bronze casting. Known for being the leading producer of Argand oil lamps throughout the United States toward 1845. During the nineteenth century it also turned to making bronze bases for candelabras, supports for furnishing porcelains, nearly always in neo-rococo style.

Corrente, Vincenzo Leonardo (1887–1967). Italian potter, trained at the potteries of → Grottaglie, in 1910 he joined the Fantechi pottery at Sesto

Fiorentino; in 1913 he founded at Querce, near Prato, his own laboratory that, after reopening following the First World War, in 1920 took the name "Aetruriae Ars", since it produced Greek and Etruscan-style pottery. After transferring the plant to Sesto Fiorentino (1925), then to Le Panche (1927) and finally to Castello (1930), Corrente executed huge vases and amphoras, explicitly → deco figures, animals rendered in geometric forms and with abstract air-brush decorations; after the end of the 1930s his motifs became ribbons and braided rope.

Corroded. Glass technique allowing to obtain, by applying hydrofluoric acid onto the glass surface on which is scattered a type of resin that crackles on drying, an "ice" glass, where the presence of acid coincides with the resin crackles. Conceived and applied in Paolo → Venini's Murano glassworks since 1933.

Cortellazzo, Antonio (1819–1903). Italian chiseller who worked at Vicenza and attended nearly all the nineteenth-century world fairs with extraordinary chiselled gold, silver, steel and enamelled pieces. He started off by copying authentic gold and silver Renaissance articles, often acquired later by collectors as authentic, whereas toward 1860 he began signing pieces of his own production, with highly original forms, although always inspired by historical tradition: the 1860 sword for Victor-Emmanuel II (Florence, Museo degli Argenti), the monumental clock shaped like a Palladian arch (signed and dated 1871, Sheffield, City Museum), and the grandiose silver tea set made for Prince Narishkin around 1865–70.

Cowan Pottery, glazed vases, painted pottery, late 1920s

Cowan Pottery. United States pottery, founded in 1912 in Ohio and closed down in 1931, characterised by a production of vases with elegant, sparse geometric forms, adorned exclusively with glazed colours.

Crace. Family of English furniture-makers whose head was John (1754–1819), the founder of one of the most important furniture factories in nineteenth-century London, and the creator, in 1788, of the furnishings for the Royal Pavilion of Brighton, an execution pursued by his son Frederick (1779–1859), also the author of the decorations of the main rooms. When the firm passed on to the latter's son, John Gregory, it initiated its eclectic-historicist stage, with groups of furnishings, textiles and wallpapers in neo-gothic style, on designs by Pugin (for the new premises of the Parliament, private residences and the installation of the medieval courtyard at the Great Exhibition of 1851), and neo-Egyptian furniture designed by the pre-Raphaelite painter Holman Hunt. In the second half of the century, under the direction of the grandson John Dibble (b. 1838), the family firm specialised in producing Italian neo-Renaissance and neo-Elizabethan furniture, as well as furnishings in the Pompeian style, not leaving aside eclectic and Orientalising experiments: at the end of the nineteenth century the London firm was charged with restoring and redecorating the Royal Pavilion at Brighton.

Cranberry. Glass processing technique, used in both Great Britain and the United States since the mid-nineteenth century, that can be found in items executed in clear red or pink glass, in a number of different shapes: bowls, glasses and vases, featuring enamelled decorations, in white and in glass filaments. The name cranberry indicates the main colour of the central body of the article, that can also be ruby red (unlike the dark red used in Bohemian glassworks), onto which handles, stems and other clear glass adornments are applied.

Crane, Walter (1845–1915). English designer, trained in the pre-Raphaelite tradition, imbued with *japonaiseries*, associated with William → Morris and the → Arts & Crafts group, in 1874 be began designing tiles, and in 1879 vases for the Broseley di Maw & Co., these last imitating William Frend → De Morgan's red glazed porcelains. During the 1890s he continued his own activity, designing rugs, embroideries, printed fabrics, wallpapers and relief moulded stucco decorations. *(Pl. 40)*

Craquelures. Crackles that appear on the surface of pottery articles owing to the difference of contraction and expansion between the clay body and the outer glaze during firing. In modern pottery they are not considered a technical fault but a special decorative element, inspired by Far-Eastern pottery.

Creil. French pottery, founded in 1795 in the Oise, specialising in the production of earthenware with transfer-printed decorations, in keeping with English models. The articles, usually white or yellow, printed in black, brown or sepia, display landscapes, city views, hunting scenes or current events and, in the late nineteenth century, satirical images as well. The factory closed down in 1895.

Cros, Henri (1840–1907). French sculptor who, fascinated by the use of polychromy in sculpture, began in 1884 to work with → *pâte de verre*, intaglioed like old gemstones, and in 1889 exhibited reliefs wrought in that material. In 1893 he opened his own studio at the → Sèvres porcelain factory, becoming acquainted with contemporary artists and especially Auguste Rodin. In the 1900 fair he was awarded first prize for the glass relief *L'Histoire du Feu* (Paris, Musée des Arts Décoratifs); whereas he preferred using this technique for sculpture, Cros also produced several intaglioed glass paste vases.

Crown Milan. Glass processing technique invented by the United States → Mount Washington Glass Co. toward 1890 and usually called *Albertine glass*: an opal glass with acid processing offering a definitely decorative effect in brown and ochre colours and eventually glazings; several exemplars were executed in white opaline paste with gilt floristic decoration. The name comes from the trademark of the items made with this technique: a "C" over an "M" topped by a ducal crown.

Cube teapots. English pottery, active at Leicester from 1917 to 1951, specialised in producing exclusively cube-shaped teapots, cups, sugarbowls, adorned with floral friezes on bright yellow, red, navy and green grounds. *(Pls 41 and 42)*

Curved wood. Technique employing sheet → plywood curved by steam, used in the early nineteenth century in the United States by Samuel Gragg, who in 1808 patented the "elastic chair". In 1874 Isaac Cole in turn patented in New York the chair made out of a single piece of curved plywood (New York, Museum of Modern Art).

Cut glass. English definition that indicates the glass technique obtained by wheel-processing with geometric motifs items in very thick glass (perfume bottles and toilet articles).

Cutler & Girard. Italian cabinet-making factory, active in Florence between the end of the nineteenth century and the 1910s, known for its rich production of dark walnut furniture (shown in Italy and abroad), with strict forms and enhanced by pods and embossed, intaglioed copper plates, in → Arts & Crafts' style.

Cymric. A Celtic term referring to a particular series of jewellery and articles in silver, successfully commercialised by the firm → Liberty & Co. of London, chosen as a tribute to the Gallic origin of John Llewellyn, who was director at that time. *(Pl. 46)*

Cyprian glass. A glass processing technique having a special decorative effect, created by Frederick → Carder for the → Steuben Glass Works around 1915–20: blue glass rings are applied around the rim of each piece.

Czeschka, Carl Otto (1878–1960). Austrian goldsmith, who became a collaborator of the → Wiener Werkstätte, where he executed a series of extremely refined gold and silver jewels featuring malachite, moonstone, agate and mother-of-pearl, with naturalist themes rendered by fretwork or mounted on enamel bases.

D

Dalovice (Dallwitz). Bohemian porcelain and earthenware factory founded in 1804; in 1805 it obtained the exclusivity for the production of ordinary earthenware, a monopoly that lasted until the 1840s with excellent quality tableware. In 1830 it began producing porcelain and, especially by the late nineteenth century the variety of items greatly grew, ranging from the most refined articles to ones for everyday use. Presently the firm belongs to the porcelain plants of Karlovy Vary.

Dalpayrat, Louis (known after 1872). French enameller, connected with the revivalist Limoges school, he is documented during the 1880s in London, where he executed an ensemble of forty round enamelled plates, signed and adorned in the *grisaille* technique, now at the Victoria and Albert Museum. He also published a handbook on the *grisaille* technique.

Dammouse, Albert-Louis (1848–1926). French sculptor, glassmaker and potter, son of Pierre-Adolphe (1817–80), a renowned → Sèvres manufactory modeller. After studying sculpture, young Albert-Louis worked in the studio of A.L. Solon where he learned the technique of *pâte sur pâte* for decorating pottery, a technique used in a small laboratory at Sèvres after the master's departure for England. In 1874 he became famous for a series of items in Italian majolica and, in 1878 began working for the Poynat et Dubreuil factory at Limoges, producing decorated tableware and large-sized majolica panels, like the one to win acclaim at the Paris exhibition that year. Beginning in 1882, in his own studio at Sèvres, he started creating a series of pieces in gres with rough surfaces in emulation of Japanese tradition, while still working for porcelain factories, like → Haviland. Having become quite famous, also because many of his works appeared in the specialised reviews of the period, in 1898 Dammouse began experimenting with modelling and decorating utterly → art nouveau pieces made in glass paste.

Darmstadt. German pottery founded in 1905 by the Grand Duke Ernst Ludwig von Hessen in the vicinity of the artists' colony of that German town. Directed from 1906 to 1913, the year it closed down, by J.J. Scharvogel, the factory produced mostly gres articles with decorations obtained by speckling the surfaces, items that, while emulating typically → art nouveau models, also featured simple, linear forms aligned on Secession taste.

Dasson. French furniture-makers that gave their name to one of the most important firms producing eclectic style furnishings (neo-gothic, neo-Renaissance, neo-rococo), yet of fine quality, where traditional Parisian craftsmanship found ample space. Active around 1850 and during the Second Empire, the laboratory produced pieces that later were shown as originals in important collections: for instance the copy of the "Louis-Quinze" desk conserved today in the Wallace Collection of London.

Daum Frères. French glassworks, founded at Nancy in 1875 by Jean Daum (1825–85), then passed down to his two sons Jean-Louis Auguste (1854–1909) and Jean-Antonin (1864–1930), producing traditional-style tableware services and glassware, up to the end of the 1880s. In 1891, under the influence of Emile → Gallé's inventions, the factory turned to producing → art nouveau style glassware, and the Atelier d'Art opened at the Verrerie de → Nancy, a training centre for new glassmasters directed first by Jean-Antonin and then in 1900 by Henry → Bergé, who had been with the factory since 1897. Between 1905 and 1930 Louis → Majorelle and Edgar → Brandt contributed to the firm, mainly providing metal mountings for glass. In 1902 the factory introduced the production of glass (especially vases) in keeping with the style and technique of Emile Gallé, decorated with floristic and abstract motifs, later adopting a purely geometric idiom, used in → deco style on thick glass.

Davenport. English pottery specialising in earthenware with navy decorations stamped on a cream-coloured ground, introduced by John Davenport in 1793 and extended in 1820 with the opening of a division devoted to porcelain. Among the painters who worked in the two productions, specialising in tea and dessert sets, of significance was Richard Steele. The factory closed in 1887.

Dawson, Nelson (1859–1942). English enameller, a member, with his wife Edith (author of a technical handbook on enamel published in 1906), of the *Art Enamellers* group, linked up with → Arts & Crafts. Dawson's works in → *champlevé* enamel are widely known, while he used the → *cloisonné* technique to make minute panels and plates then inlaid in larger, embossed steel and copper articles; he also created, up to 1914, jewellery, brooches, pendants, belt buckles, clasps for coats and cloaks in the medieval-floristic Arts & Crafts style. In 1901 he founded the Artificers Guild.

Day, Lewis Foreman (1845–1910). English architect and designer, a member of the → Arts & Crafts; unlike the others, however, Day was especially drawn to industrial production, offering a series of designs for furniture, textiles, potteries, wallpapers and decorative items in iron, linked up with → Morris' models.

Debschitz, Wilhelm von (1871–1948). German painter and designer active in education, as a teacher of decorative arts, and known for the creation of items with daringly abstract forms. After starting off as a late-romantic painter, he was drawn to the production and artistic ideals of Walter → Crane and William → Morris. Settling in 1891 at Munich, he opened, in partnership with Hermann → Obrist, an institute for artists and artisans: Lehr- und Versuchsateliers für angewandte und freie Kunst, that in 1904, after Obrist departed, became Debschitzschule, known for being at the avant garde for training and creation, offering a metalwork laboratory, followed in 1906 (the year Debschitz opened with Lochner the Atelier und Werkstätten für angewandte Kunst) by one for weaving and in 1907 another for creating pottery. After the Second World War, Debschitz was called to the direction of the Hanover Handwerker- und Kunstgewerbeschule.

Deck, Joseph Théodore (1823–91). French potter, he began working for a textile factory in Strasbourg and, after a series of travels through Europe, in 1856 opened a pottery studio in Paris where he immediately began to experiment with various glazes, achieving in 1861 a particular shade of blue called "bleu de Deck". He is known for a production emulating Saint-Porchaire tableware, Turkish Iznik and Persian ware, but also for having employed a number of artists to decorate his early production of earthenware dishes (among whom Eléonore Escallier and Félix → Bracquemond). By 1870 Deck had become one of the leading spokesman of the Japanese style, decorating his own pieces with very bright-coloured naturalist motifs and, after 1878, making vases and large decorative dishes with gold grounds that became highly popular. As of 1880 he also began executing *flambé* glazes for porcelain articles. In 1887, having become director of the → Sèvres manufactory, he left the direction of the family firm to his brother Xavier. *(Pl. 43)*

Deco. → Art deco.

Décorchemont, François-Emile (1880–1971). French glassmaker, first close to the → art nouveau manner, by 1900 he began producing items in → *pâte de verre*, massive and with opaque surfaces; however in 1904, after countless experiments, he developed new colouring techniques for glass, using metal oxides, that rendered the items opaque and translucid, producing the effet of semi-pre-

François-Emile Décorchemont, vase, etched pâte de verre, ca. 1920. Paris, Musée des Arts Décoratifs

cious stones. This technique in the mid-1920s and 1930s was well-suited to a series of → deco pieces with more geometric forms, incised decorations and reliefs endowed with a special compositional liveliness.

François-Emile Décorchemont, bowl, pâte de verre, ca. 1930

Dedham Pottery. United States pottery, active in Massachusetts between 1895 and 1943, known for a production of dishes and articles adorned with stylised navy decorations on blue or crème grounds and an eggshell effect on the unpainted surfaces (*Peacock Pattern Plate*, ca. 1896).

Dedham Pottery, Peacock Pattern Plate, *ca. 1896*

De Feure, Georges (1868–1928). French writer and designer, of Dutch birth, at an early age he joined the circle of artists and aesthetes surrounding the figure of Samuel → Bing in Paris: not only as a Symbolist writer, but above all as a creative graphic artist and designer of furnishings and decorative articles in the most varied materials (wood, ivory, porcelain, fabric, bronze, glass, paper and silver). A highly refined colourist, also in emulation of French eighteenth-century, he enhanced wooden furniture, featuring lightly incised and carved plant motifs, with gildings and delicate tints (mauve, green, blue).

De Köngelige Porcelainfabrik. Danish porcelain factory founded in 1760 near Copenhagen; after becoming Royal property in 1799, it is still active today. Under the art direction of Emile Arnold Krog (1856–1931) and with the collaboration of the chemists Adolphe Clément and, later on, Knud Valdemar Engelhardt, at the end of the nineteenth century the plant executed original decors drawn from nature and inspired by the spare line of Japanese etchings to which, alongside its crystal production, it owes its fame.

Delaherche, Auguste (1857–1940). French potter, a student of the Ecole des Arts Décoratifs of Paris from 1877 to 1883, he is considered one of the major potters of the late nineteenth century. After first working in Ludovic Pilleux's L'Italienne factory at Beauvais, producing tiles and architectural elements, in 1886 he was named director of the electroplating department at → Christofle's, and the following year he purchased the → Chaplet pottery where he began creating groups of gres vases decorated with various glazes, not omitting occasional floristic compositions. In 1890 he opened a laboratory near Beauvais and in 1894 transferred permanently to Armentières, where he continued producing gres and porcelain articles. As of 1904, after countless acknowledgements obtained in the world fairs, he devoted himself exclusively to one-offs, collected in Europe and in the United States. First influenced by geometric patterns in emulation of fifteenth- and sixteenth-century Italian pottery, then turning to occasional floral motifs, from the 1890s on he decisively adopted highly simplified forms, also inspired by Far-Eastern pottery, enhanced by decorations produced by crystalline, *flambé* glazes, or with → *aventurine* that randomly, and depending on the surfaces, traces forms that are always different: these items, precisely owing to their specific modern style, exercised a determining influence on a great deal of the 1920s pottery production. *(Pl. 45)*

De Morgan, William Frend (1839–1917). English potter, an influent personality in the → Arts & Crafts movement, trained at the Royal Academy Schools, acquainted around 1860 with the historic group of the pre-Raphaelites. His first London production was limited to pottery and tile architectural decorations, but in 1862 he shifted from William → Morris to Merton Abbey, then opening his own factory at Fulham in 1888. His affinities with Morris' inventions can be seen particularly in the decorative motifs: animals, plants, fish, birds and antique ships, always elegantly stylised but with an exuberant, lively appearance and in perfect harmony with the form and surface they adorn. One of his fundamental experiences was working in Florence, as of 1892 and for every following winter, with → Cantagalli who enabled him to get away from the widespread Victorian taste combining neo-medieval and neo-eighteenth-century reproductions, and to find new models in Hispano-Moresque, Persian and Greek potteries, aligned on the style of the Tuscan and Emilian pottery production at the end of the nineteenth century. Specialising in the invention of tile prototypes, he also made splendid vases finished with lustre-glazing (that he contributed to revive) and in colours defined as "Persian", like turquoise, green and black.

Denby Pottery. English pottery opened in 1809 at Denby (Derbyshire), with gres household ware emulating forms and models used in Staffordshire. It adjusted after a while to the prevailing → deco taste: in the 1920s with the production of large vases adorned with metal glazes that shifted from orange to turquoise to navy, and in the 1930s with a series of vases, statuettes of animals and bookends shaped like animals adorned with pastel colours. The factory is still active, specialising in kitchen ware with very plain forms and especially vivid colours.

De Porcelayne Fles. Dutch majolica factory founded at Delft in 1653. In 1876 Joost Thooft took over the plant, employing Adolf → Le Comte as art director: he would precisely be the one to mark the rebirth of Delft pottery until 1915. Toward the 1890s they tried out Berbas pottery (bare forms, handmodelled on the wheel and coated with fluid glazes of various shades) and later the so-called "biscuit porcelain": an impasto of opaque porcelain, unglazed but with graffito decorations (the first pieces were shown at Turin in 1902); yet the main production is still the traditional blue and white figured pottery, typical of the Delft area.

Derby. English pottery active by 1750, that in the course of the nineteenth century went through a

particularly rich stage: with new investments and the opening of several laboratories, some being devoted to imitations of the pieces belonging to the great eighteenth-century tradition, reproductions rendered even more credible by the use of trademarks of the historic Derby period. The most famous of these laboratories was Crown Derby, opened in 1877 and, as of 1890 named → Royal Crown Derby Porcelain (still active), specialised in the production of tableware, with richly gilt and painted decorations emulating *japonaiserie* themes.

Denby Pottery, vase of the Oriental *series, ca. 1926*

Deruta. Italian potteries active since the fifteenth century, but that went through a prolonged slump during the nineteenth century; it was not until the end of that century, with the creation of the Museo Civico della Maiolica and the establishing of the Scuola di Disegno Applicato, that the plants had a productive rebirth aimed at reviving Renaissance motifs and techniques, particularly metal glazes. At the dawn of the twentieth century, the improved economic situation led to the opening of the Società Anonima Cooperativa Maioliche Deruta and, subsequently, of the Società Anonima Combattenti Grazia; toward 1920, in fact, the Maioliche Deruta (founded in 1904) took over the few factories that were still active in the town and, in 1922–1923, recruited Davide Fabbri, a native of Faenza, who was furthermore responsible for opening the → La Salamandra manufactory, presided by Giovanni Buitoni, founder of La Perugina; the latter formed an entire production unit for making luxury pottery containers for sweets. The merging in the single large consortium C.I.M.A. (Consorzio Italiano Maioliche Artistiche), then become C.I.M.A. - Maioliche Deruta, with laboratories also in Perugia, Gubbio and Gualdo Tadino, allowed to continue reviving the iconographies, models and techniques of the historical tradition, revised in keeping with the geometric simplification of the artistic avant gardes, but also retaining an extensive market of copies, period revivals and large panels, decorative dishes and furnishing amphoras, with the reproduction of masterpieces of Italian Renaissance painting. *(Pls 44 and 108)*

De Salvo, Giovanni Battista (b. 1903). Italian potter, art director of → La Casa dell'Arte at → Albisola, in 1929 he began trying out new pottery glazes, ranging from blue to yellow to red to purple, with fluorescent features, and new kinds of surfaces for vases, called *mats* or *craquelés*, adorned with hippocampi, ships, palms and farmhouses.

Després, Jean (1889–1980). French jeweller, who at Avallon (Bourgogne), his home town, opened right after the First World War a laboratory where he made, in an unmistakable style influenced by cubism and the mechanistic trend, jewellery and → *bijouterie* (costume jewellery) with flat forms, and adorned with geometric patterns executed in malachite, onyx, coral, turquoise and lacquer completely attuned to → deco style. His most famous pieces include the *bijoux glacés* (that use glass or crystal to imitate ice, incised by Etienne Cournaul between 1929 and 1937), the *bijoux moteurs* (in emulation of the various components of airplane engines, that he had designed during the war and shown for the first time in 1931) and the *bijoux céramiques* (in 1937), all usually signed and stamped (a lozenge with the initials "J.D." in the middle for the precious metals; a square for silver-plated items).

Despret, Georges (1862–1952). French glass-maker, born in Jeumont, he signed his own pieces engraving the name "Despret". Specialising in the execution of *overlay* glass vases, that is, with the outside surface overlaid with one or more layers of coloured glass that show through the incision, characterised by abstract designs and cased air bubbles, in 1890 he began making articles in vitreous paste inspired by dancing female figures, dubbed "Tanagras", and by → art nouveau models: female nudes, fish and animals. Demolished during the First World War, Despret's factory opened again in 1920, closing down permanently in 1937.

Diatreta glass. Special glass technique, invented in 1952 by Frederick → Carder for the → Steuben Glass Works and that took its inspiration from Roman glass; a technique however already experimented both by → Tiffany and → Venini. For the execution of these particular items, especially vases, the *cire perdue* or lost wax process is used, so that the adorned part, fretted and etched, is held to the surface of the article by glass stalks.

Dixon James and Sons Ltd. English silver factory, founded in 1806 at Sheffield and that soon became the most important Britannia metal tableware factory, for the most part exported to the United States by the mid-nineteenth century. In the Great London Exhibition of 1851 it became known for its pieces drawn from plants, such as aquatic plant leaves and flowers executed in silver or silver plate. Toward the end of the century the factory marketed several series of plated silverware, based on designs by Christopher → Dresser.

Doat, Taxile (b. 1851). French potter, after training in the pottery schools of Limoges, he worked at the → Sèvres manufactory in 1877, staying on until 1905, when he moved to the United States. In 1892 he opened his own studio in Paris, later transferred for reasons of convenience to Sèvres (1898). A specialist in the production of porcelain, he favoured decors in relief and white on coloured grounds; based on his enormous production (around two thousand pieces), he wrote a book titled *Grand-feu Ceramics*, published in English in 1905; in 1909 he became director of the pottery school of the University of Saint Louis. *(Pl. 105)*

Dolcetti Giovanni. Italian pottery, founded in Venice in the first years of the twentieth century under the name "Bottega del Vasaio", soon changed to the name of the owner who raised the laboratory to a high-quality level. Between 1921 and 1924 Giovanni Polidori, a skillful potter from Pesaro, worked for the firm, bringing it the entire tradition of decorated pottery from the Marche. The pro-

metric forms, highlighted by apparent riveting, far in advance of solutions adopted in Germany at the → Bauhaus, designs conceived for various specialised factories, including → Elkington (1875 to 1888) and → James Dixon & Sons Ltd. (1879 to 1882).

Dreyfuss, Henry (1904–72). United States industrial designer, after his debut as a scenographer on Broadway, in 1929 he was able to open an industrial design studio. Launched on the international market in 1930 thanks to a telephone designed for Bell (re-elaborated up to the 1950s with many imitations and variants in Europe), Dreyfuss also designed alarm clocks for the Ingraham firm, household electric appliances for Hoover (vacuum cleaners and washing machines), sinks for Crane, air conditioners and television sets for R.C.A. (as of 1946). Also active in the field of transportation, he designed a number of automobile models, farm machines, aircraft furnishings, always working on the theory of the ergonomic value of the articles combined with their aesthetic qualities.

Ducrot-Golia. Italian furniture factory active in Palermo since the end of the nineteenth century, it won outstanding fame with furniture designed by Ernesto → Basile and shown at the Turin fair of 1902. During the First World War, the crisis of modernist style and the slump in the market incited the laboratory to produce quality period furniture, specially conceived for furnishing embassies, hotels and steamers. In the midst of the 1920s the firm turned to → deco taste, and the last important furnishings were for the Hotel Columbia in Genoa and the luxury liner *Rex*; in 1939 the owner passed on the company to Tiziano de Bolis, who was to use the historical name up until the 1950s.

Dufaux. Swiss family enamel manufactory active in Geneva. Founded in 1853 by Louis (1802–84) for the production and sale to all the enamel and jewellery laboratories in Europe of pigments for enamels, the firm was also engaged in producing miniatures and small enamelled items emulating the Limoges tradition, particularly under the direction of the founder's sons, Marc-Louis (1833–87) and Pierre, an expert enameller on porcelain.

Dufrène, Maurice (1876–1955). French designer, a student at the Ecole des Arts Décoratifs of Paris, he was among the first to display his exasperation toward the henceforth worn out → art nouveau styl-istic features, and to seek a more essential, rigorous expressive manner in decoration. During his teaching activity (from 1912 to 1923) at the Ecole Boulle and as a regular collaborator in the review *Art et Décoration*, he exerted a deep influence on a whole generation of designers and artists, presenting himself as one of the founders of French → art deco. That style also appeared in the inexpensive furniture and in several especially precious one-offs, executed, since 1921, by the studio *La Maîtrise*, inside the Galeries Lafayette department store, in which his models were several inventions by Henry → van de Velde, enhanced with combined decorative elements.

Dunand, Jean (1877–1942). Furniture designer, a student of the Geneva school of decorative arts, after moving to Paris he worked in Jean Dampt's studio. After a brief début as a sculptor, in 1902 he went back to making decorative art items, especially in lacquer and metal, first connected with late- → liberty *imagerie*, then decisively directed toward the dryer, barer forms of → art deco. He mostly produced metal vases with gold, silver or enamel geometric decorations, beginning to exhibit them, along with Jean → Goulden, around 1921.

Ernesto Basile, Ettore De Maria Bergler, Antonio Ugo (for Ducrot-Golia), writing-desk, engraved mahogany, brass and oil paint, 1902. Rome, Galleria Nazionale d'Arte Moderna

France, and by his son Frédéric-Louis, who transferred the porcelain production to Turin in 1820, forming a company with Luigi Richard. The manufactory, that also counted among its partners César Prelaz, was active from 1824 to 1846, when it wound down and was taken over by Luigi Richard and Carlo Imolda, to whom Dortu passed on the family-tradition secrets for porcelain production, henceforth under the name Luigi Richard & C.

Doulton Pottery and Porcelain Company.

English pottery opened in 1815 at Lambeth, near London, with the trademark Doulton & Watts (active until 1858), for producing gres household and sanitary ware; in 1860 it also launched an imitation, still in gres, of brownish coloured containers, various forms of which had been already designed in the eighteenth century, and in 1862 began the well-known series of stanniferous glazed tableware with blue decorations. The arrival in the factory of George → Tinworth, trained at the Lambeth School of Art, gave a qualitative boost to the production, by a number of models of pitchers, jugs, vases, but also monumental fountains with relief decorations. In 1870 they also began a production using the graffito technique, introduced by the French painter J.C. Cazin and improved by the sisters Hannah and Florence Barlow who, specialising in animal scenes, created *Barlow Ware*; in those years the manufactory's commercial and collector-items success began, from six potters in 1873 growing to three hundred and forty-five in 1890, offering ever new typologies and techniques, such as glazed earthenware (since 1873), tableware called *silicon* (since 1879), *marquetry* ware (1887) and tiled panels (executed in 1900 by William James → Neatby). The factory then also continued to produce porcelain (opened in 1884 at Burslem, Staffordshire).

Drahonovsky, Josef (1877–1938).

Bohemian glassmaker, an expert in glyptics (that is, the technique of etching stones and glass, learned at the school of Turnov), in 1904 he opened his own sculpture studio in Prague, having become that same year a teacher of sculpture and glyptics in the decorative arts school of that city. Generally the glass items bearing his signature were executed by the pupils and finished by the master: this is true in particular of the cameos and triple-layer vases in glass with acid and wheel decorations. At the Paris fair of 1925 he was awarded the *Grand Prix* for his etched gems and glass.

Drawing. Technique consisting of embossing with a hammer or a punch a metal sheet so as to obtain a certain shape or a relief.

Dresser, Christopher (1834–1904). English designer and renowned scholar of the decorative arts, he immediately grasped the qualities and weaknesses of industrial production, counting on the development of design rather than on art craftsmanship. A student at the London School of Design, he started off as a very skillful botanical draughtsman, but influenced by Owen → Jones' art, he permanently turned his creativity toward the decorative arts, displaying it in production as well as in the theoretical ambit: in fact he published in 1862 *The Art of Decorative Design* and in 1871–72 *Principles of Design*. Toward 1867, he began working as rug designer for the firm Messers Brinton & Lewis, but, attracted to Japanese art, in 1877 he travelled to Japan, where he purchased articles for the → Tiffany firm of New York; in 1879, in partnership with Charles Holmes, he opened a company to import to Great Britain Oriental wares, about which he furthermore published a critical essay. A brilliant, swift inventor, he produced an endless series of designs for wallpaper, household tableware, furniture, glass, metals and potteries, the latter inspired by either Japan or the recent finds of Inca pottery in Peru (for the → Linthorpe Pottery between 1879 and 1882). Instead, for James Cooper & Sons of Glasgow he designed glass articles in the current → art nouveau style, especially with plant forms. Yet his most well-known activity is that connected with the creation of items in silver or electroplated ware, all characterised by extremely modern, functional and geo-

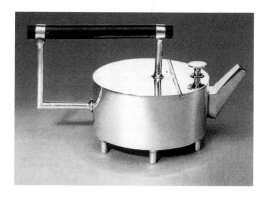

Christopher Dresser (for James Dixon & Sons Ltd.), teapot, plated metal and ebony, 1879

ries that were still active in the town and, in 1922–1923, recruited Davide Fabbri, a native of Faenza, who was furthermore responsible for opening the → La Salamandra manufactory, presided by Giovanni Buitoni, founder of La Perugina; the latter formed an entire production unit for making luxury pottery containers for sweets. The merging in the single large consortium C.I.M.A. (Consorzio Italiano Maioliche Artistiche), then become C.I.M.A. - Maioliche Deruta, with laboratories also in Perugia, Gubbio and Gualdo Tadino, allowed to continue reviving the iconographies, models and techniques of the historical tradition, revised in keeping with the geometric simplification of the artistic avant gardes, but also retaining an extensive market of copies, period revivals and large panels, decorative dishes and furnishing amphoras, with the reproduction of masterpieces of Italian Renaissance painting. *(Pls 44 and 108)*

De Salvo, Giovanni Battista (b. 1903). Italian potter, art director of → La Casa dell'Arte at → Albisola, in 1929 he began trying out new pottery glazes, ranging from blue to yellow to red to purple, with fluorescent features, and new kinds of surfaces for vases, called *mats* or *craquelés*, adorned with hippocampi, ships, palms and farmhouses.

Després, Jean (1889–1980). French jeweller, who at Avallon (Bourgogne), his home town, opened right after the First World War a laboratory where he made, in an unmistakable style influenced by cubism and the mechanistic trend, jewellery and → *bijouterie* (costume jewellery) with flat forms, and adorned with geometric patterns executed in malachite, onyx, coral, turquoise and lacquer completely attuned to → deco style. His most famous pieces include the *bijoux glacés* (that use glass or crystal to imitate ice, incised by Etienne Cournaul between 1929 and 1937), the *bijoux moteurs* (in emulation of the various components of airplane engines, that he had designed during the war and shown for the first time in 1931) and the *bijoux céramiques* (in 1937), all usually signed and stamped (a lozenge with the initials "J.D." in the middle for the precious metals; a square for silver-plated items).

Despret, Georges (1862–1952). French glassmaker, born in Jeumont, he signed his own pieces engraving the name "Despret". Specialising in the execution of *overlay* glass vases, that is, with the outside surface overlaid with one or more layers of coloured glass that show through the incision, characterised by abstract designs and cased air bubbles, in 1890 he began making articles in vitreous paste inspired by dancing female figures, dubbed "Tanagras", and by → art nouveau models: female nudes, fish and animals. Demolished during the First World War, Despret's factory opened again in 1920, closing down permanently in 1937.

Diatreta glass. Special glass technique, invented in 1952 by Frederick → Carder for the → Steuben Glass Works and that took its inspiration from Roman glass; a technique however already experimented both by → Tiffany and → Venini. For the execution of these particular items, especially vases, the *cire perdue* or lost wax process is used, so that the adorned part, fretted and etched, is held to the surface of the article by glass stalks.

Dixon James and Sons Ltd. English silver factory, founded in 1806 at Sheffield and that soon became the most important Britannia metal tableware factory, for the most part exported to the United States by the mid-nineteenth century. In the Great London Exhibition of 1851 it became known for its pieces drawn from plants, such as aquatic plant leaves and flowers executed in silver or silver plate. Toward the end of the century the factory marketed several series of plated silverware, based on designs by Christopher → Dresser.

Doat, Taxile (b. 1851). French potter, after training in the pottery schools of Limoges, he worked at the → Sèvres manufactory in 1877, staying on until 1905, when he moved to the United States. In 1892 he opened his own studio in Paris, later transferred for reasons of convenience to Sèvres (1898). A specialist in the production of porcelain, he favoured decors in relief and white on coloured grounds; based on his enormous production (around two thousand pieces), he wrote a book titled *Grand-feu Ceramics*, published in English in 1905; in 1909 he became director of the pottery school of the University of Saint Louis. *(Pl. 105)*

Dolcetti Giovanni. Italian pottery, founded in Venice in the first years of the twentieth century under the name "Bottega del Vasaio", soon changed to the name of the owner who raised the laboratory to a high-quality level. Between 1921 and 1924 Giovanni Polidori, a skillful potter from Pesaro, worked for the firm, bringing it the entire tradition of decorated pottery from the Marche. The pro-

Giovanni Dolcetti, box with lid figuring an eighteenth-century Venetian lady, painted majolica, 1926–27

duction of the factory in the 1920s and 1930s, mainly ornamental dishes, boxes with lids, cache-pots and vases, was characterised by the presence of multicoloured birds, exotic flowers, but above all Venetian architectures and figures in eighteenth-century costumes, rendered with bright colours and the kind of summary forms that were typical of twentieth-century taste. He signed his own works with the sentence "Botega del Vasaio G / Dolcetti in Venezia Bela / a Riva di Biasio" and then "GD" on the prow of a gondola.

Dolnì Chodov (Chodau). Bohemian porcelain factory and pottery founded in 1810, and by 1827 active also in producing porcelain articles under the direction of Jan Huttner, a master porcelain decorator at → Slavkov. Today it belongs to the Karlovy Vary porcelain manufactory group.

Don. English pottery specialised in the production of crème household ware, sometimes with transfer-printed decorations, and more rarely in black gres; all the items made here always bear the inscription "Don Pottery". Opened in 1790 at Swinton, it closed down in 1893.

Dorflinger, Christian (1828–1915). Alsatian glass-maker, he emigrated to the United States in 1846; in 1860 he was able to open the Greenpoint Glasswork at Brooklyn, known for the excellent quality of its etched or cut glass, and in 1865 opened another glassworks at White Mills in Pennsylvania, named (in 1873) Wayne County Glass Works, and finally, in 1881, C. Dorflinger & Sons.

Dortu. Italian porcelain factory, established by Jacob Dortu (1749–1819), active in Germany and

E

Eastlake, Charles Lock (1836–1906). English architect and designer, architecture scholar (he published *History of the Gothic Revival* in 1872) and interior decorator, he contributed to the transition from Victorian fondness for redundant, frilly furnishings to a revived simplicity of form and craftsmanship faithful to medieval tradition, applied also to wallpaper, tiles and wrought iron. His furniture, all featuring broadly gothicising references and style, was widely diffused in Great Britain and especially in the United States between the 1860s and the end of the century.

Ecanada Art Pottery. Canadian pottery, active between 1926 and 1952 at Hamilton (Ontario), known for its production of a series of furnishing items and vases with strictly cylindrical forms, made in dark green, powder blue, brown and white paste, with overlaid white decorations intaglioed in emulation of jasper cameos and following → Wedgwood models.

Echardt, Edris (b. 1910). United States glassmaker and potter, born in Cleveland (Ohio), he is renowned for having developed new processes for making "gold" glass (*Zwischengoldglas*), that is, gold leaf cased between two colourless layers of glass, offering the particularity of casing the precious laminas within several layers of different glass; furthermore he made glass sculptures using the *cire perdue* method.

Eckmann, Otto (1865–1902). German designer, after training to be a painter, in 1894 he switched to creating decorative art items in pottery, glass and metal, as well as furnishings, jewellery and tapestries. Between 1895 and 1900 he worked as graphic artist for the reviews *Pan* and *Jugend*, and in 1897 published the handbook *Neue Formen. Dekorative Entwürfe fur die Praxis*, closely reflecting → Jugendstil theories. Aside from preparing cartoons for tapestries in modernist taste for the weaving school of Scherrebeck, in 1897 he exhibited at the Glaspalast of Munich a refined series of metal articles and designed the modernist furnishings for the study of the Grand Duke Ernst Ludwig von Hessen at the Darmstadt Neues Palais. *(Pl. 8)*

Eclectism. The term defines a particular phase in nineteenth- and twentieth-century European culture, whose roots go back to historical Romanticism and that, crossing the entire century, lasted until the 1920s. The quest for origins, for historical and linguistic traditions, and the assertion of national awareness, urged the European cultures, by the 1830s, toward a rehabilitation of medieval civilization: it was identified, as opposed to the internationalism of classical and Mediterranean culture, as being at once the common cradle of communal liberties and the bastion of Christian faith, the background for the purest, most virtuous knightly existence and the best-suited atmosphere for the most extreme felonies and treacheries. Those were the Middle Ages of historical novels, opera, historical painting. But those "ages-in-the-middle" had left a great number of traces on the land: from strongholds to parish churches, convents to courts of justice and cathedrals, yet testimonies that were reduced to fragments, overwhelmed by radical alterations or even in ruins, but that increasingly became symbols of the glorious pasts of nations and cities, exercising all the while the fascination of a world forever lost. In the field of architectural restoration, during the nineteenth century, this approach led to returning, often in an arbitrary, artificial manner, to the original state, as in the case of the city and walls of Carcassonne in southern France rebuilt by Eugène-Emmanuel Viollet-le-Duc between 1846 and 1858, but at the same time to a more profound knowledge of the materials, techniques and styles of the past. These experiences gave an impetus to architectural revival, that is, to the production of period architectures and furnishings imitating various historical periods: including neo-Egyptian, neo-Romanesque, neo-Gothic, neo-Renaissance and neo-Rococo. In the second half of the nineteenth century and the first decades of the twentieth, along with this manner of taste an authentic eclectism appeared, that tended to juxtapose and combine in a same building elements and decorations belonging to different styles and periods.

Edinburgh Crystal Glass Co. Scottish glass-works founded in 1864 in the town of Penicuik, near Edinburgh, merging a series of small glassworks of Leith, including Norton Park, taken over in 1919 by Webb's Crystal Glass Co. Its present name goes back to 1955.

Edinburgh Weavers. Scottish weaving loom opened in 1932 as a branch of Morton Sundour Fabrics; specialised in printed furnishing fabrics, the firm is still outstanding for the high quality of its designs and colours. Under the direction of A. Morton, that lasted until 1963, the factory availed of the graphic designs of artists such as Jo Tilson, Marino Marini, Keith Vaughan and Victor Vasarely.

Egermann. Two important glass decorators in Bohemia were known by this name: Friedrich (1777–1864), born in Blottendorf near Haida, began his activity as enamel decorator of glass items in the wake of the fame gained by the production of Anton Kothgasser's manufactory, but very soon, after a number of experiments, he began producing at the Haida glassworks a group of coloured glass articles that became particularly popular. 1828 is the year → *lithalyn* was invented, a shiny, non transparent red-marbled glass, imitating semi-precious stones, whose production lasted until the 1870s under his patent. In the years 1820–1840 Friedrich also patented the method for brush-painting glass in yellow and red, producing the effect of a very thin coating. Anton Ambros (d. 1888), known as an expert decorator of enamel on glass, ran his father's laboratory at Novyj Bor in Bohemia, and after 1878 worked also for the → Lobmeyr factory.

Eglomisé glass. Glass technique invented by the French art dealer Jean-Baptiste Glomy at the end of the eighteenth century, consisting of securing a gold or silver leaf onto a layer of glass, after having drawn the decoration with a drypoint, this then being protected by a second vitreous layer that is soldered to the first by firing, sometimes coated over with a black glaze.

Ehrenfeld. German glassworks erected near Cologne, toward the middle of the nineteenth century it began producing articles in pressed glass or emulating the style of Bohemian factories. Under the direction of Oskar Rauter, in 1872, it began producing series of hand-made pieces imitating models connected with the German and Venetian glass tradition, especially tall goblets that won awards in many exhibitions (Nuremberg, 1881; Paris, 1900). Along with utterly plain-shaped drinking services, in 1899–1900 series of smoked glass, therefore linked up with → art nouveau taste, were produced.

Erlich, Christa (b. 1903). Austrian potter, she attended the Kunstgewerbeschule from 1920 to 1925, following the courses of Josef → Hoffmann (for whom she executed the stuccoes of the Sonia Knips house, in 1924–25), and of Michael → Powolny. Creator of pottery and fabrics at the → Wiener Werkstätte, in 1927 she moved to Holland, where she designed silverware for the Zilver-Fabriek, potteries for Regout & Maastricht, tapestries for Max Schmidt and items in precious metals for the Royal Dutch manufactories; she participated in the 1925 Paris fair.

Eiff, Wilhelm von (1890–1943). German glass designer known for having collaborated with a number of glassworks, including → J.& L. Lobmeyr and René → Lalique, for which he sometimes signed his pieces with the initials "W v E". In 1922 at Stuttgart he began teaching glass decoration techniques, of which he was a celebrated expert, both in etching and intaglio, designing items that were then decorated with miniature portraits or high-relief figures, created with new carving techniques or the use of *Geschnitzt*, that is, a way of chipping that he perfected in 1930 after patenting a flexible tool adapted to rendering with the utmost delicacy the most varied types of etching.

Eisenlöffel, Jan W. (1876–1957). Dutch metalwork designer, working in 1896 as designer at the Hoecher en Zn. jewellery firm in Amsterdam; after attending a specialisation course in enamel and niello at Saint Petersburg, in 1900 he became art director of the metalwork laboratory of the → Amstelhoek factory and a collaborator of → 't Binnenhuis, defending strictly modernist options in models that could be adapted to mass production, handles and spouts being attached with hand-hammered rivets. In 1904 he signed a contract with the C.J. → Begger firm, for which he designed countless groups of pieces in silver, whereas between 1903 and 1908 he designed copper and brass articles for the De Woning company; in 1909 he also began producing precious one-offs.

Jan Eisenlöffel, coffee set, silver, ca. 1910. The Hague, Haags Gemeentemuseum

Elgin. The name of a series of articles produced by the Bohemian etcher Frederick E. → Kny for the Dennis factory of Thomas → Webb & Sons in the 1870s, and in emulation of the Parthenon friezes purchased by Lord Elgin, exhibited at the British Museum in London: wine carafes and amphoras with long necks and curved handles in clear glass adorned with ribbings, palmettes and acanthus leaves, with at centre a large frieze reproducing the Panathenaea horse race. The items, shown unfinished in Paris in 1878, would be completed in 1879; exemplars are conserved at the Victoria and Albert Museum in London and in Birmingham.

Elkington. English metalworks factory founded by George Richard Elkington (1801–65), inventor of the electroplating processing method (1840) that enabled to either gild or silver articles in metal without using the dangerous mercury mixture, or to restore items at a low cost. After patenting the new technology (used also by the French company → Christofle and the English → Dixon & Sons), in 1842 the factory became a partner in the firm of Josiah Manson, that made pens, and in 1847 the new company Elkington, Manson & Co. launched their own large-scale production of electroplated tableware inspired by a variegated → eclecticism, ranging from Moresque to neo-rococo, from neo-Renaissance to

neo-medieval, as is evidenced in the sales catalogues appearing that year. Official supplier of leading hotels, restaurants, steamer companies and clubs, but also of private parties, the rather prosperous firm began equally to reproduce antique pieces using galvanoplasty, patented also, calling more and more often on artists, many being French, for designs of solid silver one-offs having an explicit, redundant decorative value (*The Bowl of the Inventions*, on a design by L. Morel-Ladeuil, 1863, London, Victoria and Albert Museum). Toward the 1870s, the manufactory, that had received many awards in international exhibitions, counted nearly a thousand employees and then, while remaining faithful to tradition, during the last two decades of the century it became receptive to the novelty of Christopher → Dresser's designs, this remaining however an exception. The company is still active.

Elmslie, George Grant (1871–1952). American architect and designer born in Scotland, he emigrated to the United States in 1884 and in 1887 began his training in the Chicago studio of J.L. Silsbee, along with G. Maker and Frank Lloyd → Wright, and in 1889 he joined Louis Henry Sullivan, becoming his main designer in the years between 1895 and 1909. He executed middle-class interior furnishings, metal and glass articles, and is known for a series of rugs adorned with stylized plant motifs, characterized by pointed, angular forms that would be repeated later in Sullivan's architectures.

Elton, Edmund Harry (1846–1920). English potter, member of the → Arts & Crafts, in the 1880s he inherited Clevedon Court in Somerset where, in collaboration with the potter G. Masters, he began producing earthenware featuring floristic decorations in liquid clay and coloured in shades of blue, green and red (*Elton Ware*).

Endell, Auguste (1871–1925). German architect and designer, working in Munich, exponent of → Jugendstil and connected with → Obrist's output. Creator of jewellery, textiles and refined furnishings

that displayed a gradual distancing from the more explicitly modernist forms, tending toward a more rarefied floral adornment and more functional forms.

Essevi. Italian pottery opened in 1934 at Turin by Sandro Vacchetti (formerly art director of the → Lenci factory) and Nello Franchini; it borrowed many of the Lenci themes (especially female figures, nude or in contemporary garb), benefitting by the contributions of the sculptors Otto Maraini and Ines Grandi. Furthermore it produced a series of figures in traditional Sardinian costume, entirely modelled by the sculptor Alessandro Mola. The prototypes produced by the laboratory amount to around eight hundred, all numbered under the base, indi-

Elkington, Manson & Co., jewel-box, gilt bronze, silver, enamel and painted porcelain, 1851

Edmund Etling & Cie, horse, glazed and gilt bronze on a black marble base, 1925. Gardone Riviera, Il Vittoriale

cating the date and stamped by the manufactory, that was closed owing to the war and in 1952 permanently wound down its activity.

Essex & Co. English wallpaper manufactory; opened in London in 1887 merely for distribution, in 1897 it became active with its own plant. It called upon numerous designers, including Lindsay Butterfly and A.J. Baker; yet the most famous is Charles Francis Annesley → Voysey, who in 1893 wrote up a contract for the production of a broad range of tapestries, hand- and machine-printed, openly aligned on William → Morris' floral taste and re-

ceptive to the solutions of European → art nouveau. The plant wound down in 1914.

Este. Italian pottery active since 1758 under the name Giovan Battista Brunello, associated with a second factory, opened by Girolamo Franchini in partnership with the Frenchman Giovan Pietro Varion, known for the production of cream-coloured tableware, pottery and porcelain statuettes and monumental centrepieces. Active during the nineteenth century with the same kind of items, the two factories merged in 1893, taking the name Este Ceramiche e Porcellane, still producing today.

Etching on glass. Technique referring to one of the most ancient processings of vitreous paste, performed either with a grinder or different-sized wheels, on a surface consisting of several layers; sometimes a mixture of abrasive paste and oil can be used as well. Decorations can either be intaglioed, that is, obtained by hollowing, or cameo, that is, in relief. Nowadays → acid etching is the preferred technique.

Etling Edmund & Cie. French glassworks, active in Paris in the 1920s and 1930s, specialising in the production of objects, small sculptures with animals, fish and female figures, nude or draped in veils, and figured caps for automobile radiators, in opalescent glass often shifting to gold and blue shades. The firm commissioned a number of sculptors for bronzes and chryselephantine statuettes as well, which were then commercialised with the label "Etling Paris".

F

Fabergé, Peter Carl (1846–1920). Russian jeweller, son of Gustav, a French goldsmith settled in Petersburg in 1842. After a long formation trip in Europe, Peter Carl took over the family firm in 1872, making it the most important jeweller's shop in the city, whose renown was consolidated by imperial recognition in 1881. The following year, forming a partnership with his brother Agathon, just back from Dresden and from having acquired a fundamental experience with Dinglinger, Fabergé began production on a large scale, backed by nearly five hundred employees, including designers, modellers, stonecutters, enamellers and goldsmiths; he opened branches in Moscow (1887), Kiev (1905), and thanks to the family ties between the Romanovs and the Windsors, in London, in 1906. Among his most celebrated creations, of great significance were the Easter eggs executed for the Czars Alexander III and Nicholas II, made with precious and semi-precious materials and featuring perpetually different decorative inventions; those one-offs would later be revisited in a serial production for ordinary sales. Mainly a supplier of the Russian and English aristocracy, but of other European countries as well, Fabergé executed with equal eclectic refinement in the choice of materials tableware, tea sets, frames, pens, cigarette holders, jewels and knick-knacks: statuettes of Russian peasants, animals and bouquets of flowers made of precious stones placed in small rock-crystal vases. While his principal model remained French eighteenth-century jewellery, enhanced by a typically Russian polychromy, a few pieces of the 1910s openly displayed an → art nouveau taste. The firm would be nationalised after the Bolshevik revolution in 1917. *(Pl. 47)*

Fabris. Italian pottery opened in Milan in 1917 by Luigi Fabris (b. 1883) who, in 1912, took over the old Passarin di Nove furnace near Bassano del Grappa, whence he had fled after the defeat of Caporetto. In 1919 he began modelling the first pieces of hard porcelain, used either in technical appliances (engine candles, insulators) or artistic, the latter with quite limited series of statuettes and plas-

tic groups — even very large ones — inspired by eighteenth-century European porcelain models. After suffering heavy bombing in 1942, the factory transferred to Bassano, where it is still active.

F.A.C.I. Italian pottery, its full name being Fabbrica Artistica Ceramiche Italiane; founded in 1926 at Civita Castellana by Carlo Guerrieri, thanks to the precious contribution of local craftsmen it obtained a certain success on the market, producing boxes and small containers adorned with masks and air-brush colours, but also with applied relief decorations.

Falize, Lucien (1839–97). French jeweller seeking to revive the technique of clear enamel, he continued to follow the most explicitly → eclectic models, even amidst the success of → art nouveau, after having taken over his father's laboratory in 1880 and forming a company with the silversmith Germain Baptiste. Carrying to extremes the revival of Renaissance, medieval and rococo styles, he executed nearly exclusively formal articles, that were largely echoed in the reviews of the times, especially in reference to their patrons.

Fallica, Alfio (1898–1971). Italian designer, born in Sicily, he moved to Rome where he took part in the 1925 Biennale, entering → Cambellotti's group; 1927 was the year he designed some dining-room furniture (shown at Monza) in briar-root and polished black wood, with square forms, and handles consisting of two extremely graceful stylised deer; on the other hand in 1930 he signed several pieces of furniture with severe forms, featuring large surfaces divided in horizontal parts by a clever contrast between light and dark woods, decorated with stylised inlays. In 1940 he returned to Sicily, settling permanently in Catania.

Fancello, Salvatore (1916–41). Italian potter, hailing from Sardegna, he arrived at the I.S.I.A. in Monza in 1930, and immediately won recognition as a very skillful modeller, especially of animals, often in groups, and Christmas crib figures with surface etchings. In 1938 at → Albisola, for the Mazzotti factory, he initiated a very abundant, imaginative production of high-relief panels and three-dimensional figures in vivid colours, but also vases with animal figures in enamelled reliefs with dark metallic hues on bright-coloured grounds.

Fantoni, Marcello (b. 1915). Italian potter, after being art director of a pottery at Perugia, in 1936 he opened his own workshop in Florence, and by the next year it had already become the most up-to-date studio in the city for its rustic style, rich in African and marine suggestions enhanced by stylised, glazed figurines.

Fattorini. English jewellery manufactory founded in London in 1827 and specialised in the production of plates and trophies, especially in period styles, and in enamelled medals on neckchains. In 1927 another laboratory was opened in Birmingham, and the firm is still in business today.

Fauré, Camille (1872–1947). French enameller, active at Limoges, known primarily for his extremely elegant enamelled vases and bowls with explicitly → deco motifs. In 1920 he tried out a technique whereby copper items were coated with silver leaf featuring areas of translucid and opalized enamels, adorned with geometric patterns and severe lines. He remained active until 1940.

Favrile. Term coined in 1894 by Louis Comfort → Tiffany for an opaque → iridescent glass that, owing to its ingredients and the type of decoration executed, is very similar to metal, analogous to the glass produced in the early nineteenth century by Lötz in Bohemia. The etymology of *favrile* is the Latin *faber*, with the aim of displaying its utterly artisanal nature (every single piece is actually made by hand by the craftsmen) and the symbolic connection with the crucible where metals are processed. Emulating naturalist themes of → art nouveau origin, these Tiffany vases, lamps and items, often stamped or fully signed by the artist, resemble Roman glass unearthed after centuries by excavations, since the antique gold, the blue, green and other colours are sprayed onto the object while it is still in the furnace, or anyway still hot, in such a manner that the metal salts, attacking the surfaces, confer on them iridescence and a mother-of-pearl effect exactly like antique glass.

Fenice. Italian pottery founded at → Albisola in 1922 by Manlio Trucco, in partnership with the painter Geranzani; however, since the latter preferred the decoration called "old Savona", after just a year he withdrew from the laboratory. From 1922 to 1926 the factory had three turners and forty designers, and in 1926, through the good offices of Mario Labò, collaboration began with the sculptor Arturo → Martini, who produced a series of terra cottas, either figurines or groups of small figures, then painted by Trucco himself. Others who worked for Fenice during the 1930s and 1940s were Romeo Bevilacqua, Francesco Di Cocco, Francesco Messina, Emanuele Rambaldi, Nanni Servetti and the Genovese painter Adelina Zandrino. In 1936 the company was taken over by Ernesto Daglio, who launched a production aimed at the American, French and English markets.

Feuillâtre, Eugène (1870–1916). French goldsmith and enameller, working for the → Lalique firm and then for → Falize, where he was director of the enamelling laboratory until 1897; in 1900 he opened his own business, and that same year displayed in the international Paris fair extremely tasteful items in → art nouveau style, made in glass, silver and clear enamels.

Fielding & Co. English pottery, founded at Stoke in 1879 and dissolved in 1982, known for a varied production of tableware and kitchenware, tea and coffee sets, decorative statuettes; during the 1930s, in particular, it was able to produce a felicitous combination of purely abstract decors, inspired by the creations of Clarice → Cliff and Susie → Cooper in cubist style, and geometric floral motifs and female figures in fashionable attire.

Figini, Luigi (1903–84) and Gino Pollini (b. 1903). Italian designers, espousing since their youth the functionalist principles of → Le Corbusier and Gropius, they became the promoters of the Italian rationalist movement, founding in 1926 the *Gruppo 7*; by 1929 they started designing furniture that was so streamlined and modernist (like the chair in steel tubular and plain padding of 1930–31, or the Olivetti sitting-room of 1932) as to be still produced and sought after today. In 1933 they won the competition of the V Triennale of Milan with a radiogramophone made in Makassar ebony supported by four tubulars in chromium-plated metal, and in 1936 the one for a writing-desk with modular elements suitable for industrial production.

39. Susie Cooper, jug with geometric decorations, majolica, 1928–29

41. Cube Teapots, the 1930 catalogue

42. Cube Teapots, teapot with floral decorations, majolica, ca. 1930

40. Walter Crane (for Maw & Co.), Skoal ("Cheers!") amphora, earthenware, 1898–1900. Budapest, Iparmüvészeti Múzeum

43. Joseph Théodore Deck, bowl imitating Iznik pottery, ceramic, 1867. Paris, Musée du Louvre

44. Deruta, dish with neo-Renaissance grotesques, polychrome majolica, 1920–25

45. Auguste Delaherche, peacock feathers vase, enamelled earthenware, ca. 1889. Paris, Musée des Arts Décoratifs

46. Archibald Knox (for Liberty & Co.), pitcher of the Cymric *series, silver and cabochon stones, 1903*

47. Peter Carl Fabergé, dolphin table lamp, silver and onyx, ca. 1890

48. *Angelo Biancini (for Società Ceramica Italiana di Laveno),*
Duck and ducklings, *earthenware and coloured glazes, 1938*

49. *Emile Gallé, vase with chrysanthemums, cameo-etched*
pâte de verre, 1890–95

52. Grueby Faïence Company, vase, gres, 1898–99. London, Victoria and Albert Museum

53. *Haagsche Plateelbakkerij Rozenburg, vase with lid, painted and glazed gres, 1887*

54. *Haagsche Plateelbakkerij Rozenburg, vase with peacocks and irises, polychrome porcelain, 1908. Karlsruhe, Museum beim Markt - Angewandte Kunst seit 1900*

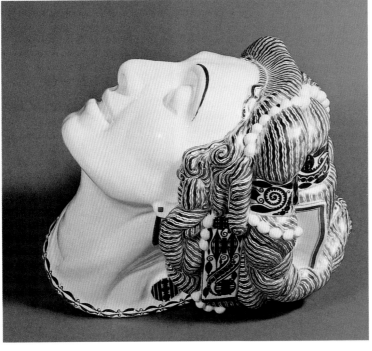

57. René Lalique, Ivy bowl, sandblasted glass, 1921

next page
58. René Lalique, perfume bottle with procession of priestesses, etched glass, 1920–22

Finch, Alfred William (1854–1930). English potter and leading figure in the evolution of the modern Finnish artisanal tradition, as well as for his teaching activity at the school of industrial art in Helsinki. Born English, he trained in Belgium under the influence of Henry → van de Velde; then after transferring to the French capital, in 1897 he settled permanently in Finland, where he had gone to supervise the Iris laboratory of Porvoo, then wound down in 1902. His production is characterised by utterly plain forms, aligned on the tradition of rustic craftsmanship, with rare ornamentations, occasionally → art nouveau.

Fisher, Alexander (1864–1936). English jeweller and sculptor trained at the South Kensington School (1881–84), after a trip to Paris to study the → Dalpayrat technique of pottery enamelling, in 1887 he opened his own studio in London where he made small enamelled statues inspired by pre-Raphaelite painting, jewellery and decorative items. In 1896 he founded his own school in Kensington, while keeping up a close collaboration with contemporary reviews such as *The Art Journal* and *The Studio* and exhibiting in numerous international events. Clearly Victorian in taste, his best-known pieces recall Byzantine tradition (triptych for the duke of Balfour), eighteenth-century style (centrepiece with mermaids, sailboats and electric lamps for Lord Carmichael) and Celtic culture (frame for the triptych with *Life of St. Pancrace*, Dublin, National Museum of Ireland); he also developed groups of articles (for household and liturgical uses) related to → eclectism.

Fishleyn E.B. & W. Fishley Holland. English pottery, active in Devon from 1861 to 1959, interesting for its production, in the 1920s, of superb vases decorated in contrasting shades with *flambé* slips, imitating chalcedony and agate.

Flat-back. Particular typology of earthenware figures produced in Staffordshire in the mid-nineteenth century, modelled so a to be seen only frontally and used exclusively to decorate fireplace architraves.

Floegl, Mathilde (1893–1950). Austrian potter and designer, attended the Kunstgewerbeschule from 1909 to 1916; from that time until 1933 she collaborated with the → Wiener Werkstätte. The author of mural paintings in the Grabencafé and the Brauner house, furnished by her master Josef → Hoffmann, from 1931 to 1935 she ran her own studio, making

pottery, items in ivory, leather and wood, caskets, *cache-pots* and painted boxes, enamels, decorations on glass, lace, tulle works, fashion accessories and tapestries; she furthermore dealt in advertising graphics, wrote for several women's reviews and took part, as in others, in the Paris 1925 fair.

Florentia glass. Definition of an art glass invented by Frederick → Carder for the → Steuben Glass Works and produced between 1920 and 1930, characterised by connected leaves, joined at the base, whose points are splayed outward; the leaves are modelled with sprayed glass that is cast on the surface of the article.

Follot, Paul (1877–1941). French designer, one of the protagonists of → art deco and pupil of the painter Eugène Grasset, he began working on his own in 1904, elaborating a highly personal version of the modernist style, consisting of simplified structures yet enriched by both the choice of materials and the added decorations. Opposed to the notion of art for everyone, Follot designed furnishings, furniture, textiles and pottery of rich elegance, winning a certain acclaim in his regular exhibitions in the Salon d'Automne and the Salon des Arts Décoratifs, and was commissioned, in 1925, to install the interiors of the *Exposition Internationale des Arts Décoratifs*. That same year he was called upon to direct the design studio "Pomone" in the Au Bon Marché department store, where he executed furnishings for the upper-middle class: furniture and

Paul Follot, chair, carved sycamore, ebony and Cayenne mahogany, ca. 1913. Paris, Musée des Arts Décoratifs

Paul Follot, chair and dressing-table, lacquered and gilt wood, 1919

articles made according to the dictates of international deco taste, but characterised by a clever recuperation of eighteenth-century models, both on the level of comfort and of decorative form. The materials are usually precious: Makassar ebony and amboina wood, intaglioed for centrepieces with flowers and fruit, baskets and capitals, always gilt. In most cases his exemplars have a rosebud, etched or stamped, usually on the back rim or under the seat of chairs and armchairs.

Fontana Arte. Italian glassworks founded in Milan under the name Luigi Fontana & C. in 1881, that took about twenty years to assert itself, presenting at the 1902 Turin exhibition elegant stained-glass in → liberty style; in 1907 the firm associated with the better-known Beltrami G. & Co. in furnishing the casino at San Pellegrino Terme, especially with the contribution of Fausto Codenotti for the stained-

glass window *The Roses*. In 1931, Gio → Ponti was called in as art director, promoting a special production of furniture and glass and crystal items with strictly geometric forms, created as one-offs. In 1933 the firm absorbed the art glass workshop of Pietro → Chiesa, who had previously worked with Gio Ponti, creating Fontana Arte, that would become enormously famous, both for furnishings and for lighting equipment, where very thick plate played a leading role by a clever, modern use of wheel-grinding. In 1934 the factory launched a production of glass wall facings for interiors and exteriors in various colours and sizes, among which the well-known *marbled* glass. The most famous pieces to be recalled are the mirror table by Gio Ponti with the *Story of the Mermaids* (1931), furniture faced with curved, coloured mirrors by Pietro Chiesa (1938), the bowl suspension lamp (1941) and the tables with a single curved plate (1934).

Gio Ponti (for Fontana Arte), dressing-table, wood, mirror and bronze, 1931

Fontenay, Eugène (1824–1887). French jeweller, he opened his own workshop in Paris in 1847, specialising by 1860 in the reproduction of various period styles and techniques of granulation, following the method patented by Pio Fortunato → Castellani, and filigree, with Egyptian motifs and precious stones to adorn the items he created (medallions, incense burners, bowls, boxes) for an international clientele, including the shah of Persia and the king of Siam.

Formica. Rigid → plastic material patented in the United States in 1913, constituted by a sheet of resin of phenyl-formaldehyde, applied with an adhesive to a layer in phenylic resin and spread onto a sheet of plywood; the surface thus obtained is water-proof, heat-proof and scratch-resistant, so therefore often used in finishing kitchen and office furniture, etc.

Fornaci di San Lorenzo. Italian pottery founded in 1906 at Borgo San Lorenzo in Mugello by Galileo and Chino → Chini; after starting off with symbolist and floristic pottery, it soon specialised in metal-glazed pottery with motifs drawn from European medieval, Far-Eastern and Arabic traditions, and in gres vases with stylised cobalt blue decorations inspired by the archaic cultures of the Mediterranean and the secessionist taste, yet not omitting to produce also modular panels with friezes in neo-fifteenth-century style. The firm (become in 1919 Manifattura Fornaci San Lorenzo di Chini e Co.), availed of the collaboration of the sculptors Gemignani (who made statues and figured panels with *putti* and animals in the Austrian secessionist vein) and Valmore. Once the management passed on to Chino's sons, Tito (1898–1947) and Augusto (b. 1904), the company went into a slump, going back to a production imitating the past and emphasising an affected, ornate approach to the → deco manner pursued by Tito, whereas Augusto's development was more solidly Novecento, with strong aspects related to futurist pottery. In the late 1930s, it began producing monumental vases coated with pink and mother-of-pearl glazes in simple geometric forms. In 1943 the factory was bombed out.

Forstner, Leopold (1878–1936). Austrian mosaicist and designer, pupil of Koloman Moser and of the Munich Academy, in 1906 he founded in Vienna the Wiener Mosaikwerkstätten.

Fouquet, Georges (1862–1957). French jeweller, active as a designer in the family workshop as early as 1885, after a decade he replaced his father Alphonse (a famous nineteenth-century jeweller); he aligned his entire production on the rules of the floristic idiom of → art nouveau, collaborating with Eugène Samuel Grasset and Alphonse → Mucha (with the very famous *Asp* bracelet for Sarah Bernhardt, Lisbon, Gulbenkian Collection); later on, when the popularity of that style began to dim, his creations became strict and geometric, directly emulating cubism; toward 1909 in fact the structure of the jewels was notably simplified, and figuration had less and less to do with nature and more and more with geometry. During the 1920s even his shop was altered, following the new → deco style and based on Jansen's ideas, eliminating Mucha's precious, ornate settings; Fouquet at that time designed and produced jewellery characterised by the combination of black and white (in white gold, platinum and black onyx) and by polychromy, but only using semi-precious stones like jade, turquoise, coral, lapis-lazuli, rock crystal and various other semi-precious stones. After the 1925 exhibition his son Jean seconded him.

France, Charles William Fearnley (b. 1898). English furniture-maker; settled in Denmark in 1936, after taking over a mattress factory he launched a production of furnishings, that he began to export

Georges Fouquet, brooch, gold and enamels, 1901. London, Victoria and Albert Museum

right after the Second World War, featuring light wood, plain forms and practicality. In 1948 he started producing chairs with spring seats.

Frankoma Pottery. Unites States pottery, active at Sapulpa (Oklahoma) since 1936 and known for its production of bowls, glassware and vases in ochre shades and etched ornaments inspired by Maya and Aztec pottery.

Fritsche, William. Glass etcher of Bohemian birth, active in the 1870s and 1880s at the Dennis glasswork of Thomas → Webb & Sons, where he tried out a new technique for deep etching in the vitreous material dubbed "rock crystal", with which he executed a series of pieces shown at the Paris World Fair in 1878, including the renowned *Fritsche Ewer* vase, on the mouth of which Neptune's countenance is engraved (Corning, Corning Museum of Glass).

Froment-Meurice, François-Désiré (1802–55). French jeweller, the most highly esteemed silversmith in Paris, celebrated by contemporary writers and known for his technical virtuosity recognisable

in all his works; he was responsible for the rediscovery of the chyrselephantine technique, presented in London in 1851 with the figure of *Leda* (ivory, silver, gold and turquoise, now at Geneva, Musée d'Art et d'Histoire), and a group of spectacular precious items in neo-gothic style, such as caskets, candelabras and the dressing-table pitcher and basin for the Duchess of Parma, in gilt silver and enamels, also shown in London. His son Emile (1837–1913) kept up his father's activity in the revivalist and neo-Renaissance styles, as in his superb *Hope* bowl, based on the story of Perseus and Andromeda, in bloodstone, gilt silver and enamels (private collection), exhibited very successfully at the Paris 1855 fair. The business lasted until the end of the century, when it was eclipsed by the success of → art nouveau.

Frullini, Luigi (1839–97). Italian carver, known for the creation of furniture, frames, cases for clocks, chests, bookbindings, cabinets and candelabras endowed with a personal, luxurious style, according to neo-fifteenth-century, neo-Renaissance and neo-mannerist models, acquired in the Florentine Angiolo → Barbetti's workshop. With Egisto Gaiani, his studio companion, he published in Paris *Panneaux et Ornements en bois sculptés*, concurrently and with wide acclaim exhibiting in the leading international fairs (London, 1862; Paris, 1867; Vienna, 1873). He counted a great many customers in Europe and the United States, where he executed, in 1875–76, the carved walnut furnishings for the dining-room and library of Chateaux-sur-Mer at Rhode Island (presently in the Philadelphia museum) and carved, in 1890, the library for 231 Madison Avenue in New York. Several of his most important pieces are conserved in the Museum für angewandte Kunst in Vienna. One of his pupils worth mentioning was Marcello Andrea Baccetti (1850–1903), whom Gabriele D'Annunzio called upon for the staging of *Francesca da Rimini* in 1901–02.

Fry Glass Company. Unites States glassworks founded at Rochester (Pennsylvania) toward 1920, specialised in the production of opalescent glass items and *foval* articles, that is, glass with applications of silver, supplied separately by the Rockwell Silver Co. The factory closed down in 1934.

Fulham Pottery. English pottery, active in the vicinity of London by 1864, producing a variety of household and garden pottery adorned with traditional floral motifs and animal figures.

Fulper Pottery Company. United States pottery opened in 1860 at Flemington (New Jersey) and closed in 1935, specialised in tableware; in 1910 it began, in emulation of European → art nouveau models, production of distinguished containers adorned with crystalline glazes, dubbed *Vasekrafts*. One of the most original items deserving mention: the mushroom-shaped table lamps with pottery bases, altered from French models, with uneven glazing and glass shades. *(Pl. 50)*

Fürstenberg. German porcelain factory, founded in 1747 by the Duke Charles I and close to the models of → Sèvres and Königliche Porzellan-Manufaktur of → Berlin, it was active throughout the nineteenth century, revisiting traditional styles, even after being taken over in 1959 by private management. It is still active today, producing modern tableware.

François-Désiré Froment-Meurice, mirror of the Duchess of Parma's dressing-table, partly gilt silver, enamels and garnets, 1847. Paris, Musée d'Orsay

G

Gaillard, Eugène (1962–1933). French furniture-maker, working for Samuel → Bing; while his pieces always featured wavy lines and low-relief carvings, his stylistic options were clearly simplified compared to models presented by the → Nancy school.

Gaillard, Lucien (1861 - after 1945). French jeweller, son of the noted jeweller Ernest Gaillard, he soon became known at the Paris fairs of 1889 and 1900 for his very special jewels inspired by Japanese art. Strongly influenced by → Lalique's creations, by 1900 he had in his studio a group of Japanese ivory and tortoise-shell carvers, creating fantastic items in all sorts of materials that won him recognition at the 1904 exhibition.

Gallé, Emile (1846–1904). French glassmaker, after learning glass and pottery processing techniques in his father's laboratory, he studied philosophy, zoology and botany. In 1867 he started working at the Meisenthal glassworks in Lorraine; after taking a significant trip in 1871 to London and Paris, where he discovered Japanese art, in 1874 he replaced his father in the firm and in 1884 opened a cabinet-making workshop, followed in 1886 by a furniture factory. His success in the Paris exhibitions (1878, 1889, 1900) incited him to found in 1901 the Ecole de → Nancy. In 1903 he made his last glass pieces, that would continue being produced up to 1931; the firm closed down in 1935. As in his furnishings and pottery, naturalist inspiration (plant species and insects) was prominent in his glass production also, inspired by the Chinese technique of → etching on glass, but obtained with his own glass plate processing, whereby transparency is not contaminated by the heightened intensity of the colours. *(Pl. 49)*

Galvani. Italian pottery, founded at Pordenone in 1811 by Giuseppe Galvani, it began in 1823 to mark with an anchor its pieces in hard earthenware; once the management was taken over by his sons Giuseppe and Giorgio in 1855, the firm notably prospered until the end of the nineteenth century, producing fine, white or coloured earthenware, and ornamental terra cotta for outdoors. In the mid-1930s the name of the factory changed to S.A. Andrea Galvani, and the pieces were stamped with a rooster head and a stylised cockerel combined with a G. The pieces produced in those years are among the most well-known and innovatory, since they borrowed the simplified forms of twentieth-century taste (spheres, cubes, parallelopipeds, geometric decorations, animals and stylised figures), associated with several graphic refinements inspired by Gio → Ponti, but executed with the air-brush glaze technique.

Gambone, Guido (1909–69). Italian potter active in the 1930s at Vietri sul Mare in the Avallone factory, in collaboration with Irene Kowaliska. In 1935 he became designer at the Industria Ceramica Salernitana owned by the Melamerson family that, having also acquired the → Cantagalli firm in

Emile Gallé, Dragonfly *coffee-table, fruit wood, 1900*

Florence, transferred him to Tuscany in 1936, where he would remain until 1939, producing several series in the traditional Vietri style, but also refined pieces in emulation of Gio → Ponti's designs for → Richard-Ginori of Doccia, as well as of metaphysical painting and that of Massimo Campigli, creating a particular decorative tone, archaic and primitivist, that he would pursue after the war, when in 1950 he settled permanently in Florence.

Gariboldi, Giovanni (b. 1908). Italian potter, he began working for → Richard-Ginori toward the end of the 1920s, collaborating with Gio → Ponti, designing pieces for production and advertising graphics appearing in the review *Domus* (from 1928); in 1946 he became its art director. For San Cristoforo in Milan he designed in 1933 series of dishes, glasses and items adorned with naturalist subjects in a definitely Impressionist vein. In the late 1930s he made in gres, coated with *mat* glazes, animal figures, centrepieces with cameo-like relief decorations, and dishware with marine allegories executed in opaque gold.

Garrard. English goldsmiths active from 1735, becoming court jewellers in 1830 supplanting the Rundell firm, they are known for the exuberant style of their creations; tea sets, table sets (especially soup tureens and very elegant dishes), articles for writing desks, but also gift items for which they challenged Hunt & Roskell's commercial primacy. For the execution of the most important pieces they called upon the collaboration of the sculptor Edmund Cotterill, replaced at his death in 1860 by W.F. Spencer. The firm was active until 1952, when it merged with the Goldsmiths' and Silversmith's Company of London.

Gate, Simon (1883–1945). French glass designer, he joined the → Orrefors Glasbruk factory in 1915, where he soon began processing and etching coated glass. Of special note were the items made in *graal* glass, a solution way in advance of → Gallé's double glass: it is coloured glass, carved and → acid etched and then coated with a layer of clear glass; using this technique he executed in 1925 the famous bowl featuring *The Procession of Bacchus*, etched with explicit → deco motifs (Orrefors, Orrefors Museum).

Gatti, Riccardo (1886–1972). Italian potter, active at Faenza, he trained at the → Minardi factory until 1909, and from 1919 to 1924 at the Manifatture Ceramiche. In 1927 he set up a small furnace, in 1928 opening with Luigi Montabilini the factory Gatti & C. (the trademark is still a stylised cat face with the inscription "Faenza" up to 1933–1935, when the signature "R. Gatti" or "Gatti R." appeared); it was here that futurist art pottery was researched, with works by Giacomo Balla and Benedetta Marinetti. One of Gatti's principal merits was the introduction of glazed majolica, extremely elegant and refined, still being produced.

Genazzi, Luigi (1876–1946). Italian silversmith, trained at the Academy of Brera and in Paris, after an extensive teaching experience, he began in the early twentieth century modelling sculptures and medals. In 1920 he left France and returned to Milan and, with Guido Colombo, in 1924 opened a workshop where, during the 1920s and 1930s, along with the production of religious furnishings in an eclectic, historicist vein (a great number being in the Vatican), he launched a very rich collection of silver tableware and furnishings (pitchers, basins, drinking services, candelabras, and so on) with stylised, graceful forms that, although recalling eighteenth-century prototypes, left aside the additional ornaments, instead highlighting flowing forms by a special processing of the surfaces, either → hammered or → glossed.

Luigi Genazzi, two-bracket chandelier, hammered silver, 1930

George W.S. Pottery Company. United States semi-porcelain factory, active from 1904 to 1960 at East Palestine (Ohio), supplying hotels and restaurants in tableware, with Victorian floral ornaments on a cream ground; it was not until the 1930s that the decorations would become sparser, having an affinity with some products inspired by futurist notions.

Ghiozzi Federico. Italian pottery active in Florence from the early twentieth century up to 1935, known for its abundant, quality production of patinated terra cotta suited for fountains and garden furniture, vases, boxes, sculptures and decorative reliefs, and interior furnishings. Along with the reproduction of antique models, there were series of modern pieces influenced on the one hand by the secessionist idiom and on the other by the cold grace of → deco style, as well as the rigourous monumentalism of Novecento taste.

Gianotti, Giovanni Battista (1873–1928). Italian cabinet-maker, he was active from the early twentieth century in Belgium, England and then in Italy where he designed frescoes, mosaics, textiles, furnishings and stained glass for Luigi → Fontana's firm; he is specially known for his activities during the 1920s in Milan, where he opened a shop. He took part in the Monza fairs and the one in Paris in 1925, offering furnishings in a hybrid → deco vein, often marked by neo-Renaissance influences.

Gillinder James & Sons. United States glassworks opened at Philadelphia in 1860 by the English glassmaker William Gillinder for executing pressed and cut glass, but later specialised in the production of ground glass on the *Westward Ho* model, owing to which it became quite famous after the 1876 Centennial Exhibition. In 1912, when his brother James entered the firm and they took over the Bronx and Royal factory at Port Jervis, the company took the name whereby it is most widely known, closing down in 1930.

Gillows. English cabinet-making laboratory, active since 1727, known for being the greatest supplier of furnishings (produced in the Lancaster factory) for English and Scotch landed nobility. In 1760 it was the first in Great Britain to experiment the processing of moulding furniture, creating series of Georgian and Regency period furniture, well-made, but plain from a decorative point of view. During the nineteenth century, adopting the Victorian fashion, it availed of the collaboration of several important designers; in 1897 it took over Collinson & Lock and immediately afterward S.J. Waring & Son. During the 1930s it began producing several series of furniture designed by S. Chermayeff and P. → Follot.

Gimson, Ernest William (1864–1919). English architect and designer, prominent member of the → Arts & Crafts, he was one of the first in England to make chairs in turned ash; in 1895, with a group of craftsmen (among whom his brother Barnsley) he

opened a studio where they made graceful furniture, with strict, thin lines, decorated with mother-of-pearl inlays and characterised by a treatment of the wood that emphasised the veins.

Ginzkey J. Bohemian textile factory founded at Maffersdorf (Bohemia) in 1843, known for having set up a *jacquard* machine for making rugs, and in 1845 a loom for producing lambswool blankets. During the 1860s the firm was also equipped with dying and washing units and a laboratory for artificial wool, winning its first international acclaim in London in 1862. In the early twentieth century the factory was remarkable for the high quality of its production, owed to the designs for knotted rugs supplied by L. Baumann, →Olbrich and → Voysey, along with the more extensive production of Persian-style and vaguely Oriental rugs, and imitations in "Louis-Quinze" and "Louis-Seize" style.

Giolli Menni, Rosa (b. 1889). Italian painter known for her painted fabrics, featuring explicit → deco rhythms in stylised flower motifs and bright, futurist-tone colours, exhibited at Monza and in Paris, where they were awarded the gold medal.

Giustiniani. Neapolitan pottery active from 1760; around 1870, thanks to the contribution of Michele, it went through a phase of particular success in international fairs, with an abundant production of ornamental articles and useful ware, along with the reproduction of some Renaissance majolicas; but the firm was forced to declare bankruptcy in 1885.

Gladding - McBean Company. United States pottery active in Los Angeles since 1875 for the production of kitchen and table ware, that during the 1920s and 1930s offered streamlined forms emphasised by glowing monochrome colours.

Glass dome. A typical turn-of-the-century furnishing item to protect compositions of dried flowers, wax figurines, mantelpiece clocks, and so on, obtained by blowing a bubble of clear paste until a cylindrical form is obtained, then cutting off one end; there are also oval ones.

Glass marqueterie. Glass technique imitating the wood inlay invented by Emile → Gallé in 1897, and consisting of pressing into a glass body pieces modelled in different-coloured glass before they have cooled, so that the surface stays smooth and ready to be processed by carving or etching.

Gloss. Coating applied on the surface of pottery, obtained by spraying on the item a layer of very fine clay soaked in illite and then firing it in an oxidising fire. It is defined metallic when the surface becomes iridescent, as in Islamic, Hispano-Moresque pottery and in Italian majolica, by using metal oxides mixed with fine ochre and applied on the surfaces of previously glazed items and again fired at a rather low temperature. This ancient technique was rediscovered during the nineteenth century by → De Morgan, followed by → Pilkington Pottery and → Ruskin Pottery in Great Britain, and in Italy by the Florentine → Cantagalli manufactory and the Faventine → Gatti. In Germany this technique is employed with success by Müller pottery of Karlsruhe and in Hungary by → Zsolnay of Pécs. It can also be applied to glass articles, with the spreading or spraying of oxides of silver (hence a straw yellow), copper, gold (producing a ruby colour), platinum or bismuth (giving a silvered effect), blended with an oily agent and subjected to heat. In modern times the gloss technique was used with magnificent results by → Tiffany, with → *favrile* glass, by the → Lötz manufactory and by → Carder in the United States.

Gmunden. Austrian pottery founded in 1863 near Salzburg, but that only became important in 1908, when Franz Schleiss (the owner's son), who had followed courses at the Vienna Kunstgewerbeschule, set up a unit inside the plant solely for the production of art pottery connected with the secessionist manner (Kunstlerische Werkstätte Franz und Emilie Schleiss). In 1912 this production was absorbed by the Viennese laboratory of Michael → Powolny, becoming the Wiener und Gmundener Keramik Werkstätte, exhibiting its pieces under that name in international fairs.

Godwin, Edward William (1833–86). English architect and designer, to whom are owed absolutely innovatory creations with respect to the Victorian manner; highly admired by Wilde and Whistler, he offered a style in furnishing, rather improperly dubbed Anglo-Japanese. Subsequent to his first neo-medievalising works and his friendship with → Burges, already by 1862 his interests as an architect and designer were directed toward Japanese culture, which he particularly admired for its asymmetrical compositions, its delicate draughtsmanship and accurate outlines. In 1868 he began devoting himself exclusively to designing furnishings, wallpaper, textiles, rugs and decorative items: for instance the series of *Butterfly* furniture, created with Whistler for the Paris exhibition of 1878, the furnishings of Whistler's own house, the White House in Chelsea (1877–78) and Oscar Wilde's house, again in Chelsea (1884). He permanently abandoned the → eclectic style, being drawn to bare, rigorous forms; his preferences went to furniture in ebonied woods and with square forms, therefore adapted to serial production, their value being in their lightness and the harmonious mass and vacuum ratio.

Goldscheider. Austrian pottery active in Vienna from 1885 to 1953 for the production, for the most part exported to the United States, of figurines for furnishings, wall masks or heads and series of household articles that during the 1920s and 1930s were associated with earthenware reproductions of bronzes by → Zach and Lorenzl. As regards themes, there were single female figures in fashionable attire and pairs of dancers; the masks, highly popular during the → deco period, consisted of stylised female countenances with bright, shiny colours and expressions borrowed from contemporary graphics and African sculpture. The trademark was usually "Goldscheider Wien. Made in Austria".

Golia (Eugenio Colmo, 1885–1967). Italian graphic artist and potter, he began his career as a decorator in 1922, taking mass-produced earthenware and porcelain articles that he turned into one-offs, signed, dated and numbered, that offered decorations — especially with figures — indebted to → liberty graphics, but that were concurrently characterised by a thoroughly → deco accuracy and balanced elegance. The artist executed nearly 1500 pieces adorned with low-fired enamels, most of which are lost, that met with success at the Paris 1925 exhibition; the themes were the typical ones of the international deco manner: Oriental dancing girls, Venetian damsels, Spanish dancers, contemporary women in 1920s apparel. His production was suddenly broken off in 1927.

Gorbunovo. Russian pottery active between 1800 and 1872. It is especially known for the production of porcelain figurines representing Russian peasants and inspired by Gardner's manufactory.

Gorham Company. United States silverworks active since 1818 at Providence (Rhode Island). Its take-off on the market, that occurred in 1841, was connected with the use of mechanical advanced technology for the execution of solid silver ware. In 1868 it called in as designer Thomas J. Pairpoint, formerly employed at the London firm → Lambert

& Rawlings, launching a production of solid silver vases in emulation of eighteenth-century models, that from then on bore its trademark and the date. As of 1900, with the arrival of William Codman, one-offs were wrought, hand-processed and called *martelé*, inspired by the strictest forms of European modernism, and with which the firm won significant recognition at the Saint Louis exhibition in 1904. It is still producing top-quality silverware.

Goss W.H. English porcelain manufactory opened in 1858 at Stoke and known under the name *Falcon Works*, because of the trademark used (a goshawk). The owner, William H. Goss, began producing ornamental articles, tobacco jars and beer mugs, using eggshell porcelain; yet the firm's success did not come about until 1880, with heraldry porcelains, that is, series of items reproducing in miniature, besides the coats-of-arms of cities and countries, also significant local monuments; sold as souvenirs, these articles gave rise to singular collections. Specialising in miniaturisation, the factory produced tableware for children as well, minute models of houses, tanks and weapons; in 1929 it was sold and came under the trademarks "England" and "W.H. Goss", winding down in 1940.

Goulden, Jean (1878–1947). French jeweller specialised in the use of enamels and lacquers; he produced table lamps, clocks and cigarette holders, using silver as a base and as executive techniques → *champlevé* and → *cloisonné* enamels. During the 1920s and 1930s his themes were always strictly geometric.

Goupy, Marcel (1886–1954). French glass designer, from 1909 to 1954 he was art director of the "Maison Géo Rouard", for which, along with useful wares in glass, he designed both forms and decorations, especially for small decorative articles, always enamelled, executed between 1919 and 1923 by the Frenchman A. Heiligenstein. At the end of the 1920s also arose a production of etched glass, but always decorated with landscapes, flowers, birds, scenes drawn from classical mythology and nudes.

Graffart, Charles (1893–1967). Belgian glass designer working at the → Val Saint-Lambert manufactory, he became master-etcher in 1926 and in the span of only three years succeeded in designing over three hundred pieces. In 1942 he was made art director of the factory: active in wheel-processed decoration, he also worked with vitreous paste and blocks of solid glass in which he made sculptures.

Grand Rapids Furniture. Name referring to the furniture production coming from the homonymous town in Michigan: the first workshop was opened in 1836, and by 1850 mechanical processing of the furniture was introduced. The merging in 1873 of a group of small and medium factories in a single large firm called Berkey & Gay Furniture, whose activity lasted until 1948, launched the commercial success of the articles (award-winning in 1876 at Philadelphia) in neo-Renaissance style, with countless machine-carved decorative parts. The production of the 1890s was characterised by more austere and simplified forms, defined "Mission Style". Between 1908 and 1929 the Grand Rapids area counted nearly fifty factories; after the economic crisis, by 1938 a significant upturn could be observed, thanks to a more modern design for mass-produced furniture.

Granite ware. Definition attributed to two different types of English nineteenth-century pottery: the earthenware produced by → Wedgwood and many Staffordshire manufactories with navy or grey lead-base glazes making the surfaces similar to granite, and a very hard and resistant white earthenware produced at → Davenport as of 1850, used mainly for equipping ships and for export.

Gray A.E. & Co. English pottery, active at Stoke between 1912 and 1961, producing kitchen and table ware with plain forms and decorated with flower patterns in bright colours and a popular vein.

Gray, Eileen (1878–1977). Irish architect and designer, a student of the Slade School of Art in London, she started her career as a restorer of antique lacquers; in 1907 she settled permanently in Paris, working in a Japanese lacquerer's studio, where she began making one-offs that in 1922, shown at the Union des Artistes Modernes, were extremely well-received. So she opened her own studio and a shop where exquisitely → deco articles ruled: shelves resting on lotus flowers, screens adorned with slender figures or else abstract compositions produced by the juxtaposition of woods lacquered in various techniques. Beginning in 1927, influenced by → Le Corbusier's architectural creations, she gravitated toward the conception of functional, very graceful furniture, like her well-known steel tubular tables with lacquer tops.

Green, Charles (1868–1957). United States architect and designer, in partnership with his brother Henry Mather (1870–1954), he worked mainly at Pasadena (California), where Gamble House, their most prestigious construction, is now a museum devoted to their works, usually associated with Bernard Maybeck and the Craftsman Style. Involved, from 1893, not only in architecture but also in designing furnishings for wealthy clients, they designed furniture that reflected an obvious Far-Eastern influence, with a certain amount of *chinoiserie* in the decorations, but also certain affinities with → Arts & Crafts, especially in the mahogany furniture with ebony pegs and splines. Their furnishings, moreover widely imitated, were often enhanced by → Tiffany glass and lamps; they also designed mats and rugs, that were usually executed in England. Their finest production was between 1893 and 1910, since after 1916, when the brother Charles moved to Carmel, the studio stopped dealing in furnishings.

Green T.G. & Co. English pottery, active by 1864 in Derbyshire, known for its production of kitchen ware, among which worth mentioning are coffee pots and sugar and flour containers adorned with wide, horizontal navy stripes on a white ground.

Grice, Edwin (1839–1913). English glass designer, he began his career as carver and etcher in 1861 at the → Northwood glassworks in Wordsley, then moving, in 1879 and up to 1904, to the Guest Bros manufactory at Brethell Lane, where he contributed relevant technical-executive improvements.

Griffen Smith and Hill Pottery. United States pottery active at Phoenixville (Pennsylvania) from 1879 to 1890, known for its production of industrial majolica articles, with relief decorations of plant elements (maple leaves, seaweed) and shells, then coated with very bright-coloured glazes.

Grimwade Bros. English pottery and porcelain manufactory active from 1886 to 1979 at Stoke, renowned for its production of vases and bowls with floristic adornments in the Victorian manner until 1910, then shifted to the series of centrepieces in → deco style with little birds and coral branches in enamelled colours (produced from 1926 on) and teapots adorned with motifs drawn from chintz textiles (*Royal Winton Hazel Teapot* of 1934) or in the shape of a cottage, produced until the 1950s. *(Pl. 51)*

Grohé, Guillaume (1808–85). German furniture-maker, with his brother Jean-Michel he was one of the leading producers of Second Empire style furniture. Moving to Paris in 1827, he began by trading in art works, later successfully presenting several neo-Egyptian and neo-gothic furnishings at the 1834 fair. By 1861, henceforth by himself, he specialised in reproducing eighteenth-century furnishings of the finest quality, availing of the collaboration of very skilful carvers, such as Liénard, and workers in bronze like Fanières; the official supplier of furniture for Louis-Philippe, Napoleon III and Eugénie, especially in "Louis-Quinze" style, as of 1862 he executed furnishings for Queen Victoria as well. Several significant pieces are conserved in the castles of Compiègne and Fontainebleau and the Musée Carnavalet in Paris.

Grottaglie. Italian potteries that in the course of the nineteenth and the early twentieth centuries upheld a traditional production connected with the formal and decorative prototypes of seventeenth-century Apulian rural tradition. During the 1920s, techniques and decorative effects were updated in → deco and then more broadly Novecento styles, such as the decoration dubbed *smarmoriata* (marbled) and the use of plumbiferous glazes rendered more vivid by the use of bright colours like yellow, navy, manganese, green and pink.

Groult, André (1884–1967). French designer, he began in 1910 exhibiting at the Salon d'Automne and in the decorative arts shows metal articles and furniture whose forms, already contrasting with → art nouveau models, instead displayed an explicit preference for Biedermeier references, that is, "Charles-Dix" and → "Louis-Philippe" styles, mainly owing to the use of very light-coloured woods assembled in structures with sweeping forms and a great deal of padding. His finest period however was the one in → deco style: he designed and furnished numerous pavilions for the Paris fair of 1925, where he simplified his earlier models, still producing gorgeous, exuberant effects, in particular by the damask velvets, decorated with stylised plant motifs used for the upholstery.

Grueby, William H. (1867–1925). United States potter; after forming a company in partnership with Atwood, he opened in 1894 the Grueby Faïence Company that specialised in producing tiles and decorative *clipei* (a type of antique shield) in a variety of styles (including Renaissance, Moresque, Chinese, medieval), nearly always polychrome and figuring landscapes, plants and stylised decorative patterns. It was not until 1898 that tableware was introduced, usually designed by George P. Kendrick, who was inspired by famous pieces by the French designers → Delaherche and → Chaplet that had been shown in the United States. The sculptural vases featured daringly elongated forms and were enhanced with opaque glazes combined with decorative compositions and colours of extreme distinction, ordinarily in shades of green, navy, brown and yellow, the pieces coloured in red being far more rare. After winning wide acclaim at the Pan-American exhibition of Buffalo (1901), the manufactory received a commission from → Tiffany as well, that planned to use its vases as bases for monumental table lamps with glass shades. Yet in 1908 the company had to declare bankruptcy: taken over by Grueby Faïence and Tile Company, it went back to its exclusive, traditional production of decorated tiles, that continued even after it was taken over, in 1911, by the C. Pardee Works of Perth Amboy, and up until 1930. *(Pl. 52)*

Grünstadt. German pottery active since 1801 and known for a particular yellowish-white earthenware

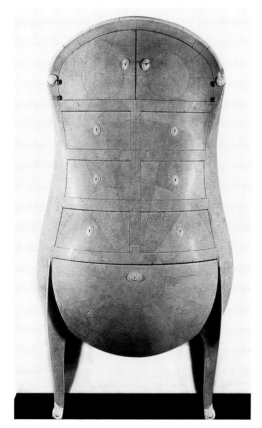

André Groult, secrétaire, shagreen and ivory, 1925

for the most part following prototypes provided by the Frankenthal firm; during the nineteenth century it executed stencilled tableware on Anglo-Saxon patterns (in particular → Spode). Still in activity, it continues to bear the trademark "GBG".

Guimard, Hector (1867–1942). French architect and designer, teacher at the Ecole des Arts Décoratifs in Paris from 1894 to 1898, he was one of the most significant representatives of the organic, floristic manner typical of the French version of → art nouveau; his style is characterised by the enveloping linearity of the forms, the emphasis on contrasts and the use of luminous effects, features found in his architecture designs, furnishings, deemed a part of the total work of art (dining-room conserved at the Musée d'Orsay), and in his urban designs (the famous entrances to the Paris underground).

Gurschner, Gustav (1873–1970). German designer, trained as a sculptor in Vienna at the decorative arts school, in 1896 he moved to Paris where he was influenced by → Charpentier's → art nouveau trends. His most renowned production includes plates, medals, busts, but also door handles and seals inspired by most ductile, attractive secessionist forms.

Gustavsberg. Swedish pottery opened in 1827 nearby Stockholm for producing household tableware and furnishings, but that in 1860 began making series of porcelain articles obtained with bone ash (on the English model of → *parian ware*) and in glaze-coloured majolica; toward the end of the century, in tune with the modernist taste, it also executed gres vases with elegant *flambé* decorations. Directed from 1897 to 1908 by Gunnar Gunnarsson Wennerberg, trained at → Sèvres, the factory initiated production of coloured pottery, on → Wedgwood models, with adornments inspired by → art nouveau (although in a simplified form), or graffito decorations on vases and monumental urns. The factory designer from 1897 to 1945 was his pupil Josef Ekberg, who excelled in extremely graceful foliage decors; whereas by 1917 the designing of forms was entrusted to the art director Wilhelm Kage. The manufactory, today still very active in the production of decorative and useful wares, during a short period also executed art pottery.

Guttaperca. Substance drawn from the sap of an Indian tree, widely used at the end of the nineteenth century for decorating furniture and wall mouldings.

H

Hadelands Glasverk. Norwegian glassworks founded in 1762 for the production of bottles, that in 1850 began making tableware and crystalware of various typologies, but also items in coloured glass with elegant new forms and decorations created by important designers. The manufactory, belonging for generations to the → Berg family, is still active.

Hald, Edward (1883–1973). Swedish glass designer and potter, he joined → Orrefors Glasbruk in 1917 and became a close collaborator of Simon → Gate for executions in coated glass.

Hammered. Glass technique invented by the Daum brothers to obtain a facetted glass — so as to produce the same visual impression as hammered iron — and used on items so that the surfaces display facetting produced by side-by-side contacts with an abrasive wheel: a widely popular processing method in late → art nouveau and → art deco items.

Hampshire Pottery. United States pottery, founded at Keene (New Hampshire) in 1871 and closed in 1923, that produced pitchers and vases modelled in keeping with plant themes or calling upon a typically → art nouveau idiom, always entirely coated with a vitrified green glaze.

Hancock Sampson & Sons. English pottery, active from 1858 to 1937 in Staffordshire, known mainly for its series of graceful vases and bowls produced in the early twentieth century in keeping with designs and themes dear to William → Morris.

Handel Company. United States glassworks active in Connecticut by 1885; its activity lasted until 1936 with the production of decorative lamps (stamped "Handel") featuring → Tiffany-style glass shades, their decoration being obtained by → sandblasting.

Hankar, Paul (1859–1901). Belgian cabinet-maker and designer, after training to be a sculptor, in 1888 he began to work as an architect with the decorator Alphonse Crespin, and in 1893 built his own

Hampshire Pottery, vases with relief figures, pottery with glazed colours, 1905–15

house, one of the first examples of → art nouveau buildings in Brussels. Also active in designing furnishings, in 1894 he began collaborating with the review *L'Emulation*, and in 1897 exhibited in Brussels along with Henry → van de Velde and George Hobé.

Hansen, Frida (1855–1931). Norwegian textile designer, trained at Cologne and with the painter Puvis de Chavannes in Paris, in 1900 she presented in the French capital her celebrated *Milky Way* tapestry. Drawing her inspiration both from Japanese tradition and English pre-Raphaelite and French Symbolist painting, the artist devoted herself to perfecting the technique of transparent weaving, that conferred on her embroidered figures a texture verging on the unreal.

Hardman. English metalwork factory active at Birmingham as of 1838; it was founded by John Hardman, who had formerly received a button factory belonging to his father, and with him and a third partner in 1837 had created a consortium with → Elkington to exploit the goldplating technique. Collaboration with A.W.N. Pugin, as of 1837, led the factory to specialise in a series of articles bound to a neo-medieval style: precious metal tableware designed by the architect (for both household and liturgical use), but also fibulas for copes, crucifixes, chalices, candelabras, furnishings usually inspired by English gothic, plated or even solid silver, the latter then being further decorated with enamels and precious stones. Beginning in 1845, for the same liturgical production but for small sculptures as well, less expensive proposals were produced, using brass, but concurrently important series of polychrome stained glass windows and embroidered articles were being made. The connection with Pugin developed further when the manufactory became engaged in the interior decoration of the new House of Parliament in London, designed by the architect with C. Berry. In 1852, when Pugin died, he was replaced as master designer of the firm by his pupil John Hardman Powell, son of the partner William Powell, who worked in the → eclectic style, backed also by neo-gothic designs suggested by the architect William → Burges. Toward the end of the nineteenth century the factory slowed down its metal production, focusing on period stained glass, still sold today under the trademark "John Hardman Studios". *(Pl. 55)*

Harker Pottery Company. United States pottery, active from 1889 to 1975 in Ohio and West Virginia, with elegant household pottery and tablesets with white grounds and featuring black rims and silhouetted figures.

Harrachov. Bohemian glassworks founded at Novyj Svet in 1712, that in 1803 had over a hundred carvers occupied in production. Directed after 1808 by Johan Pohl, it had a period of remarkable growth, seizing the opportunity to become one of the leading producers of cut glass, decorated in Biedermeier style. Taken over in 1887 by Josef → Riedel, it became one of the most important factories for glassware, popular all over Europe.

Haviland. Franco-North-American porcelain manufactory specialised in household tableware; it was founded by David Haviland, who in 1842 at Limoges opened Haviland & Cie for the decoration of pottery and the manufacturing of porcelain (by 1865) intended for the United States market (his brother Robert had founded at Augusta, in Georgia, R.B. Haviland & Company). Emulating Biedermeier models, its tableware sets were highly successful (worth mentioning are the two sets executed for the White House in 1861 and in 1881). In 1873 the factory set up a workshop for decorating porcelain at Auteuil (later transferred to Paris in 1881), with which a number of artists collaborated, including → Chaplet and → Dammouse; it was precisely Chaplet (in 1875) who introduced a group of pieces inspired by Japanese pottery. Run by the founder's three sons, the firm was wound down in 1892. The nephew, Charles Field Haviland, trained at Limoges, and having joined his uncle's company by marriage, succeeded in restoring the important Alluaud firm of Limoges, enabling him to found in 1870 the "Charles Field Haviland Co." in New York.

Heal, Ambrose (1872–1959). English furniture-maker, he was able to turn his father's furniture business into Heal & Sons, one of the most important English factories producing middle-class furnishings. He made a strong entry on the market in 1898, owing to the publication of the catalogue titled *Heal's Plain Oak Furniture*, displaying oak furniture (sometimes darkened by smoking and enhanced by ebony and pewter elements), simple and strict in form in keeping with → art nouveau but in a more linear version, offered as a less expensive alternative to both the very costly → Arts & Crafts pieces and the more commonplace imitations of international modernism. Presently the manufactory has modified its sales activity, importing and selling particularly high-quality household ware, and initiated a productive unit devoted to average-quality, reasonable-priced framed prints for furnishing.

Heaton, Clement J. (1861–1940). English designer specialised in producing stained glass windows and enamel decoration of metal items. Son of Clement Heaton, the founding partner of Heaton, Butler & Bayne manufactory that produced and decorated polychrome stained-glass windows in connection with the renewed ecclesiastical construction in mid-nineteenth century England (Cambridge, Trinity College chapel), young Clement initiated his own career, producing decorative metal items (the bronzes for the court building in Victoria, Australia) and using with great skill the technique of → *cloisonné* enamel decoration. He was associated with Arthur Heygate→Mackmurdo, whom he supplied in designs for enamels, and with the Century Guild, for which he made a number of designs. After having founded Heaton's Cloisonné Mosaics Ltd., specialised in producing metal covers, lamps, medallions, but also embossed wallpaper imitating antique treated leather, in 1893 he moved to Neuchâtel, in Switzerland, where he executed the complicated decoration of the stairway of the

Musée des Beaux-Arts with *cloisonné* mosaics on designs by P. Robert. In 1912 he settled permanently in the United States, where he worked nearly exclusively making stained-glass windows for churches; collaborating with his son Maurice, he created the stained-glass windows for Rockefeller Center in New York and the Court Rooms of the Bay Court Building of Bay City, in a graceful → deco style. In 1931 Maurice began making decorated glass walls and lighting equipment, and in 1947 tried out a processing, then perfected in 1961, enabling to model directly in the furnace items decorated and enamelled with graffito figures and then coated with several layers of glass.

Heckert, Fritz (1866–1900). Bohemian glass enamel decorator, active at Petersdorf in Bohemia, he set up in 1886 a decoration studio and in 1889 a glassworks, producing a vast range of traditional German articles, like for instance tall beer glasses (*Humpen*); a group of pieces wrapped in metal mesh and marked in enamel "1616" have been attributed to this artist.

Heider. German pottery founded in 1890 at Schongau am Lech by the chemist and potter Maximilian von Heider, a teacher since 1907 at the Kunstgewerbeschule of Magdeburg, and his sons Hans and Fritz (who later would work as a painter) and Rudolph (who later was to become a sculptor), under the name Max von Heider & Söhne. Producing gres items coated with burnished or dry-processed glaze or occasionally with relief decorations of masks or else birds' heads, the factory also made majolica tiles, fireplaces and wall fountains, appearing in many international exhibitions (Paris, 1900; Turin, 1902; Saint Louis, 1904).

Heisey A.H. Glass Co. United States glassworks active by 1860 at Newark (Ohio) where at first pressed glass and etched crystal were produced, and later crystal drinking services in modern taste.

Henningsen, Poul (b. 1894). Danish architect and designer, one of the most significant personalities of the production renovation in Denmark in the ambit of arts applied to industry, especially while he was director at the Kritisk Revy manufactory, between 1926 and 1928, where he was willing to restore traditional forms, but only when they were functional with respect to modern life. Of significance among his best-known designs were the lighting installations (then executed by Pousen & Co. of Copen-

hagen), the first one being the *PH* lampshade in 1924 for a table lamp, followed by countless prototypes of either table or wall lamps equipped with three or more concentric shields, opaque and transparent, allowing to diffuse and reflect the ray of light; many of these are still being produced today.

Herend. Hungarian pottery opened in 1838 by Moritz Fischer for the creation of household ware in various European and Oriental styles, besides bowls, vases and ornamental dishes embellished with gilding and plant motifs reminiscent of neo-eighteenth-century taste; with their redundant forms and showy decorations, these pieces were often used as precious gifts. However, during the 1920s and 1930s the manufactory, also producing quality porcelain, turned to themes related to Hungarian tradition, in particular the floral patterns of the Kalosha area, revisited by a → deco geometric style.

Herman Miller Inc. United States furniture company erected at Zeeland (Michigan) in the early twentieth century and run by G. Nelson, who was responsible for introducing in the factory innovatory designs by Charles Eames for series of chairs, among which the → plastic stackable one became immediately famous, and for the → curved wood and padded couch. A great success greeted *Action Office*, a complete office furnishing (desk, files, table for meetings, etc.) with homogeneous, utterly modern lines, executed by an elegant combination of wood and plastic, and characterised by its glossy cast aluminium legs. Production, in the spirit of this prototype, was extended to furnishings for libraries.

Herter Brothers. United States furnishings factory formed in 1866 in New York by two brothers, sons of a furniture-maker from Stuttgart: Gustav, whose share in the business was taken over in 1870 and who returned to Germany, and Christian (1840–1883), who had moved to New York around 1860 and then returned to Europe in 1868 to study with the Parisian decorator Pierre-Victor Galland. The furniture factory was one of the first in America to give up traditional styles and models, offering furnishings similar to those being made at the same time in Great Britain, with plain lines and inspired by the → Arts & Crafts movement, yet not leaving aside the use of Far-Eastern motifs as well. Very well-known was the series of carved furniture made in 1877–82 for the railroad tycoon Jay Gould (New York, The Metropolitan Museum of Art), featuring a graceful floral *ramage* spread over the surfaces, but contained within the severe, stark lines of the furniture.

Heubach. German pottery founded at Lichte (Thuringia) in 1822, whose production was limited to useful wares with a modest decorative quality; thanks to the owners, the Heuback family, at the dawn of the twentieth century it underwent a radical transformation, with the introduction of ornamental pieces close to those concurrently being produced by the → Copenhagen manufactory: mainly animals and birds, as well as female figures and *Commedia dell'Arte* masks, modelled by masters like Otto Pech, Paul Zeiller, William Krieger, Sigismund Wernekinck and Wera von Bartles.

Hewitt & Leadbeater. English pottery, active at Longton between 1906 and 1926, known for its production of tableware and small figures of minute animals.

Hibjan, Samuel (1864–1919). Hungarian goldsmith, while teaching enamelling and jewellery at the Budapest school of decorative arts from 1895 until his death, he produced important examples of jewellery inspired by the Magyar tradition, but revised by French-style modernism, as well as bowls, bracelets, pendants, in enamelled silver and gold.

Historismus. A German expression connected with historicism or revivalism and that refers to that special cultural mood that characterised European design in architecture and decorative arts from the 1830s to the early twentieth century. The trend, already wide-spread in Biedermeier, thrived in the 1860s owing to the restoration yards of historical buildings and monumental areas. Experience with old buildings and the aim to bring back to life the sense of history through architectural and decorative typologies, inspired many designers and decorators to accentuate the original models, sometimes producing architectural pastiches and scenographic effects that recreated in an utterly imaginative, unscientific manner, an ideal notion of the Middle Ages, classicism, rococo and the Renaissance.

Hitchcock, Lambert (1795–1852). United States furniture-maker; in 1826 he founded a factory at Barkhamstead (Connecticut) specialising in the production of chairs that by 1829 bore the inscription "Hitchcock, Alford and Company, Hitchcockville, Conn". His most famous model had rounded front legs, and back legs squared and extended upward

to form the back, the middle section of the outside being turned; the seat was wicker, Vienna straw or wood, then painted black and decorated, on the front and outside of the back with painted or printed flowers and fruit, polychrome or gilt.

Hobbs Brockunier & Company. United States glassworks opened by 1863 at Wheeling (Virginia) for the mass production of useful pressed glassware, along with, toward the turn of the century, → *peach blow glass*: cameo glass containers with the milk-coloured body coated with dull or glossy glass, reddish-yellow in emulation of the porcelain items made under the K'ang Hsi dynasty.

Hodgetts, Richardson & Co. English glassworks opened in 1870 at Wordsley, near → Stourbridge; that same year Henry Richardson patented a type of decoration involving an application inside a glass container, therefore covered, always from the inside, with an air bubble blown in such a way that the decorative element adhered entirely to the body of the object, which only later was shaped in the desired form. In 1878 William Hodgetts patented a tool enabling the application of glass filaments onto items, also glass, in order to create designs and decorations. Beginning in the 1880s next to the manufactory there was a school devoted to the use of cameo glass, directed by the French glassmaker Alphonse Lechevrel.

Hoffmann, Josef (1870–1956). Austrian architect and designer, one of the fathers of the Viennese Secession (1897), and founder with Koloman → Moser of the → Wiener Werkstätte that he ran until 1931, exerting an extraordinary influence on the development of the decorative arts in the secessionist and → Jugendstil context.

Honesdale Decorating Co. United States glassworks founded by C. → Dorflinger in Pennsylvania in 1901 and taken over in 1916 by Carl Prosch, an Austrian glassworker and former employee, who performed → acid decoration and gilding of items produced by other glassworks. Each piece bears the full inscription "Honesdale", or else the single initials "HDC" or yet just a "C" set in a shield. The factory was active up until 1932.

Horejc, Jaroslav (b. 1886). Hungarian glass decorator, who specialised in the decoration of glass articles with human figures made in relief; a processing that entailed the tracing of the drawing and then its execution by cutting the base, as in relief cameo; defined *Hochschnitt*, it was to become one of the most famous techniques used in Bohemia and Germany, and was practically identical to processings adopted by Emile → Gallé. From 1922 Horejc was employed in the Stefan Rath factory of Stein-Schönau, directed by → Lobmeyr.

Josef Hoffmann, Chair no. 322, durmast-oak and leather, 1904. Vienna, Museum für Angewandte Kunst

Horta, Victor (1861–1947). Belgian architect and designer, the most famous → art nouveau designer in Belgium, after studying in Ghent and Paris, in 1881 he moved to Brussels where he worked for A. Balat's studio. Appointed professor of architecture in 1893, that same year he began building the Tassel house (completed in 1895), considered to be the manifesto of art nouveau architecture, and between 1894 and 1898 the Solvay house: in those constructions he applied the concept of total art, his aim being for furnishings, decorative elements and bearing structures to all follow the same organic, asymmetrical idiom, inspired by nature and intensely fascinating.

Horti, Paul (1865–1907). Hungarian designer, trained in Budapest, Paris, Munich and London, in 1890 began teaching at the Budapest school of graphic art, all the while being an → eclectic artist who created designs for furnishings, glazed pottery, silk rugs and wallpaper; he also collaborated in the execution of enamelled silver and gold jewellery, works close to traditional Magyar decorative typologies and motifs yet that were deeply renewed by the Viennese Secession.

Hot water plate. Food warmer patented in Great Britain during the nineteenth century and consisting of a silver or silverplate basin, oval or round, with two handles and a lid, in which a red-hot iron was introduced or boiling water was poured in order to keep the food hot.

Hunzinger, George (active between 1861 and 1880). United States furniture-maker of German birth, he specialised in designing and executing chairs often with imaginative shapes, for which he used turned wood imitating bamboo and usually padded backs and seats; he patented a model of a reclining chair (1861) and many of his pieces were published in 1876 in the *Book of Design*.

Hutton, John (b. 1906). Australian glass decorator known for having made the glass panels for the cathedral of Guilford, processed by → sandblasting, and the one at Coventry, decorated with a mobile wheel expressly made; several designs of his panels were borrowed on vases and articles executed by → Whitefriars.

Hyalithe. Bohemian glass processing technique that, as of 1820, produced a sealing-wax red or black glass, imitating the antique red tableware and so-called *black basaltware* from the → Wedgwood factory, a monopoly of southern Bohemian glassworks.

I

Iittala. Finnish glassworks active since 1881 and that in 1888, after having resumed the production of art glass and household ware of the Karhula factory, became Karhula-Iittala Glasbruck; in 1917 it joined the industrial group Ahlstrom and is still active today, known for its production of quality glass and tableware with original, innovatory designs, and in particular for the treatment of surfaces. Several items were designed by Alvar Aalto; Tapio Wirkkala began his collaboration in 1947 and Timo Sarpaneva in 1950.

Ikora-Kristall. A typology of thick glass articles with inclusions of coloured stripes and air bubbles arranged in regular patterns, produced around 1930 by the glass division of the → Württembergische Metallwarenfabrik factory of Göppingen (W.M.F.).

Ilmenau. German pottery founded near Weimar in 1777 and taken over in 1808 by Christian Nonne; it remained active up to 1871 with the trademark Nonne & Roesch.

I.L.S.A. Italian pottery founded at → Albisola toward the 1930s by Franco and Rinaldo Perotti; after the war it was transferred to Carcare, where it produced tiles decorated with glass tesseras, and in the 1960s it made the five million tiles for the covering of the Passeggiata degli Artisti at Albisola Marina, reproducing works by artists like Luzzati, Sassu, Capogrossi, Fontana.

Incalmo. Literally "graft", it is the Murano glass processing technique allowing to perfectly join two open hot-blown glass objects of the same diameter and thickness, obtaining items decorated with two or more coloured zones.

Inlaid linoleum. Name of a special laminate consisting, like linoleum, of oxidised seeds of flax, used mainly for wall facings; it was patented by F. Walton in 1877 with embossed or else relief decoration, obtained by die-printing, imitating solid wood pan-els, treated leather and stucco panels. Some of the most renowned works with this material worth mentioning are several reliefs with abstract patterns in → art nouveau style by Hector → Guimard in 1900.

Inset. Pottery decoration invented at the royal manufactory of → Sèvres by Cotteau (its art director during the reign of Louis XVI) around 1781, revisited at → Worcester and in the William H. → Goss porcelain factory in the mid-nineteenth century; it consists of the application and the fusion of drops of enamel on a silver or gold leaf.

Intarsia glass. Invented in 1920 by Frederick → Carder for the → Steuben Glass Works, it is a highly complex technique that consists of → acid etching a design set upon a dark ground (amethyst, black or navy) and casing it between two layers of colourless glass (casing).

Intercalaire décor. Invented in France, it is a type of decoration obtained with a layer of glaze, spread cold on an article that, heated in the furnace, is then covered with a second layer of clear glass; also dubbed *verre intercalaire*, this technique was widely used in → art nouveau glass.

Iribe, Paul (1883–1935). French designer, interior decorator, creator of wallpaper, furniture, jewellery and textiles, he started off in the Parisian → art nouveau mood, producing comfortable upholstered chairs, in soft, graceful shapes and decorated with carvings or inlays. Arriving in 1914 in the United States, he worked in the field of scenography and costumes for theatrical performances or film sets: some of his executions for Cecil B. de Mille are very well-known. His influence on the features of French → art deco is unmistakable, both in several formal options and in the use of precious materials. Back in France in 1930, he created jewellery and quality bijouterie for Coco Chanel's *maison*.

Iridescent. Glass of this quality was made for the first time by the → Lobmeyr firm in 1863, by treat-

Paul Iribe, brocade with baskets of roses, 1914

ing the vitreous surfaces with metal oxides and then reheating them in a reduced atmosphere; then came a series of patents, yet the finest level of production was reached by the United States manufactories of → Tiffany and → Carder and the Hungarian one of Lötz, that succeeded in making items creating silvered and gilt iridescent effects, in emulation of beetles' elytrons and butterfly wings.

Ironstone China. Pottery technique patented by Charles James Mason in 1813, and up to 1817 the monopoly of his factory in Staffordshire. Later applied in numerous English and United States manufactories, it is a technique introducing in the hard porcelain impasto glass scoriae of iron minerals; the material deriving from it is suited for tableware and, owing to its resistance, also for large-sized articles such as amphoras, bottles and monumental vases for entrances and hallways, and frames for fireplaces.

Isabelline. Definition of a fashion in furnishing, remained popular nearly up to the end of the nineteenth century, owing its name to Isabelle Queen of Spain, ruling between 1833 and 1868. Contemporary and akin to Second Empire style in France, Central European Biedermeier and Victorian taste in Great Britain, the isabelline style offers furnishings that sought to combine comfort with a profusion of ornaments and decorations drawn from the international rococo tradition — but in a languid, worn-out version — and at the same time from the resurgence of a neo-medievalism, especially gothic, displayed in carvings with plant motifs, pinnacles and pointed arches.

Islington. English glassworks, active in 1803 and become in 1960, after many different ownerships, Islington Glass Co. Ltd., specialised in the production of → paperweights, usually marked "IGW".

J

Jack, George (1855–1932). English architect and designer, born in the United States, he studied at Glasgow and toward 1880 joined Philip → Webb's London studio; in 1890 he was put in charge of the project and design unit for furnishings at Morris & Co., that he characterised with furniture based on an explicit return to the "Queen Anne" style, laden with adornments and floral carvings directly drawn from textiles and designs by William → Morris.

Jack-in-the-pulpit. Typical form of vase, with a very slender stem and large fleshy corolla-shaped mouth for holding a single flower, made by → Tiffany and → Carder (the latter for → Steuben glassworks) in → *favrile* or → iridescent glass, between 1890 and 1910. These were emblematic → art nouveau items inspired by American flora and in particular *Arisarum vulgaris*.

Jeanselme, Charles-Joseph-Marie (1827- after 1871). French cabinet-maker, son of the furniture-maker Joseph-Pierre-François; in 1847 he took over the Jacob-Desmalter factory and launched one of the largest nineteenth-century Paris laboratories, producing a good part of the furnishings for the royal residences with period furniture, in particular pieces in the Boulle and "Louis-Seize" manner. In 1863 he associated in the firm the cabinet-maker Godin, who in turn took over the company in 1871, when Jeanselme retired.

Jelliff, John (1813–93). United States furniture-maker active in New Jersey between 1836 and 1890, known for a production of fairly well-made furniture, usually walnut and rosewood in neo-gothic, "Louis-Quinze" and "Louis-Seize" styles.

Jenär Glaswerk. German glassworks active in Mainz by 1884, specialised in mass-production of glass for industry and optics; during the 1920s it completed that activity with the production of earthenware and tableware, generally on designs by Wilhelm → Wagenfeld. The firm's productions were particularly popular during the 1950s and 1960s.

Jennens & Bettridge. English → *papier mâché* factory active since 1816 (after H. Clay from Birmingham took over the factory), that opened several shops in London and was active up to 1864. At the Great London Exhibition of 1851, it won acclaim with its boxes, trays, an armchair, a piano and a cradle in papier mâché with decorations designed by the sculptor John Bell. In 1847 the firm patented a decorative technique with inclusions (previously invented by an employee in 1831) with tortoise-shell, mother-of-pearl, ivory, coloured glass and, on occasion, precious stones.

Jensen, Georg (1866–1935). Danish silversmith who gave his name to a specific style, widely imitated in the United States and Europe. Trained in Copenhagen as a goldsmith, he worked with → pewter and

Georg Jensen, bowl, silver, 1914. Paris, Musée des Arts Décoratifs

M.H. Kühne, Jugendstil candelabra for the new city hall of Leipzig, silver, 1905. Leipzig, Museum für Kunsthandwerk

J

Jack, George (1855–1932). English architect and designer, born in the United States, he studied at Glasgow and toward 1880 joined Philip → Webb's London studio; in 1890 he was put in charge of the project and design unit for furnishings at Morris & Co., that he characterised with furniture based on an explicit return to the "Queen Anne" style, laden with adornments and floral carvings directly drawn from textiles and designs by William → Morris.

Jack-in-the-pulpit. Typical form of vase, with a very slender stem and large fleshy corolla-shaped mouth for holding a single flower, made by → Tiffany and → Carder (the latter for → Steuben glassworks) in → *favrile* or → iridescent glass, between 1890 and 1910. These were emblematic → art nouveau items inspired by American flora and in particular *Arisarum vulgaris*.

Jeanselme, Charles-Joseph-Marie (1827- after 1871). French cabinet-maker, son of the furniture-maker Joseph-Pierre-François; in 1847 he took over the Jacob-Desmalter factory and launched one of the largest nineteenth-century Paris laboratories, producing a good part of the furnishings for the royal residences with period furniture, in particular pieces in the Boulle and "Louis-Seize" manner. In 1863 he associated in the firm the cabinet-maker Godin, who in turn took over the company in 1871, when Jeanselme retired.

Jelliff, John (1813–93). United States furniture-maker active in New Jersey between 1836 and 1890, known for a production of fairly well-made furniture, usually walnut and rosewood in neo-gothic, "Louis-Quinze" and "Louis-Seize" styles.

Jenär Glaswerk. German glassworks active in Mainz by 1884, specialised in mass-production of glass for industry and optics; during the 1920s it completed that activity with the production of earthenware and tableware, generally on designs by Wilhelm → Wagenfeld. The firm's productions were particularly popular during the 1950s and 1960s.

Jennens & Bettridge. English → *papier mâché* factory active since 1816 (after H. Clay from Birmingham took over the factory), that opened several shops in London and was active up to 1864. At the Great London Exhibition of 1851, it won acclaim with its boxes, trays, an armchair, a piano and a cradle in papier mâché with decorations designed by the sculptor John Bell. In 1847 the firm patented a decorative technique with inclusions (previously invented by an employee in 1831) with tortoise-shell, mother-of-pearl, ivory, coloured glass and, on occasion, precious stones.

Jensen, Georg (1866–1935). Danish silversmith who gave his name to a specific style, widely imitated in the United States and Europe. Trained in Copenhagen as a goldsmith, he worked with → pewter and

Georg Jensen, bowl, silver, 1914. Paris, Musée des Arts Décoratifs

silver at the workshop of Mogens → Ballin, and after a trip to France and Italy opened in 1900 his own porcelain factory, but it went bankrupt right away. In 1905, after a successful exhibition of his pieces, Jensen developed a profitable friendship with the painter Johan Rohde, who urged him toward a dryer, more linear and graceful style compared to his first jewellery and silverware marked by → art nouveau taste. Knives with shorter handles and forks with wider-spaced teeth, pitchers and vases with harmonious forms, displayed that special glossy appearance obtained in tempering the piece by soaking it in sulphuric acid, and immediately burnishing it to prevent a slight oxidation. The firm, with its premises in Copenhagen, is still in business, producing top quality silverware.

Jersey Glass Co. United States glassworks opened in New Jersey by the New York glass carver George Drummer in 1824 and active until the 1860s, specialised in the production of fairly good ground, etched and pressed glass.

Jersey rose. Particular decoration of some → paperweights of the → Millville manufactory, characterised by a base on a foot upholding a bowl containing a glass sphere in which is placed a rose. The flower, executed in ruby or yellow glass, has opalescent petals and is accompanied by buds and three green leaves, producing a hyperrealistic impression. This type of article was produced by Ralph Barber between 1905 and 1918.

Jones, Owen (1809–74). English architect and designer, he published in 1856 the staple *Grammar of Ornament*, an authentic repertory of decorative motifs gleaned during his travels in the Middle East (1833) and Spain (1834), widely used by Victorian craftsmen. He is known for having been William → Morris' forerunner in offering stylized floristic themes for ornamenting fabrics and wall paper, as opposed to the Victorian naturalistic bunches of flowers.

Jourdain, Francis (1876–1959). English architect and designer, son of the Belgian architect Frantz, he was the designer for the modernist building of the Paris department store La Samaritaine; after starting as a painter, in 1911 he turned to the decorative arts, designing furnishings, wallpaper, textiles and pottery in an anachronistic → art nouveau style. He was one of the leading figures of the Paris fair of 1925, where he was noted for the conception of furniture with streamlined, highly simplified forms for mass-production.

Jugendstil. German expression that identifies the Munich Secession movement, hence the German version of modernism; the title of a wide-spread review still published in the 1920s, the term was extended to include more specifically → deco trends

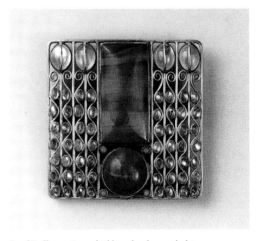

Josef Hoffmann, Jugendstil brooch, silver, malachite, moonstone, lapis-lazuli and coral, ca. 1904

as well. The style is akin to that of the Austrian Secession even though it emphasises its geometric tendency, making the forms more rigid, favoring empty or monochrome spaces, forcing the typically French → art nouveau naturalistic themes into symmetrical, regular, rhythmic and repetitive grids, which explains how by the late 1910s it had already turned to openly deco forms. *(Pl. 56)*

Juhl, Finn (b. 1912). Designer of French birth known for having renovated the furniture production in Denmark, backed by Arne Jacobsen and Hans Wegner, up to the 1940s. His creations were an alternative to the stark, functional style imposed by Kaare → Klint, presenting furniture conceived as sculpture, with free forms and abstract linear designs based on crossing diagonals; to produce the fascinating impression of simplicity characterising this furniture, they must be made of precious wood and be perfectly handcrafted.

K

Kähler, Hermann August (1846–1917). Danish potter who had a fundamental influence on the development of Danish and European art pottery. After working in → Berlin and Zurich potteries, in 1872 Kähler took over the family factory at Neestved, where he started producing ornamental elements for architecture, trying out various colours and decorative glazes; among his most renowned pieces it is worth mentioning high-fired earthenware vases decorated with polychromies ranging from copper brown to purple blue, with speckled red glazes or painted according to modernist formulas. A number of artists worked for his manufactory, including Thorvald → Bindensboll and Otto → Eckmann, who offered delightful → art nouveau designs; several important pieces were shown in international exhibitions (Paris, 1889; Munich, 1899).

Kastrup & Holmegaards. Danish glassworks founded in 1825 on the island of Zeeland under the name Holmegaards Glasvaerk, specialised, employing Norwegian glassblowers, in the production of beer bottles in green glass; with the arrival of Bohemian and German master glassmakers production turned to tableware. Kastrup Glasvaerk was opened in 1847 near Copenhagen exclusively to continue the bottle production, and in 1907 it controlled nearly the entire Danish glass production, except window panes. By 1924, after signing a contract with Royal Copenhagen, the porcelain factory, it took on as head designer Orla Juul Mielsen, then replaced in 1925 by Jacob E. Bangche, who introduced a very abundant production of tableware, ornamental glass and decorative items in the modern vein, raising the manufactory to a European level during the 1930s thanks to a rigorous, sparse style applied to blown glass, decorated with deep carvings and → acid etchings. The manufactory is still in business.

Kayser, Engelbert (1840–1911). Owner and manager of the leading German → pewter factory, working since the late nineteenth century at Bochum, near Krefeld, on designs executed in the homonymous studio active in Cologne; in 1896 it in-

troduced a production of pewter items with exquisite → art nouveau forms, winning considerable success in the exhibitions of Paris (1900) and Saint Louis (1904), marking the international triumph of style applied to metal articles.

Kew Blas. Name of → iridescent glass made in 1893 by the → Union Glass Company and decorated with leaves and feathers motifs rendered in different shades of green and brown. Each piece bears etched (not incised, that being typical of the fakes) the trademark "Kew Blas" drawn from an anagramme of the name of the factory director, William S. Blake.

Kimble Glass Co. United States glassworks created in 1931 when Evan F. Kimble took over the → Vineland Flint Glass Works; he gave up the production of art glass for more commercial series that however borrowed certain themes from → *clutha* glass (inspired by Japanese decorations) and → Tiffany, in particular polychrome glass balls.

Kirk & Son Inc. United States silver company founded by Samuel Kirk in 1815, that in 1828 began making containers in various shapes featuring very ornate embossed decorations, known as "Baltimore silver".

Klablena, Eduard (1881–1933). Austrian potter, after studying at the Kunstgewerbeschule of Vienna, he was hired by K.P.M., the royal porcelain manufactory (Königliche Porzellan-Manufaktur) in → Berlin as modeller of small furnishing sculptures. In 1901 he became independent, opening his own pottery at Langenzerdorf, called Langenzerdorfer Keramik, specialised in representing animals, often dubbed "imaginary animals"; as of 1912 his articles were sold through the → Wiener Werkstätte.

Klint, Kaare (1888–1954). Danish designer, son of the architect P.V. Jensen, he began dealing with furnishings in 1916, suggesting the revolutionary use of unvarnished wood, leather and natural-fibre textiles, illustrating the value of the basic principles of ergonomics. In 1924 he founded the furnishing department at the Danish Art Academy, where he also taught, an essential fact for understanding the worldwide popularity of Danish furniture in the 1920s and 1930s. Careful to recover traditional models (though entirely without decorations) and heedful of constructive features, he drew his inspiration from the furnishings found in Egyptian tombs and Greek culture, but also from English eighteenth-century furniture (especially Chippendale), the stark chairs and tables made by the Shakers in America and nineteenth-century nautical furniture. One of his most famous pieces is the teak deck-chair executed in 1933 inspired by → Le Corbusier's 1929 *chaise longue*.

Knobs. Glass knobs for doors and windows or else to adorn the ends of stairway bannisters, fashionable toward the mid-nineteenth century and produced in France by the → Baccarat, → Clichy and → Saint-Louis manufactories, they were characterised by the use of the → *millefiori* technique. In the United States the → Stourbridge Flint Glass Works of Pittsburgh obtained the patent for making clear glass or moulded coloured knobs.

Knowles, Taylor & Knowles Company. United States porcelain factory opened in 1872 at East Liverpool (Ohio), known for a large produc-

Knowles, Taylor & Knowles Company, toiletry pitcher, pottery, 1905

tion of household and ornamental ware, and later on active in executing pieces drawn from → Belleek models, to which it would owe its fame. After all its furnaces burned down in 1889, production resumed, making translucid porcelain obtained with bone ash, sold under the name *Lotus ware* and very often featuring relief or painted decorations, with plant themes and decorative geometric patterns.

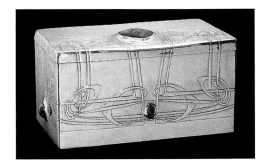

Archibald Knox, cigarette case, embossed silver and opal, 1903–04. London, Victoria and Albert Museum

Knox, Archibald (1864–1933). English silversmith, after moving from his birthplace on the Isle of Man to London in the 1890s, he first worked for Christopher → Dresser and then for → Liberty & Co., a firm for which he produced until 1912 nearly four hundred designs for the most part used for the → *Cymric* line of silver items and after 1903 for the *Tudric* series in → pewter, but also for the execution of rugs, pottery, fabrics and jewellery in which the Celtic tradition merged with → art nouveau stylistic features. *(Pl. 46)*

Kny, Frederick Engelbert (active between 1860 and 1879). Bohemian glass etcher, specialised in etching on rock crystal and glass carving, he signed his own pieces with the stamp "Fek"; having moved to Great Britain, he worked for the → Whitefriars glassworks and, by 1860, at the Dennis glassworks of Thomas → Webb & Sons, where he made his most famous piece, the *Elgin Jug*, completed in 1879.

Kok, J. Jurrian (1861–1919). Dutch designer and potter, after training as an architect, he directed from 1894 to 1913 the pottery Haagsche Plateelbakkerij → Rozenburg in The Hague. A collector of Javanese art, he enthusiastically studied subtropical landscapes, Javanese craft traditions, batik textiles and shadow theatre (Wayang), and with the purpose of transferring those inventions onto a light pottery support he opened a porcelain factory where, with the chemist M.N. Engelden, he studied solutions for obtaining a material having the right kind of consistency for that type of decoration: in 1899 he succeeded in producing a very thin, ivory-coloured porcelain (called eggshell) having a consistency similar to glass. In his creations the forms of the porcelain coincide perfectly with the decorations, nearly always floristic in inspiration, and whose motifs always appear sideways, like silhouettes.

Köpping, Karl (1848–1914). German glassmaker, after several years in Paris he attended the Berlin Akademie in 1890, where he began designing very elegant glass articles, characterised by extreme thinness and typically → art nouveau organic forms: his most famous piece is a rather soaring glass, thin and very light, with a flower-shaped bowl, the foot being formed by the stem of the flower, tall and very fine, with the leaves applied with the "lamp" technique, executed, as other models, by Friedrich → Zitzmann at Wiesbaden and, after 1896, at Ilmenau in Thuringia, and a few United States glassworks. Having studied glazes applied by Japanese craftsmen on pottery, he tried out unusual colour combinations on clear items. As of 1896 he belonged to the editorial staff of the review *Pan*.

Körmöcbánya. Hungarian pottery, active since 1800 at Kremnica (in Bohemia), in the late nineteenth century it was taken over and modernised by Janos Kossuch, who changed its name to J. Kossuch Pottery Co. and exhibited at the 1896 Millennium Fair in Budapest several of its products adorned with traditional Magyar patterns, featuring experiments with metal glazes as well, that launched it on the international market. The trademark is "Cömötz" and in German "Kremnica".

Kosta Glasbruck. Swedish glassworks founded by Anders Koskull and Georg Bogislaus Stäl von Holstein (whose initials gave the laboratory its name) in 1742, at first active in a rather run-of-the-mill production (pane glass for windows, then chandeliers and drinking services). In 1864 → Boda Glasverk opened, and in 1870 merged with Kosta in the Afors group. The Swedish painter Gunnar Gunnarsson Wennerberg was responsible for a significant quality production, with a group of vases in coated glass made between 1898 and 1903. Under the direction of innovatory designers, like Elis → Berg from 1927 and Edvin Ollers and Ewald Dahlskog from 1926 to 1929, it became, along with

the → Orrefors factory, one of the leading glassware and glass vase factories in Sweden, with characteristic essential, organic forms.

Kraka. Glass technique invented around 1944 by Sven → Palmqvist for the → Orrefors Glasbruk: inspired by a female character of the Viking sagas who appeared to her lover draped in a fishing net, it consists of *reticella* (filigree) cased between two layers of opalescent glass. Later pieces were given a gilded or bright navy colouring.

Kuhnt, Georg Gottlieb (1805–85). Bohemian glass mosaicist, born in Bratislava, known for the execution of mosaic panels and compositions representing views of the Bohemian spa towns.

Kuznecov (also known as Kuznetsoff). Russian family, owner of countless porcelain factories and potteries opened at the beginning of the nineteenth century, that absorbed two thirds of the entire production of the Russian Empire. These factories are known for their production of a large range of commercial tableware based on an imitation of European models, but also of a series of ornamental statuettes representing Russian peasant life, like the ones made by the Gardner factory, moreover taken over by the Kuznecov family in 1891.

L

Labino, Dominick (b. 1910). United States glass designer, active since 1936 in his workshop at Grand Rapids, where he made highly original pieces, elegant decorations with → "combed threads" and handles and feet applied onto the body of the object. His production also dealt in items in *reticello* (filigree) glass and very refined pieces decorated with colloidal gold.

La Casa dell'Arte. Italian pottery founded at → Albisola in 1920 by Giuseppe Agnino and Guido Barile, two financiers who to launch the laboratory called back from Paris Manlio Trucco (1884–1974), then joined by the painters Roggiapane, Pacetti and Ravano. Active from the start in a modern production, both in the forms and the glazes used, the factory was guided by the art directors Manlio Trucco, then Pietro Rabbia (until 1932), and finally Giovanni Battista → De Salvo; yet outside artists and designers were frequently called in, like for instance Gio → Ponti, who designed some pottery made in 1937. It participated successfully in the Monza Biennales and the Milan Triennales, crafts exhibitions in Florence and the Paris fairs; it also produced on cartoons by the Tuscan painter Giuseppe Cesetti the large paving in pottery tiles presented in Paris in 1937.

Lace-de-Bohême. Bohemian technique, introduced between 1880 and 1890, consisting of the decoration with white enamel, on a coloured or → glossy ground, used to imitate more costly cameo glass. A second technique, again Bohemian, consists of the use of a coloured glass with a thin opalescent layer, upon which a design is traced, then coated with acid-proof ink; therefore, after soaking in hydrofluoric acid, when the piece is removed there is a thin relief on the reserved parts.

Lachenal, Edmond (b. 1855). French potter, art director for → Deck, he opened his own laboratory at Chatillon-sous-Bagneux in 1880, where he produced gres items in emulation of Japanese pottery, that met with worldwide success. He also ex-ecuted pottery and porcelain with painted decors representing birds, flowers and insects in → art nouveau style, as well as small sculptures, some made in collaboration with Auguste Rodin.

Lacy glass. Characteristic objects in pressed glass adorned with relief decorations, like small spheres, arabesques and leaves, that just barely stand out on a ground of minute rhombs formed by the dots of the mould. The effect is that of lace that is extended over trays, dessert dishes, pitchers, bowls and small basins. Made nearly exclusively between 1830 and 1850 by the → New England Glass Company and the → Boston and Sandwich Glass Company, these objects were borrowed and imitated in France and other European countries.

Laeuger, Max (1864–1952). German potter, interior decorator and architect; trained at Karlsruhe, where later he was to teach (1885–98), he is known for vases with Orientalising forms — although simplified — decorated in a limited range of colours: yellow and green on a navy ground, black and white on a green ground, outlining stylised flowers, especially tulips, suited for the purpose because of their long stem and the compact bowl of the corolla. He further executed a series of very elaborate tiles and other decorative elements for religious architectures and for interiors he designed himself. In 1921 he began working at the Karlsruhe Majolika-Manufaktur, but a great deal of his later work was figurative and sculptural in dimension. He was also the author of essays on the art of pottery, and his influence on the development of art pottery in Germany would be remarkable.

La Farge, John (1835–1910). United States painter on glass, son of a painter, he studied in Paris in T. Couture's studio, beginning with painted stained glass and frescoes in the pre-Raphaelite manner. From 1870 to 1880 he worked in his own studio at New York, executing → iridescent → *opaline* glass panels, onto which abstract ornamentations were painted, representing stylised flat figures and leaves

113

and flowers in emulation of William → Morris' textiles, then mounted as windows or screens in the homes of rich magnates (the Vanderbilts and the Whitneys, for instance). The author of essays on decorative art, he had a determining influence on the formation of the modernist style in the United States.

La Fiamma. Italian pottery opened at → Albisola by Ivos Pacetti in 1929; by its documented participations in the Milanese Triennales, especially in 1933, it was known for articles strictly inspired by rationalist models and → deco-style decorations (cornucopias, small Oriental heads), with a small futurist interlude.

Lalique, René (1860–1945). French jeweller and glassmaker, he started off in his own laboratory opened in 1885 as jewellery designer in the most exquisite → art nouveau style (dragonflies, beetles, peacocks, overblown flowers, female nudes) and asymmetrical forms, enhanced by semi-precious stones, enamels and glass overlays. Later on he would make

a number of pieces for the Samuel → Bing firm, but his name did not become famous until 1902, with the creation of perfume bottles for the Maison Coty. In 1908 he opened a factory at Combs-la-Ville, in the vicinity of Paris, specialised in producing pressed glass vases and articles, moulded and etched, as well as very thick, etched panels for windows, all treated with a special → sandblasting technique and acid baths producing the opalescence of ice. Fascinated by → Gallé's glass, he made a very rich series of vases imitating the art nouveau style of the → Nancy master, and sculptures using the lost wax technique with coloured glass. In 1918 he took over a glassworks at Wingen-sur-Moder, that was to pursue his serial production under the direction of his son Marc and under the name Cristallerie Lalique & Cie., becoming one of the most important → deco manufactories in Europe. All the pieces modelled after 1925 were in colourless glass, but with an opaque surface and an azure or pink opalescence, especially bottles and small ornaments, but also large vases, statuettes, bowls adorned either with naturalist themes (birds, fish,

René Lalique, radiator cap shaped like a peacock head, moulded blue pâte de verre, 1928

René Lalique, Senlis vase, fumé glass, ca. 1925

plant elements) or female nudes, soft and evanescent but always having explicit deco features. The articles always bear the inscription "R. Lalique" and after 1945, just "Lalique". The factory is still active and its finest pieces are conserved in the Gulbenkian Collection of Lisbon. *(Pls 57 and 58)*

Lambert & Rawlings. English jewellery laboratory active since the mid-nineteenth century, founded by Francis Lambert and William Rawlings in 1842 (who that year had inherited the commercial activity of the Rundell, Bridge & Rundell firm), that produced a huge quantity of silver items, both for liturgical and household use, all inspired by neo-medieval taste, some of which were shown at the Great London Exhibition in 1851 and widely admired. The firm continued its activity in the twentieth century, under the name Harman & Lambert.

Lamp-blown glass. Glass technique that consists of the execution of small items and ornamental groups realised with glass threads and canes, easily molten and re-heated on the flame of a lamp or an incandescent blowpipe, blown, joined and hand-shaped.

Lancaster. United States glassworks opened in New York in 1849 for producing drug-pots, cups and carafes with *lily pad* decorations. The factory wound down in 1900.

Lancetti, Federico (1817–92). Italian carver and cabinet-maker, born in Umbria, he specialised in the use of → glass *marqueterie* for floral decorations with ivory overlays; a table of his shown in Florence in 1861 was purchased by Vittorio Emanuele II and today is at Palazzo Pitti.

Lancia, Emilio (1890–1973). Italian architect and designer, a longtime friend of Gio → Ponti, he was co-owner of the studio between 1927 and 1933, and in 1927, again with Ponti, he opened the "Domus Nova" department in the La Rinascente department store in Milan for selling mass-produced furnishings, and founded the artistic association *Il Labirinto* with the participation of Pietro → Chiesa, Tomaso → Buzzi, Michele → Marelli and Paolo → Venini, that produced furnishings, textiles, chandeliers, vases in refined, precious materials. At the Monza Biennale Lancia displayed furniture emulating eighteenth-century or neo-classical typologies executed in elm wood, briar-root, walnut, with bronze decorations, giving rise to one of the most elegant → deco-style productions of the 1920s in Italy.

Landberg, Nils (b. 1907). Swedish glass designer, active until 1936 at the → Orrefors Glasbruk, where at first he executed etched decorations and blown pieces without using a mould; particularly known for his modelling of large vases and crystal drinking services with very long stems and different shades of colour.

Larsen, Emil J. (b. 1877). Swedish glassmaker, emigrated to the United States in 1887, he worked at the → Dorflinger factory until 1918, then at the → Pairpoint Manufacturing Co. until 1926, and the → Vineland Flint Glass Works until 1933. In 1935 he opened his own laboratory at Vineland (New Jersey), creating decorative articles, either moulded or free-blown, and very well-known → paperweights famous under the name *Jersey Rose*.

La Salamandra. Italian pottery, opened in Perugia in 1923 and active until 1931; in 1932 it changed its partnership organization and marked its pieces "C.I.M.A. Perugia", → "Deruta Perugia" or merely "Perugia", up until the end of its activity in 1955. Created by the founders of the Perugina confectionery company, the pottery had first been conceived for producing packaging for sweets, and it marketed items (boxes, vases, dishes, baskets) featuring an openly popular, "homemade" → deco taste, highly attractive however by their colour range. *(Pl. 59)*

Lauensteiner Hütte. German glassworks founded near Hanover in 1701 for the preparation of objects and drinking services imitating English glass, with a facetted knob and long stem. The pieces are occasionally stamped with a rampant lion and a capital "C", indicating the Principality of Calenberg where the glassworks, active until 1870, was located.

Lava glass. Glass technique invented by → Tiffany and characterised by a smooth surface obtained by melting basalt powder in the glass impasto. Once completed, the object, always an uneven shape, takes on a special gilt iridescence with decorative gold striped motifs or else abstract elements giving it the appearance of molten lava, whereby its original name "volcanic glass".

Laveno. Italian pottery, active since 1856 with former employees of → Richard of Milan, become in 1883 Società Ceramica Italiana di Laveno. In 1924 Franco Revelli merged his own Società Ceramica

Stand design of Società Ceramica Italiana di Laveno set up for the first Monza Biennale, 1923

Revelli with the Società Ceramica Italiana di Laveno; this partnership remained alive until 1932, producing earthenware table sets and porcelain ware (since 1925). After successfully focusing on producing pottery vases and articles in an explicit → art nouveau style, in 1923 the factory took on as art director Guido → Andlovitz, who turned the entire production toward a homogeneous, refined → deco idiom. Between 1937 and 1940 the factory was directed by the sculptor Angelo Biancini; in 1965 it was incorporated by Richard-Ginori. *(Pls 5, 48 and 60)*

Leach, Bernard Howell (1881–1979). English potter; born in the Orient, after his schooling in Great Britain he went to Japan in 1909, where he studied pottery at the studio of Ogata Kezan VI. Back in England in 1920, he founded the Leach pottery at Saint Ives with his Japanese pupil Shoji Hamada, who later on his return to Japan asserted himself as the best potter. Mainly inspired by

Japanese *Raku* pottery, Leach was also interested in medieval English pottery and seventeenth-century production, in particular the *slipware* kind, making household ware and vases in simple, compact forms, whose decorative effect was owed to the glazes and the motifs, etched or sprayed on the surfaces. His *Potter's Book*, that appeared in 1940, is a key to the theorisation of art pottery.

Le Bertetti. Italian pottery, active in Turin after 1931, founded by Clelia Bertetti after she had worked for three years at the → Lenci manufactory, producing patinated terra cotta one-offs and series of multiples signed "Le Bertetti", for the most part languid, graceful female nudes. In 1942 Clelia Bertetti permanently closed the laboratory to entirely concentrate on sculpture. *(Pl. 61)*

Le Comte, Adolf (1850–1921). Dutch potter, after studying in Karlsruhe, Nuremberg and Paris, he was appointed artistic director of the porcelain factory → De Porcelayne Fles at Delft from 1877 to 1915, producing a wealth of designs in emulation of Renaissance culture, but rarely executed in the factory, that was more drawn to traditional floral decoration. In 1885 he developed a new type of ceramic paste, similar to the one produced by the → Rozenburg factory, inspired by Persian pottery, and later produced series of designs for facing tiles, including the ones mounted in the Hamburg zoo.

Le Corbusier (1887–1965). Architect and designer, resolute champion of modernism and promoter of the convergence of design and industry, theoretician in the debate on architecture as well as

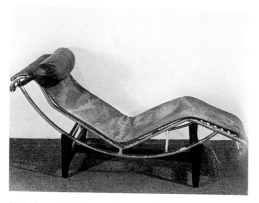

Le Corbusier, chaise longue, chromium-plated steel, black steel and leather, 1928

in that of design production, he envisaged furnishing as an ensemble of modular container units placed against or recessed in the walls, or at the centre of a space: the *casiers standard*, in emulation of office furniture. World-famous are his chaise longues that slide on the base and can be gradually transformed, the *grand confort* armchair and the small rocking chair, all designed for industrial production in 1929. The *chaise longue* exemplifies the rationalist trend, by blending durability with an essential sense of lightness, by the combination of several materials, but mainly because of its utter functionality and adaptability to the various movements of the human body.

Leerdam. Dutch glassworks founded by the royal family near Utrecht in 1765 for producing all types of glass: from bottles to vases, from ornamental crystals to tableware. After P.M. Cochius was named director in 1915, the factory shifted decisively toward the execution of high quality items

and mass production of first-rate tableware, calling on designers like A.D. → Copier, responsible in 1917 for the art direction of the factory and known for his heavy crystal vases and blown glass. The factory, that benefitted by the creations of numerous designers, including K.P.C. de Bazel in 1915, C.J. Lanoy in 1919 and H.P. → Berlage in 1923, is still in business with a connected museum for its own production.

Legrain, Pierre (1889–1929). French furniture designer, one of the founders of → art deco. Joining Paul → Iribe's studio, where he worked between 1908 and 1914, in 1917 he designed book bindings for Jacques Doucet, whose house he had also decorated, and who in 1925 engaged him to furnish his own studio in Neuilly. Influenced by the austere essentiality of African sculpture, but attracted to precious materials and monumental forms, during the 1920s he designed a great quantity of furniture to be executed with unusual materials and sometimes featuring geometric decorations.

Lenci. Italian pottery, founded at Turin in 1919 by Elena and Enrico Scavini for the production of wooden toys, cloth dolls and furnishings for children's rooms, that met with immediate success, confirmed by a number of awards at the 1925 Paris fair. In 1928 the manufactory launched its pottery production, hiring alongside its former collaborators (Gigi → Chessa, Sandro Vacchetti and Riva) new artists, including Mario Sturani, Claudia Formica, Lino Berzoini, Giovanni and Ines Grande, Massino Quaglino, Beppe Porcheddu, Clelia Bertetti (who later founded → Le Bertetti studio), Giulio Da Milano, Teonesto De Abate, Bona Sancipriano and Felice Tosalli (who further on would specialise in fascinating precious wood sculptures in an exotic vein), whose works were presented in 1929 at the Galleria Pesaro in Milan. In 1930, Ronzan, Ghigo, Bologna, Fany and Jacopi joined the Lenci team. Production, backed up by skilled craftsmen, was extremely varied, offering furnishing statuettes, vases, boxes, very well-crafted tiles featuring underglaze decorations and the use of a bright palette. Especially in its three-dimensional figures, the most famous product of the firm, the perfect rendering of details and the quality of the modelling succeeded in blending the masters' individual styles with the mood of contemporary taste; that is apparent, over time, in the female nudes inspired by the Orient and presenting typically → deco wavy lines (like Sandro Vacchetti's creations) or in Mario Sturani's

Lenox Company, coffee set, porcelain and silver, 1920

more strictly Novecento still lifes and figurines. In 1933 the manufactory joined up with the Garella brothers, who in 1937 took over the trademark that was still owned by the founders: henceforth production repeated stereotyped models and forms without the slightest innovations up to today. *(Pls 62 and 63)*

Lenox Company. United States porcelain factory active since 1889 at Trenton (New Jersey) and directed by Jonathan Coxon and Walter Scott Lenox; the latter being art director at the → Ott & Brewer Company, he had learned there the processing technique for making → Belleek porcelain: this led to a production, still under way, of tableware and decorative articles modelled in very thin, quality porcelain.

Lessore, Emile-Aubert (1805–76). French pottery and porcelain designer, pupil of D. Ingres, he worked for the Laurin factory at Bourg-la-Reine, at → Sèvres, and the → Minton factory in Great Britain. But his most important connection was with → Wedgwood, that toward the mid-nineteenth century sent him in Paris crate-loads of porcelain and pottery for him to decorate, especially dishes, that he composed like paintings, mostly on mythological themes.

Lethaby, William Richard (1857–1931). English designer, in 1900 he began teaching at the Royal College of Art in London, where he was responsible for spreading the ideas of William → Morris and the → Arts & Crafts; he was also active in the decorative arts, making models for embroidery, metal items, decorations of → Wedgwood pottery, but equally furniture inspired by Chippendale, although in a slightly rustic, simplified interpretation, decorated with non-coloured relief elements representing floristic subjects.

Léveillé, Ernest Baptiste. French glassmaker, pupil and, in 1885, successor of François-Eugène → Rousseau, he pursued the application of the glass technique developed by his master, with a stylish production in the → art nouveau manner, like his graceful vases with fish and animals made of colourless crystal, blown, carved, → glossed and burnished. After 1900 the firm, under the same name, was taken over by Harand and Guignard, who kept up the activity well into the twentieth century.

Libbey Glass Co. United States glassworks, sprung up in 1878 within the → New England Glass Company, it took its final name in 1888 when it transferred to Toledo (Ohio) and became the biggest ground-glass factory in the world (between 1890 and 1915). It met with a huge success when, in 1893, it employed about a hundred and thirty glassblowers and grinders for the execution of the Glass Pavilion at the Chicago World Fair and a series of souvenir-items all trademarked "Libbey Glass Co. World's Fair 1893". In the period between 1883 and 1940 the manufactory's output was elegant articles in coloured glass, modelled by Joseph → Locke, including → *maize*, → *amberina*, → *peach blow*, → *agata* and → *pomona*. In 1925 ownership passed from the Libbey founders to the Robinson partners, and after 1931 production benefitted by the glass creations of A. Douglas → Nash, especially with → *Libbey-Nash* glass, of the very finest quality (1933). In 1936 owing to financial losses the firm passed under the control of Owens-Illinois Inc., that is still producing popular glass and crystal ware in contemporary style (series of pieces with lead ornamentations designed by E.W. Feurst in 1940–45). Presently the production cycle has eliminated items in hand-crafted glass.

Libbey-Nash. Trademark that relates to ornamental and luxury ware, produced as of 1933 by A. Douglas → Nash for the → Libbey Glass Co., having exceptional technical quality and finishing, both as to the grinding and the etching of the surfaces, signed with the name "Libbey" in italics and surrounded by a circle. The drinking service series features eighty-two different models, some produced in four colours, whereas regarding ornamental articles produced in limited numbers, the material used is clear, colourless glass.

Liberty. Term referring to the Italian version of international modernism (derived from the trademark of → Liberty & Co., the well-known London department store that exported → art nouveau articles and furnishings to Italy also), featuring stylistic traits extremely similar to those of French-speaking cultures, yet retaining, within an utterly modernist manner, a special interest in naturalistic themes and the human figure, typical of the academic, late-romantic tradition of Italian art. In architectural design (above all Fenoglio and D'Aronco in Turin and Sommaruga in Milan and Lombardy) as well as in the decorative arts (in particular for furnishings by → Basile in Sicily and by → Zen and → Quarti in Milan, for pottery by → Chini in Tuscany, → Zecchin glass at Murano, and for ironwork by → Mazzucotelli and → Rizzarda in Milan and → Bellotto in Venice), Italian liberty, between 1890 and 1906, developed a great variety of creations, that had their counterparts in painting as well (we should mention in particular the symbolist Gaetano Previati, and the Venetian group revolving around Cesare Laurenti), and equally in sculpture (especially Leonardo Bistolfi, Italian plastic symbolism's spokesman), and were frequently receptive to the various Central European Secession productions, as could be seen in the pieces shown at the great Turin fair of 1902 and, later, the 1906 Sempione fair in Milan. Those exchanges, particularly apparent in Venice and Trieste, facilitated the smooth transition from the last, repetitive residues of Italian liberty to the → deco taste of the very early 1920s. *(Pl. 46)*

Liberty, Arthur Lasenby (1843–1917). English dealer who was to London what Samuel → Bing was to Paris. After starting off as a clerk, in 1862 he took over the direction of the Oriental department in the Farmer & Rogers store; in 1874 he opened his own sales space on Regent's Street, called *East India House*, specialised in *japonaiseries* and Oriental items, but at the same time retailing furniture, textiles and furnishing articles in the → eclectic manner. In 1884 to renew his stock, he took on C.F.A. → Voysey as textile designer and in 1889 opened his own shop in Paris that would be a sort of launching pad for spreading throughout Europe the English version of → art nouveau: for instance for silverware (produced by 1894) inspired by the Celtic tradition (→ *Cymric*, meaning Welsh) and a new → pewter series featuring a high

Jessie M. King (for Liberty & Co.), buckle with birds and flowers, silver and enamels, 1906

Umberto Bellotto (for Pauly and Co.), clear green glass liberty vase with lateral scroll handles

percentage of silver, dubbed *Tudric*. A strong believer in joining the beautiful to the useful and the inexpensive, he commissioned and sold furnishing textiles (with characteristic floral patterns, including tulips, irises and waterlilies), metal items with Celtic-type abstract decorations and navy or turquoise enamels, furniture with tapering shapes provided with large-sized, brass or bronze hinges and handles.

Libisch, Joseph (active between 1921 and 1947). Hungarian glass etcher, after training in Vienna and Prague he moved to the United States, where in 1921 he began working at the → Steuben Glass Works. Frederick → Carder, who held him to be the finest living etcher, charged him with the execution of the *Gazelles Bowl* and *Zodiac Bowl* (both executed in 1935 on designs by Sidney Waugh), the *Acrobats Bowl* (designed in 1940 by Pavel Tchelitchev); again in 1944 he etched, on a design by Epstein, the *Orchids Bowl*.

Lime glass. Name for "calcic glass", a technique previously used in Bohemia and Silesia during the seventeenth century, that began to be wide-spread in 1864, when in Virginia for the first time light glass replaced lead glass for making bottles.

Lind Jenny. Defines a historic kind of flask, manufactured in the United States toward the mid-nineteenth century in three different sizes and adorned with the relief portrait of the Swedish singer Jenny Lind. The bottle, with a flattened globular body and a long neck, can also present a relief laurel wreath, the name of the singer portrayed and a lyre below. In 1925 a series of counterfeits in several colours were produced by the Fislerville Glass Works in New Jersey.

Lindstrand, Vicke (b. 1904). Swedish glass designer, working between 1928 and 1941 at the → Orrefors Glasbruk, where he produced his very famous "ice cubes". In 1950 he joined the → Kosta glassworks.

Linthorpe. English pottery founded in 1879 in Yorkshire, directed by Henry Tooth; the models by Christopher → Dresser, art director, were often inspired by Japanese and Inca pottery. The manufactory continued to produce items of this type, including teapots with graceful, utterly simple lines, up to the end of the century, although those two directors had retired in 1882.

Lion Cahet, Carel Adolph (1864–1945). Dutch furniture designer, active at Vreeland, near Utrecht, by 1897, producing a richly ornate form of → art nouveau in which rare, precious materials were used (rosewood, Coromandel), for single pieces as well as for entire furnishings, especially conceived for steamer interiors. Interesting exemplars are conserved at the Rijksmuseum in Amsterdam.

Liporesi. Italian furniture factory, active at Bologna since 1890 in the production of commissioned furnishings; despite not having its own stylistic line the firm worked for important designers like for instance Duilio → Cambellotti, who in 1931 had the Bologna factory execute the furnishings for the Acquedotto Pugliese at Bari, including the stuccoes, pavings and lighting fixtures. It is still in business.

Lithophanes. Porcelain panels carved with motifs, often drawn from famous paintings, that can be seen with backlight. Their production began at → Meissen in 1828 and → Berlin between 1827 and 1850; made also by the English manufacturers → Minton and Copeland, and the German Gotha and Plaue, a number of exemplars are conserved at The Blair Museum of Lithophanes in Toledo (Ohio).

Lithyalin. Glossy glass, marbled with red or other bright colours, imitating semi-precious stones. Produced in Bohemia between 1825 and 1840 by Friedrich → Egermann, it was used in the production of countless articles in different styles; a variant dubbed "chameleon glass" was presented in 1835.

Lobmeyr, J. & L. Austrian glassworks founded in 1823 by the glassmaker Josef Lobmeyr (1792–1855) in the vicinity of Linz. Commercial success took off under the direction of the founder's two sons, Josef (1828–64) and Ludwig (1829–1917); the latter, in charge of designing, commissioned designs for articles from the leading Viennese artists, among whom the architect Theophil von Hansen. Most of the pieces were produced by the Meyrs Neffe glassworks, in Bohemia, owned by Lobmeyr's son-in-law, on the most widespread Bohemian models and in various period styles, although several series of glassware and carafes were outstanding by the particular sobriety of their forms and decorations. When Ludwig retired in 1902, the direction of the factory passed down to his grandson Stefan Rath (1876–1960), very closely connected to Secession artists, even

J. & L. Lobmeyr, octagonal Bronzite *vase, decoration by Josef Hoffmann, ca. 1910. Vienna, Museum für Angewandte Kunst*

having as co-director, in 1910, Josef → Hoffmann, and as his collaborators Adolf Loos (famous series of strictly cylindrical glassware) and Michael → Powolny. *(Pl. 64)*

Locke, Joseph (1846–1936). English glassmaker; after training as of 1858 in the pottery of → Worcester, in 1865 he began working in the firm for the decoration of glass by the Guest brothers at → Stourbridge, then switching to the → Hodgetts, Richardson & Co. glassworks, for which he executed in 1876 a glass copy of the British Museum *Portland* vase, shown in Paris in 1878. In 1882 he moved to the United States, joining the → New England Glass Company, where he made countless coloured glass articles; later, at the → Libbey Glass Co., he created → *amberina*, and → *agate*, → *maize*, → *pomona* and → *peach blow* (the name of a wild rose) glass. In 1891, after moving to Ohio, he opened his own glassworks, signing the pieces "Locke" or else "Locke Art".

Lonhuda. United States pottery founded at Steubenville (Ohio) in 1892, specialised in art pottery featuring under-glaze coloured stripes and modelled vases imitating Indian pottery, although the decorations were inspired by Japan. In 1905 Long, one of the founders, opened the → Clifton Art Pottery at Newark (New Jersey), that produced

(or "Charles-Dix"), but emphasising the more decorative effects and giving a kind of "bourgeois" character to utterly aristocratic furnishings. Basically inspired by a fabled Middle Ages, the Troubadour style was soon replaced by a more accurate reproduction of gothic, late-gothic and Renaissance style. During the reign of Louis Philippe, coinciding with the diffusion of Biedermeier in Central Europe, there was a return to rococo, and particularly of the elegant, refined Pompadour version.

Lundgren, Tyra (1897–1979). Swedish glass designer and potter endowed with remarkable distinction and creativity, after the success obtained at the Milan Triennale in 1933, he was called to Murano by Paolo → Venini. His favourite themes related to the animal world (especially snakes, fish and birds), but also to the plant world, like in the large bowls with leaves decorated with glazes and his remarkable Phoenician glass vases. *(Pl. 118)*

Lunéville. French pottery founded in 1731 and specialised in the production of tableware with graceful rococo forms. During the nineteenth century the factory went back to offering traditional models, like life-size lions and dogs made of polychrome majolica to be placed in entrances of buildings and in gardens. The pieces usually bear the name of the manufactory, followed by the designer's initials.

Lurçat, Jean (1892–1966). French painter and tapestry-designer, trained at → Nancy with Emile-Victor Prouvé, he began his career making book bindings in → art nouveau style; in 1912 he settled permanently in Paris. Drawing his inspiration from fourteenth-century Parisian tapestries, but pre-Columbian geometricising fabrics as well, during the 1930s he introduced a radical renovation in the making of modern tapestries, beginning with *The Illusions of Icarus*, designed in 1936 for the Gobelins manufactory, and pursuing with a series of designs for the → Aubusson manufactory, characterised by the choice of ordinary materials for weaving and a sparse, modest colour range.

Lustre. Term that during the nineteenth century referred to a chandelier with a structure in gilt bronze or wood adorned with glass drops hanging from the rim, garlands of small beads or minute balls.

Lutz, Nicholas. French glassmaker, he emigrated in 1869 to the United States and joined the → Boston and Sandwich Glass Company, specialising in the creation of striped glass articles and in → paperweights with fruit and leaves represented in a naturalistic manner and in miniature. In 1888 he switched to the → Mount Washington Glass Company and later to the → Union Glass Company.

Lynn. Definition referring to glass tableware, especially drinking services, carafes and bottles, characterised by the presence of circles (from two to eight) stamped on the surfaces, probably by the processing instruments.

Lyon. Silk manufactories active since the fifteenth century; at the end of the eighteenth century, with the introduction of *jacquard* looms for processing, they were able to produce huge quantities of Empire-style silk for the Napoleonic residences. Many of these fabrics, not even entirely completed nor purged of their imperial symbols, were used by the Bourbons during the Restoration; during the nineteenth century the factories were active producing silks richly adorned with flowers or copying eighteenth-century models, woven in the faded shades of the originals that in time had lost their bright colours. In the 1920s the Bianchini-Férier firm began using graphic designs by Raoul Dufy, thus initiating collaboration with contemporary artists. They still produce today the finest silks in Europe.

Lion Cahet, Carel Adolph (1864–1945). Dutch furniture designer, active at Vreeland, near Utrecht, by 1897, producing a richly ornate form of → art nouveau in which rare, precious materials were used (rosewood, Coromandel), for single pieces as well as for entire furnishings, especially conceived for steamer interiors. Interesting exemplars are conserved at the Rijksmuseum in Amsterdam.

Liporesi. Italian furniture factory, active at Bologna since 1890 in the production of commissioned furnishings; despite not having its own stylistic line the firm worked for important designers like for instance Duilio → Cambellotti, who in 1931 had the Bologna factory execute the furnishings for the Acquedotto Pugliese at Bari, including the stuccoes, pavings and lighting fixtures. It is still in business.

Lithophanes. Porcelain panels carved with motifs, often drawn from famous paintings, that can be seen with backlight. Their production began at → Meissen in 1828 and → Berlin between 1827 and 1850; made also by the English manufacturers → Minton and Copeland, and the German Gotha and Plaue, a number of exemplars are conserved at The Blair Museum of Lithophanes in Toledo (Ohio).

Lithyalin. Glossy glass, marbled with red or other bright colours, imitating semi-precious stones. Produced in Bohemia between 1825 and 1840 by Friedrich → Egermann, it was used in the production of countless articles in different styles; a variant dubbed "chameleon glass" was presented in 1835.

Lobmeyr, J. & L. Austrian glassworks founded in 1823 by the glassmaker Josef Lobmeyr (1792–1855) in the vicinity of Linz. Commercial success took off under the direction of the founder's two sons, Josef (1828–64) and Ludwig (1829–1917); the latter, in charge of designing, commissioned designs for articles from the leading Viennese artists, among whom the architect Theophil von Hansen. Most of the pieces were produced by the Meyrs Neffe glassworks, in Bohemia, owned by Lobmeyr's son-in-law, on the most widespread Bohemian models and in various period styles, although several series of glassware and carafes were outstanding by the particular sobriety of their forms and decorations. When Ludwig retired in 1902, the direction of the factory passed down to his grandson Stefan Rath (1876–1960), very closely connected to Secession artists, even

J. & L. Lobmeyr, octagonal Bronzite *vase, decoration by Josef Hoffmann, ca. 1910. Vienna, Museum für Angewandte Kunst*

having as co-director, in 1910, Josef → Hoffmann, and as his collaborators Adolf Loos (famous series of strictly cylindrical glassware) and Michael → Powolny. *(Pl. 64)*

Locke, Joseph (1846–1936). English glassmaker; after training as of 1858 in the pottery of → Worcester, in 1865 he began working in the firm for the decoration of glass by the Guest brothers at → Stourbridge, then switching to the → Hodgetts, Richardson & Co. glassworks, for which he executed in 1876 a glass copy of the British Museum *Portland* vase, shown in Paris in 1878. In 1882 he moved to the United States, joining the → New England Glass Company, where he made countless coloured glass articles; later, at the → Libbey Glass Co., he created → *amberina*, and → *agate*, → *maize*, → *pomona* and → *peach blow* (the name of a wild rose) glass. In 1891, after moving to Ohio, he opened his own glassworks, signing the pieces "Locke" or else "Locke Art".

Lonhuda. United States pottery founded at Steubenville (Ohio) in 1892, specialised in art pottery featuring under-glaze coloured stripes and modelled vases imitating Indian pottery, although the decorations were inspired by Japan. In 1905 Long, one of the founders, opened the → Clifton Art Pottery at Newark (New Jersey), that produced faithful copies, both in shape and in adornment, of Pueblo Indian pottery.

Loreti. Italian furnishings factory, active since the early twentieth century in Rome and known for its production of period and floristic-style furniture for the royal family. Mario Loreti worked with his father Fernando as of 1925, enlarging the factory and launching the production of one-offs he designed himself, like the 1928 furnishings for the Venchi shop on Via Veneto in Rome, a typical combination of neo-Renaissance elements and → deco style. Beginning in the 1930s the furniture became squarer, personalised by bosses, embossed surfaces, metal finishings, veins of different woods, from walnut to rosewood. The factory was wound down in 1952.

Lötz Witwe. Bohemian glassworks active at Klostermühle in 1836 and taken over in 1840 by Johann Lötz (1778–1848); at his death the business passed down to his wife Suzanne under the name "Johann Lötz Witwe" (that is, widow). Her nephew Max Ritter von Spaun became director in 1870, and the factory notably increased production, executing top quality pieces. In the last decade of the nine-teenth century they were making art glass imitating semi-precious stones, like → *aventurine* and → *agate*, and concurrently the factory was given a patent for the production of items in → iridescent glass, similar, but chronologically earlier, to the noted → Tiffany → *favrile* glass; this production of iridescent glass vases, imitating insects' elytrons, creating a great visual effect and with at times extravagant forms, was exported all over the world. Alongside strictly → Jugendstil decorations, particularly in abstract motifs rendered with soft, irregular and → combed lines, there were decorative themes typical of the → Wiener Werkstätte, on designs by → Powolny and Polek, but black and white items as well; in 1914 production was halted. Right after the war the firm reopened, but was then destroyed in a fire in 1932. From 1891 on, a good number of the pieces meant for export bear the trademark "Lötz-Austria", whereas the ones for the domestic market present "Lötz Klostermühle" beside two crossed arrows inside a circle. *(Pls 65 and 66)*

Louis-Philippe. The stylistic name of the period coinciding with the reign of Louis Philippe, between 1830 and 1840, an extension of the Restoration style

Lötz Witwe, vases, green iridescent glass, ca. 1900

M

Macdonald, Margaret (1865–1933). English designer, after studying at the Glasgow School of Art, in 1900 she married C.R. → Mackintosh and became very active in the field of designing metal articles and embroideries, often collaborating with her sister Frances (1874–1921), a skilled metal craftswoman, she also married to a member of the Glasgow School, J. Herbert McNair, a furnishings designer. With their two husbands-to-be they founded in 1893 the group dubbed *The Four* and in 1894 a workshop on their own.

Macintyre James & Co. English pottery, active between 1852 and 1913 at Burslem, offering an interesting production of bud- and chalice-shaped →

art nouveau vases (around 1910), hand-decorated with flower motifs (especially tulips, irises and violets), and milk jugs and coffee pots (after 1902), decorated either with traditional English scenery motifs, navy on a white ground, or with floristic patterns inspired by William → Morris' textiles.

Mackintosh, Charles Rennie (1868–1928). English architect and designer, leader of the Glasgow School and outstanding figure of international modernism. After graduating in architecture in 1889, he participated in the → Arts & Crafts exhibition of 1896, and the following year designed the furnishings for the Glasgow School of Art (extended in 1907); between 1897 and 1910 he designed sev-

William Moorcroft (for James Macintyre & Co.), Pansy Vase, *polychrome pottery, ca. 1910*

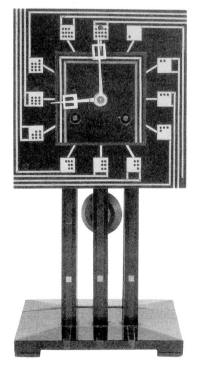

Charles Rennie Mackintosh, table clock, 1917

eral tearooms, again in Glasgow, for Miss Cranston, and a number of private residences. Mackintosh had started designing furniture for himself toward 1890, and a while later he began to collaborate with the Guthrie & Redwells firm; always inspired by → Godwin's models and the characteristic use of colours in Whistler's furnishings, he had a preference for furniture painted white (the opposite of Arts & Crafts, fond of hand-crafted oak) with inserts of colour, occasionally of amethyst-colour glass or else paintings, outlining strictly two-dimensional floral patterns, emulating Japanese *imagerie*. The chairs present very high backs, narrowing toward the top, the tables thin legs, the sideboards projecting frames. His strict, gracefully virginal furniture was more popular abroad than in Scotland (Venice, 1899; Turin, 1902; Vienna, 1900). He moved to London in 1914, and five years later began designing printed fabrics for W. Foxton.

Mackmurdo, Arthur Heygate (1851–1942). English architect and designer, after a trip to Italy with Ruskin and the dawning of a friendhip with William → Morris, in 1882 he founded the Century Guild, a group of artists and craftsmen committed to a rad-

Arthur Heygate Mackmurdo, chair, mahogany and silk, 1886. Paris, Musée d'Orsay

ical transformation of the arts and the decorative arts, whose official mouthpiece was the review *The Hobby Horse*, that began appearing in 1884. The artist designed furniture in tune with Morris' conceptions, book covers and textiles where the prevailing themes were "whiplash" ribbons and withered or wind-swept leaves: features that connotate the style that would later be called → art nouveau. Conspicuous among his pieces are the essential screen in natural wood with panels lined in textiles featuring a decoration of flaming thistle-stalks (1885–90), the mahogany chair with fretted back figuring a floral composition arranged in a snake-like pattern, executed by the Collinson & Lock firm in 1882–83 (London, William Morris Gallery) and the ultra-modern writing-desk in natural wood with tapering legs dated 1886.

Maddock John & Sons. English pottery, founded at Burslem in 1855 and dissolved in 1982, whose production is known under the name "Royal Ivory" for the cream-coloured grounds of its useful ware and tableware, usually adorned with schematic floral patterns in a popular vein. *(Pl. 67)*

Mafra. Portuguese pottery founded in 1854 at Caldas da Rainha, known above all for its remarkable and nearly indistinguishable copies of B. Palissy's sixteenth-century pottery, highly prized by collectors and connoisseurs in the second half of the nineteenth century for the naturalist rendering of fauna and flora.

Maize glass. Glass technique invented by Joseph → Locke for the → New England Glass Company, patented in 1889 and subsequently by the → Libbey Glass Co., that allows to obtain opaque white or cream-coloured glass items whose surface is stamped with dots imitating maize-cob kernels, and featuring leaves with green or brown, or else red or blue involucres.

Majolica. English term defining a highly processed type of pottery, coated with coloured glazes, very often with a lead base. Created by → Minton, that displayed several exemplars at the Great London Exhibition of 1851, the majolica technique was enormously diffused especially for making umbrella handles, *cache-pots* and flower basins, but also large-sized articles like statues and garden fountains. It was also used by other English manufactories, and then in the United States (mainly, as of 1853, by G. & W. → Bennett of Baltimore) and in Sweden (not until 1860, by the Rörstrand and → Gustavsberg factories).

Majorelle, Louis (1859–1926). French cabinet-maker and designer, son of the cabinet-maker Auguste active at Nancy and working in the reproduction of eighteenth-century furniture, after studying painting in Paris he returned to Nancy in 1879 to run the family business, maintaining period furniture until 1890. But the influence of → Gallé's creations, in furniture as well, led Majorelle

Louis Majorelle, Orchid *writing-desk, mahogany, gilt bronze and leather, 1903–05. Paris, Musée d'Orsay*

to a radical change of register, so that by 1900 he had become the leading producer of → art nouveau furniture in France and perhaps even in Europe. Such a success was owed to the complete mechanisation of his laboratories, capable of turning out furniture in quantity but without losing the processing quality, and making luxury furniture, but accessible to the middle-class. The shapes Majorelle adopted were always designed with particular care for both the practicability of the article and the inspiration drawn from natural forms (like the waterlily coffee-table), and adorned with fretwork that appeared to surface spontaneously from the form in which the material was shaped; however, amidst his conformance with art nouveau models and rules, a constant reference to the wavy, pretty lines of rococo furnishings can be detected. The factory was practically entirely destroyed in 1916 because of the war, but returning to Nancy in 1919 Majorelle initiated its reconstruction, leaving aside the now dated modernism to embrace the new → deco style, whereby the forms, once wavy, became

squared and geometric without losing the wealth of materials and compositional elegance that insured, in this instance as well, the popularity of the manufactory with its middle-class clientele.

Maling C.T. & Sons. English pottery, opened at Newcastle-upon-Tyne in 1857 and dissolved in 1963, offering a varied production of gift items, furnishings, kitchen and tableware, that in the period between 1920 and 1940 featured an exuberant floristic decoration or rustic scenes in bright colours (red, pink and yellow) on cobalt blue or white grounds (*Windmill Plate*, 1935), along with a series of vases with explicitly → deco etched or relief decorations and an inclination for American ethnic traditions. *(Pls. 68 and 69)*

Mallard, Prudent (1809–79). United States cabinet-maker trained in France, and at New York from 1829 to 1838; he subsequently moved to New Orleans, where he opened his own workshop, specialised in producing furnishings in neo-Renaissance and neo-rococo style.

Malmsten, Carl (b. 1888). Swedish interior designer, teacher and founder of three crafts schools, in 1916 he won the competition for the execution of the furnishings for the Stockholm Town Hall, a task that took him until 1923, followed, in the years 1924–25 by the furnishings for the concert hall of the Swedish capital. A stubborn opponent of rationalism, Malmsten produced furniture featuring explicit references to peasant craftsmanship and folklore, but without spurning the creation of very expensive inlaid furniture.

Malta lace. Typical article of the island, pillow-made, in silk after 1833, usually white or black and featuring in the design the Malta cross, widely imitated during the nineteenth century in France, Great Britain and Ireland.

Mal'tsev. Russian glassworks active in the vicinity of Moscow since 1724, transferred to Gusev in 1747 and enlarged with a new plant at Diat'kov in 1792, producing household ware, but equally some pieces of noteworthy quality. Toward the mid-nineteenth century the two factories of Gusev and Diat'kov produced etched crystals following the Bohemian exquisitely Biedermeier models, but at the end of the century they went back to making traditional Russian enamelled ware, some pieces being designed by Elizabeth Böhm.

Mandarin yellow. Type of glass invented by Frederick → Carder for the → Steuben Glass Works, translucid and having a monochrome yellow colour imitating the principal colour of Ming Dynasty Chinese porcelain.

Manifattura Santa Lucia di Dino Rofi e Co. Italian pottery, active at Siena in the 1920s with a particular production of metal glazes, adorned with decorative patterns inspired by the Orient and the Renaissance or else with figures, closely following the creations of the → Cantagalli and Galileo → Chini potteries. Beginning in 1930 Dino Rofi permanently gave up revivalism, launching a production featuring stylised forms representing themes from classical myths or local folklore.

Manifattura di Signa. Italian pottery, active at Signa near Florence as of 1895 and under the direction of Camillo Bondi, who successfully exhibited in Paris in 1900 a vast repertory of three-dimensional terra cottas executed with a special impasto and patination technique rendering the surfaces refined and resistant. The manufactory, already involved since the turn of the century in revisiting classical and Renaissance models, during the 1920s initiated the production of → deco-style majolica articles, all the while keeping up the profitable activity of imitations in great demand for the foreign market. At the 1933 Triennale in Milan its display of large vases and garden seats in a strictly Novecento style met with great success, along with refined, rigorous sculptures modelled by Italo Griselli.

Manzana-Pissarro, Georges (1871–1961). French painter, son of Camille, active in the field of the decorative arts, executing either tapestries or painted glass, often with exotic themes.

Mappin & Webb. English business firm, active in London since the late nineteenth century in the trade of enamelled items, tableware and silverware, including plated ware, cigarette holders, opera glasses, little boxes, exported all over the world. The series generally reflected an eclectic taste, revisiting eighteenth-century and neo-classical models, even if there was no lack of items inspired by the floristic and → art deco vogue. *(Pl. 114)*

Marblehead. United States pottery founded in 1905 inside a clinic; at first merely a hobby for the patients, it soon became an independent business producing series of vases and other containers characterised by bare forms, with a simplified colour range, designs inspired by nature, with dragonflies and stylised flowers, or else from an abstract repertory, often etched on the surface and then painted. The articles are coated with a opaque dotted glaze.

Marcotte, Léon (active between 1848 and 1880). United States furniture-maker of French birth; after graduating in architecture, he married the daughter of a well-known Parisian furniture-maker who exported furnishings to the United States and attended the great international exhibitions. In 1849 the Ringuet Le Prince firm opened a branch in New York, adding to its name Margotte's, that in 1861 became the only name of the firm, active either in import from France or in the creation of its own "Louis-Seize" furniture in ebonied wood with refined gilt bronze decorations and rich *capitonné* upholstery.

Marelli, Michele (1897–1977). Italian architect and designer, associate of Tomaso → Buzzi with whom in 1924 he opened a studio, he would soon join up with the → Ponti- → Lancia pair, adopting a shared expressive idiom: pillar, pilaster, arch, gable, obelisk. A member of the *Il Labirinto* group, Marelli appears to have been the most austere, severe designer working in Milan in the 1920s, while reinterpreting in modern terms eighteenth-century models from which he borrowed the cleft foot, bronze points, truncated-pyramid supports.

Marinot, Maurice (1882–1962). French glassmaker, first a painter belonging to the *fauve* group, in 1911 at Troyes he chose to work in art glass in collaboration with the V.I.A.R.D. laboratory. He executed ornamental items, mainly cups, small flasks and vases with massive, spare forms, in clear or coloured glass, sometimes enamelled or else etched with freehand-drawn figures. In order to create characteristic effects he would case a nucleus of coloured glass between two clear layers, and use air bubbles and the veins of the vitreous paste for decorative purposes. He retired from the business in 1937.

Marsh & Jones. English furniture-makers active at Leeds and London since 1864, mainly in the ambit of the neo-gothic manner and the revival of other periods of the past, in most cases designed by Bruce James → Talbert and Charles Bevan; in the 1880s, on the other hand, they made rosewood furnishings on designs by William Richard →

59. Daniele Fabbri (for La Salamandra), Little Lady, *polychrome majolica, ca. 1922*

60. *Guido Andlovitz (for Società Ceramica Italiana di Laveno),*
vase with lid, earthenware, 1925–30

61. *Le Bertetti,* Mermaid with dolphin,
painted and air-brushed earthenware, 1934–36

62. Lenci, The tritons, *painted and air-brushed earthenware, ca. 1930*

63. Sandro Vacchetti (for Lenci), The two tigers,
painted earthenware, 1930

*64. J. & L. Lobmeyr, bowl, painted and gilt green glass, 1893.
Hamburg, Museum für Kunst und Gewerbe Hamburg*

65. Lötz Witwe, guttae vase, iridescent glass, ca. 1900   *66. Lötz Witwe, amphora with handles, green and pink glass, ca. 1900*

*67. John Maddock & Sons
(for Lamberton China),
serving dish of the Hotel
Baltimore, at centre Ramses
II on a chariot, porcelain,
ca. 1915*

*68. C.T. Maling & Sons,
Windmill dish, majolica,
1935*

69. C.T. Maling & Sons, vase with lid of the Ginger *series, polychrome pottery, ca. 1930*

70. *Arturo Martini (for I.L.C.A., Nervi)*, Heron, *painted pottery, 1929*

71. *Napoleone Martinuzzi (for Venini),* Cactus, *red and black glass paste, 1925–27. Gardone Riviera, Il Vittoriale*

72. *Napoleone Martinuzzi (for Venini),* Elephant, *blue glass paste and gold leaf, 1928. Gardone Riviera, Il Vittoriale*

73. L. Vierthalen (for Meissen), box with lid featuring
a Hindu holding a melon, porcelain, 1914. Dresden,
Kunstgewerbemuseum

74. Minardi, box with anthropomorphic lid,
majolica terra cotta, 1911–13

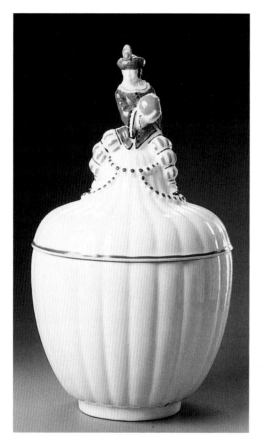

75. Pietro Melandri, vase with antilopes, glazed majolica,
1924–26

76. *Francesco Nonni,* Andalusian woman, *painted and gilt majolica, 1923–25*

77. *Francesco Nonni,* Indian dancing girl on an elephant, *painted and gilt majolica, 1925*

Arturo Martini (for La Fenice), Visitation, *enamelled pottery, 1927*

Lethaby. Receptive to changes of taste and style, they produced several series of → liberty style furnishings, enhanced by Edwin Luytens' suggestions (1907), and collaborated equally in the furnishing of the steamer *Saturnia*. Every piece, besides the factory trademark, usually bears the name of the craftsman.

Martens, Dino. Italian glass designer, active by the 1930s at the → Salviati firm where he executed a series of blown glass exhibited at the Venice Biennales of 1932 and 1936. On the other hand the 1950s and 1960s were the years of the asymmetrical-shaped forms composed according to a patchwork technique produced for the → Barovier glassworks as well as for the Aureliano → Toso manufactory.

Martin. English pottery erected at Fulham in 1873 for producing salt-glazed gres articles by Robert Wallace Martin (1843–1923) who, after some time at the → Doulton manufactory, studied sculpture and was involved in the House of Parliament yard, an experience that inclined him to a neo-gothic style and a fondness for grotesqueries. In 1877 he transferred the firm to Norwood (Middlesex) and enlisted his brothers in a production of medievalising pieces, never identical, such as traditional

sixteenth-century German pitchers, owl-shaped tobacco-jars, grotesque chess-pieces, sneering faces as jars; but by the 1890s the presence of floristic decorations and birds reveals the influence of the → art nouveau style. The firm wound down in 1914.

Martini, Arturo (1889–1947). Italian sculptor, occasionally working in creating art pottery, he began in 1902 at Treviso in the Cacciaporti and Sebellin manufactories, then between 1908 and 1912 worked at the Gregorj pottery. A brief contact with Faenza in 1918 preceded his arrival, after 1921, at La → Fenice factory of Albisola, where he executed a series of one-offs, including low-relief still lifes on tiles, along with occasional dishes and small decorated basins. *(Pl. 70)*

Martinuzzi, Napoleone (1892–1977). Italian sculptor and master glass-maker from a long line of Muranese glass-makers, he trained at Murano in Giacomo Vivante's pottery, whose style was openly → liberty, and at the Tamburlini e Carbonaro manufactory of architectural and galvanoplastic terra cottas. In 1910–11 he worked in Rome at the studio of the Brescia sculptor Angelo Zanelli, and on his return to Venice developed a manner inspired by both Klimt and the neo-Michelangelism of Ivan Mestrovich. In 1917 in his own Murano studio he met Gabriele d'Annunzio, with whom he initiated a fruitful collaboration that would last until the mid-1930s, creating dozens of glass articles placed in the Vittoriale degli Italiani: ranging from fruit to luminous baskets, pumpkin-lamps to animals, candelabras to vases. In 1925 in partnership with Paolo → Venini he formed the Vetri Soffiati Muranesi Venini & C., becoming its art director and producing pieces of outstanding beauty with sculptural forms updated with the slender elegance of → deco along with Novecento tectonic shapes: such as the famous *Cactus* in multicoloured vitreous paste (furnishing items and monumental lamps for post offices and public buildings) and the large vases in → *pulegoso* glass of his own invention. In 1932 he left Venini right after completing a catalogue of the series under production, founded with Francesco Zecchin a new glassworks, then giving up art glass permanently to return to sculpture, by the end of the Second World War, aside from occasional collaborations with Gino → Cenedese's glassworks, between 1953 and 1958, where he made glass paste panels for facing furniture, stained-glass windows in glossy glass and vases featuring organic forms. *(Pls 71 and 72)*

Marussig, Guido (1885–1972). Italian painter and designer, born in Trieste, a many-sided artist working in graphics as well as in the decorative arts. In 1910 he furnished the pavilion of the city of Trieste at the Venice Biennale with small streamlined, strictly Secession armchairs. In 1923 at Monza he exhibited Pietro → Chiesa's *La vetrata delle navi* executed on one of his cartoons, and also created lamps and stained-glass windows produced at the Parma art institute of which he was director. From 1923 to 1935, Marussig was active, even if just off and on, at the Vittoriale degli Italiani executing the decorations commissioned by Gabriele d'Annunzio.

Massier, Clément (1844–1911). French potter, active at Vallarius, near Cannes, with his brother Douphin, his cousin Jérôme and Gaetano Gandolfo; he created interesting metal-lustre glazed pottery since 1880, and from 1890 on his output was deeply influenced by Japanese art and a modernist taste.

Mathews, Arthur Frank (1860–1945). United States architect and designer, inventor of a Californian version of → art nouveau. After studying draughtsmanship in Oakland and Paris (1885), in 1890 he became director of the California School of Design, and toward the late nineties began executing mural decorations and painting on furniture, an activity that he continued at San Francisco after the 1906 earthquake. From 1906 to 1920 he ran *The Furniture Shop*, a studio with nearly fifty employees specialised in the execution of entire furnishings and complete interior decoration designs, including tapestries, stained glass, ornamental caskets, all adorned with bright-coloured floral patterns (in particular California tulips) in emulation of Japanese models, but equally influenced by European art nouveau. Many pieces by Mathews are conserved at the Oakland Museum.

Mathsson, Karl Bruno (b. 1907). Swedish designer known for a striking series of furnishings in → curved wood, inspired by Alvar Aalto's specimens, made during the 1930s.

Matsu-no-ke. Glass processing technique consisting of the application, on vases and containers, of clear crystal or superficial decorations with iridescent effects, representing the knotty branches of an ornamental pinetree dubbed *matsu* in the Japanese culture; invented by Frederick → Carder for the → Stevens & Williams Ltd. in 1880, it was continuously used by the → Steuben Glass Works after 1922.

Mauder, Bruno (1877–1948). German glass-maker, distinguished interpreter of → Jugendstil, he executed a number of articles in keeping with naturalist models, either plant or animal, and experimented a particular frosted effect on the surfaces, dubbed *crystalline*, obtained by the use of hydrofluoric acid.

Mayer China Company. United States semi-porcelain manufactory, active at Beaver Falls (Pennsylvania) between 1881 and 1989 in the production of tableware and ware for hotels, usually characterised by a wide, monchrome rim (orange-red or black) and Chinese-style decors.

Mazzolani, Enrico (1876–1968). Italian potter, sculptor and modeller of terra-cotta or polychrome majolica female figures, working at Milan and Varese between the 1920s and the 1950s.

Mazzucotelli, Alessandro (1865–1938). Italian ironwork designer, trained in Defendente Oriani's workshop, he took over the firm in 1891, creating a laboratory that produced some of the most fascinating wrought iron → liberty-style pieces, among which we should mention the roofing for the Calderoni jewellery store. He attended important exhibitions beginning with Turin in 1902, taught in Milan at the Umanitaria for nearly twenty years, collaborating with Carlo → Rizzarda, and undertook study trips to Paris and London. In the course of his career, Mazzucotelli worked with the architect Sommaruga (Palazzo Castiglioni in Milan, Villa Faccanoni at Sarnico), producing extremely elegant liberty-style articles, but also neo-Renaissance and neo-Medieval wrought iron for monumental edifices; right after the First World War, he worked for the ensemble of the Vittoriale degli Italiani and took part in the Monza Biennales with pieces that show his receptivity to → deco style.

McCoy Nelson Pottery Company. United States pottery, active at Roseville (Ohio) from 1910 to 1990, producing a variety of kitchen and tableware, useful pottery, vases and furnishing items. The founder's sons were responsible for introducing floral decorative motifs in an → art nouveau vein (between 1910 and 1915) and, subsequently, → deco-style geometric forms.

McLaughlin, Mary Louise (1847–1939). United States potter, writer and painter; in 1872, influenced by William → Morris' writings, she tried out pottery

Alessandro Mazzucotelli, torch-holder with dragonflies, iron, ca. 1910. Genoa, Wolfsonian Foundation

Nelson McCoy Pottery Company, deco vase, air-brushed pottery, ca. 1930

and in 1879 created the *Women's Pottery Club* of Cincinnati, a group of amateurs who executed under-glaze decorations on pottery items produced by the Rockwood manufactory, between 1880 and 1883, and enamel paintings on porcelain. In 1898 she introduced a porcelain production dubbed *Losanti Ware* (derived from the old name for Cincinnati, L'Osantiville), enhanced with leaves and flowers etched in keeping with the most up-to-date Parisian → art nouveau models. She exhibited at Buffalo (1901), Turin (1902) and Saint Louis (1904); she also created embroideries and lacework.

Meakin. English potteries, active in Staffordshire: the one connected with the name of Meakin, founded in 1874 and merged with other groups in 1976, is interesting because it created a combination of → deco taste and local decorative traditions, linked up with floral motifs; on the other hand the J. & G. Meakin factory, opened in 1851, was taken over by the → Wedgwood group in 1970, producing tableware and articles, especially in the 1930s, inspired by United States design.

Medalta Potteries. Canadian pottery, active in the State of Alberta from 1916 to 1955, known for a serial production of ordinary kitchen and table ware supplied to hotels.

Meeks Joseph & Sons. United States furniture manufactory in business since 1797; it first dealt in the production of Regency furniture, in 1840 inclined to the neo-gothic taste (that characterises also a group of chairs designed for the White House, 1846–47), and subsequently to neo-rococo, executing furnishings in laminate rosewood similar to the ones by → Belter. The business was wound down in 1868.

Meigh. English pottery founded in Staffordshire in 1780; it was taken over in 1843 by Charles Meigh who, one of the first to embrace the neo-medieval manner, had patented in 1842 the church-jug (*Minster Jug*) made in gres adorned with reliefs reproducing full-size figures of saints inside gothic niches, that became quite popular, as were the articles in neo-Renaissance style, in particular the 1847 prize-winning Bacchic jar. At the Great London Exhibition of 1851 he presented a remarkable number of porcelain items, → *parian ware* and gres; in this last material he furthermore executed two gilt vases a meter-high featuring the painted portraits of Victoria and Albert and views of the Crystal Palace.

Meissen. German porcelain manufactory, founded in 1710 (the first in Europe) at Meissen, near Dresden, by Augustus the Strong, elector of Saxony, for a remarkable production of furnishing sculpture and knick-knacks along with tableware of unmatched elegance and distinction, purchased by all the ruling families and aristocracy of Europe. The manufactory went in a slump during the Napoleonic wars, but the Restoration led to a revival of its traditional rococo models during the period from 1833 to 1870, at which time the mechanical repetition of the original designs led to a mawkish excess of ornament. In the decade of 1870–80, production was updated with statuettes of Prussian soldiers or bathers, and by the end of the century resolutely looked to modernism, combining the elegantly flowing style of rococo with the modernism of → art nouveau: conspicuous among these pieces are the *Crocus* tableware, designed in 1896 by Julius Konrad Hentschel, or the white porcelain dishes with delicate gilt decorations by Henry → van de Velde of 1904, but equally so are statuettes of women performing winter sports (by Alfred Otto König), musicians and dancers (by Paul → Scheurich), or else birds and animals. Along with a production of tiles for furnishings and items more and more influenced by → Jugendstil, and soon → art de-

co — as in the boxes with anthropomorphic lids or candlesticks with stylised figures — reproduction of its eighteenth-century models continues to this day. In 1945 the factory changed its name to Porzellan-Manufaktur Meissen, while still using the trademark with two crossed blue swords (adopted in 1724). (*Pls 56 and 73*)

Melandri, Pietro (1885–1976). Italian potter, trained at Faenza at the Minardi manufactory, he first went South, and then moved to Milan — where he began his artistic activity as a decorator and scenographer — later on returning to Faenza, in 1919, to work with → Zoli and → Nonni; in 1922, with the backing of the industrialist Umberto Focaccia, he took over the Minardi furnaces, founding the Melandri e Focaccia company (that was in business for eight years), the trademark being a stylised dragon head in a circle combined with the initials "MF". The forms and decorations created by Melandri during the 1920s and 1930s are absolutely some of the most original of the Italian pottery production: comprising jars and vases, centre-pieces and table services and coffee sets, anthropomorphic boxes and small classical-style statuettes, Melandri painted and composed Orientalising, neo-Renaissance, floristic, archaeological and neo-eighteenth-century decorations, always freshened by and intelligent, rigorous → deco spirit for their cohesive, graceful forms and the use of gold, navy and green, sometimes producing metal-lustre effects. (*Pl. 75*)

Pietro Melandri, tile with dolphin, polychrome majolica, 1928–30

Pietro Melandri, bowl with woman's face, glazed majolica, 1925

Ferruccio Mengaroni, Medusa, *polychrome majolica terra cotta, 1925*

Melis, Melchiorre (1889–1982). Italian potter, one of the most important artists of Sardinian pottery, after training in Rome he attended the Monza Biennales with the circle of Roman potters as of 1925, his products masterfully and cleverly combining the tradition of Sardinian folklore with the cold, bare idiom of international → deco style. He was very active until 1942 in Libya where he was director of the Tripoli arts and crafts school and the artisanal pottery school, seeking to create a modern version of the Arabic style.

Mengaroni, Ferruccio (1875–1925). Italian potter, trained at the Molaroni workshop at Pesaro, he initiated his own career in 1906 trying out the techniques of metal-lustre and glazes on the ancient models of Della Robbia; in 1916 he founded his own company, that closed down at his death in 1925.

Meriden Britannia Company. United States metalwork manufactory founded in Connecticut in 1852 for producing articles in *Britannia metal* (an alloy of tin, antimony and copper, used as a cheap substitute for → pewter), but that in 1855 began producing plated articles and later on silverware. The policy of taking over other silver and silver-plated items factories, such as the Rogers brothers firm, turned the manufactory into the International Silver Company, still today one of the leading producer of silver articles.

Methey, André (1871–1920). French potter, who after a few experiments in sculpture succeeded in opening, although with great difficulty, his own pottery furnace at Asnières, that allowed him to present in 1901 a series of pieces decorated in the manner of the *fauve* painters, with whom he was closely acquainted; a friendship that would enable him, among other things, to obtain from artists like Denis, Van Dongen, Derain, Rouault, Vlaminck, Valtat, Bonnard and Renoir, painted dishes then shown at the Salon d'Automne in 1907. Beginning in 1908 he executed a series of painted potteries with lead glaze and then enamel glaze, in simple forms and extremely vivid colours emulating Persian and Turkish (Iznik) ware, but equally Italian majolica and French eighteenth-century rustic pottery.

Methven David & Sons. Scottish pottery, opened at Kirkaldy in 1850 and wound down around 1930, active in the execution of household ware with openly popular shapes and colours, generally in red, green and black on a cream ground; the 1920s introduced the production of several series of large-sized drinking services, decorated with floral motifs in the traditional Scottish vein (for instance the *Gallion* series), hand-painted with orange and yellow tints.

Metlox Potteries. United States pottery, active from 1927 to 1989 at Manhattan Beach (California) in the production of kitchen and table ware imitating English models, but also ornamented with motifs drawn from the Aztec civilisation; in 1934 Carl Romanelli intoduced a series of terra-cotta figurines and animals.

Midwinter W.R. English pottery, founded in 1910 at Burslem and closed down in 1987, specialised at least until the 1930s in mass production of teapots and tableware, as well as supplying the Navy with useful ware, generally stencil- and transfer-decorated with navy or black rims.

Mies van der Rohe, Ludwig (1886–1969). German architect and designer, in 1936 the successor of W. Gropius at the → Bauhaus, he moved to the United States in 1928 where he became a Professor at the Illinois Institute of Technology. His designs for furnishings date back to the 1920s and 1930s; 1926 was the year of the famous cantilever chair in steel tubular with a wicker seat, and 1929 of the *Barcellona* chair, in chromium-plated curved steel rods and cushions supported by leather straps (designed for the German pavilion at the Barcellona fair of that year), one of the symbols of twentieth-century design.

Ludwig Mies van der Rohe, Barcelona *chair plus stool, chrome-plated flat steel and red leather, 1929. Paris, Musée des Arts Décoratifs*

Milk glass. Glass technique whereby the glass paste, by using tin oxide, turns an opaque, milky white, completely like porcelain, whose first applications were experimented at Murano in the fifteenth century.

Millefiori. Mosaic glass technique obtained by introducing in a mass of clear white glass bright-coloured disks composed of glass canes sections. Venetian furnaces and then Bohemian ones were the first to execute *millefiori* → paperweights, and the same process was gradually taken up by French, English and United States manufactories. This decoration can be found in drinking services, vases, inkstands, perfume bottles, door handles, various sizes of cups and seals.

Millville. United States glassworks active from 1806 in New Jersey, that in 1857, changing ownership, took the name Whitall, Tatum & Co.; it is known for its production of → paperweights.

Minardi. Italian pottery opened at Faenza in 1900 by the brothers Virginio and Venturino Minardi, in which the finest talents of Faventine pottery would work: Domenico → Baccarini, Paolo → Zoli, Pietro → Melandri, Amerigo Masotti, Anselmo Bucci and Riccardo → Gatti, active not just in the routine of the local decorative tradition but also updating to the new European trends. The trademark bears the sign "MF. Faenza"; the manufactory went out of business in 1922. *(Pl. 74)*

Minghetti, Angelo (1821–85). Italian potter, he began at Bologna as an interior decorator and restorer of antiquarian pottery; later he worked at a manufactory at Imola, and finally at Bologna, in 1858, he opened his own furnace where he produced an abundant series of dishes and tableware, so cleverly ornamented in the manner of the Faenza and Urbino Renaissance factories that they were often sold as originals. Beginning in 1870 he also made large-sized majolicas for architectural decoration: cornices, caryatids and busts on clipei following Della Robbia models, all marked "M". At his death the business passed under the direction of his son Gennaro, up until 1925.

Minton. English pottery founded in Staffordshire in 1796 by Thomas Minton (1765–1836) to produce porcelain tableware. The items coming from this manufactory, still in business, range over the most diverse historical styles (Italian Renaissance majolicas, "Henri-Deux" style, → Sèvres "Louis-Seize" porcelain) and are always trademarked: statuettes and centrepieces in → *parian ware*, some gigantic compositions measuring nearly ten meters for fountains and stairways, tableware with polychrome, ornate decorations. In the 1890s it successfully adopted the → art nouveau manner, recognisable in the interesting *Secessionist Ware* series,

executed in 1904 by Léon Solon and John Wadsworth with gaudy colours and openly contrasting, in the dishware, adorned in *pâte-sur-pâte* in 1911, with highly elegant gold "Napoléon-Trois" *ramages*, bearing at the centre a classical-style cameo. In the 1920s the manufactory went back to table services inspired by Delft pottery with navy decors on a white ground or else floristic decors in country taste on a cream ground.

Mission Furniture. Unadorned oak furniture produced in the United States at the turn of the century, on English → Arts & Crafts models, by G. → Stickley and E. Hubbard.

Mocha. Earthenware similar to Mocha stone (moss-agate, a variety of chalcedony with green and reddish-brown colour banding like moss), produced since 1780 in England and used in France and the United States during the entire nineteenth century, especially for useful wares. It is obtained by pouring onto coloured bands of wet clay droplets of Mocha tea (a mixture of tobacco juice, turpentine and urine) that, in spreading, draw on the surface of the object images suggesting fern sprays, feathers, trees and, precisely, moss.

Molaroni, Vincenzo (1859–1912). Italian potter, founder of his own manufactory at Pesaro — still in business — in line with the local tradition of the city, who in the early years of the nineteenth century

Vincenzo Molaroni, formal dish, polychrome majolica terra cotta, 1910–12

offered female busts in polychrome glazed terra cotta and anthropomorphic boxes with lids recalling some of → Nonni's and → Dolcetti's inventions; in the mid-1920s his laboratory revived the great Renaissance tradition in floristic decoration of monumental formal dishes.

Moncrieff. Scottish glassworks founded in 1864 at Perth (Scotland), active in the production of household ware; it underwent a substantial upheaval in 1922 with the arrival of the Catalan Salvador Ysart (1887–1956), who introduced the production of *monart* glass, an art glass used after 1920 for creating art items decorated with polychrome stripes and spots. In 1948, after leaving the direction to his son Paul Ysart, with another son he founded Vasart Glass Ltd.

Mondovì. Italian pottery active with a group of furnaces between 1808 and 1897, producing earthenware decorated with traditional themes in the Anglo-Saxon floral manner. At the turn of the century, associating with → Richard-Ginori, it differed from it and the two other factories of the group, San Cristoforo of Milan and San Zeno of Pisa, by an original, independent production, completely 1920s in manner, of soft earthenware featuring rustic decorations, achieving the formal and chromatic synthesis of Novecento style. Giovanni → Gariboldi and F. Brown were commissioned to design vases, decorative dishes, tableware and furnishing items for the manufactory.

Moorcroft William. English porcelain manufactory, founded in 1913 at Burslem and still in business, that took its name from its founder, one of the outstanding interpreters of the → art nouveau manner in Great Britain, as illustrated by the 1902 *Florian Ware Vase*, in cobalt blue pottery, and the 1904 *Tulip Vase*, explicitly → liberty with its swollen bud form and gilt and navy decoration on a cream ground with tulip stems. During the 1920s and 1930s, the manufactory updated to → deco taste, adopting decorations inspired from the natural world and scenery, but described in intentionally condensed, decorative forms with *flambé* effects in the background tones (*Claremont Ware* in 1935 and the *Flambé Hazeldene Vases* in 1932).

Moore Bernard. English pottery, founded in 1905 at Stoke and wound down in 1915, to which are owed bowls, vases, amphoras, snuff boxes, boxes, minute animals made in porcelain with decorations inspired by *chinoiserie* themes (*Exotic Bird Vase* in 1908) on a ruby-red and gilt ground, or by historical themes with orange *flambé* effects.

William Moorcroft, vases of the Hazeldene *series, polychrome pottery, ca. 1932*

Morris, William (1834–96). English designer, one of the most conspicuous figures in the decorative arts field during the second half of the nineteenth century, he founded in 1861 the Morris, Marshall, Faulkner & Co. for the production of ornamental articles; the manufactory, that met with immediate success, was reorganised in 1875, taking the name Morris & Co., and in 1881 it was permanently transferred to Merton Abbey, where it was active until 1940. Production initiated with embroideries, in 1862, continuing with wallpaper (printed by the Jeffrey & Co. firm on Morris' designs), stained glass, woven and printed fabrics (in 1883), furniture, tapestries (the looms for their production were set up in 1881) and rugs; for these last articles Morris founded a special factory at Hammersmith in 1880, while ten years later he launched the Kelmscot Press, specialised in printing books of great distinction. *(Pl. 9)*

Mosaicised glass. Very ancient glass technique consisting of coloured glass threads, molten and cut into minute pieces on whose surface a floral decoration appears; scattered over a metal surface, they are absorbed in a vitreous mass rolled over them, to then blend during firing and blowing.

Moser, Koloman (1868–1918). Austrian designer, one of the founders of the Viennese Secession (1897), and with Josef → Hoffmann of the → Wiener Werkstätte (1903), teacher at the Kunstgewerbeschule as of 1899, and book illustrator, designer of jewellery featuring particularly refined shapes and materials, metal objects, glass, furniture (resembling, by their dry linearity, the ones designed by Hoffmann and then executed by the Viennese firm Portois & Fix), and furnishing textiles characterised by intricate plant patterns swarming with birds, recalling those → Morris and → Mackmurdo produced in London.

Moser, Ludwig (1833–1916). Bohemian glass etcher, active at Karlsbad and pupil of Andreas Mattoni. Having been appointed official supplier of the Imperial Family of Austria, he opened his own factory at Meierhöfen in 1857. Of great significance were his pieces modelled in the midst of the → art nouveau period: the large trunco-conical vases decorated with flowers, especially irises, arranged unevenly over the surface with deep → acid etching, and moulded bowls and drinking ser-

Koloman Moser (for Wiener Werkstätte), writing-desk with armchair, Makassar ebony, inlaid with Madagascar ebony, boxwood, mahogany, ivory, tortoise-shell and brass, 1903–04

vices in keeping with Biedermeier models, carved with folklore motifs.

Moss agate. Glass technique that consists of introducing in several layers of glass different fragments of coloured glass; it was invented by John → Northwood, in partnership with Frederick → Carder, between the 1910s and 1920s, in likeness with some French glass production by F.-E. → Rousseau and E.B. → Léveillé.

Koloman Moser (for Wiener Werkstätte), vase, citrine brass, 1903–04

Mougin Frères. French pottery, active in Paris since 1900, it met with instant international success for its → art nouveau models exhibited at that year's fair. After transferring to Nancy in 1904, the manufactory worked with local artists, then launching an important production of → deco pottery. It remained active until 1960.

Mount Washington Glass Company. United States glassworks opened in New Bedford (Massachusetts) for producing useful ware in blown, carved and pressed glass, along with art glass made in → *amberina* and → *peach blow*. In 1885 → *burmese glass* was patented, a glass used for creating drinking services and decorative items, its colour ranging from yellow to pink; this glass was produced with permission by the Thomas → Webb & Sons manufactory of → Stourbridge as well, but under the name *Queen's Burmese*.

Mounting. Glass technique relating to making stained-glass items, whereby, to hold together the various glass elements constituting the decoration, lead rods are used, shaped like a U, a T or a double T or round, sometimes coated with brass or → nickel silver. For minute works requiring special accuracy, for instance lamps and lampshades, in order to obtain very thin attachments, the mounting is made with copper wire, that → Tiffany used successfully for the first time toward the 1880s.

Müller Frères, mushroom-shaped lamp, triple-layer etched glass, ca. 1910

Mountmellick. Embroidery executed with white cotton on a base of satinised cloth for the execution of decorations with fruit, flowers and leaves, made by hand for the first time at Mountmellick (Ireland) in 1840, but revived on an industrial scale between 1880 and 1890.

Moustiers. French pottery active in the region of Marseilles since the seventeenth century, known for its majolicas, often imitated in Spain and Italy, decorated in underglaze navy and used for formal dishes, ornamental panels and drug-pots. During the first half of the eighteenth century production diversified in the various typologies of household tableware borrowing Bérain-style decorations, that is, navy *grotesqueries* and arabesques on light grounds. In 1779 Jean-Gaspard Féraud's factory opened, active until 1874 in the production of pottery adorned with naturalist figures and flowers in a broad range of colours. The manufactories of the area are still flourishing.

MT Clemens Pottery Company. United States semi-porcelain manufactory, founded in 1914 in Michigan and wound down in 1987, producing tableware in white and crème porcelain with flower decorations.

Mucha, Alphonse (1896–1939). Bohemian designer, one of the main figures of European → art nouveau; after studying in Munich he went to Vienna and Paris, where he became acquainted with the actress Sarah Bernhardt, for whom he designed stage costumes and sets, jewellery and clothes; in 1901 he designed Georges → Fouquet's superb shop, later demolished, and then extremely elaborate jewellery drawn from nature and using precious materials, such as opal. His naturalist inspiration, at times highly realistic, like in the table sets and chairs imitating tree trunks, was always transformed by an elegant, striking graphic interpretation, typically → liberty, easily recognisable in his posters, for which he is famous, and wallpaper, sometimes executed in twelve colours.

Müller Frères. French glassworks opened in 1910 in Lorraine by the brothers Henri and Désiré Müller, near Lunéville, with the intention of associating it with the one that already existed at Corismare, run by Henri, producing art glass adorned with overlaying of two or three colours (*overlay*), etched with hydrofluoric acid and the abrasive wheel and decorated in themes linked up with → art nouveau configurations.

Muncie Clay Products Company. United States pottery, active in Indiana between 1919 and 1936 in the production of tableware, flower vases and useful household ware. Of particular significance were several vases called *Ruba Rombic*, fashioned toward 1930 in a manner inspired by cubism.

Murray, Keith (1892–1981). English pottery designer, during the 1930s he worked for the → Wedgwood manufactory, creating table services endowed with a severe, classicising distinction, but also designing vases and drinking services for the → Stevens & Williams firm at Brierley Hill. The pieces dated 1933–35 are *potiche* vases and spheric vases with sharp horizontal edges in an unusual

Keith Murray, vases, air-brushed majolica, 1933–35

leaf-green colour, or else vases with strictly geometric forms in grey and basalt black adorned with concentric circles etched on the body of the article.

Murrine. Glass technique invented in Roman times in emulation of vases in *murrha* (a substance found in the Orient, held to be mysterious and then found to be a variety of fluorite emanating a certain scent owed to the resins used during processing as bonding agents). *Murrine* are created by cutting across polychrome glass canes, that are then molten while being placed on a form and according to a determined design. During the sixteenth century Murano glassworks began imitating Roman *murrine*, a technique then revived at the end of the nineteenth century by Vincenzo Moretti at the → Salviati & C. and used by the → Venini and → Barovier works during the 1920s and 1930s, consisting of the arrangement of a mosaic (or a hot-inlay) of pieces of profiled glass fired so as to be soldered together.

Mutz, Richard (1872–1931). German potter, in 1896 he took over the direction of his father's firm located at Altona, near Hamburg, that produced gres containers inspired by Japanese pottery, and in turn introduced the execution of pottery adorned with very colourful liquid glazes. He moved in 1904 to Berlin, where he opened a shop and a laboratory that by 1906, while still modelling gres items inspired by the Far East, began producing gres statuettes on models of Russian peasants executed by E. Barlach.

Alphonse Mucha and Auguste Truffier, La Princesse lointaine, *wall-lamp, gilt and chiselled bronze, precious stones and enamels, 1904*

N

Nailsea. English glassworks opened at Bristol in 1788 (and active up to 1873), producing glass sheets for windows (by 1844) and flat rolled glass (after 1860); a lateral activity was making bottles, vases, pitchers, decorative items in dark glass with white spots or stripes, or else in clear glass with dark and light alternating stripes, and by 1844 articles in *crown glass* with polychrome decorations.

Nancy, School of. Group of designers and creators of art objects under the influence of the personalities of Emile → Gallé, Louis → Majorelle, Emile-Victor → Prouvé and the → Daum brothers, responsible for the finest, most consistent exemplars of French → art nouveau, from 1880 up until the early years of the twentieth century.

Nash, Arthur J. (1849–1934). English glass designer, after having directed the Glass House at → Stourbridge, he moved to the United States in 1895, joining the → Tiffany company at Corona, for which he designed art glass, among which the *Cypriots*, in different colours and with a partly rough surface imitating mother-of-pearl recalling antique Roman glass having been buried at length.

Nash, A. Douglas (d. 1940). English glass designer, he worked with his father Arthur at the → Tiffany manufactory in New York until 1919, the year in which Tiffany retired from the direct direction of the firm and the company took the name Douglas Nash Associates until 1920 (the year of the constitution of the Louis C. Tiffany Furnaces Inc.). Nash continued to produce Tiffany-style art glass while designing new ones, like *Silhouettes*, usually drinking glass stems executed in black glass and shaped like animals, and *Chintz*, formed by many multicoloured stripes emulating the Indian textile of the same name, for which he used the trademark "Corona", "ADNA" and "Nash". The firm having been dissolved in 1931, he moved to Toledo (Ohio) where he worked as a technician and designer for the → Libbey Glass Co.

Navarre, Henry (b. 1885). French glass designer influenced by Maurice → Marinot's explicitly → deco models, he executed in the 1920s and 1930s articles in clear glass, at times reheating them in the flame or directly processing them in the furnace.

Neatby, William James (1860–1910). English designer; after an initial training at an architect's studio he joined the pottery of Burmantoft; having moved to London, between 1890 and 1900 he was director of the architecture unit of the → Doulton manufactory at Lambeth, a fact that unquestionably contributed to the development of a productive line in→art nouveau style permeated with pre-Raphaelite strains, observable in tiles and panels for architectural decoration with elaborate decorative programmes inspired by nature, adorning the Winter Gardens at Blackpool (1896), the Everard Building at Bristol (1901) and, especially, the monumental meat arcade on the ground floor of Harrods department store in London (1901–05).

Newbery, Jessie R. (1864–1919). Scottish embroiderer and textile designer, daughter of a shawl producer, she married in 1889 Francis H. Newbery, dean of the Glasgow School of Art, where she taught from 1894 to 1908, becoming one of the leading figures in the revival of decorations applied to furnishing fabrics.

New Chelsea Porcelain Co. English porcelain manufactory, active from 1910 to 1951 at Longton (Staffordshire), both producing juvenile ware decorated with childhood scenes and toys, and executing table services in traditional style.

Newcomb College. United States pottery founded at New Orleans in 1895 as a women's laboratory of Tulane University: in the workshop, directed by Ellsworth Woodward and the potter Mary G. Sheerer, design teacher, the vases were modelled by master potters, whereas the decoration was executed by the pupils. The articles thus produced, decorated with floriated models inspired by → art nouveau, began being sold by 1897, and in 1900 several vases were awarded the Bronze Medal at the World Fair in Paris, winning fame and popularity. The forms elected for the vases were inspired by either Far-Eastern pottery or the country tradition, while the subjects, restricted to the flora and fauna of the Southern United States, but reproduced with a typically → liberty fluidity, were first etched and subsequently coloured in navy or green; in 1910 the colours of the decorations became brighter. Each piece bears the label "the designs are not repeated". The laboratory closed in 1930.

New England Glass Company. One of the largest United States glassworks, active at Cambridge (Massachusetts) since 1871, it initiated its activity bringing out essentially clear lead-glass articles with deeply etched ornaments, in the English style, but in blown and moulded glass as well. Toward the middle of the nineteenth century it also produced → *millefiori* → paperweights and cameo glass (*flashed glass*) in the Bohemian manner. To one of its employees, the Bohemian etcher Louis F. → Vaupel (working in the manufactory from 1856 to 1885), is owed a decoration with hunting scenes executed with the grinder, whereas Joseph → Locke developed on an industrial scale several types of coloured glass: → *amberina* (from pale amber to ruby red, 1883), → *pomona* (pale amber with navy decorations, 1885), → *peach blow* (from white to purple) and → *agate*. The firm, taken over by William T. Libbey, was transferred to Toledo (Ohio) in 1888 under the name → Libbey Glass Co.

Newport Pottery Co. English semi-porcelain manufactory active at Burslem beetween 1920 and 1964 specialising in the production of table services with naturalist floral decorations on a white ground, and as of around 1928, with typically → deco themes.

Niderviller. French pottery founded in 1754 in Lorraine, specialised in the production of dishes with fretted rims imitating woven wicker, soup tureens topped with vegetables and with lids modelled with open-work floral compositions. During the nineteenth century the factory, still running today, focused on the reproduction of eighteenth-century models based on original prints.

Niederer, Roberto (b. 1928). Swiss glassmaker, owner of manufactories in Zurich and Calabria, he specialised in blown glass, rather thick and with in-

tentional surface flaws: worth mentioning for instance are his water and wine carafes, displaying the veins of the moulds in which they were blown.

Nieuwenhuis, Theodore (1866–1951). Dutch designer, pupil of the architect Cuypers, he designed in Amsterdam buildings and planned countless interior designs; in 1908 he became director of the leading applied arts manufactory in the city, for which he drew articles and furnishings featuring a sober interpretation of the modernist idiom: curved lines, peacock feathers, coiled snakes, plant elements, whiplashes. He supplied executive designs to the De Distel pottery as well.

Niloak Pottery. United States pottery, founded in 1911 at Benton (Arkansas), specialised in the production of furnishing articles, candelabras, ashtrays and gift items executed with an impasto imitating the veins of agate and a mosaic effect. In the 1920s production of *Mission Ware Vases* was launched, decorated with varied shades of ochre streaks on a yellowish ground.

Noke, Charles John (1858–1941). English potter, he initiated his career at the → Worcester porcelain factory, and in 1889 joined the → Doulton Pottery and Porcelain Company, later becoming its director (between 1914 and 1936, succeeded by his son Cecil Jack until 1954). He concentrated in particular on the production of two kinds of heavy earthenware: *Holbein* pottery from 1895, and *Rembrandt* pottery from 1898, as well as small bowls and dishes decorated with single figurines copying the ones in the so-called *Tapisserie de la Reine Mathilde* (conserved at Bayeux), or with episodes and characters taken from Shakespeare's tragedies or Barham's work; the use of *flambé* glazes was frequent.

Nonni, Francesco (1885–1976). Italian potter, but above all graphic artist, between 1919 and 1922 he worked for several Faventine manufactories, in particular → Zoli, Giuseppe Fiumi's Ca' Pirota, the workshops of Aldo Zama, of Castelli e Masini, the Focaccia e → Melandri manufactory and the → Fabris laboratory in Milan, modelling single figures with intentionally flattened forms in tune with the German version of → deco style, like the *Pierrots* and the *Spaniards*, along with composing spectacular centrepieces like the famous *Oriental Procession* (Faenza, Museo Internazionale delle Ceramiche, and Milan, Pinacoteca Ambrosiana). In the 1920s he of-

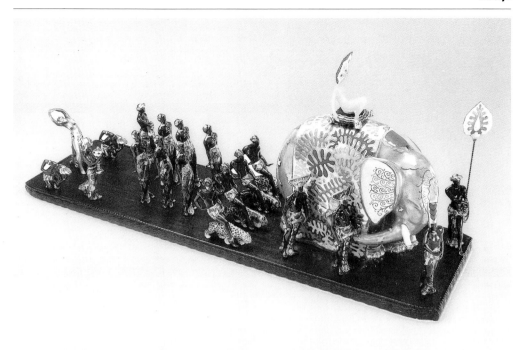

Francesco Nonni, Oriental Procession, *polychrome majolica, 1927. Faenza, Museo Internazionale delle Ceramiche*

Francesco Nonni, Pierrot, *polychrome majolica, 1925. Gardone Riviera, Il Vittoriale*

ten called upon the collaboration of Anselmo Bucci, as painter decorator of his own models; furthermore he met with great success at the Paris fair of 1925. *(Pls 76 and 77)*

Northwood, John (1836–1902). English glass decorator responsible for the revival of etched cameo glass in England. He founded his own laboratory toward 1860 and won fame in 1873 with the *Elgin Vase*, in clear crystal etched in low relief in emulation of the horsemen of the Panathenaea frieze by Phidias (London, British Museum), and the *Portland* Vase (1873–76), executed with the same technique as the Roman original. Northwood created an abundant series of other works, always in cameo glass (for instance the *Pegasus* vase in 1882) and concurrently running a glassworks with his brother Joseph. His son John became in turn a cameo glass etcher and director of the → Stevens & Williams company; last of all, the grandson William was to follow in their footsteps.

Notsjo. Finnish glassworks active since 1793, that by the mid-nineteenth century became one of the most important glassworks in Finland. Its production prevailingly consisted of tableware with mod-

Notsjo, vase, bubble glass, early 1940s

ern, essential forms, alongside art glass designed by Kaj Frank, Heikki Orvola and Oiva Toikka. In 1950 the factory was taken over by the Wartsila group, and since 1971 its products are sold under the trademark → "Arabia".

Nuutajarvi. Finnish glassworks, active since 1793, in the second half of the nineteenth century it became the leading glassworks in Finland. Around 1900 the new company "Costiander & Co." was founded, that while maintaining its serial production of table glassware, also launched art items in the → art nouveau vein, designed by Helena Willenius, that were successfully serial-produced as well. During the 1920s its cut glass articles were very popular, but lost favour in the 1930s.

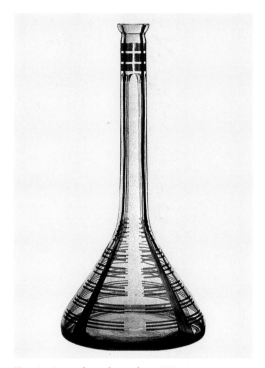

Nuutajarvi, vase, glass and enamels, ca. 1900.
Helsinki, Taideteollisuusmuseo

Nyman, Gunnel (1909–48). Finnish glass designer formerly creator of furniture, working at the → Riihimaki glassworks, she obtained a certain popularity at the Paris exhibition of 1937 and began collaborating with the → Iittala manufactory and → Notsjo. She used a variety of executive techniques and styles, among which it is worth mentioning the

folded-over glass (a strip is folded over like the flap of an envelope), ground and → sandblasted glass, heavy clear glass with a symmetrical array of air bubbles (the 1940s).

Nymphenburg. One of the most important European porcelain manufactories during the eighteenth and early nineteenth centuries, it was erected in 1747 in the vicinity of Munich; in 1862, no longer backed by the Bavarian State, it was rented to Ferdinand Scotzniovsky, who limited the production to household useful ware, whereas a revival of several models of the past and equally the creation of decorative articles was again initiated in 1888, under the direction of Albert Bäuml. During the → Jugendstil period even the ancient porcelain factory followed the formal models and especially the ornamental elements inspired by nature, executing in particular small animal sculptures and birds modelled by Theodore Kärner, an employee between 1905 and 1918, and statuettes with figures in up-to-date attire, works by Paul → Scheurich and Josef → Wackerle. The manufactory is still running and producing along with quality tableware and decorative items an abundant reproduction of eighteenth-century models. *(Pl. 78)*

Nyon. Swiss porcelain factory opened toward 1780 by Ferdinand Muller (joined in 1781 by his partner Jacob → Dortu who had formerly worked in Berlin, Marseilles and Marieberg), active in the production of bowls, coffee pots and cups decorated with sprigs of flowers and butterflies; in the final stage of its activity (it wound down in 1860) the main production was cream-coloured earthenware and gres imitations of → Wedgwood models.

Obrist, Hermann (1863–1927). Swiss embroidery designer, employed by the Kunstgewerbeschule of Karlsruhe from 1888, in 1892 he opened an embroidery workshop in Florence, in 1894 moved to Munich and in 1897 was one of the founding members of the Vereinigte Werkstätte für Kunst im Handwerk, that he subsequently directed. A designer of furnishings as well, his true specialties were graphics for the execution of embroideries, nearly entirely inspired by plant themes, always displaying wavy lines and the whiplash.

Offenbach. German pottery opened in 1739 near Frankfurt, specialised in the production of high-fire tableware painted with themes linked up with country life and nature, rendered with simple, slightly rustic expressiveness. It was active until the end of the nineteenth century.

Olbrich, Joseph Maria (1867–1908). Austrian architect and designer, collaborator of Otto Wagner, one of the leading personalities of the Viennese Secession, he designed its exhibition premises in 1898. The year after he was invited by the Grand Duke of Hessen to take up residence at the → Darmstadt artists' colony where he was to remain his whole life, designing furnishings, table silverware, lamps and metal-wrought articles, all characterised by the refusal of the slightest naturalist inclination, to the benefit of abstract patterns rendered in rhythmic compositions of lines and rounded elements; in 1906 he also designed several prototypes of automobiles for Opel. A good part of his production can be seen at the Heissisches Landersmuseum in Darmstadt.

Omega Workshops. English manufactory founded in London in 1913 by the art critic Roger Fry, in conformity with William → Morris' model, aiming at improving the quality of decorative design and providing a professional opportunity for a number of young talents, including Vanessa Bell, Henri Gaudier-Brzeska, Duncan Grant and Wyndam Lewis. The products of the manufactory com-

Joseph Maria Olbrich, sideboard, durmast-oak, glass, brass and embossed copper, 1902. Genoa, Wolfsonian Foundation

prised furniture and pottery, the latter usually with abstract decors, but especially rugs, produced at Wilton, and furnishing textiles, printed in France, featuring abstract designs rendered in quite vivid colours, closely linked up with the *fauve* and cubist pictorial experiments; nonetheless the company, badly managed and with too popular prices, was dissolved in 1920.

Onondaga Pottery Co. United States porcelain manufactory and pottery, founded in 1871 at Syracuse (New York), hence the trademark "Syracuse China", and still in business producing tableware and supplies for hotels, schools, hospitals, railway companies and restaurants; decorations range from English traditional floral themes to strikingly → de-

Onondaga Pottery Co., Marathon *serving dish, painted pottery,* 1926

Lamp, iron and opaline glass, 1930–31. Milan, Stazione Centrale

co geometric compositions (*Marathon Pattern Plate* in 1926), and views of scenery and historical scenes (*Mayflower Hotel Service* in 1930).

Onyx glass. Term defining → *chalcedony* glass, but also the name of a particular decorative glass patented by George W. Leighton in the United States in 1889 — and used in the Dalzell, Leighton & Co. and Gilmore glassworks in Findley (Ohio) — obtained by mixing various metal components in the bolus, or basic vitreous mass.

Opaline. Slightly translucid glass opacified with bone ash and coloured with metal oxides in pastel or white tones, or else black and navy. The term appeared for the first time on the antiquarian market in 1907, but derives from the nineteenth-century definitions of *cristal d'opale*, of the Empire and Restoration periods, and from the German *Opalglas* used in the late eighteenth century. Opaline reached its peak in France between 1820 and 1870 owing to the production of the → Baccarat, → Saint-Louis and → Choisy-le-Roi manufactories, whose most frequent colour schemes were *gorge de pigeon* (dapple-grey), *bulle de savon* (soap bubble), turquoise, green, powder blue, bright blue, pink, coral, ruby and yellow, applied in various useful shapes: vases, basins, boxes, candle-sticks, bottles, pitchers, bowls, caskets. The articles, sometimes ornamented with cold-paintings or enamelled and mounted on a copper-, zinc- and tin-alloy base having the appearance

of gilt bronze (*ormolu*) — used also for the handles — were moulded, blown or pressed. Since the late nineteenth century opaline is produced all over the world.

Orlov. Russian glassworks of Miliatino, known for making useful tableware and in particular bottles for vodka, clear or in coloured, enamel-decorated glass; it was taken over toward 1828 by M.F. Orlov, who introduced an interesting production of art glass and table crystalware. In 1840 it passed on to S.I. → Mal'tsev, becoming imperial property between 1884 and 1894.

Orrefors Glasbruk. Swedish glassworks that has been producing tableware and inexpensive glass since 1898. Acquired by Johan Ekman in 1913, the manufactory initiated an important production of art and ornamental glass, availing of the artistic collaboration of Simon → Gate (from 1915), Edward → Hald (from 1917), Vicke → Lindstrand (between 1928 and 1941), Sven → Palmqvist (from 1928) and Edvin → Öhrström (from 1936). Under Hald 's direction (from 1933 to 1944), the glassworks became known worldwide for its coated ornamental glass and table crystalware, with facetted forms, dark green or smoked brown (usually executed in a partner factory at Sandvik), as well as for the elegance of the bubbled or smoked glass with deeply etched designs. Its most significant period can be identified in the 1920s and 1930s when the most diversified articles were created, comprising *graal* glass (coloured glass, → acid etched and carved under a thin layer of clear glass), → *ariel* (cased glass with inlays of air bubbles forming abstract or figurative patterns), → *kraka* (opalescent white or navy glass with *reticella* decoration) and *Ravenna* (heavy coloured glass with inlays of abstract motifs in clear glass, invented after the Second World War by Sven Palmqvist). The firm is still in business, producing also candelabras and lighting fixtures of particular significance, benefitting by the creativity of Nils Landberg, inventor, among other things, of gorgeous bowls made of steel-blue potassic crystal.

Osler F. & C. English glassworks founded at Birmingham in 1807, specialised in the production of large-size glass and metal furnishing articles, like the monumental fountain and candelabra exhibited and widely acclaimed at the London exhibition of 1851.

Ott & Brewer Company. United States porcelain manufactory in New Jersey, opened in 1863 for the production of earthenware; in 1871, with the arrival of William Bromley, who brought with him significant professional experience acquired when working at the Irish → Belleek factory, production

was aligned on the latter's models, from then on become particularly popular all over the United States. A number of artists collaborated with the manufactory, creating interesting pieces in the → eclectic manner: the Canadian Isaac Broome, to whom is owed a gilt Cleopatra bust in → *parian ware*, shown with other items at the Philadelphia Centennial Exhibition (1876), and the United States artist Walter Scott Lenox, who opened his own laboratory, → Lenox Company, in 1889.

Öttingen-Schrattenhofen. German pottery opened in Bavaria in 1735, specialising in the production of high-fired beer mugs, painted in bright colours and featuring highly imaginative rococo motifs, along with brown useful majolica ware. During the nineteenth century it mainly produced cream-coloured tableware.

Orrefors Glasbruk, pitcher and small bottle, etched glass, 1925. Paris, Musée des Arts Décoratifs

P

Paden City. United States pottery, active in West Virginia from 1914 up to 1963 making semi-porcelain tableware, usually on a pink ground with polychrome floral ornamentation arranged unevenly over the surface of the plates.

Pairpoint Manufacturing Co. United States glassworks founded in 1865 at New Bedford for the marketing of useful ware; in 1884 it took over the → Mount Washington Glass Company, one of the biggest producers of glass → paperweights using various techniques.

Palme, Franz Josef. Bohemian glass etcher, known for pieces — that he always signed — adorned with animals in a naturalist vein aligned on the Biedermeier tradition, working as of 1882 at the English Dennis laboratory owned by Thomas → Webb & Sons.

Palmqvist, Sven (b. 1906). Swedish glass etcher, pupil in the school connected with the → Orrefors firm, in 1928 he became an employee of the manufactory, where he patented → *kraka* and *Ravenna* glass, with which he produced a series of articles in rather thick material with inserts of bright-coloured abstract designs (*Light and Shadow*, with two hundred pieces of *Ravenna* glass mounted in Geneva); meanwhile he tried out a new technique for the execution of glass bowls exerting on the vitreous paste merely centrifugal force, barring any hand-finishings.

Pankok, Bernhard (1872–1943). German designer, extremely active in the Munich → Jugendstil and co-founder with other artists of the Vereinigte Werkstätte für Kunst im Handwerk, he was the author of executive designs for wooden furnishings with modernist forms, yet interpreted in an excessively plastic sense. In 1902, at Stuttgart, he was appointed director of the Staatliche Kunstgewerbeschule.

Pannaggi, Ivo (1901–81). Italian designer, having adhered to futurism in 1918 and signed the *Manifesto of Mechanical Art* (1922), he was one of the most interesting interior decorators of his generation, by his capacity to transfer the language of futurism inside a housing ensemble: it is worth mentioning his furnishings for the Zampini house at Esanatoglia (in the province of Macerata), executed between 1925 and 1926 and today for a large part destroyed, where lamps, furniture, textiles and articles cleverly and impeccably blended → art deco models with the elements of the futurist syntax.

Pantin. French crystalworks founded in 1851 by E.S. Monot in the Paris suburb of La Villette; in 1855 they were transferred to Pantin, where a number of changes of ownership occurred; they dealt mainly in the production of water and wine carafes of great, essential distinction, and by the early twentieth century of drinking services with ultramodern lines, designed by the Dutch architect Hendrik Petrus → Berlage. In 1900 the manufactory permanently took the name Cristallerie de Pantin, under the direction of St. Hilaire, Touvier, De Varreux & Cie., and became prominent on the market especially with its original → paperweights with flowers, lizards and minute insects, in line with the favourite naturalist themes of → art nouveau. Right after the First World War, in partnership with the Legras & Cie. firm, it became Verreries et Cristalleries de Saint-Denis et Pantin Réunies. The pieces produced by the laboratory can bear the trademarks "Pantin", "Degué" (the name of a master glassmaker) and "De Vez" (the name of the art director De Varreux).

Paperweight. Small decorative object made in lead glass, usually round, having a diameter of about 8 centimetres and the typical dome-like form that serves as a magnifying glass for the decoration cased in the glass. The oldest paperweights were produced in Bohemia (the first Bohemian exemplar dates from 1848) and Murano: the most famous ones are those made by Pietro Bigaglia, toward the 1840s during the Biedermeier period, immediately followed, in 1843 by the ones produced by the → Baccarat and → Clichy factories, and after 1850 by English and United States firms. Paperweights in time had different forms and decorations, and would be executed with various techniques, but several traditional types can be identified: → *millefiori*, → *opaline*, *overlay*, *sulfure*.

Papier mâché. A material obtained with paper soaked in water with an addition of glue, plaster and occasionally sand, that after being modelled and fired can be painted or lacquered, acquiring an unusual solidity and water-resistance. Probably of Eastern origin, the technique arrived in Europe in the seventeenth century, particularly in France and Italy. Having become widely popular during the nineteenth century, *papier mâché* was used for furniture, furnishing items, trays (in England by 1830), for sculpture and architectural-decorative elements (Faventine *papier-mâché* manufactories), and for an overall production of tableware and various-sized boxes in Russia, a production inspired not only by the folklore tradition of floral motifs on black and gold grounds (Palec school), but also an important expression of the pictorial style of the so-called "Itinerants".

Paragon China Co. English porcelain manufactory and pottery, opened at Longton (Staffordshire) toward 1899 and taken over in 1968 by the Royal Doulton Group, specialised in the execution of cups and tea sets with roses on a navy ground or buttercups on a white ground, it is also renowned for the production of juvenile ware with designs by J.A. Robinson focusing on the world of childhood.

Pargeter, Philip (1826–1906). English glassmaker specialist in the manufacturing of cameo glass, that usually was then etched by his cousin John → Northwood (the two also collaborated in the execution of the copy of the *Portland Vase*) at the → Stourbridge glassworks. Conspicuous among the pieces signed and dated by the etcher (once stored in the British Museum and then sold on auction) are the *Milton Vase* (1878) and a series of cups in navy cameo glass with etched portraits of famous Englishmen (between 1878 and 1882).

Parian ware. Identifies a typical English porcelain, white and with a fine-grained surface, rather similar to statuary marble and for that reason mostly used for modelling whole figures and busts, in some rare cases for vases and formal dishes, and buttons and jewellery (the latter highly appreciated by Queen Victoria). It was used for the first time

in 1844 at the Copeland factory, and later by → Minton, → Worcester, → Wedgwood and, in the United States, by → Bennington.

Pâte de cristal. Particular type of glass, produced by using powdered glass of excellent quality and brilliancy, elected for the execution of very special items on an excellent creative level by the French workshops of Gabriel → Argy-Rousseau, Alméric → Walter and François-Emile → Décorchemont.

Pâte de riz. Type of → *opaline* glass in a grey tint used after 1843 in the → Saint-Louis manufactories.

Pâte de verre. Paste obtained with powdered clear glass (then coloured in the die with various powders to create the effect of semi-precious stones) or coloured glass, amalgamated by a binder insuring a quick fusion of the mixture, in turn poured into a die. Items thus produced can feature layers of polychrome reliefs, obtained by overlaying materials in the die, and etchings as well. This extremely ancient technique was very successful-

Perfume bottle made in pâte de verre, 1930–35

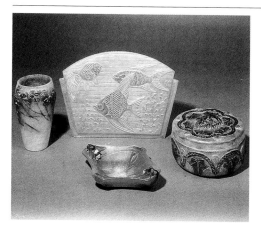

Writing-desk articles made in pâte de verre, France, 1925–30

then heating it and handling it until the desired form (especially vases and bowls, sometimes with precious metal mountings) and decoration are produced, the latter presenting a polychrome "combed" version with at the centre a dark glass imitating the so-called "peacock eye" on the kaleidoscopic feathers.

Peche, Dagobert (1887–1923). Austrian designer, active for the → Wiener Werkstätte as of 1915, between 1917 and 1919 he also ran the separate department of the school in Zurich. Toward 1912 he designed pottery and rugs in the secessionist vein, intended for industrial production, but right after the war he inclined toward an utterly innovatory trend both in the forms (in an absolutely fantastic vein) and in the materials (typically → art deco), displaying a special proneness toward art craftsmanship and hand-production of articles, in blatant opposition to modernist objectives. His most original designs were for furnishings drawn from a clever revival of rococo trends (later widely imitated by the Milanese → Ponti, → Buzzi and → Lancia) and for silverware: his *potiche* vases, with their geometric ribbings, suggest pleated paper.

ly revived in the second half of the nineteenth century, especially in France owing to Henri and Jean → Cros, followed by Albert-Louis → Dammosue, François-Emile → Décorchemont, Gabriel → Argy-Rousseau and Emile → Gallé.

Paul, Bruno (1874–1968). German designer, co-founder of the Deutsche Werkstätten and collaborator of the *Jugend* review, the official mouthpiece of the German version of international modernism; as director of the Berlin Kunstgewerbeschule (1907) and the Vereinigte Staatsschule für freie und angewandte Kunst, in Berlin also (1924–33), he had a significant influence on the modes and forms of the development of design in Germany. He designed a series of furnishings planned for an inexpensive, serial production, with intentionally simplified forms and reminiscences — but merely ornamental — of → Jugendstil.

Peach blow glass. United States glass processing technique invented toward the mid-nineteenth century to imitate the effect of Chinese porcelain dubbed "peach blossom", dating back to the K'an Hsi dynasty (1662–1722), but that offers, instead, a broad colour range by the use of glass coated with pastel colours, in tones from blue to pink (utilised especially by → Mount Washington Glass Company), and from yellow to rose, executed after 1885 by the → New England Glass Company.

Peacock feather. Type of → iridescent glass invented by A. → Nash for the → Tiffany manufactory; it is obtained by adding to the bolus small quantities of molten glass of different colours and textures,

Dagobert Peche (for Wiener Werkstätte), Small deer, *silver, 1918*

Pelikan, Franz Anton (1786–1858). One of the most renowned members of a family of Bohemian glass etchers, he was the great interpreter of the Biedermeier trend; for decorating drinking services, bowls, dishes and bottles he favoured hunting scenes and horsemen.

Pellat, Apsley (1791–1863). English glassmaker, he was active in the Falkon laboratory at Southwark, that his father had taken over in 1790; there he researched the French processing of *sulfures*, obtaining a monopoly. The articles turned out by the manufactory, especially pitchers, candelabras, → paperweights, dishes and perfume bottles with etched adornments or portraits, were given the name *cameo incrustation* or *crystal-ceramic*; besides the cameos executed with this technique, Pellat presented at the London exhibition of 1851 items executed with a type of glass dubbed "Anglo-Venetian".

Peloton. Glass technique entailing the application on the surface of an article in clear, opaque or coloured glass, of thin segments of glass by spinning the item, while still soft, on a sheet scattered over with filaments; reheated, it is then pressed in a mould and finally → glossed. The technique was patented by William Kralik in Bohemia in 1880.

Perles (broderie de). Bead embroidery, an executive technique that, using extremely minute glass beads of different colours, designs decorations, very similar to needle embroidery, on handbags, powder compacts, lipsticks, jewel cases, clothing; toward 1850 the technique was revived in Bohemia for decorating drinking vessels, and in Great Britain, for prints and etchings with views and floristic compositions. At the turn of the century glass beads and → *murrines*, of different colours and sizes, were used, aside from embroidery and flat decoration also to adorn ribbons, strings, and hairstyles (memorable for instance the cloaks, tunics and lamps made in Venice by Mariano Fortuny y Madrazo).

Perry, Mary Chase (1868–1961). United States potter, at the beginning of her career, at Detroit, she was active in porcelain decoration, firing each piece in rented furnaces until the agreement with Horace Caulkins, with whom she opened the Revelation Kilns factory; after a number of marketing successes, she created Pewabic Pottery, devoted exclusively to art pottery linked up with the models of → Tiffany and → Grueby, as well as antique Chinese pottery. Adopting the manner of → art nouveau imported from Europe, during the rest of her career the artist produced graceful items — especially vases — adorned merely with exuberant iridescent glazes.

Pesaro. Italian pottery known and documented since 1480–1490, whence in all probability originated the majolica tiles of Isabella d'Este's apartment at the Palazzo Ducale of Mantua. Throughout the nineteenth century the Pesaro territory counted numerous flourishing workshops and laboratories, like those of the Benucci and Latti, Reggiani, Frongini, Magrini-Bernacchi-Micoletti-Uguccioni and Molaroni families. Toward 1860, conspicuous among the other personalities was Terenzio Bertozzini (1816–1901), working in a laboratory near Villa Imperiale (later transferred to Pesaro), where he executed refined vases ornamented in the style of the Pesarese models of the Renaissance and majolicas with shifting reflections and lustre-glazed, such as the ones made by the master majolica maker Giorgio da Gubbio; in the same laboratory, after 1866, worked Vincenzo → Molaroni and his sons Eliseo (1865–1957) and Telesforo (1848–1933). In 1899 Oreste Ruggieri opened a factory, renowned for its production in the Italian → liberty floristic manner (worth mentioning the extremely elegant stuccoes and ornamental majolicas of the Ruggieri house on the Pesarese seawalk) and, for the pottery models, Galileo → Chini's works. During the twentieth century Ferruccio → Mengaroni (1875–1925) also opened his workshop-laboratory, engaged in imitating and counterfeiting fifteenth-century traditional pottery of the Pesaro and Marche area.

Peters & Reed Pottery. United States pottery active at Zanesville (Ohio) — hence the trademark "Zaneware" — from 1898 to 1957; in 1901 it began producing *cache-pots* and flower vases, and between 1905 and 1912 it introduced the *Moss Aztec* series, that brought it fame: the vases are made to be water-resistant on the inside and finished on the outside with a delicate glaze over ornaments modelled in relief and drawn from insects and plants, in an exquisitely → art nouveau vein. Toward the 1920s the factory tried out a series of vases adorned with a dripping technique in contrasting colours going all around the body of the article.

Petersburg. Russian porcelain manufactory founded by the Imperial family (1744), it was active until the 1917 Revolution producing pieces of the finest quality inspired by the classicising culture of which Catherine II was fond. The tableware was very similar to what was produced at → Sèvres, while it was owing to the head-modeller Jean Rachette (employed at the manufactory from 1899 to 1804) that was introduced a production of small statues figuring Russian peasants that were very popular throughout the nineteenth century, monumental amphoras, vases and ornamental dishes nearly always adorned with personalities and episodes belonging to the History of Russia. Pottery production was resumed in the 1920s, with series of tableware (mainly plates and coffee and tea sets) inspired by the Russian avant garde and constructivism, whose themes were linked up with the revolution and propaganda. In the 1930s several classicising models came back in fashion, yet simplified, in which navy and gold colours were prevailing.

Petersdorf. Bohemian glassworks opened in 1866 in the area bordering with Poland by Fritz → Heckert, member of a dynasty of German glassmakers famous all over Europe for the production of glass items inspired by various historical styles, ranging from the German tradition of Renaissance large enamelled pitchers to Indian drinking services of the Moghul dynasty. In 1923 the company merged with the Schreberhau glassworks.

Pewter. Alloy made with tin combined with copper ("English pewter", the best that, once polished, is as bright as silver), or else with lead, and in this case usually having a blackish-grey colouring. Used since the Middle-Ages, pewter was revived at the end of the nineteenth century and particularly in the → liberty era as the right material for expressing the modernist taste and lines in tableware, owing to the reasonable cost of the basic materials used and the possibility of imitating silver.

Pfaltzgraff Pottery. United States pottery, opened at York (Pennsylvania) by a European family of potters in 1894 and still in business, specialising in kitchen, useful and table ware, as well as in furnishing vases in different sizes (in the period from 1932 to 1937) decorated in delicate shades ranging from pink to sea-green. *(Pl. 79)*

Pfohl, Karel (1826–94). Bohemian etcher working at Stein-Schönau and known for a rich production of drinking services in coated glass, wheel-etched and ornamented nearly exclusively with hunting scenes and equestrian subjects.

Phoenix Glass Work. Name chosen by three different United States glassworks in the early nineteenth century: one opened in 1820 at South Boston by the Englishman T.Caines and specialising in the production of etched glass, articles decorated with → *lacy glass* and pressed items, a second one at Bristol executing etched glass, and a third active between 1832 and 1868 at Pittsburgh, also dealing in moulded glass and etched articles.

Pickard China Company. United States porcelain manufactory, founded at Chicago and still active, known especially since the 1910s for its refined tea sets and tableware in white porcelain, with gilt decorations drawn from European → liberty floristic themes.

Pickled furniture. Definition referring to furniture that, particularly in the 1910s and in the Anglo-Saxon world, was coated with white decorations obtained by scratching the colour applied on the wooden surface revealing the plaster preparation underneath.

Pilkington Brothers Ltd. English glassworks, that took that name in 1901 — after the merging of British Cast Plate Glass (founded in 1771) and Saint Helens' Crown Glass (active since 1826 at Liverpool where the headquarters remained) — and that became one of the greatest English suppliers of industrial and flat glass, of optics, optical fibre and pressed crystal. The firm is associated with an interesting glass museum that in fact is located at Saint Helens, near Liverpool.

Pilkington Pottery. English pottery opened in the vicinity of Manchester in 1892 by the Pilkington family (that owned coal mines and glassworks) and directed by William Burton, formerly working as a chemist in the → Wedgwood manufactory. First involved in the industrial production of floor and roof tiles, it choose the path of artistic creation in 1897, presenting at the Paris exhibition of 1900 a series of ornamental vases that were quite successful. Beginning in 1903, and on designs by artists such as W.S. Mycock, W. → Crane, → C.F.A. Voysey and L.F. → Day, they executed large decorative vases using a new clear glaze technique and application of metal lustres researched by Burton and his brother Joseph, continuing throughout the 1920s and 1930s with forms inspired by antique Greek pottery, → art nouveau and the spare → deco style of Central European origin. The manufactory wound down in 1938.

Pilkington Pottery, a page of the catalogue with the Royal Lancastrian *series, 1930s*

Pisa. Italian pottery in all probability dating back to the twelfth century, when the Pisans were in contact with the products of the Arabo-Spanish majolica on the island of Mallorca (hence perhaps the term used to identify that type of ceramic product), and active until the sixteenth century. The same name was given to another manufactory, devoted to the use of white clay, set up, in 1841, by the Palme family and taken over in 1887 by the Milanese Società Ceramica Richard, later become → Richard-Ginori.

Plant R.H. & S.L. English pottery, opened at Longton in 1881 and still in business today under the trademark "Royal Tuscan", exclusively specialising in the creation of tableware and tea sets in porcelain with Victorian decors. In the 1920s it introduced production of a series of furnishing statuettes with animals, birds, butterflies and children in polychrome porcelain.

Plastics. Modellable artificial materials, the first of which, being celluloid (used mainly for eyeglass frames) was discovered in Great Britain by Alexander Parkes in 1862. Acetate of cellulose was patented in 1894 (and used for cutlery handles), casein in 1897 (coloured when used for making buttons). The first entirely artificial material was bakelite, or phenylic formaldehyde, in which was launched a huge production of costume jewellery, purses, eyeglasses and furnishing articles, patented in 1907 by the Belgian chemist Baekeland, to whom the formula was owed; whereas the basis of the modern plastic industry was founded in the 1930–40 decade with the invention of polyvinyl chloride (PCV). *(Pls 24 and 81)*

Plated amberina. United States glass technique patented by Joseph → Locke in 1886 for the → New England Glass Company: a slightly blueish opalescent glass ground is coated with a layer of → *amberina* glass, so the surface is decorated with vertical veins.

Plywood. Produced by overlaying three or more layers of wood with crossed fibres, then pressureglued, the board is flexible and resistant. Already used by the eighteenth century, plywood was at its peak during the Biedermeier period, when it was utilised for modelling hollow chair backs, as at the end of the nineteenth century the Viennese → Thonet used it in rods, whereas → Belter used it in sheets. In the twentieth century Aalto and → Breuer adopted it.

Poli, Flavio (b. 1900). Italian glass designer, active from 1934 for the → Seguso Vetri d'Arte manufactory and known for his heavy glass or ground crystal items representing animals, as well as for enamelled objects.

Pomona. Glass processing technique patented by Joseph → Locke in 1885 for the → New England Glass Company whereby items are made in clear glass, presenting a surface in part coloured in pink and amber, in part etched with polychrome wreathes of flowers and fruit. Two typologies of these can be found: in the first the article is coated with a material resistant to the action of acid, in which grooves are made so that the corrosive process takes place in those pre-arranged places; in the second the piece, after having been coated with very minute particles of a resistant substance, is soaked in the acid to obtain a bare surface.

Ponti Gio (Giovanni, 1891–1979). Italian architect and designer, one of the most outstanding personalities in the Italian decorative arts during the 1920s and 1930s. After obtaining his degree at the Politecnico of Milan, in 1923 he became art director of the → Richard-Ginori manufactory of Doccia, San Cristoforo and Mondovì where, during the fifteen years of his collaboration, he renovated the entire line of production, signing a huge, very eclectic quantity of pieces, including bowls, amphoras, vases, dishes, table sets, chinaware, jewel cases, inkstands, paperknives and decorative sculptures either in porcelain or majolica, featuring the same rarefied distinction with a → deco flavour. His favourite subjects were ironic quotations of the classical repertory, often executed with an agate point on white and gold porcelain, with eventual touches of navy, purple and grey. Under the term "Pontesca", his variations of the theme of grotesques, just as his theme of "my women", elegant, mannerist female nudes gently reclining on ropes or clouds, belonged to his highly personal interpretation of Renaissance tradition. After having opened a studio with the architects Fiocchi and → Lancia in 1922, between 1927 and 1933 all the designs for furnishings and decorative art articles were done in association with Lancia. Joining in 1927 the art board of the Monza Biennale and founding the group *Il Labirinto*, Ponti worked in designing furnishings and items for the Luigi Fontana firm of Milan, transforming it, with Pietro → Chiesa's collaboration, into → Fontana Arte in 1933. Creator and director of the review *Domus* in 1928, Ponti displayed an openness to rationalism yet without giving up the neoclassic grace of his personal style, that soon developed into a Novecento line apparent in the architectural designs and designer products created between 1930 and 1939, in which he remained faithful to the principle of comfort that each item must have, yet created increasingly personal articles, each one different, introducing novel elements like scallop-edging, latticework and coils, along with new materials like steel and iron. *(Pls 80 and 84–86)*

Poole Pottery. English pottery, active in Dorset as of 1873 under the direction of the Carter family; to Owen Carter is owed an interesting group of furnishing vases, in geometric forms drawn from → art deco, decorated with metal glazes (between 1900

and 1918). In 1921 Charles Carter, Harold → Stabler (in partnership) and John Adams introduced a production of table and furnishing ware in → art nouveau style, especially in its luxuriant flower designs (by Truda Adams) in very vivid colours emulating South American folk art and Persian civilisation; in the second half of the 1930s there were a number of coffee sets and furnishing vases inspired by utterly geometric forms in the → Bauhaus manner. *(Pl. 82)*

Pope-Gosser China Company. United States pottery, opened at Coshocton (Ohio) in 1902 and closed down in 1958, specialised in the production of semi-porcelain table ware inspired by models either in Victorian style or with *chinoiserie* themes.

Poppelsdorf. German pottery opened in 1755 near Bonn, renowned for its production of cream-coloured earthenware; taken over by Ludwig Wessel in 1825, it began using the trademark of an anchor combined with the initial B, and is still active.

Poschinger, Ferdinand von (1815–67). German glassmaker, known for a magnificent production of → iridescent glass imitating → Gallé and → Tiffany models; he was active at a factory located at Buchenau, in Bavaria, taken over by his father Benedikt in 1856 and later bequeathed to his son, Ferdinand Benedikt (1867–1921).

Potschapple. German porcelain manufactory opened by Carl Thieme near Meissen between 1870 and 1880 under the name Porzellanfabrik Carl Thieme, active in the imitation of ornamental statuettes based on models belonging to eighteenth-century → Meissen series, and large vases with extremely ornate decoration, often marked with the inscription "Dresden".

Potsdam. German pottery founded toward 1739 and active up until the late eighteenth century, known for its production of pottery imitating Delft majolicas. The same name applied to a glassworks instituted by Frederick William of Brandenburg in 1674 for the production of crystal items and glass for mirrors and useful ware; the glassworks was active until 1736, the year it was transferred to Zechlin where, under State management, it kept up the same production until 1890.

Pottier & Stymus. United States cabinet-makers company. Auguste Pottier, cabinet-maker, and

William Pierre Stymus, upholsterer, were active in New York between 1840 and 1850 at the Rochefort & Skarren laboratory, that they took over in 1859; the success of their articles incited them to open a large store on Lexington Avenue (1871) and an office on Fifth Avenue (1883), becoming one of the most fashionable furnishing companies in New York society, since they supplied furniture overflowing with decorations drawn from the most varied historical styles, from Hellenism to Renaissance to rococo: of great fame were the *fumoir* in Moresque style made for John D. Rockefeller (New York, Brooklyn Museum) and the *Henri-Deux* chair (New York, The Metropolitan Museum of Art).

Pountney & Co. English pottery, opened at Bristol (Avon) in 1849 and closed down in 1971, specialised in kitchen and table ware; in the course of the 1910s it used vaguely → liberty shapes with decorations inspired by country life.

Powolny, Michael (1871–1954). Austrian potter, in 1906 he founded in Vienna, where he had studied, the Wiener Keramik laboratory in partnership with the graphic artist Berthold Löffler (1874–1960), specialising in the production of small white majolica sculptures, for the most part decorated in black in keeping with the Viennese Secession manner; later on several designs were contributed by Josef → Hoffmann and Dagobert → Peche, and his articles were sold by the → Wiener Werkstätte. In 1912 he entered in partnership with the pottery studio of his pupil Franz Schleiss, under the name Wiener und Gmundener Keramik Werkstätte; right after the war, in collaboration with → Lobmeyr, he introduced decoration on glass using grinding and carving; he also modelled small bronze figures. *(Pl. 87)*

Price Brothers. English pottery, founded at Burslem in 1896 and dissolved in 1960, specialised in useful and kitchen ware with floral decorations.

Primavera. Type of decorative glass invented in 1927 by Ercole Barovier for the Vetreria Artistica → Barovier, consisting of a clear surface covered with crackles, whereas handles, mouth and base are executed in black glass paste.

Prouvé, Emile-Victor (1858–1943). French painter and designer, born in Nancy, after his studies in Paris he returned to his home town in 1901 to work with Emile → Gallé, at whose death, in 1904, he took over the manufactory, continuing to produce "Gallé-style"

glass articles, jewellery and furniture that bear, next to the master's name a star, precisely to distinguish them from the works made before 1904. After a research trip to Munich (1905), between 1908 and 1909 he organised a congress at Nancy to publicise the features of German Werkbund. In 1918 he was appointed director of the Ecole des Arts Appliqués at → Nancy, a position he occupied until 1930. His son Jean, architect, created interesting inventions in the field of furnishing, in particular the graceful, essential chair executed in 1925, along with experiments with aluminium and → plastic materials.

Prutscher, Otto (1880-1949). Austrian designer, a pupil of → Hoffmann in Vienna, in 1903 he became a member of the → Wiener Werkstätte. He prepared a remarkable quantity of designs for the Vienna pottery and porcelain manufactory, but in 1900 began creating art glass, influencing a good part of Austrian art glass up until the First World War, working for the → Lobmeyr, → Bakalowitz & Söhne and Carl Schnappel firms as well. A very famous creator of jewellery and silverware, in which he expressed to the utmost his very special version of modernism, both highly refined and barbaric, he also designed furnishing textiles and wallpaper.

Otto Prutscher, wine glass, hand-painted glass, 1905

Pucci, Francesco (1817–86). Italian inlayer, born at Calvi, he worked at the same time at Lancetti and Falcini, using a → *marqueterie* technique in the floristic manner with ivory inlays. In 1873 at Vienna, during the World Fair, he was awarded a prize for a precious carved round table, adorned with inlays of precious woods, mother-of-pearl and metal profilings, based on a design by the painter Alessandro Venanzi (Cagli, Museo Civico).

Puiforçat, Jean (1897–1945). French goldsmith, one of the most famous silversmiths and goldsmiths in → deco style, he successfully exhibited at the great Paris event of 1925, but was also a great collector of eighteenth-century silverware, conserved today at the Louvre. He began his career in 1922, on his own, and in 1925 executed the silverware for the Hotel du Collectionneur in Paris; his admission to the group *Les Cinq*, with Pierre → Legrain and Pierre → Chareau came about in 1926, and in 1928 to the Union des Artistes Modernes, a controversial group with regard to the ruling art deco. His articles have timelessly retained their utter formal distinction, strictly geometric lines, precious materials, technical perfection suited to a luxury clientele, several exemplars being conserved in New York, The Metropolitan Museum of Art, and in Paris at the Musée des Arts Décoratifs.

Pulegoso (bubble glass). Type of opaque glass characterised by the insertion of countless air bubbles (*puleghe*) that give an uneven appearance to the surface; when it is covered with a layer of clear glass it is called *vetro pulegoso sommerso* (cased bubble glass). This technique, invented by Paolo → Venini and Napoleone → Martinuzzi in 1928, is used for producing amphoras, bowls, vases and lighting fixtures of rare distinction.

Pull, Georges (1810–89). German potter, in 1856 he opened a factory in Paris where some of the finest imitations of Bernard Palissy's Renaissance ornamental potteries were created.

Napoleone Martinuzzi, vase with handles, green pulegoso glass and gold leaf, 1930. Gardone Riviera, Il Vittoriale

Q

Quarti, Eugenio (1867–1931). Italian cabinet-maker; in 1888, after some experience in Paris, he settled in Milan where, after a short period in Carlo → Bugatti's laboratory, he opened his own factory, gradually extending it as a result of the prizes won in several international exhibitions (Paris, 1900; Turin, 1902; Milan, 1906). His furnishings, among the most felicitous inventions of Italian → liberty, while referring to Belgian and Austrian models, were characterised by the use of refined mother-of-pearl and silver inlays, elegantly floristic intaglios and bronze adornments. Often collaborating with architects (with Giuseppe Sommaruga he furnished, in 1903, palazzo Castiglioni in Milan), Quarti also worked in creating furniture to be mass-produced, in particular for hotels, and in a variety of furnishing items, including chandeliers, pottery and textiles.

Quetzal Art Glass and Decorating Company. United States glassworks founded in 1918 at Brooklyn to imitate glass items produced by → Tiffany. It wound down in 1918.

Quilted. Type of glass produced by Thomas → Webb & Sons and Stevens & Williams toward 1880. It is a coated glass with a mould-blown opaque interior reproducing a diamond-shaped motif, in turn coated with a thin vitreous layer containing an air bubble; ultimately the surfaces are glossed with hydrofluoric acid.

Quimper. French pottery opened in Brittany in 1690; in 1743, after Pierre-Paul Caussy took it over, it began producing majolicas similar to the ones from Rouen, with *chinoiserie* decorations and an overall rococo style. In 1792 it introduced series of pieces imitating its own eighteenth-century articles, that from then on would bear the trademark "H.B."

Eugenio Quarti, glass-case, ebony inlaid with mother-of-pearl and metals, handles in bronze, 1902

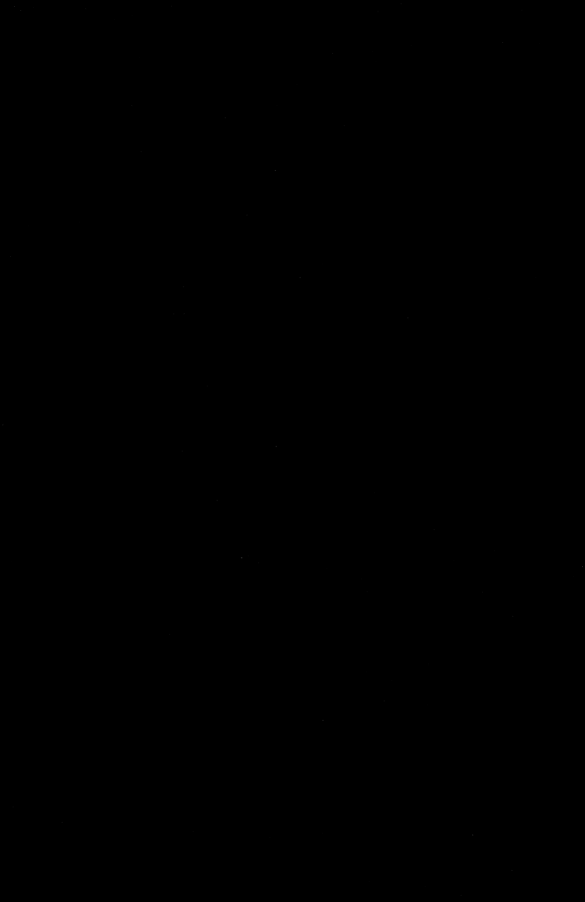

R

Radford E. English pottery, founded at Burslem (Staffordshire) in 1930 and wound down toward 1928, known for a production of household ware in country style, based on polychrome plant and floral themes on a yellow, grass-green or white ground.

Radford Samuel. English pottery, founded at Fenton (Staffordshire) in 1879 and dissolved in 1957, it specialised exclusively in the production of tableware, its model being Chinese porcelain, with red, gilt and navy floral and "lattice-work" ornamentations on a white ground.

Radi, Lorenzo (1803–74). Italian glassmaker, at length collaborator of the "Laboratorio d'Arte Musiva → Salviati dott. Antonio", he is known for having rediscovered in 1846 the executive technique of → *agate* glass and → *chalcedony* glass, whereas in 1850 he experimented with a polychrome vitreous paste and with gold leaf suitable for the formation of mosaic tesseras, that in fact would be used in the restoration of the mosaic walls of the Basilica of San Marco in Venice.

Raeren. German pottery opened at Aachen in the first half of the sixteenth century for the execution of brown, salt-glazed gres containers; after an uninterrupted activity, in the eighteenth century production focused exclusively on beer mugs. During the nineteenth century a few manufactories in the area directed their marketing strategy to the reproduction of Renaissance models and in any case period pottery items: in 1887 the laboratory directed by Hubert Schiffer began making and selling gres tableware with relief friezes, featuring either mythological or religious themes, circulated as originals, and toward the end of the century the Nuremberg firm of C.W. Fleischmann continued, with the selfsame models, the former production of the Raeren manufactory.

Ramsden, Omar (1873–1939). English goldsmith, specialised in the production of silver one-offs. Trained at the Sheffield School of Art, after a trip through Europe he opened in London, with his school mate Alwyn Charles Ellison Carr (1872–1940), a laboratory whose first major commission was the creation of the symbolic mace for the mayor of Sheffield (1899); from then on the laboratory would be crowned with success, both on the market and on the two artists' personal level, for a varied production of hand-crafted silver articles, in which it is easy to identify direct influences of → Arts & Crafts models and several decorative and structural elements relating to international modernism. The firm's masterpiece is the gilt silver monstrance enhanced with enamels, executed in 1907 for Westminster Cathedral. Carr having enlisted at the outbreak of the First World War, Ramsden ran the laboratory by himself, until the company was officially dissolved in 1919. Returning from the war, Carr initiated his own business as designer of silver and wrought iron articles, whereas Ramsden devoted himself to the production and marketing of a variety of useful, liturgical and decorative ware, influenced by the different English period styles, usually with the inscription "Omar Ramsden me fecit". Many pieces of the manufactory are conserved at the Victoria and Albert Museum in London, at the City Museum in Sheffield and the City Museum of Birmingham.

Randall, John (1810–90). English porcelain decorator renowned for his extraordinary skill in representing birds, both in the stylistic modes elaborated at the → Sèvres factory during the eighteenth century, and in a more precisely nineteenth-century naturalist manner. After working in Staffordshire in the workshop of his uncle Thomas Martin Randall (1786–1859, a specialist in the imitation of Sèvres pieces), toward 1830 he joined the pottery of Rockingham, between 1835 and 1880 he worked as decorator in the → Coalport manufactory, and subsequently, for reasons of health, he retired. A good number of his pieces, including magnificent vases and dishes, are conserved at the Clive House Museum of Shrewsbury.

Rateau, Armand-Albert (1882–1938). French designer and cabinet-maker, renowned for the legendary gorgeousness of his creations presenting a highly elegant → deco style. After his studies at the Ecole Boulle of Paris, in 1898 he began working as a professional man and, from 1905 to 1914 took over the direction of the Maison Alavoine, an interior decorating workshop. He became famous when, be-

bronze articles of the Roman period, in an opulent blending of imperial classicism and stylised forms inspired by Japan and China.

Ravasco, Alfredo (1873–1958). Italian goldsmith, son of a renowned Milanese goldsmith , he studied at the Academy of Brera and won important awards at the exhibition of Sempione in 1906, asserting him-

Armand-Albert Rateau, ottoman for Jeanne Lanvin's boudoir, bronze, ca. 1922

Alfredo Ravasco, bracelet, platinum, brilliants and cabochon emeralds, 1938–40

Armand-Albert Rateau, armchair, bronze, 1919–20

tween 1920 and 1922, he equipped with furniture displaying exceptional elegance and sumptuousness the *maison* of the fashion designer Jeanne Lanvin (now Paris, Musée des Arts Décoratifs); henceforth, as decorator of Lanvin-Décoration, he designed and installed numerous, well-publicised interior decorations in New York and Paris, Spain and the French Riviera. By his use of precious, sought-after materials, his particular style was receptive to the influences of the Far-Eastern cultures, but equally to

self as one of the most celebrated jewellers of his day. Also active in restorations of precious testimonies of the past, like the *Gold Altar of Saint Ambrose*, he executed necklaces, reliquaries, caskets, shrines, jewellery and furnishing items, using the most miscellaneous materials (including semi-precious stones, jade, coral and pearls, ivory and enamels, malachite and opals) and seeking his inspiration either in nature (*Centrepiece with octopi*, 1925–35, Milan, Castello Sforzesco), or in the late-Renaissance Italian tradition (*Shrine for Lucrezia Borgia's lock of hair*, 1934, Milan, Pinacoteca Ambrosiana).

Ravasi, Guido (1877–1946). Italian textile designer, son of a weaver, he trained in Germany, and in the early 1920s asserted himself as one of the leading designers of silk textiles of the Como industries. He took an active part in the Monza Biennales and the Paris fair of 1925, and founded the Bottega d'Arte, a laboratory specialising in the production of damasks and processed silks that, while being made with traditional techniques, offered models and decorative themes that were utterly modern and inclining to abstraction.

Ravilious, Eric (1903–42). English pottery decorator, he began his career as a designer at the → Wedgwood manufactory; after a trip to Italy, in 1926 he received several commissions to illustrate books and, in 1928, to execute mural decorations for the Morely College in London. In 1933 he turned to designing for pottery production, and the following year presented an exhibition of his works in Harrods department store. From 1936 until his death he worked for the Wedgwood manufactory, utilising a number of decorative techniques (including transfer-printing): including the group of cups executed in 1936 on the occasion of the coronation of Edward VIII, tea sets and tableware and letters of the alphabet for the nursery.

Reactive glass. Type of art glass that has the particularity of changing colour if re-heated; invented by → Tiffany, it is also known under the name *Tiffany flashed glass* or *Pastel Tiffany*. With this material articles are fashioned with glaze-finished interiors or present a polychrome interior decoration (therefore called *under-the-water*), whose decorative motifs, inspired by nature in an exquisitely → art nouveau vein, are named *Opalescent Optic, Rainbow, Morning-glory* and *Gladiola*.

Red Wing Potteries Inc. United States pottery, active at Red Wing (Minnesota) between 1877 and 1967, specialised in the serial production of household ware, table services and art pottery, featuring plain, strict forms and usually adorned with stylised plant patterns.

Reed, Henry Gooding (1810–1901). United States metal-processing expert, in 1834, with three partners, he took over a small plant in Massachusetts specialising in the production of Britannia metal articles, that in 1840 took the name Reed & Burton, becoming very famous for its production of electrolytic-plated objects (between 1850 and 1860) and subsequently of pieces in solid silver; the models imitated refer prevailingly to the production of the contemporary English manufactories, in particular → Elkington. The company is still in business.

Rhead, Charlotte (1885–1947). English pottery decorator, coming from a very well-known family of pottery decorators from Burslem, she worked in decorating jars, vases, ornamental dishes and *cachepots*, generally on cream-coloured, blue or white grounds, featuring plant patterns (thistle flowers, roses, pomegranates, persimmons) rendered in keeping with naturalist formulas, in some instances gracefully stylised.

Richard-Ginori. Italian majolica and porcelain manufactory, active since 1896. It sprung up as an extension of the Richard factory, erected in Milan in 1840 by taking over the San Cristoforo laboratory of the Tinelli brothers, transformed in 1873 by Giulio Richard in the Società Ceramica Richard, specialised in the production of table and useful ware. It was his son, Augusto, in 1896, who associated the firm with the old Ginori porcelain factory, active at Doccia since 1737, thus creating the Società Ceramica Richard-Ginori, that took over three other plants: the San Michele and the Santa Marta earthenware manufactories (both in Pisa) and the Mondovì pottery, having a long-established tradition in producing household ware. For the direction of the Doccia porcelain manufactory, Augusto Richard elected Luigi Tazzini, who strived toward a substantial industrial renovation of the firm and an updating of production in strictly → liberty terms, which was to allow the new company to triumph at the exhibitions of Turin (1898 and 1902), Milan (1903 and 1906) and Bologna (1907). The R.-G. underwent a period of exceptional creative and technical renewal between 1923 and 1930, the years during which the architect Gio → Ponti was its art director. The countless letters (conserved in the archives of the Museum of Doccia) Ponti sent from the Milanese San Cristoforo manufactory and from his own office defined an organic, boundless creative line, a heed for problems of marketing and technical innovations, a constant control — even from afar — exercised on his collaborators, master potters, modellers and decorators. The production of porcelains, in small series of very fine quality, is perhaps one of the most fascinating and accomplished of Ponti's creations and of Milanese → deco style, among the most connotated and connotating of a time of intense cultural and artistic discussion, evidence of the relationship, often problematic, between industry and craftsmanship. Ponti did not just design updated series of pieces for the Richard-Ginori production, concurrently developing new graphic strategies for advertising the manufactory, but extracted from the classical and pre-classical tradition extremely modern archaic forms adaptable to contemporary living spaces: the majolica jar with a triple circle in relief and decorated with spurs appears drawn from Cretan jars, while the pictorial decoration, the so-called *Archaeological Promenade*, is a clever *mélange* of Roman candelabras, obelisks, amphoras, dancing *putti*, fluttering fabrics, on a background of geometric designs that looks like a mysterious hieroglyphic writing. The success of Richard-Ginori products, displayed with great acclaim in Paris in 1925, as well as in the three Monza Biennales (1923, 1925, 1927) and the

Venice Biennale in 1928, related to furnishing articles and sculptures in white and polychrome porcelain, along with dishes, amphoras, boxes, statuettes, jars, arranged in different families that usually appeared in the trademark: *Pellegrino stanco, Gentilesco, Doccia, San Cristoforo, Tre Fiori, Pisa, Ermione, Maiolica, Ruresco, Velasca, Aretium, Augusta Cuore* and *Mondovi*. The titles of each series, within which appeared pieces of different sizes and uses, were conceived by Ponti with the explicit intent to suggest a fabled antiquity blended with utterly contemporary models and shapes, for which the iconographic sources and cultivated quotations were boundless; yet their unquestionable elegance and their still explicit and extraordinary modernism were precisely justified by that graceful irony, that delicate cynicism, that sought-after, opulent chromatic distinction that are the most original distinguishing features of deco taste. The large *cistes* fashioned between 1928 and 1930 by Libero Andreotti, in navy porcelain with gilt agate point decorations, are the most striking examples of Ponti's production, that always availed of outstanding modellers and decorators such as Italo Griselli (modeller), Elena Diana (agate point decorator), Radames Brettoni, Giuseppe Sciolli (author of one-offs in gres for San Cristoforo) and especially Giovanni → Gariboldi (who replaced Ponti at the beginning of the 1930s), Alfredo Brown (author of soft porcelain pieces in black and gold *biscuit* and *céladon*) and Fausto Melotti (*Babbuino*, in *céladon*, dated 1930). *(Pls 80, 85 and 86)*

Richardson A.G. English pottery, active at Tunstall by 1915 and taken over by → Wedgwood in 1974, known for an abundant production of tableware: *Crown Ducal* (since 1930), usually a cream-coloured ground with floral adornments (navy and/or red) on the rim, and *Chintzware Tray* (since 1935), whose fastuous floral ornamentations in the naturalist vein recall the contemporary production of country-style printed cottons.

Richardson Henry G. & Sons Ltd. English glassworks active at → Stourbridge, known for having been the first in Great Britain to make → iridescent glass. In 1830 it was taken over by Thomas → Webb & Sons.

Richardson W.H.B. & J. English glassworks taken over in 1830 by Thomas → Webb, that in turn sold to a Richardson heir the White House Glass Works laboratory in 1842, then taking its definitive name. Active in the manufacturing of → milk glass, on which then painted, printed or gilt ornamentations representing views and landscapes were executed, the firm exhibited several exemplars of its production in London in 1851 and 1857; subsequently Benjamin Richardson obtained the patent for making moulded and etched glass with some new equipment. Conspicuous among the designers for the manufactory were Philip → Pargeter and John → Northwood.

Ricketts Henry & Co. English glassworks sprung from the merging of the Phoenix glassworks, active since 1780 at Bristol in the production of quality cut glass, and the Soapboiler's Glasshouse, in Bristol as well, specialised in making bottles; it was in business until 1923.

Ridgways. English pottery, active at Shelton (Staffordshire) since 1838, taken over in 1964 by the Royal Doulton Tableware Group, for the production of household tableware (especially plates and tea and coffee sets) decorated with landscapes and scenes of rustic life framed with flowers.

Rie, Lucie (b. 1902). Austrian pottery designer, after attending the Kunstgewerbeschule of Vienna, in 1939 she moved to Great Britain, where she came under the influence of Bernard H. → Leach. She is renowned for her production of delightful items in cream-coloured, thin porcelain, and coated with a raw glaze, but above all for vases and gres tableware featuring rather simple, linear forms and decorations.

Riedel. Bohemian glassmaker dynasty, involving Josef (active from 1830 to 1848), famous for using uranium to obtain a green or yellow fluorescent glass (dubbed *Annagrün* or *Annagelb*, for his wife's name); Franz Anton (1786–1844), glass etcher, active with his own laboratory in an openly Biedermeier style; his nephew, Josef (1816–94), who founded a glassworks in Bohemia where he made articles that were then given to decorators and jewellers of different laboratories, and in 1887 took over the important → Harrachov glassworks (active since 1712), known for its luxury production intended for export; last Claus Josef (b. 1925), who designed glass for the Austrian Tiroler Glashütte manufactory of Kufstein.

Riemerschmid, Richard (1868–1957). German architect and designer, founder in 1897 of the Vereinigte Werkstätte für Kunst im Handwerk in

Richard Riemerschmid, rug, wool, chenille and linen, 1904. Dresden, Kunstgewerbemuseum

Munich, was one of the first designers involved in mass market industrial production. He designed cutlery, glass articles, lighting fixtures and wood furnishings, first inspired by the purest forms of international modernism, always with a particular heed for the functional: worth mentioning is his 1899 armchair (New York, Museum of Modern Art), still sold today. In 1905 he created a series of furnishings for industrial production with the Deutsche Werkstätten at Hellerau, near Dresden; later he was appointed director of the Kunstgewerbeschule of Munich (1914–24) and the Cologne Werkschulen (after 1926).

Reissner & Kessel. Bohemian porcelain manufactory active since 1892, specialising in the production of earthenware vases featuring imaginative → art nouveau shapes adorned with stylised floristic motifs; it is known for its execution of porcelain ornamental statuettes.

Riihimaki. Finnish glassworks founded in 1910 and subsequently named Riihimaen Lasi Oy. Starting off as a factory for useful glassware and window glass, as of 1928 it launched a production of art glass, comprising the celebrated *koralli* and *kubiikki*. Conspicuous among the designers who worked for the manufactory were Arrtu Brommer, Gunnel Nyman and Henry Ericsson, connected with the so-called Swedish functional style.

Rippl-Rónai, Jozsef (1861–1927). Hungarian pottery decorator, after studying in Munich he moved to Paris in 1887, where he was in touch with the Nabis and → art nouveau; back in Hungary, although mainly devoting himself to painting, he was active as a decorator at the → Zsolnay pottery of Pécs, executed book bindings and tapestries, and designed furnishings and interior decorations that in the early 1920s inclined to a manner explicitly aimed at reviving forms and decorations of Magyar folklore.

Rizzarda, Carlo (1883–1931). Italian iron-work master, pupil of Alessandro → Mazzucotelli at Milan, he soon became known as one of the most important masters in the processing of art ironwork, attaining the level of the Matteuccis of Faenza, the Gerardis of Rome and → Bellotto of Venice. He made gates, gratings, lights and lamps, flower vases and household furnishings in a taste that ranged from a late- → liberty naturalist idiom to the sleeker, more refined → deco manner. In 1939 at Feltre, his native town, his own museum with the collection of art works and his creative repertory was opened.

Carlo Rizzarda, fountain with little birds, wrought iron, ca. 1925. Genoa, Wolfsonian Foundation

Robineau, Adelaide Alsop (1865–1929). United States pottery decorator, she began her career painting naturalist themes on porcelains; in 1899 she married Samuel E. Robineau and took over the *China Decorator* review, that right away became *Keramic Studio* and was published at Syracuse (New York).

Attracted to imported French contemporary pottery, she turned with determination to → art nouveau strains, executing, as of 1903, porcelain vases, also in large dimensions, with etched decorations under crystalline glazes. After 1911, the year in which she won flattering appreciation in Turin, presenting a repertory of nearly fifty pieces, her interests shifted to decorative modes inspired by Chinese art and Maya civilisation. Many of her creations are conserved at the Everson Museum of Art in Syracuse.

Robinson, Gerard (1834–91). English carver and cabinet-maker specialised in carving oak furniture, literally covering them with figured scenes all drawn from the Romantic literary repertory. Highly admired at the world fairs, his anti-modern furniture coincided perfectly with the revivalist, neo-gothicising taste that was highly appreciated throughout Queen Victoria's lengthy reign.

Robinson-Ransbottom. United States pottery, opened at Roseville (Ohio) in 1901 and still active in the production of pots and table and kitchen ware adorned with geometric patterns and *flambé* colours.

Rockingham ware. United States definition relating to nineteenth-century tableware generally coated with a crackled brown glaze.

Rogers, John (1829–1904). United States sculptor; his work inspired a New York manufactory for the production, in the years 1859–93, of plaster figures dubbed *Rogers Groups*, reproducing subjects inspired by a sugary, sentimental interpretation of the American Civil War, becoming enormously popular throughout the entire nineteenth century for decorating drawing-rooms.

Rohlfs, Charles (1853–1936). United States designer, a leading figure in the American → Arts & Crafts group, he began his career designing cast-iron stoves; in 1890 he initiated, in his own laboratory at Buffalo, a production of furnishings made of solid oak, with apparent joints and a few abstract ornaments in the modernist style, that were quite well-received in a number of international events (Buffalo, 1901; Turin, 1902; St. Louis, 1904).

Rometti. Italian pottery founded at Umbertide in 1927 by Settimio and Aspromonte Rometti and still active today. From the start it was directed by Dante Baldelli, trained in Rome as a sculptor, who pro-

moted the factory's production on the occasion of the most important national and international decorative arts exhibitions; in 1936 the firm took the trademark "S.A.C.R.U". (Società Anonima Ceramiche Rometti, Umbertide). Production focused on furnishings and useful ware characterised by ultra-modern forms and attuned to international → deco taste, but adorned with designs strongly influenced by the themes and modes of futurist art, in particular by Depero and Balla, with very bright colours, hand-painted or air-brushed. In the late 1930s began the production of vases and tableware inspired by purely geometric Novecento forms, with a wide use of red, green and greenish tints. *(Pl. 83)*

Rontjen van Beek, Jan (b. 1899). Potter born in Denmark but always active in Germany, by the 1920s he launched a production of gres articles featuring refined glazes. He was appointed director of the Hochschule für angewandte Kunst in Berlin in 1945.

Rookwood. United States pottery opened by Maria Nichols Storer at Cincinnati (Ohio) in 1880 (and active up to 1967), it is considered one of the most important producers of art pottery in America. Arisen as a crafts studio where articles were fired and then decorated by the Women's Pottery Club (at least until 1883), it became a commercial firm with the arrival of the decorator Albert R. Valentien (1862–1925). Taken over in 1890 by William Watts Taylor, the manufactory specialised in producing pitchers and ornamental vases whose forms were inspired by Eastern culture and characterised by superb green or brown glazes, but above all the crystalline one known as "tiger's eye", used after 1884. The decorative motifs reveal a striking Japanese influence, but also refer to the representation of themes linked up with American culture (for instance chiefs of Indian tribes). Generally each piece bears the initials of the decorator and a symbol referring to the year it was made. *(Pls 88, 89 and 92)*

Rörstrand. Swedish pottery active near Stockholm in 1725 and specialised in the production of English-tradition cream-coloured earthenware, that lasted well into the nineteenth century, and, between 1830 and 1840, of tableware with English-style landscapes printed in black; beginning in 1857 instead it marketed ash-bone porcelain tableware, and by 1870–1880 hard paste porcelain. Initially known for the use of period styles and drawn from the English tradition, the manufactory went through a radical change as of 1895, when the art direction was taken over by Alf Wallender (1862–1914), who supplied models for the forms and decorations of one of the most fascinating → art nouveau productions in Europe: vases with relief decorations, featuring underglaze leaves and flowers in dim colours on designs by Nils Erik Lundström, Anna Katarina Boberg and Karl Lidnström, but also ornamental statuettes representing animals. In 1932 the manufactory transferred to Lidkoping, where it is still active, later specialising in the production of tableware — always of excellent quality — in different materials (earthenware, porcelain, gres), sometimes on designs by Edward → Hald, who worked at the same time for the → Orrefors glassworks. *(Pl. 93)*

Rosati, Roberto (1890–1949). Italian potter, devoted pupil of Duilio → Cambellotti, he began working on his own in 1910; with Giuseppe Sprovieri he opened a pottery at Treia (Lazio), and in 1914 presented several pieces of high-fired earthenware in Rome. After exhibiting large vases in the Roman section of the first Monza Biennale in 1923, he began a collaboration with Fiamma, Ferruccio Palazzi's Roman furnace, that lasted about ten years. His style is easy to identify owing to his use of dots to outline and rhythm forms, these usually being zoomorphic. Some vases were signed in full, others simply with the initials "RR" and others marked "Fiamma" or "Palazzi". *(Pl. 91)*

Rosenthal. German porcelain manufactory opened in 1879 at Selb, in Bavaria, by Philip Rosenthal (1855–1937), and still in business. Its first successes on the market in the early twentieth century were owed to two typologies of very well-made, attractively decorated products: statuettes of various sizes, polychrome or in two colours, representing female nudes or women in modern attire or in bathing-suits (but mythological or allegorical scenes as well, with explicitly modern characters) and table services with forms highly simplified compared to → art nouveau models. Thus were created the *Darmstadt* service (1905), a clear tribute to the secessionist artists' colony led by the Viennese → Olbrich, and the *Donatello* service (1907), executed in white porcelain or decorated with an underglaze fruit-laden branch. At the same time series inspired by eighteenth-century factories' designs were also marketed; in the 1920s and early 1930s, with the art direction of Gerhard Schliepstein, the register changed, inclining toward white porcelain, modelled in the shape of female heads and figures,

Algot Eriksson (for Rörstrand), porcelain vase mounted in silver in Paris by E. Lefèbvre, ca. 1900. Berlin, Bröhan-Museum

dedicated to the fashionable female typology: close-clinging clothes, masculine hairstyles, almond-shaped eyes and pointed faces, and rhythmic attitudes recalling Egyptian sculptures. After the Second World War the manufactory entirely renovated its repertory by calling on important designers, including Löwy and Wirkkala. *(Pl. 95)*

Rose-teinte. Type of glass similar to → *amberina*, with a pale pink, slightly amber colouring, created by the → Baccarat factory in 1916 and produced again in 1940.

Roseville. United States pottery, active in Ohio from 1890 to 1954 for the production of art pottery, flower vases and *cache-pots*, first following → art nouveau models, like the *Persian Flower Bowl*, in 1916, or else decorated by the sole use of colour, like the *Cornelian Vase*, executed by Henry Rhead in 1910. Later on the *Pinecone* series of the 1930s and the *Wincraft* series of the 1940s would be highly popular.

Rouge flambé. Glass technique developed by Frederick → Carder for the → Steuben Glass Works in 1916–17 and in emulation of the Chinese vases of the so-called "Pink family": the glass is permeated with cadmium and selenium sulphates that produce shades ranging from bright red to orange and to pink coral, while the surface remains glossy, but not iridescent.

Rousseau, François-Eugène (1827–91). French glass and pottery decorator; fascinated by Japanese art, he executed a series of pieces in the most exquisite *japonaiserie* manner, creating with glass — nearly always champagne-coloured — imitations of jade, but also pieces with inlays of polychrome glass and decorative effects produced by the use of metal oxides, then coated in colourless glass and wheel-finished. Rousseau made his most celebrated works drawing his inspiration from *Raku* pottery: large vases in solid glass ornamented with sprays of colour and → *craquelures*. When he retired in 1885, his laboratory and his models were pursued by his pupil Ernest Baptiste → Léveillé, who signed each piece "Léveillé-Rousseau".

Roux, Alexandre and Frédéric. French cabinet-makers, brothers, active in New York by 1837; in 1857 they founded the Roux & Company, active in the production of period furniture so highly appreciated by the American clientele that they had to import some from France. Between 1840 and 1850 they mainly executed furnishings in the gothic style; then, between 1850 and 1860, they turned to the Elizabethan, rococo and French Mannerist styles; finally, between 1860 and 1870, neo-Greek and "Louis-Seize" prevailed, with inserts of porcelain plates and *ormulu* decorations. The Roux & Company was active until 1881.

Royal Albert. English pottery, founded at Longton in 1896 and taken over in 1972 by the Royal Doulton Group, specialising in the production of tableware, especially tea sets, in the various versions of the *China* décor.

Royal Crown Derby Porcelain. English pottery, founded at Derby in 1877 and taken over by the Royal Doulton Group in 1973, specialising in the production of tea services, trays, dessert dishes and small furnishing sculptures in polychrome porcelain, generally ornamented with naturalist flower bouquets on a white ground and decors inspired by eighteenth-century *chinoiseries*.

Royal Doulton. English pottery, founded in Staffordshire in 1815 and transferred in 1826 to Lambeth (London) under the name Doulton of

Watts, it focused on a varied production of high quality: from tableware (such as dessert plates with marine landscapes painted by J.H. Plant in 1916) to enthralling vases and containers in emulation of Sung and Chang period pottery, executed in the 1920s with a *flambé* glaze technique obtained by high-firing, to typically → deco female figurines or little female nudes in the 1930s manner modelled by the sculptor Gilbert Bayens. In 1956 the plant was dissolved. *(Pl. 97)*

Royal Flemish. Glass technique that entails acid-processing of the surfaces with the introduction of lines of gilt enamel in relief often framing scenes with an Oriental flavour, ducks in flight and abstract designs. The technique was researched by the → Mount Washington Glass Company toward 1890, whereas the patent was granted in 1894 to Albert Steffin, who henceforth signed his pieces "RF".

Rozenburg. Dutch pottery opened near The Hague in 1883 for the production of blue and white majolica in the Delft tradition, yet more known for a series of articles decorated with abstract patterns, executed in 1889 on designs by Theodorus → Colenbrander. Under the direction of J. Juriaan → Kok (from 1894 to 1919) the manufactory underwent radical change, introducing a production of porcelain dubbed "eggshell" and choosing rigorously → art nouveau models, in particular protruding, angular forms of German secessionist origin. Ornamentation, including peacocks and lilies, full-blown poppies and insects, was mostly executed by J. Schellink and R. Sterken. *(Pls 53 and 54)*

Rubian Art Pottery. English pottery, active at Fenton from 1906 to 1933 in the production of vases, bowls, *cache-pots* and toilet articles in a broadly floristic taste.

Rugiadoso (dewy). Type of glass invented by Ercole Barovier for the Vetreria Artistica → Barovier toward 1920, characterised by the presence on the surface of countless glass scales that, once molten, take on the appearance of dewdrops.

Ruhlmann, Jacques-Emile (1879–1933). French designer and furniture-maker, one of the leading personalities of the 1920s in Paris; forming right after the war a partnership with M. Laurent, he created the *Maison de Décoration*, that by 1925 had become the most important in the capital, with laboratories for cabinet-making, tapestries, *japonaiseries*.

Jacques-Emile Ruhlmann, dressing-table, Makassar ebony and ivory, 1918–19

Ruskin Pottery, vase with flambé decoration on a base, ca. 1925

He always selected, for his furnishings featuring refined, precious lines, rare and extremely costly materials (Makassar ebony, ivory, amboina wood), blending them with a special chromatic care, whereby grey was always combined with silver and gold with black. Often inspired by rococo models, Ruhlmann designed sideboards, coffee tables and writing-desks featuring sinuous legs, slightly curved and ending in silver points, whereas his armchairs and couches related to Empire style; all of his articles are always marked, as in the eighteenth-century tradition. Several important pieces of his production are conserved in Paris, Musée du Louvre and Musée des Arts Décoratifs, and in London, Victoria and Albert Museum.

Ruskin Pottery. English pottery, active at Birmingham from 1898 to 1935 in the production of very graceful vases inspired by Japanese models with *flambé* colourings ranging from blue to ruby red, especially during the period from 1920 to 1930; in the first two decades of the century, instead, its source of inspiration, besides Japanese culture, was Chinese. The 1910s was the period for several pottery plaques and items mounted in silver as brooches or pendents for necklaces.

Russell, Gordon (1892–1980). English designer, linked up with → Arts & Crafts, in 1925 he began designing furniture of extreme simplicity compared to the models of the past, and in 1930 he introduced a decidedly modern programme intended for industrial production. Russell was the inventor of the *Murphy* radio sets (1930), the first of their kind; in 1939 he opened a group of shops where he also sold → Thonet furniture, → plywood chairs by Aalto, pottery by → Leach and textiles by the → Edinburgh Weavers.

S

Sabino, Marius Ernest (1878–1961). French glass designer, in 1923 he opened his own workshop where he made a series of table glassware, automobile radiator cowlings and decorative articles in opalescent glass comparable to René → Lalique's. Each piece was stamped with his full name or the capital initial S, the rest being etched in italics. The laboratory closed down in 1939.

S.A.I.A.R. (Società Anonima Industrie Artistiche Riunite) Ferro Toso. Italian glassworks sprung from the transformation of the Ferro Toso & C. manufactory, founded in 1902, transferred from Venice to Naples during World War I under the trademark Vitrum S.A.I.A.R. Ferro Toso, and finally restored to Venice right after the war under its definitive name. Active in the production of lighting fixtures and furnishing glass, the factory called upon the collaboration of a number of designers, to whom are owed outstanding pieces like traditional blown glass then etched by → S.A.L.I.R., blown glass animals and vases by Guido → Balsamo Stella that were acclaimed at the first Milan Triennale in 1930, Novecento monochromes by Anita Antoniazzi and Vittorio Donà, and clear vases with → *murrines* by Anna Akerdhal. In 1933 the factory was taken over by the Toso brothers, Artemio, Decio and Mario, and in 1936 merged with the → Barovier manufactory, creating in 1939 the Barovier Toso & C., which in 1942 became Barovier & Toso, its current name. *(Pl. 96)*

Saint-Amand-les-Eaux. French pottery founded in 1781 and dissolved in 1882; after the Revolution it began producing counterfeit → Sèvres porcelains.

Saint-Louis. French glassworks, called Compagnie de Verrerie et Cristallerie de Saint-Louis, founded in 1767, it created a splendid kind of crystal in 1782, widely imitated by the English. Having become one of the leading French manufactories producing table glassware of an unmistakable quality, in 1839 it also began turning out coloured glass items and, subsequently, → paperweights in *filigree* or → *millefiori* glass. Located at Munzthal, in Alsace-Lorraine, the manufactory belonged to German territory from 1871 to 1918, and the articles were marked "Saint-Louis-Munzthal", "Arsale" or "Arsal", or even "D'Argental". Working in collaboration with the → Baccarat manufactory since 1825, by the mid-nineteenth century the plant began producing → *opaline* glass and wheel- and → acid etched items with landscapes and flower arrangements. The manufactory is still running.

Saint Petersburg. Russian imperial glassworks founded by Peter I, it focused on the production of huge chandeliers and crystals for the Court and the aristocracy. During the nineteenth century, it manufactured drinking services in colourless glass decorated with etchings and enamels reproducing mainly the two-headed eagle and the Czar's initials, but also enamelled glass or glass coated with two or three colours. In 1890 the manufactory was taken over by the Imperial Porcelain Factory, until it wound down in 1917.

Sala, Jean (b. 1895). Spanish glassmaker, son of the master glassmaker Dominique, he settled in Paris; for his own articles he used a blue-green material, flawed, and with many cased air bubbles. Of great significance the series of fishes executed for the aquarium of the Principality of Monaco.

Salem China Company. United States pottery, active in Ohio from 1898 up until 1960, specialised in the production of semi-porcelain household ware on a white ground with polychrome, country-style floristic decorations.

S.A.L.I.R. (Studio Ars Labor Industrie Riunite). Glass decoration laboratory opened at Murano in 1923 by Guglielmo Barbini, Giuseppe D'Alpaos, Gino Francesconi (decorators already working in the grinding unit of the Cristalleria Franchetti) and Decio Toso, where collaborators were Guido → Balsamo Stella from 1926 to 1931, the Bo-

Guido Balsamo Stella (for S.A.L.I.R.), vase with side handles, blown glass (the etched decoration figures women on stairs), 1930. Murano, Museo Vetrario

Salviati, vase, blown glass and glass paste, 1915

hemian Franz Pelzel from 1926 to 1968; during the 1930s it availed of the precious creative support of artists and designers such as Vittorio → Zecchin, Pietro Fornasetti and Gio → Ponti. The manufactory, still active, from the start focused on variations of etching techniques (wheel, sandblast, diamond-point), executing some of the most enchanting pieces in → deco and Novecento style. *(Pl. 11)*

Salviati. Glassworks opened at Murano in 1859 by the Vicentine lawyer Antonio Salviati (1816–90) as Laboratorio d'Arte Musiva Salviati dott. Antonio. In 1866, with the collaboration of Antonio → Barovier, Salviati opened a new glassworks that in 1872, with English sponsorisation, took the name Venice & Murano Glass & Mosaic Company Ltd. and specialised in turning out glass for mosaics, for which it received numerous commissions from Great Britain (Memorial Chapel at the Windsor Castle, altar at Westminster Abbey, 1867) and from Germany (Aachen, Palatine Chapel, 1870–75). In 1877, separating from his two English partners, Salviati founded his own business, called Salviati dott. Antonio, that became one of the most prestigious emblems of Venetian glass production, attending all the turn-of-the-century world fairs, and producing ornamental articles and tableware in coloured, enamelled, gilt and coated glass attuned to the historicist

manner: therefore reviving Renaissance and eighteenth-century specimens, but also imitating antique Roman glass (after 1870) and amphoras in semi-precious stones (with *cornelian* or → *agate* glass) mounted in gilt bronze. The manufactory, taken over by the Camerinos in 1920, is still in business.

Samson, Emile (1837–1913). French porcelain designer, son of the decorator Edmé (1810–90), he is known for the execution of admired romantic scenes and as a specialist in the reproduction of pieces from the most famous eighteenth-century manufactories (from → Sèvres to → Meissen) and of Chinese objects executed for export to Europe: all having such quality and executive delicacy as to be often mistaken for originals. The manufactory he erected at Montreuil is still active today in the sector of the reproduction of eighteenth-century enamels, gilt bronzes, majolicas, porcelain tableware and statuettes. All the pieces coming from the factory bear a trademark referring to the founder's name rendered with a series of variants of the letter "S".

Sandblasting. Glass processing technique that consists of directing onto the glass surface a blast of sand or ground iron, while the reserved parts are coated with a steel or rubber masking or a glaze.

Tried out for the first time in the United States in 1870, it has always been used for large sheets of glass serving for architecture and mass-produced tableware.

Sandoz, Gérard (b. 1902). French goldsmith, known for the creation, in the 1920s, of elegant cigarette-lighters, boxes, cigarette holders, pendents and brooches, articles for which he used precious stones and gold, but mainly enamels and niello work, combining several elements on the metal surface, achieving highly refined effects, close to cubist aesthetics and Léger's painting. The trademark is usually "Gérard Sandoz", in full and in capitals.

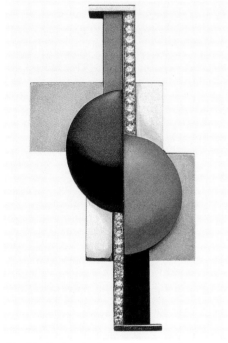

Gérard Sandoz, brooch, platinum, diamonds and jet, 1925

Sarreguemines. French pottery opened in Lorraine in 1778 and managed up to the end of the nineteenth century by the Utzschneider family. From the dawn of the nineteenth century on, it produced tableware with printed English-style landscapes or subjects inspired by sixteenth-century Italian majolicas; in 1867 its presence on the market made it one of the leading industrial porcelain manufactories in France. The region being annexed to Germany after 1870, new premises of the factory were opened at Dijon (1876) and Vitry-le-François (1900).

Sassuolo. Italian pottery founded in 1741, it produced earthenware and tableware up until 1852, the year it was taken over by the Carlo Rubbini manufactory, whose activity was making large majolica stoves, decorative items and tableware.

Satin-glazed. Glass processing technique consisting of soaking the glass article (upon protecting the decoration) in a bath of hydrofluoric acid that only attacks the bottom, producing an opaque surface resembling frost.

Satsuma. Japanese manufactory, founded in the sixteenth century, specialised in the production of terra-cotta vases with utterly simple forms for the domestic market and of showy pottery articles with lead-base glazes for the foreign market. Among the pieces executed since the early nineteenth century conspicuous are the censers, wine bottles, incense-burners, painted with a charming delicacy, and especially the so-called "brocade pottery" (produced continuously since 1870), in cream-coloured majolica with ample crackles decorated in gold and enamels, sometimes artfully aged by smoke, tea or sulphuric acid.

S.A.V. (Società Artistico-Vetraria). Italian glassworks opened as a cooperative at → Altare in 1856 and engaged in hot-blown glass; the subsequent introduction of mechanisation did not prevent the pursuit of crafted glass; authentic masterpieces were made also with off-hand blowing. The factory produced either articles for chemical and pharmaceutical laboratories or bottles, vases and furnishing articles. In 1978 the name changed to S.A.V.A.M., dissolved in 1992.

Savonnerie. French rug manufactory active since 1627, it is held to be one of the most important European factories of knotted rugs; in 1825 it merged with Gobelins, but during the reign of Louis Philippe and Napoleon III the quality of production went into a significant decline, in particular as regards the decorative standard. In the second half of the nineteenth century, owing to excessive costs, it broke off its rug production, replacing it by that of tapestries, which in the early twentieth century was enhanced by pieces drawn from paintings by Monet, Van Gogh, Manet and Odilon Redon.

Scarpa, Carlo (1906–78). Italian architect and designer, he initiated his connection with glass in 1927 at the → Cappellin firm in Murano, leaving it in 1934

Carlo Scarpa, Corroso, *clear glass, 1936–38*

to replace Napoleone → Martinuzzi in Paolo → Venini's manufactory, where he stayed until 1947. In that period he executed a rich series of items using new techniques: *corrosi* (corroded), *velati* (satin-like), *battuti* (stippled), *tessuti* (woven), *granulari* (grained) and → *murrine* glass, displayed in a special room at the 1940 Venice Biennale. In 1942 he presented, again at the Biennale, *pennellati, zigrinati* and *a fili* vases. *(Pls 90 and 117)*

Scharvogel, Jacob Julius (1854–1938). German pottery designer, employee at the → Villeroy & Boch manufactory, he founded his own plant in Munich toward 1898 to produce articles — especially vases — in gres decorated with speckled glazes allowed to drip over the surface. Transferred to Darmstadt in 1904, he ran the Grand Duke's pottery, then returning to Munich in 1913. He was the first German potter to have brought to perfection high-fired colours; by 1900, after putting aside *japonaiserie* décors, he mainly devoted himself to the execution of → liberty-style interior decorating items. His trademark is generally a stylised bird (*vogel*) combined with the initials "S.K.M." (Scharvogel Keramik München).

Scheurich, Paul (1883–1945). German pottery designer, born in New York but trained in Berlin, he

is a well-known interpreter of → deco taste with exemplars of statuettes figuring ballerinas, goddesses and negro figures that he supplied to the porcelain manufactories of → Berlin, → Meissen, → Schwarzburg and → Nymphenburg.

Schmidt, Karl (1873–1948). German furniture-maker, he began his career as a cabinet-maker in the wake of the → Arts & Crafts experiences, and in 1898 opened at Dresden a firm for mass-production of furniture designed by top-ranking architects, among whom Bruno Taut and Bruno → Paul, his purpose being to launch a quality production but at reasonable prices for a wide public.

Schneider. French glassworks erected in 1908 at Epinay-sur-Seine by Charles Schneider (who studied decoration with Emile → Gallé and the → Daum brothers at → Nancy and was influenced by Maurice → Marinot's models), it first engaged in a commercial production that by 1920 was replaced by series of articles still affected by → art nouveau taste, with glass coated in two or three colours, at times etched with hydrofluoric acid, featuring vaguely geometric forms and a rich ornamentation produced by air bubbles and, occasionally, monochrome colourings. The pieces usually bear the signature "Schneider" or else the name "Le Verre Français", or again a filigree design, whereas the superior-quality articles are signed "Charder" and the first and last initials of the creator of the piece. In 1962 the manufactory was transferred to Lorris, in the Loiret.

Schreiberhau. German glassworks active since the fourteenth century; in 1840–42 it was transferred to Marienthal, with a new set-up called Graeflich Schaffgottsche Josephinenhütte, directed by Franz Pohl (1813–84), becoming one of the leading German glassworks, where traditional techniques, even Venetian sixteenth-century ones, blended with the novelties of Biedermeier. Its international reputation was confirmed by the Great London Exhibition of 1851, where monumental ruby-coloured glass vases and → *millefiori* → paperweights were displayed. After 1870 its turn-out began focusing on glazed glass and, between 1880 and 1890, on → iridescent glass, not coming under the influence of → Jugendstil's expressive manner until after 1900. In 1923 it merged with the → Petersdorf and the Neumann & Staebe glassworks. The company, today in Polish territory, is still active.

80. Gio Ponti (for Richard-Ginori, Doccia), formal dish with The gentle activities, *painted porcelain and agate point gold, 1925*

81. *Deco-style bakelite rigid bracelet, United States, ca. 1930*

82. *Truda Adams (for Poole Pottery), vase, polychrome ceramic, ca. 1930*

83. Rometti, centrepiece with Dance of the mermaids, *enamelled and air-brushed pottery, 1934–36*

84. *Gio Ponti (for Venini), glasses, blown glass with canes, 1955*

85. *Gio Ponti (for Richard-Ginori, San Cristoforo),*
Venus, painted pottery, 1926–28

86. Gio Ponti (for Richard-Ginori, Doccia), Hospitality Bowl, *white porcelain and agate point gold, 1924–25*

87. Michael Powolny (for Wiener Werkstätte), Putto with cornucopia, *bronze, ivory and white marble, 1905–10*

88. Harriet Elizabeth Wilcox (for Rookwood), vase with freesias, painted pottery, 1900. London, Victoria and Albert Museum

89. Rookwood, pitcher, polychrome pottery, silver mount, 1895

90. Carlo Scarpa (for M.V.M. Cappellin & Co.), black glass vase with red glass cables and oxidised silver leaf, 1930

92. *Artus van Briggle (for Rookwood),* Loreley *vase, pottery,*
1898. London, Victoria and Albert Museum

93. *Alf Wallender (for Rörstrand), vase with starfish, porcelain,*
1897. Copenhagen, Det Danske Kunstindustrimuseum

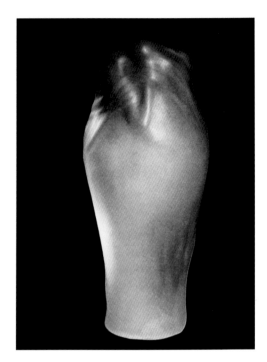

91. *Roberto Rosati (for Fiamma), cache-pot with tigers,*
polychrome majolica, 1925

94. Agathon Léonard (for Sèvres), The game
of the scarf *centrepiece, porcelain, 1898*

95. Gerhard Schliepstein (for Rosenthal), Prince and princess,
porcelain, 1926. Berlin, Bröhan-Museum

96. Anna Akerdbal (for S.A.I.A.R. Ferro Toso), chalice-shaped vase, clear aquamarine tessera glass and crystal with navy glass finishings, 1920

next page
98. S.P.I.C.A., vase with lid, polychrome air-brushed majolica, 1930

Schrezheim. German pottery founded in 1752 in the Württemberg, known for its production of monumental altars and sculptures in polychrome majolica, tableware, with original soup tureens shaped like animal heads and vegetables, of tiles imitating paintings with spiralled frames. Decorations for the oldest pieces were high-fired, and glazed for the more recent ones. The manufactory kept up the same production until 1872.

Schwarzburg. German porcelain manufactory opened in 1908 by Max Adolf Pfeiffer under the name Schwarzburger Werkstätte für Porzellankunst, specialised in the production of small statues, usually depicting Russian peasants. The original drawings for the statues were by Ernst Barlach (1870–1938), who always planned them in white, and then by other designers such as Otto Thieme and Paul → Scheurich, theirs sometimes featuring enamelled or underglaze colours. The laboratory merged with the Volkstedt factory in 1913.

Seguso, Archimede (b. 1909). Italian glassmaker active since the 1920s; of great significance are the polychrome groups of the years 1930–35, the vases *a rete, ad anelli, a piuma, a nastro, a merletto*, the animals in *bulicante* glass and sculptures in solid glass.

Seguso Vetri d'Arte. Italian glassworks, formerly Vetreria e Soffieria Barovier Seguso Ferro founded in 1933 under the art direction of the painter Vittorio → Zecchin, replaced in 1834 by Flavio → Poli who, with the change of name to the present one (1937), also became a partner. The manufactory's production comprised thick glass sculptures and animals, frequently adorned with a regular pattern of air bubbles or else with surfaces corroded by hydrofluoric acid. Poli addressed particular attention to the invention of new forms, by the use of → *corroded* glass and so-called *bulicante* glass. The factory is still in business.

Seignouret, François (1768 - post 1853). French cabinet-maker and furniture-maker, he settled in New Orleans, opening a laboratory for turning out and marketing solid wood furniture covered with carvings in a neo-rococo style taken to extremes; notwithstanding his period furnishings, like those by Prudent → Mallard, were remarkably popular. There is no available information after his return to France in 1853.

Serrurier Bovy, Gustave (1858–1910). Belgian designer formed by → art nouveau, active at Liege. During a trip to London, in 1884, he was very impressed by → Arts & Crafts products, but once back home he began simplifying the lines of the furniture and the character of the furnishings in a manner that was definitely more geometric than Victor → Horta's creations.

Seto. Japanese pottery active in the region of Nagoya by the ninth century, whose most famous products are gres wares for the tea ceremony, in brown or grey decorated with iron or copper oxides and coated with thick feldspath glazes, at times opaque. Nineteenth-century production focused on a great quantity of kitchen earthenware (often decorated with pleasing themes like landscapes, birds and other animals painted with a great sense of freedom in underglaze black, brown or navy), and on navy and white porcelain.

Sèvres. French porcelain manufactory active since 1783 and specialised in luxury articles; first erected near the castle of Vincennes, in 1759, after having been raised by the king, it transferred to other premises. The factory trademark, until 1793, was the royal monogramme (a crossed double L), and then the monogramme "R.F." (République Française) was adopted. In 1800, under the direction of Alexandre Brogniart (1770–1847), it interrupted the production of soft porcelain, too costly, researching new techniques for the preparation of hard paste porcelain and new pigments allowing the execution of decorations similar to those of oil painting. Napoleonic commissions, the bent for spherical and cylindrical forms, the echoes of classicism and Egyptian civilisation constituted a repertory of Empire style, imitated by nearly all the other European porcelain manufactories. The factory was re-organised in 1848 and, renouncing to the imitation of painting, turned to a lighter, more delicate adornment that could enhance the aesthetic values of the porcelain paste; eighteenth-century specimens were revived, imitating prototypes of the → Meissen manufactory and Chinese "eggshell" porcelain, yet alongside the decoration dubbed *pâte-sur-pâte* developed by M.L. Solon. In 1876 it transferred to the present Saint-Cloud premises and took on as art director the sculptor → Carrier-Belleuse, who provided a stimulus for a highly elaborate production of vases adorned with plastic decorations and Chinese-style tableware decorated with *flambé* glazes; on the

Henri Rapin (for Sèvres), vase, polychrome pottery, 1925. Berlin, Brohän-Museum

Shagreen. Term referring to the skin of a small shark with a slender body and blackish colour, widespread in the Mediterranean and the north Atlantic, that after proper tanning, in particular during the → deco period that appreciated its even texture and fine grain, was glued to furniture and frequently dyed green or occasionally blue.

Shaw & Copestake. English pottery, active at Longton from 1894 to 1928 with, after 1930, the trademark "Various Sylva Ware", it is known for a diversified production of vases and furnishing bowls, small sculptures with animals and table services. The 1930s in particular introduced some vases featuring geometric forms and shaded chromatic decorations, such as the *Diamond Flower Vase*.

Shawnee Pottery Company. United States pottery, active at Zanesville (Ohio) between 1937 and 1961, in the production of containers and flower vases and household ware, usually in a single colour. Renowned is the series, executed in the

other hand, the influence of Far-Eastern cultures, in particular Japanese, can be discerned in a number of pieces created by Félix → Bracquemond and Albert-Louis → Dammouse. When the potter Joseph Théodore → Deck became art director in 1887, the productive cycle admitted new materials, like soft-paste porcelain and gres for the execution of decorative architectural elements. Toward the 1890s the renovatory → art nouveau wave also swept over the ancient manufactory, that attended the Paris 1900 exhibition with a rich series of products in the modern taste, including the well-known series of twelve small statues of dancing girls fashioned by Agathon Léonard. The change in taste brought about by → deco style in the early 1920s also influenced the factory, particularly receptive to the novelties and demands of the market: in fact it commissioned of cabinet-makers like → Ruhlmann a series of designs for decorative articles. However, the current production that lasted throughout the twentieth century, and even today, was committed to copies and simplified revivals of eighteenth-century models. The manufactory, since its foundation, has always carefully marked every single piece produced, except for the *biscuit* figurines that instead were only signed after 1860. *(Pls 94 and 105)*

Jean-Michel Frank, two-door cabinet, wood and shagreen, 1925–28

1940s, of vases adorned with animal figures in relief and dazzling, monochrome glazes.

Shelley Potteries. English pottery, founded at Longton in 1853 and taken over by the Royal Doulton Group in 1972, for the production of a variety of articles: decorative little statues inspired by Mabel Lucie Atwell's designs with children as subjects (1920s), and the so-called *Shelley Girls* (one of the most famous series of the manufactory after the 1930s), tableware and tea sets beholden to the octogonal forms of the "Queen Anne" period, with landscapes (*Sunrise and Tall Trees* service in 1929), with → *cloisonné* ornaments (toward 1930) and floral decorations and gold inside (1930–1933), and finally services linked up with rationalism, such as the *Mode Teaware* (toward 1930) inspired by the Russian constructivists.

Shenango China Company. United States pottery and porcelain manufactory, active at New Castle (Pennsylvania) between 1901 and 1990; particularly conspicuous is its serial production of tableware and furnishing articles for hotels and restaurants, adorned with white or light green flower patterns imitating *céladon* porcelain.

Shorter & Son. English pottery founded at Stoke (Staffordshire) in 1878 and taken over by the Devon Works Company in 1964; it produced kitchen and table ware, either adorned with geometric motifs recalling American Indian terra cottas on ochre, white or green grounds, or influenced by the typical 1930s' fondness for techtonic and ultra-modern forms (*Thisbe Vase*, a green, spiralled vase belonging to a series imitating geometric solids) and by the link-up with the exotic mood (*Stag Ware Vase*, from the mid-1930s, with sketchy naturalist motifs and in low-relief on the surfaces).

Silk glass. Type of glass experimented by Frederick → Carder for the → Steuben Glass Works toward 1903 and produced until 1918; it is a lead glass with a surface that feels silky and is made iridescent by spraying lead chloride on the article during firing. The pieces are generally finished with an aquamarine ring on the rim and decorated with beading, filaments or etching.

Silver nickel. Metal alloy made of copper, nickel and zinc, whose colour varies from yellow to silver depending on the percentages of the materials. Ir is used for the creation of ornamental items, cutlery and supports for decorative enamels, especially in German and Austrian artisanal workshops at the end of the nineteenth century, and in the early twentieth century for items such as cigarette holders.

Silvered. Glass processing technique conceived in 1849 by F. Hale Thompson of London, working at E. Varnish & Co., who signed several pieces thus processed. In 1855 William Leighton of the → New England Glass Company patented the process that over the next thirty years would be acquired by Belgian, French, English and Italian firms, and called "mercury glass", the technique used for making thermos bottles. The process involves inserting a solution of silver nitrate inside a double-walled glass object, sealing with a glass bubble the entry hole to prevent the metal from oxidising. Sometimes these items are etched or coated with colours through which the silvered layer can be seen.

Silveria. Type of silvered glass formed by two layers of clear glass containing a silver leaf, at times decorated with ribbings or vertical green threads. It is an extremely delicate glass and easily attacked by devitrification (that can also attack the silver leaf), produced toward 1900 by John Northwood II for → Stevens & Williams Ltd., whose articles generally bear the trademark "S & V" followed by "England" or else by a small etched lily.

Silverina. Type of glass invented by Frederick → Carder in 1920 for the → Steuben Glass Works by placing on the bolus mica scales in turn coated in a layer of clear coloured glass, to which are frequently added air bubbles as adornment.

Simm, Anton (1799–1873). Bohemian glass etcher, renowned member of a family of glass etchers active at Jablonec; to him are owed items of high quality and inspired by the Biedermeier style with etched views of cities (Prague, Karlovy Vary and Teplice-Sanov), Italian landscapes, nobiliary coats-of-arms and mythological scenes.

Sinceny. French pottery erected near Laon in 1733, known for its output of tableware painted with *chinoiseries* featuring high-fired colours, and large cider jugs. It turned out the same items until 1864.

Slag glass. Type of glass imitating marble obtained by inserting in the vitreous paste metal bits recovered from furnace residues. Produced in

Great Britain between 1875 and 1890 by several manufactories in the North-East (Henry Greener & Co.; Teams glassworks; → Sowery's Ellison), it was used for inexpensive moulded articles in navy, black or purple.

Slavkov. Bohemian porcelain manufactory active by 1800, where toward the year 1842, under the direction of Georg Lippert, neo-rococo style porcelain began being produced.

Slip. Pottery technique consisting of the application of a fine clay impasto on vases of coarser material so as to make them less porous; it is a kind of → white washing and can be decorated with the graffito technique.

Smith, William. English glassmaker who, after working at length in Birmingham glassworks, moved to the United States and in 1855 was employed at the → Boston and Sandwich Glass Company. Subsequently he opened his own laboratory for gilding and glaze-decorating glass lamps. His sons Henry and Alfred followed their father's career: they worked for the → Mount Washington Glass Company as of 1871, and later founded at New Bedford their own workshop where, on glass executed by other factories, they painted views, flowers, fruit and scenes with an Oriental flavour, marking their pieces with a lion rampant on a shield or else under the name "Smith Bros".

Soho Pottery. English pottery, first active at Tunstall (1901–06) and later at Cobridge (1906–44), that created series of beer beakers, cups, household ware and small coffee cups, the latter in particular featuring, during the 1930s, the language of abstraction. It is still in business.

Sowery's Ellison. English glassworks active in the second half of the nineteenth century at Gateshead-on-Tyne for the industrial production of inexpensive pressed glass, all bearing a trademark featuring a peacock head and sometimes also the registration number of the design utilised. In 1883 it obtained from the → New England Glass Company the patent to produce articles in pressed → amberina glass.

Spangled glass. Type of glass characterised by a layered coating of coloured glass covering the inner, clear body adorned with the insertion of mica scales; created in 1883 by William Leighton Jr., it

was used by → Hobbs Brockunier & Company, sometimes with relief applications of leaves and flowers as well.

S.P.I.C.A. Italian pottery, founded at Albisola Marina in 1927 under the name Società per Industrie Ceramiche Artistiche; the art director between 1929 and 1932 was the Parmesan painter Romano di Massa. The manufactory was in business up to 1955; its production featured primarily vases, amphoras, writing-desk articles, boxes with lids and small furnishing sculptures, all these items presenting broadly deco themes and lines, that in the 1930s tended increasingly to the geometric. The trademark, along with the initials of the name, features an ear of corn. (*Pl. 98*)

Spode. English pottery erected in Staffordshire in 1776 for the production of cream-coloured earthenware, replaced after 1783 by a new turn out of *pearl ware* featuring a pearly gloss, particularly suited as a ground for navy decorations. In 1833 the manufactory was taken over by W.R. Copeland and T. Garrett (today called W.T. Copeland & Sons Ltd.), and among the most conspicuous articles produced after the mid-nineteenth century figured countless statuettes in → *parian ware*, table services adorned with flowers, birds, landscapes, a great deal of common tableware and garden furnishings; all the pieces bear the name of the plant, stamped or painted. The manufactory is still active.

Stabler, Harold (1872–1945). English pottery designer, linked up with the → Arts & Crafts, in his own laboratory at Hammersmith, in collaboration with his wife Phoebe, he made jewellery, pottery statuettes and enamels. He is known for having designed the tiles for the underground station at Saint Paul's Cathedral, tableware then modelled and hand-decorated at the → Poole Pottery (a manufactory of which he was a co-founder in 1921), silver gift items, steel cutlery and porcelain statuettes for the Worcester manufactory.

Staffordshire Potteries. English pottery constituted by a number of potteries active since the seventeenth century and that, faithful to tradition, went on producing throughout the nineteenth century — especially the smaller firms — large quantities of plain-shaped tableware and popular-shaped decorative statuettes to adorn mantlepieces: favourite subjects were dogs, mainly spaniels and poodles, and famous personalities of contemporary Anglo-Saxon history, including Queen Victoria and the North American John Brown, General Gordon and Garibaldi. These articles were produced between 1840 and 1900 with moulds, then brightly coloured and coated with a thin glaze leaving the backs uncoloured.

Staite Murray, William (1881–1962). English pottery designer, engaged as of 1919 in the production of gres items in the Kensington area; so determining was his encounter with the works of Bernard H. → Leach and Shoji Hamada that he was induced to adopt an idiom and executive techniques of clearly Japanese inspiration; this is well exemplified in his large vases, that are astonishingly akin to *Raku* potteries by their ultra-simple decorations featuring etched and/or painted motifs.

Stam, Mart (b. 1899). Dutch designer, inventor of the steel tubular spring chair (designed in 1924 but executed for the first time only in 1926), contemporary of the well-known spring chair by → Mies van der Rohe and borrowed by Marcel → Breuer who, in 1928, tried out his own version of a steel tubular chair (*Wasily* series).

Sterling China Company. United States pottery, active at Wellsville (Ohio) from 1917 to 1975, in particular for the production and supplying of tableware for hotels.

Steuben Glass Works. United States glassworks opened at Corning (New York) in 1903 under the direction of Frederick → Carder, specialising in the production of → *aurene* glass decorative items. Taken over in 1918 by the Corning glassworks, the name "Steuben" was restored in 1913 for a productive unit, directed by Sydney Waugh (1904–63), engaged in the execution of ornamental articles in very thick, wheel-decorated colourless glass; several of these pieces were particularly appreciated when shown at the Paris exhibition of 1937, drawing the attention of some artists (including Matisse), who began supplying it with designs for etchings. *(Pl. 99)*

Steubenville Pottery Company. United States pottery, active in Ohio between 1879 and 1959, mainly in the execution of kitchen ware and toilet articles in pottery imitating granite.

Stevens, Alfred (1817–75). English designer, especially known for the invention of iron-ware stoves and fireplaces decorated with an abundance of greenery, figures and many different architectural motifs in a kind of neo-Renaissance style; his true masterpiece is the furnishing of Dorchester House in London (1858–62, torn down in 1929), where he painted the ceilings and made the mantlepieces.

Steuben Glass Works, glasses and chalices, opalescent and painted glass, 1903–05

Stevens & Williams. English glassworks active in Worcestershire by 1846 with a vast production of cameo glass, etched by John → Northwood and Frederick → Carder, vases with decorations made with silver deposits, tableware adorned with the → *craquelure* technique. The carving unit was at length directed by William Hodgetts (1857–1933), who executed a significant series of floral designs in a naturalist vein; in the 1930s and '40s production focused on vases, cups and useful ware designed by Keith → Murray, in keeping with international modernism's precepts but with → deco and Novecento leanings. The manufactory is still in business.

Stevensgraphs. English manufactory that is at the origin of the term defining figures executed on silk, produced by Thomas Stevens by 1879 on an improved *jacquard* loom; production lasted until 1938, but the factory was bombed out in 1940.

Stickley, Gustav (1857–1942). United States furniture designer, after some experience building chairs and furnishings in different period styles, in 1898 he opened his own firm at Eastwood (New York) named Gustav Stickley Company; during an updating trip to Europe he had the opportunity to meet several designers, including Charles Francis Annesley → Voysey. Turning his back on historicist and → eclectic styles, he engaged in the conception of plain, massive modernist furniture, featuring a moderate use of floral decorations, that he presented at the 1900 Paris exhibition. The following year he coined the expression "Craftsman" to distinguish his own creations from the furniture turned out by his brothers at the L. & J.G. Stickley firm at Fayetteville, and started up publication of the review *The Craftsman*, where he theorised views influenced by William → Morris and Ruskin. His furniture then related to English → Arts & Crafts models: solid forms, oak, highlighted plugs and inlays, undecorated leather or cloth upholstery, and all called → *Mission Furniture*. He published countless catalogues of his production, addressed to a very broad public, and patented an armchair with an adjustable back. Widely imitated also owing to his popularity, he opened premises in New York in 1905, yet that after a decade went bankrupt.

Stoltenberg Lerche, Hans (1867–1920). Designer of Norwegian origin, he was born in Germany, studied in Paris, then settling permanently in Rome, where he became one of the leading figures in Italian → liberty. In 1895 he began exhibiting bronzes and pottery; he furthermore collaborated with the → Toso manufactory with several projects and designs for glass decorations.

Stourbridge. English glassworks active since 1612, that despite their different company identities were known under the name of the region where they were active; they had an impressive development as of 1845, the year the tax on lead-glass was abolished, a circumstance that enabled Stourbridge to compete with Bohemian glassworks. Conspicuous among the items from this part of England are the articles in cameo glass, drinking services, bowls, pitchers, candle-sticks, perfume bottles and dishes in a vast range of colours. In 1851 the Richardson glassworks introduced relief decoration of lead-glass and in 1857 a machine to produce filigree glass according to the Venetian technique; while as of 1880 technological evolution made industrial production of cameo glass possible. The products of the second half of the nineteenth century always responded to a market demand inclined to exoticism and period styles.

Subes, Raymond (1893–1970). French metalwork artist, with → Brandt he is held to be one of the greatest creators of metalwork in France during the prime of → art deco. Responsible for the metalwork production for the Borderel et Robert construction company, he is especially famous for the interior decorating of the transatlantic liner *Normandie*, launched in 1935. Although preferring iron, he occasionally used bronze and copper as well, and in the 1930s he turned to aluminium and oxidised or lacquered metal. He made tables, with wood tops and metal supports, mirrors, lamps, radiators, radiator covers whose models were inspired by nature; by the 1920s he sought more geometric and elegant forms.

Süe, Louis (1875–1968). French architect and designer, an emblematic name of → deco taste in France, in partnership with André Mare (1887–1932), he founded in 1919 the Compagnie des Arts Français Süe et Mare for producing furnishings. The company, that had its peak in the early 1920s (closing down in 1928), pursued a moderate quest for modernism, yet that generally was limited to merely the decorative accents, instead respecting the dictates of tradition, especially the models in "Louis-Philippe" style and neo-classicism, attuned with the like revival → Ruhlmann had introduced. One of the particularities of his furniture was in the supporting elements, usually pro-

Louis Süe, room in the Château de la Foujeraie, Brussels, 1911

truding from the body of the object as if applied from the outside, regardless of whether they were made in wood, bronze, aluminium or other metals. The Compagnie, engaged in the execution of entire ensembles, also produced tapestries, rugs, pottery, metal items, wallpaper, glass and lamps coordinated with the furniture, the latter often connotated by an exuberant decoration in mother-of-pearl, metals, poor lacquers made with cellulose-base paints, gildings, inlays, vein patterns and dazzling glosses.

Sunderland. English potteries, the most renowned of which, Dixon, Austron & Co., active from 1800 to 1865, specialised in the production of large jugs and bowls decorated with pink lustre mottled with white, whereby a marbled effect is obtained; the decorations, always printed, were nearly always exclusively views of the surrounding area: the most frequent was the iron bridge of Sunderland. The items are countersigned with the trademark of the pottery of origin printed on the surface.

Swinnertons. English pottery, active in Staffordshire from 1906 to 1955, especially for tableware and tea sets with Victorian-style decorations, in particular *corbeilles* of roses and wildflowers, on a white ground.

T

Talbert, Bruce James (1838–81). English furnishings designer, after working as planner at the Diverton, Bird & Hull furniture factory (from 1862 to 1865), in 1866 he joined the London Holland & Sons manufactory; he became famous when, in 1867, he was awarded the silver medal in the Paris exhibition, displaying a sideboard and other furnishings in a strict English neo-gothic style, and published in London the book *Gothic Forms Applied to Furniture, Metal Work and Decoration for Domestic Purpose*. His period creations, far simpler and more severe than → Burges' and Pugin's contemporary inventions, featured inlays and low-relief panels that were extremely plain even compared with historicist specimens turned out in France and Germany (for instance the *Pet Sideboard* by the Gillows firm, 1967, London, Victoria and Albert Museum). Toward the 1870s Talbert was drawn to other period styles, but less successfully so; in 1876 he published *Examples of Ancient & Modern Furniture*.

Tams John. English pottery, erected in 1874 at Longton and still in business, renowned especially for a varied output of tableware and furnishing items under the influence of eighteenth-century *chinoiseries*.

Taylor, Howson (1876–1935). English potter, who opened in 1898, near Birmingham, the → Ruskin Pottery, specialising in the production of vases with spare forms and inspired by Chinese pottery, decorated merely with monochrome or speckled or *flambé* glazes, that won it great fame in the period between 1901 and 1914 (some pieces are conserved at the Victoria and Albert Museum in London and at Manchester, Manchester City Art Gallery). The factory was officially dissolved in 1933, although production went on until 1935.

Taylor, Smith & Taylor Company. United States pottery active from 1899 to 1981 at Chester (Virginia) in the production of semi-porcelain dishes, tableware and kitchenware, usually on a cream-coloured ground. Typical of the 1930s was the decoration with black outlined figures on a crème ground.

Teague, Walter Dorwin (1883–1960). United States designer, held to be one of the founders of American design, in 1911 he opened his own graphic design studio in New York; his activity as industry consultant only initiated in 1926 with Eastman Kodak, a company for which he invented in 1933 the *Baby Brownie* photographic camera. The range of his activity was boundless, especially after the crash of 1929 and the subsequent economic upturn, comprising furniture (he patented a chair in aluminium and Lucite, a transparent acrylic resin), interiors of railway cars and aircrafts (Boeing 707), hospital fixtures and glass articles for Corning glassworks, and the ten thousand service stations created for Texaco in the mid-1930s. He summed up his thoughts and fundamentals of his style in *Design this Day*, published in 1940.

Templier, Raymond (1891–1968). French goldsmith, celebrated jeweller of the luxury Parisian market (beginning with his grandfather's activity since 1849), he made strictly geometric brooches, earrings, pendents and bracelets, and after 1929 inspired by Manhattan skyscrapers. In his jewellery, where the influence of Georges → Fouquet's taste is obvious, the contrast between the shiny and dull surfaces and the vertical and circular lines created aesthetic effects of an impressive quality, emphasised by the use of white gold and platinum with *pavés* of diamonds and black enamels. In 1929 he called in as designer Marcel Pecheron, who remained with the firm (dissolved in 1965) for thirty years.

Thayaht, Ernesto Michahelles (1893–1959). United States designer, after studying painting and sculpture in Florence, Paris and the United States and entertaining close contacts with the futurist milieu, in the very early 1920s he began creating designs for furnishings, metal-wrought items, fabrics and pottery, working at the same time as a graphic artist for the review *Vogue* in New York and as a textile designer for the Paris couture house Vionnet. After following at first a futurist manner, he later firmly embraced → deco taste; he exhibited at the

1923 Monza Biennale and founded in 1939 the "Ars Fiorentina" firm, with the explicit aim of buoying up the Italian decorative arts production and artistic craftsmanship.

Thesmar, André-Fernand (1843–1912). French enamel artist, after working in a textile factory, then at the → Aubusson manufactories and a foundry at Barbédienne, toward 1872 he opened his own laboratory at Neuilly, specialising in works with → *cloisonné* enamels, that later on he was to execute on → Sèvres porcelain as well. After winning admiration in international exhibitions, in 1888 he began making his first items in *plique à jour* enamel, later patenting a clear enamel on metal, thereby becoming one of the major exponents of → art nouveau taste.

Thonet, Michael (1796–1871). German cabinetmaker, renowned for having brought to perfection and made the finest use of the technique of → curved wood in furniture construction and for creating an industrial furniture production. Thonet began his career in 1819 as an inlayer specialised in geometric patterns, and in 1830 made his first experiments in steam-curving of beech wood — or boiling it in a mixture of water and glue — forming long, curved boards to be used for chair frames. The possibility of making the back legs and the back out of a single board permanently eliminated hand-crafted joints, while the seat was made of woven narrow strips of rattan bark (at the time dubbed Vienna straw). Turning his back on the usual ornamentation, in 1859 he patented the so-called *Chair no. 14*, an exceptional industrial prototype, since it consisted of six components that could be packed, shipped and mounted using merely ten screws. The very low cost of the piece, the facility of transportation and its sober elegance imposed Thonet's success; in 1841 he had his method patented also in France, Great Britain and Belgium. The Prince of Metternich persuaded him to leave Germany and settle in Vienna, where he first formed a partnership with the furniture-maker Carl Leistler, known for his neo-rococo furnishings; it was not until 1849 that he was able to form, with his four sons, the Gebrüder Thonet company; in 1850 he patented *Chair no. 4*, that was to become the prototype for all the café chairs in Central Europe and France, and is still being produced today (one of the first specimens, commissioned by the Café Daum, is at the Vienna Museum of Decorative Arts); a while later he designed the small armchair *B9*, whose utter modernism anticipated →

Hoffmann's and → Moser's furniture. His clamorous success inspired him, between 1850 and 1860, to open other factories in the Hungarian and Moravian beech forests and, in the following decade, a great number of stores all over Europe (Brussels, Milan, Rome, Marseilles, Barcelona, Madrid, Moscow, Odessa, Petersburg) and in the United States (Chicago and New York). At his death, his sons maintained the business with their father's models: the sole novelty being, in 1888, the patent for a folding chair for theatres. Right after the war, the main factory transferred to Brno and in 1923 the manufactory merged with Mundus; still very active in Austria, the company keeps on producing its own classical repertory alongside excellent modern models, conspicuous among them being models designed by → Breuer.

Thorn-Prikker, Jan (1868–1932). Dutch painter and graphic artist, trained at the Academy of Fine Arts of The Hague, he moved to Germany where he began his artistic career, working in particular for church interiors, all the while teaching at Munich, Dusseldorf and Cologne. He executed, aside from frescoes and mural paintings, numerous stained-glass windows, mosaics and works in → *eglomisé glass*.

Tiffany, Charles Louis (1812–1902). United States goldsmith, highly skilled producer and tradesman rather than craftsman, he began his career in 1837, as Tiffany, Young & Ellis, selling luxury items in New York, and opening in 1848 a workshop for the creation of jewellery with a branch in Paris. Having become in 1853 the sole owner of the company, he decided to measure himself with a vaster public, taking part in a number of world fairs (he won first prize for silverware in the 1867 Paris exhibition) and opening a second branch in London. Between 1890 and 1900 he was the most famous and acclaimed United States jeweller, and the names of nearly all the ruling dynasties figured on the list of his customers; however in those same years he adopted electroplating, a technology offering him a larger production for a huge public of average buyers. His pieces, careful to follow the newest trends, ranged from the revival of all the period styles, from Greek antiquity to Empire, French rococo to exotic models, Moghul jewellery to Central-American goldwork, even adjusting to the vocabulary of → art nouveau, especially when he began selling glassware and lamps produced by his son Louis Comfort → Tiffany.

*Louis Comfort Tiffany, table-lamp with peacocks and scarabs, favrile glass, bronze and enamels, 1900–02.
Richmond, Virginia Museum of Fine Arts*

Tortoise-shell. Type of glass imitating the shell of a turtle with black, yellow and brown spots cased between two layers of clear glass; created in 1880 by Francis Pohl in Silesia, it was taken up with variants by United States glassworks, in particular by the → Boston and Sandwich Glass Company.

Tosin, Tarcisio. Italian potter active in the Veneto; in 1922 he was called upon to direct the Vicentine manufactory La Freccia, where he produced a series of small pottery sculptures, knick-knacks and bookends, in a popular taste and very bright colours using the air-brush technique under glaze. These items were strongly influenced by the futurist spirit, streamlined and featuring its amusing play of abbreviated forms and sense of dynamism, as in the fish, the elephants and the *Alpinist*, fashioned by Spolverato in the years 1934–36. The factory trademark is a vertical arrow with the initials of the modeller. *(Pl. 100)*

Toso Aureliano Vetri Decorativi. Italian glassworks founded in 1938 by Aureliano Toso; under the artistic direction of Dino → Martens, a Murano painter, interesting series of articles were produced in *zanfirico* glass (presented at the 1940 Venice Biennale). In 1966 Martens was replaced by the designer Gino Poli.

Toso Fratelli. Italian glassworks founded in 1854 by the brothers Liberato, Carlo, Angelo, Ferdinando, Giovanni and Gregorio Toso for the production of household glassware and drug-pots and, toward the end of the century, copies of antique glass. Updating to the new floristic manner, the manufactory introduced chandeliers, *appliques* and → liberty-style furnishing items, often executed with the → *murrine* technique. A remarkable success was obtained by the glass sculptures by the Norwegian artist Hans → Stoltenberg Lerche, presented at the Venetian Biennales of 1912 and 1914. During the 1920s the factory produced series of *Trasparenti* in traditional forms, yet finding a new vein on the occasion of the 1934 Biennale with articles in crystal decorated with strips of silvered glass. Under the artistic direction of Ermanno Toso in 1936, the manufactory engaged in the revival, in a modern idiom, of traditional Murano techniques, that were widely popular after the Second World War. The business wound down in 1982.

Tostrup, Olaf (1842–82). Norwegian goldsmith, son of a gold chiseller, he studied sculpture in Oslo and from 1854 to 1862 at the Berlin Academy, then working with a Parisian goldsmith (1864) and Michelsen in Copenhagen (1865). In 1878 he joined his father's laboratory, producing jewellery and silver items in the eclectic manner, but by 1880 he turned decisively to the modern style. At Tostrup's death the draughtsman Torolf Prytz (1858–1938) took over, being particularly interested in filigree enamel after seeing Hungarian enamels at Budapest in 1884 (works shown later in the 1889 Paris fair).

Treviso. Italian potteries active since the fifteenth century that comprise, from the later eighteenth century and the early nineteenth, the activity of a porcelain factory run by the brothers Giuseppe and Andrea Fontebassi, and that of a laboratory for cream-coloured earthenware producing tableware similar to → Wedgwood's. With the advent of the Restoration, the porcelain factory assumed a leading role in the execution of furnishing statuettes and table services, first to the Hapsburgs, then to the Savoias (whose coat-of-arms would figure in their trademark until 1943). Extremely active in the 1910s and 1920s were the Cacciaporti and Sebellin firm and the Gregorj pottery, where the sculptor Arturo → Martini designed models between 1908 and 1912.

Tyneside. English potteries opened on the banks of the Tyne in 1730. In 1830–40 the Richard Davis manufactory executed an important group of tiles whose models were Flaxmans's etchings; among the other factories in the area, the most important ones were Thomas Fell & Co., active from 1817 to 1890, C.T. → Maling & Sons, opened around 1860 and active up to 1963 and, above all, Adamsek Ltd. (still in business) specialised since 1880 in the production of sanitary ware and as of 1904 in an elegant production of art pottery in the → art nouveau manner, sold under the trademark "Adamsek".

Tyrian glass. Type of two-coloured glass, green and purple, sometimes decorated with leaves and branches in → *aurene* glass, invented by Frederick → Carder for the → Steuben Glass Works between 1916 and 1917. All the pieces produced with this technique were signed.

Louis Comfort Tiffany, table-lamp with peacocks and scarabs, favrile glass, bronze and enamels, 1900–02. Richmond, Virginia Museum of Fine Arts

Tiffany, Louis Comfort (1848–1933). United States decorator, son of the jeweller Charles Louis whose business he continued after 1902, active nearly exclusively in designing jewellery; he started his career in Paris as a painter, but, under William → Morris' influence, in 1878 he switched permanently to the decorative arts. In 1879 he founded a firm that furnished, in an → eclectic style comprising neo-Moresque, neo-Romanesque, neo-Byzantine, a number of buildings in New York, both private and public, and several rooms in the White House at Washington. In 1880, inspired by Emile → Gallé's creations, he patented *favrile*, a hand-crafted iridescent glass, and in 1892 opened Tiffany Furnaces, where he executed the spectacular glass mosaics of the neomedieval chapel created for the Chicago World Fair of 1893, and the polychrome stained-glass windows for → Bing's *Art Nouveau* shop in Paris, executed in 1895 on cartoons by Nabis painters. His most celebrated, diffused production was that of goblets and drinking services featuring oblong forms and decorated with wavy lines in → iridescent greens, reds, mother-of-pearls and golds coated with glossy glazes; but also of vases, bowls and articles fashioned on floral themes where the fluidity of the vitreous material rendered the soft, apparently uneven, growth of grass and flowers. A second productive typology, widely imitated in Europe, was that of table lamps and chandeliers, usually with a bronze structure, decorated with lighting fixtures emulating the corollas of tulips and calla lilies, in iridescent glass, and with shades in opalescent glass mosaics, with abstract patterns or linked up with nature: a system that Tiffany also used in the creation of screens, furniture, stained-glass partitions, along with designing furnishings textiles and wallpaper, thus creating an extremely personal interpretation of the → art nouveau manner that was the most authentic American form of international modernism. *(Pl. 104)*

Tinworth, George (1843–1913). English carver and potter, working, as of 1866, at the → Doulton manufactory; he is known for an extremely abundant production of gres articles and statuettes with the most diverse subjects: comprising religious, lofty themes, fashioned in some large panels that Ruskin greatly admired, and grotesque or popular subjects like figures of grimacing musicians, and delightful, minute sculptures of animals: extremely popular was the series devoted to the "humanised" world of white mice.

Tobey Furniture Company. United States furniture manufactory opened in 1875 at Chicago by the brothers Charles and Frank Tobey, specialised in everyday products mostly inspired by English → Arts & Crafts models, with their massive, severe forms and the use of oak. In 1888 the two partners launched, under the name Tobey & Christianson Cabinet Company, a production of quality furniture in emulation of international modernism, interpreted at the same time in Chicago by Louis Henry Sullivan.

Toft, Charles (1832–1909). English potter working in the years 1860–70 at the → Minton manufactory; he executed a group of reproductions of late-Renaissance pieces of the French Saint-Porchaire manufactory, featuring a lavish use of plastic elements and mannerist decors. His pieces are all signed.

Torquay Terracotta Co. English pottery active in Devon between 1875 and 1939 with articles drawn from British country life: collector items of little cottages, vases and teapots adorned with rustic scenes.

Louis Comfort Tiffany, calla lily vase, favrile glass, 1920–30

U

Union Glass Company. United States glass-works founded at Sommerville in 1851 and active up until 1924, producing quality cut glass. Its finest products were the moulded glass, clear crystals and silvered glass of the years 1870–85.

Union Porcelain Works. United States porcelain manufactory opened at Greenpoint in 1848, it took the name Union Porcelain Works. in 1862 when Thomas C. Smith took it over and, especially when it successfully presented, at the Philadelphia Centennial Exhibition in 1876, several pieces emulating → Wedgwood, in its neo-Greek models, and drawn from American History. Later the firm produced luxury tableware, also sold in → Tiffany stores, until it was dissolved in 1910.

Universal Potteries Inc. United States pottery, active at Cambridge (Ohio) from 1934 to 1960, specialised in serial production of table and kitchen ware in semi-vitreous porcelain, generally in one colour or with stylised floral decorations on a crème ground.

Upchurch Pottery. English pottery active in Kent between 1913 and 1961, known, during the 1920s and 1930s, for its production of extremely refined vases and containers featuring spare forms inspired by Japanese pottery and decorated with glazed monochromes and a slight *flambé* effect.

Urania. Dutch metalwork manufactory, founded at Maastricht in 1895 for making wrought-iron articles and particularly untreated → pewter, gilt and silvered; its market was predominantly Germany, having opened stores in Aachen and Berlin. Linked up with artists like Victor → Horta and Henry → van de Velde, the manufactory always used for its products original designs by artists and designers.

Urban, Joseph (1872–1933). United States designer, born in Vienna, he moved to the United States on the occasion of the erection of pavilions for the Saint Louis fair. A widely admired architect for his planning of theatres, including the one for the *Ziegfeld Follies*, and stage sets, he was called upon to run the New York store of the → Wiener Werkstätte, for which he created interior and furnishing designs. In his design archives (presently at Columbia University) are conserved a great number of projects for the interior decoration and furnishings of restaurants and hotels in the Middle West and New York.

Universal Potteries Inc., Cat-Tail Plate, painted ceramic, 1940

V

Vallin, Eugène (1852–1922). French furniture designer, active at Nancy by 1891, first as creator of neo-gothic and neo-eighteenth-century furniture, and after 1895, under Emile → Gallé's influence, of magnificent → art nouveau furnishings displaying a spirited, elegant floreated manner, foregone in the early twentieth century for the sake of plainer, more rigorous lines omitting adornment.

Val Saint-Lambert. Belgian glassworks opened in 1825 near Liege, toward 1830 it began printing catalogues of its production, consisting mainly of pressed glass and English-style crystal; at the end of the nineteenth century it inclined to the → art nouveau idiom, and in the 1920s unreservedly took up → deco style, creating both furnishing articles and quality table services. Today it is one of the leading producers in the sector of crystal ware and cut and etched glassware.

V.A.M.S.A. (Vetri Artistici Muranesi SpA). Italian glassworks arisen from the transformation in 1937 of the S.A.V.A.M. (a furnace opened in 1925 for producing traditional Murano glass), that secured the collaboration, as designers, of Luigi Scarpa Croce and Ermenegildo Ripa (responsible for the rich production of *sommersi* (cased) glass and figured glass), backed up by the master glassmaker Alfredo → Barbini. Production of three-dimensional female nudes in crystal, solid glass sculptures with animals and large vases in *sommerso* glass ended in 1947.

Van Briggle, Artus (1869–1904). United States potter, he began his career at the → Rookwood pottery as an under-glaze decorator, and in 1893 won a three-year scholarship to study in Paris; back in Cincinnati, he started experimenting with opaque glaze decorations in his own studio. In 1899, owing to a sickness, he withdrew to Colorado Springs where, over a period of five years, he executed a considerable number of vases in an exquisite modernist vein in both form and ornamentation, featuring birds or plants in flowing patterns, etched or mod-

elled, coated with opaque glazes over delicate colours. At his death, his wife took over the management of the firm, transferred in 1907 to larger premises, and still active today reproducing moulded original models, along with an ordinary production in modern taste. *(Pl. 92)*

Van Cleef & Arpels. French jewellers, whose manufactory took the name of the brothers Julien, Louis and Charles → Arpels, born in a family of diamond traders, and of their brother-in-law Alfred van Cleef, with whom they took over and launched in the early 1920s a jewellery store on Place Vendôme in Paris, followed in the years 1924–25 by branches at Cannes, Deauville and Montecarlo. Outstanding among the jeweller-artists of the 1920s-1940s, they became famous for creating magnificent

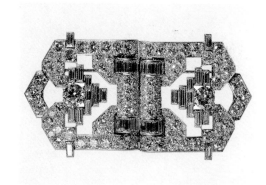

Van Cleef & Arpels, brooch dividual in two clips, platinum and brilliants, 1930

Egyptian-style jewels (influenced by the discovery of Tutankhamen's tomb) and precious evening bags, and for inventing a technique for mounting stones so close one to another that the gold is entirely invisible, dubbed *serti mystérieux. (Pl. 101)*

Van de Velde, Henry (1863–1957). Belgian architect and designer, trained at Antwerp and Paris, he came in touch with the → Arts & Crafts movement and with William → Morris; in 1896 he collaborated in furnishing Samuel → Bing's *Art Nouveau* Paris gallery and in 1898 opened several laboratories for the applied arts in Brussels (followed in 1899 by a branch in Berlin). Called to Weimar in 1902 to found an applied arts school, he directed it between 1906 and 1914 and, after a trip to Switzerland and the Netherlands, was invited back

Henry van de Velde, candelabrum, electro-plated bronze, 1898–99. Brussels, Musées Royaux d'Art et d'Histoire

to Brussels to renovate the local school of decorative and applied arts, under his direction in 1926. After a long career, during which he was active in architecture as well as in the decorative arts, he retired to Switzerland in 1947. Van de Velde adhered to the fundamental principle that the form of objects must coincide with both their function and the material constituting them, inventing a series of prototypes featuring sweeping, dynamic forms, at once naturalist and abstract.

Van Erp, Dirk (1860–1933). Dutch designer, he emigrated to the United States in 1886 and settled in San Francisco, working as a sheet metal worker in shipping yards; he started producing small cop-

per decorative items until, in 1908, he was able to open at Oakland a store called *Copper Shop*, transferred to San Francisco in 1910, where his daughter Agatha and his son William worked as well. His production comprised desk items, vases, table lamps with mica shades, decorative articles in which the apparent hammerings and joining nails contributed to the aesthetic effect of streamlined forms in tune with the modernist idiom.

Vaupel, Louis F. (1824–1903). German glass etcher; he began working at his father's glassworks, subsequently becoming an etcher and glass-blower in the glassworks his family erected in 1836 at Breitenstein; then in 1850 he emigrated to the United States, and in 1853 was employed as an etcher at the → New England Glass Company, where he remained until 1885 when he began working on his own for another five years. While his first documented pieces were in colourless glass, he soon learned to etch coloured, coated glass in keeping with Bohemian models, but mainly ruby red articles; only a few exemplars are signed.

Vechte, Antoine (1800–68). French silversmith, he started as a chiseller and bronze caster but in 1835 took up silverwork, in particular for the reproduction of Renaissance pieces, sometimes even purchased as originals; engaged at the prestigious Wagner and → Froment-Meurice laboratories in Paris, he also produced luxury articles for an aristocratic clientele, beginning to sign them. After the events of 1848, he moved to London joining the Hunt & Roskell firm, where he executed prestigious and formal pieces displayed in world fairs, beginning with the Great London Exhibition of 1851. A few of his loveliest pieces would later be reproduced by electroplating. In 1861 he retired to France.

Venini & C. Italian glassworks erected by Paolo Venini, Italian glassmaker (1895–1959), born in Milan, lawyer, who as art director, and in partnership with the antique dealers → Cappellin and Vittorio → Zecchin, founded in December 1921 the Vetri Soffiati Muranesi Cappellin Venini & C. (V.S.M.), a company that over the years would avail of the collaboration of great designers and would remain in the family until 1986, then being taken over by other owners; it is still in business. One of Venini's great merits was the renovation of the Murano tradition in modern taste, while using traditional techniques. Between 1921 and 1925 the art director was Vittorio Zecchin, who created extremely elegant blown glass inspired by Renaissance Venetian painting: the *Veronese*, *Holbein* and *Tintoretto* vases. That year, after breaking off with Cappelin and Zecchin, the art direction was entrusted to Napoleone → Martinuzzi, who introduced a remarkable production of vases, furnishing articles, chandeliers, sculptures, large lighting fixtures shaped like cactus for public buildings, and drinking services, also experimenting with new techniques like that of → *pulegoso* (bubble) glass. In 1932 the company, firmly managed by Venini, also creator of glass pieces, engaged the architect Tomaso → Buzzi, who offered a highly refined series of items, including the *Coppa delle mani* (Hands Bowl) and *laguna*, *alga* and *alba* glass. In 1934 the advent of the Venetian architect Carlo → Scarpa introduced substantial novelties in the invention of forms and the creation of new techniques, like the one for → *murrines*, and → *corrosi, battuti, variegati* glass, Paolo Venini frequently intervening directly in the experiments. The relationship with Scarpa ended in 1947. *(Pls 20, 26, 27, 71, 84, 112, 117 and 118)*

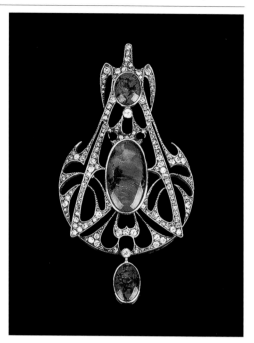

Pierre-Paul and Henri Vever, pendant, diamonds and opal, 1900–10

Vereinte Kunstgewerber Darmstadt. German decorative arts laboratories founded in 1902 by Alfred Konch and other pupils of Peter → Behrens, extremely active in the ambit of the creation of furnishings, pottery, wrought metal and book illustrations aligned on → Jugendstil principles.

Vernon Kilns. United States pottery, active in Los Angeles from 1931 to 1958, especially in the production of kitchen and table ware featuring geometric patterns. The early 1930s were the years of the series of plates in two colours (navy, orange or brown on a crème ground) with scenes drawn from Melville's novel *Moby Dick*.

Vever. French jewellers active at Metz by 1831 with the goldsmith Pierre, who transferred the business to Paris in 1871, then handing down the property of the laboratory in 1881 to his two grandsons Pierre-Paul (1851–1915) and Henri (1854–1942), who, under the influence of René → Lalique's creations, made a great number of necklaces, brooches, bracelets, combs, pendents figuring with extraordinary gracefulness flowers, insects and animals, for the most part designed by masters such as Eugène Samuel Grasset, Lucien Gautrit, Henri Vollet, by enamel painters like Etienne Touret and the sculptor René Rozet. *(Pl. 102)*

Vietri sul Mare. Italian pottery active since the eighteenth century, that underwent a profound and significant stylistic and formal renovation during the 1920s, mainly thanks to the fundamental contribution of a German artists' colony, especially of Dölker and Malamerson, the latter having previously converted the I.C.S. (Industria Ceramica Salernitana) company. Conspicuous among the articles produced in the early 1930s were the useful ware with illustrations of country scenes, highly simplified, or vases with modern, elegant forms adorned with extremely stylised geometric or plant motifs, usually in two colours (black/white, yellow/black) and generally marked "Cas.Vietri". *(Pl. 106)*

Villeroy & Boch. German pottery and glassworks active since 1748 as Boch manufactory; consolidation with the Villeroy manufactory gave rise to the new name of the company, extended by subsequent take-overs during the nineteenth century, and able to produce a large assortment of objects, comprising sanitary ware and gift items, tableware and elegant services in the most varied materials and featuring decorations and forms never very far from the average ruling fashion.

Vineland Flint Glass Works. United States glassworks, founded in New Jersey in 1897 by Victor Durand Jr. (1870–1931) sustained by the competency of Martin Bach Jr. (formerly at the → Quetzal glassworks), it engaged in the production of art glass similar by its models and forms to Quetzal glass. In 1931 the factory was taken over by the Kimble Glass Co., art production being permanently abandoned. The manufactory turned out table lamps and floor lamps with shades in different shapes and colours, but above all articles in lustreglaze glass, either yellow, dubbed *Ambergris*, or coated with a spider-web décor, called *Spider Webbing*. Some pieces are trademarked with a "W", but more frequently with the name "Durand".

Vistosi. Italian glassworks erected at Murano in 1830 for the execution of filigree glass; it continued throughout the century with a traditional production, until in 1945 Luciano Vistosi founded the Vetreria Vistosi, availing of designs by famous architects. The glass of this manufactory is usually colourless, with a sparse design and characterised by alternating smooth and rough surfaces.

Volkmar, Charles (1841–1914). United States potter, after studying in Paris he opened at Long Island in 1879 a laboratory where he produced a group of vases painted under glaze representing wooded landscapes inspired by the paintings of the Barbizon school; all the while maintaining his interest in soft, atmospheric landscapes painted on tiles, the artist, drawn to Japanese pottery, gradually set aside his naturalist repertory to focus on stylised, geometric motifs, creating an outstanding series of pottery items featuring colours and glazes giving rise to decorative and tactile effects. In 1903 he transferred the factory to New Jersey.

Volkstedt. German porcelain manufactory founded in Thuringia in 1760 for the production of interesting imitations of → Meissen models, an activity that it carried out with particular vigour around the mid-nineteenth century, at a time when the interest in the eighteenth-century manner was at its height, as was porcelain collecting. The firm is still in business.

Voysey, Charles Francis Annesley (1857–1941). English architect and designer influenced by William → Morris' conceptions, he produced attractive wallpaper and furnishing textiles enlivened by plant racemes with birds and flowery fields,

W. Kreis and K. Cross (for Villeroy & Boch), column, polychrome majolica, 1900. Dresden, Kunstgewerbemuseum

characterised by a freshness of imagination that was highly appreciated by his contemporaries. The furniture with emphasised metal hinges, the chairs with straw-seats and high backs possessed a rustic, unsophisticated look that made them comparable to the School of Glasgow's creations. Actually Voysey never shifted from that balanced position, halfway between Morris and → Mackintosh and, although reflecting on the modernist idiom, he never wholeheartedly embraced that new style.

Charles Francis Annesley Voysey, cabinet, mahogany, 1898

Wackerle, Josef (1880–1959). German pottery decorator, after a wood carver's training, the applied arts school in Munich and a trip to Italy, in 1906 he became director of the → Nymphenburg porcelain manufactory, where he was influential in its evolution from an imitative production of eighteenth-century models to an extremely interesting renovation in terms of modernism. He modelled figures of *belle époque* ladies or dressed in fashionable attire, and masks, like the famous *Pierrot* and *Pierrette*; in 1909 he resigned — although still supplying the Munich factory with models for many years — so as to work in the decorative arts museum of Berlin. Between 1909 and 1917 he produced a group of female figures in modish garb for the → Berlin porcelain manufactory.

Wade. English pottery, erected at Burslem in 1867 and still in business, producing an assortment of household items: kitchen ware and table sets and furnishing articles.

Wagenfeld, Wilhelm (b. 1900). German designer counting a great number of experiences in the decorative arts field, he was engaged at the → Bauhaus of Weimar as silversmith and chiseller, working in a style rather similar to Edgar → Brandt's, and executing in the very early 1920s a tea and coffee set and a streamlined coffee pot, as well as a pillar-shaped tea box. His most famous work however was a glass and chromium-plated metal table lamp, produced between 1923 and 1924 with J.K. Jucker, along with the design (1932) for a heat-resistant glass tea set, still being produced, for reinforced glass tableware and cutlery influenced by → Jensen. Having left the Bauhaus, from 1931 to 1935 he taught at the Berliner Kunsthochschule and in 1934 became head designer at the → Fürstenberg porcelain manufactory.

Wallendorf. German porcelain manufactory active in Thuringia since 1764 for the production of imitations of → Meissen models, although with simpler forms and decorated in an underglaze dark blue, more rarely enamelled. The firm is still in business.

Walter, Alméric (1859–1942). French glassmaker, working at the Nancy and → Sèvres manufactories where he executed → *pâte de verre* articles shaped like crabs, green lizards, frogs and wall lizards, as well as female figures often placed on the rim of glass basins. Employee of the → Daum factory from 1908 to 1914, right after the war he opened his own laboratory where he produced a rich series of articles with abstract forms and very bright colours, but also copies of the famous Tanagra pottery statuettes in vitreous paste. Several exemplars bear his signature, whereas others the name of his collaborator Henri → Bergé.

Walton, George (1867–1933). Architect and designer linked up with the Glasgow School, he founded in that city a firm for ecclesiastical and household decoration, creating metal-wrought articles in affinity with → Mackintosh's sensibility. In 1897 he moved to London where, aside from designing façades and interiors for shops, he turned out embroideries, glass items, furniture and furnishing fabrics reflecting the Glasgow manner.

Wardle & Co. English pottery founded at Hanley in 1871 and dissolved in 1935, to which is owed in the early twentieth century an interesting production of majolica vases, with figurative motifs inspired by Italian folklore traditions and other exquisitely → liberty patterns, like peacocks and flowers.

Wardour Street. Street in London occupied by stores selling ecclesiastical furniture that gave its name, toward the mid-nineteenth century, to a debased version of neo-gothic style characterised by its excessive ornateness which roused → Morris' and → Mackintosh's indignation.

Wassmus. French cabinet-makers working in Paris as of 1816, quoted toward 1840 as highly skilled imitators of the Boulle, "Louis-Quinze" and "Louis-Seize" styles; they achieved a remarkable success with Henri-Léonard Wassmus, furniture-maker who was a favorite of Napoleon III and the Second Empire Court. The firm remained in business until ca. 1870.

Webb, Philip (1831–1915). English architect and designer closely associated with William → Morris, since they were both employed in the studio of the architect G.S. Street until 1858, when Webb opened his own where besides designing houses, he engaged

Philip Webb and William Morris, buffet, mahogany painted black and polychrome panels, 1885. Paris, Musée d'Orsay

in the creation of furniture in collaboration with Morris and the painter Burne-Jones. In 1861 he joined the Morris, Marshall, Faulkner & Co. as designer of furnishings, embroidery, metal and glass items, and jewellery, that were entirely devoid of nostalgic revivals of the English Middle Ages, featuring utter simplicity: the furniture is in solid wood without upholstery, with apparent joints, in oak and coloured green or black, or else with paintings, stuccoes (as in the pianos, often covered with silvered and lacquered plaster decorations) or lacquered leather. He retired from the firm in 1875 but continued producing designs, thus explicitly influencing the → Arts & Crafts movement as well.

Webb Thomas & Sons. English glassworks founded in 1837 at Stourbridge by Thomas Webb for the execution of household ware and decorative articles, several of which were exhibited in London

in 1851. After inheriting the firm in 1869, his sons Thomas Wilkes and Charles Webb concentrated on decorative glass, meeting with noteworthy success at the Paris fair of 1878, in particular for their candelabras. In 1876 the firm had already introduced a precious production of cameo glass, supervised by T. and G. Woodall and started off with the commission to John → Northwood for a vase that, completed in 1882, was sold to → Tiffany (presently in Washington, Smithsonian Institution); that production, which drew great fame to the glassworks and required up to seventy glassworkers, was wound down in 1906, while a relevant production of tableware is still under way. *(Pl. 114)*

Weber, Karl Emmanuel Martin (1889–1963). United States silversmith, considered one of the founding fathers of modernism in the United States; he was born in Berlin where between 1908 and 1910 he was a pupil of Bruno → Paul. He created prototypes for industrial production, designs for interior decoration and film-set decoration in Hollywood, along with exuberantly decorative articles, especially furnishings, in particular chairs, in → plywood or steel tubular with springs. After visiting the Paris 1925 fair he began to be attracted to → deco taste: from zigzag patterns to typical 1930s aerodynamic forms. His major works date from after 1927 and are silver coffee and tea sets designed for the Porter Blanchard Company and the International Silver Company, featuring severe, spare shapes aligned on → Bauhaus stylistic dictates.

Webster, Moses (1792–1870). English draughtsman, porcelain decorator at → Derby and → Worcester with flower patterns in the naturalist manner, he worked in London at the Robins & Randall decorating store, painting tableware produced by the Nantgarow and Swansea manufactories.

Wedgwood. English pottery, founded in 1759 and still active after the transformation into an industrial group in 1989, celebrated for its eighteenth- and early nineteenth-century production imitating cameo glass of the Roman period and jaspers; during the nineteenth century it participated in all the world exhibitions with furnishing articles and tableware inspired by the Victorian-style → eclectic manner. The formal and stylistic revolution of → art nouveau also implicated the traditional manufactory, that executed pieces endowed with particular beauty and distinction, accrued in the course of the 1920s also under the influence of a kind of Chinese taste well il-

99. Steuben Glass Works,
bowl, iridescent glass
with filament decorations,
ca. 1914

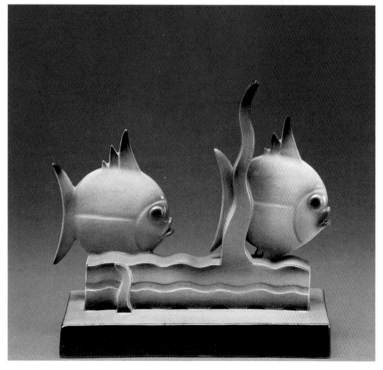

100. Tarcisio Tosin
(for La Freccia), Fishes,
polychrome air-brushed
pottery, 1935

103. Weller Pottery, vase of the Sonevo *series, terra cotta with graffito and painted decoration, 1909*

104. *Louis Comfort Tiffany, rose-water spray, favrile glass,*
ca. 1897. Vienna, Museum für Angewandte Kunst

105. *Taxile Doat (for Sèvres), perfume phial, polychrome*
porcelain, 1900. Copenhagen, Det Danske Kunstindustrimuseum

106. Vietri sul Mare, vase, two-colour majolica, 1935–38

107. Wedgwood,
"wickerwork" dish, white
majolica with reliefs,
1920–30

108. David Zipirovich
(for Deruta), dish with the
portrait of Beatrice d'Este,
polychrome majolica,
1922–27

109. Wedgwood, glazed ginger vase of the Fairyland *series, porcelain, ca. 1920*

110. Ugo Zaccagnini, umbrella stand, cold-decorated terra cotta, 1938–42

111. Zsolnay, vase, polychrome porcelain with glazes, 1900

112. Vittorio Zecchin (for Venini), Dragonfly *vase, blown glass, 1921–22. Gardone Riviera, Il Vittoriale*

113. *Jan Kotera (for Wiener Werkstätte), punch bowl and glasses, grinded crystal, 1904*

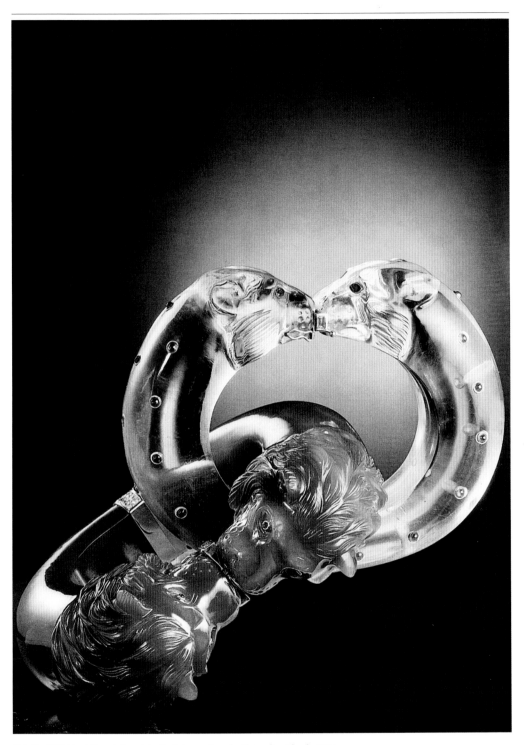

114. David Webb, rigid agate bracelet with fastener adorned with two lions' heads, 1940

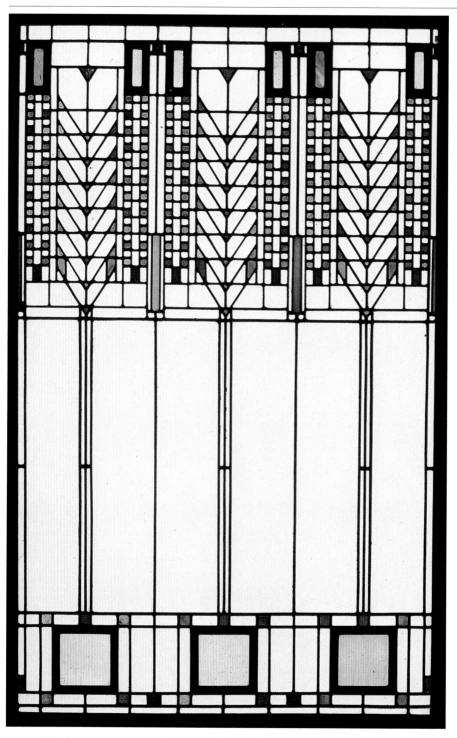

115. *Frank Lloyd Wright, stained-glass window for Darwin D. Martin's house, 1904*

116. Zsolnay, vase, porcelain painted with enamels and acid-treated, 1901

117. Carlo Scarpa (for Venini), Little owl, *1943.*
Padua University, meeting room

118. Tyra Lundgren (for Venini), Fish, *1938.*
Milan, Galleria In Arte

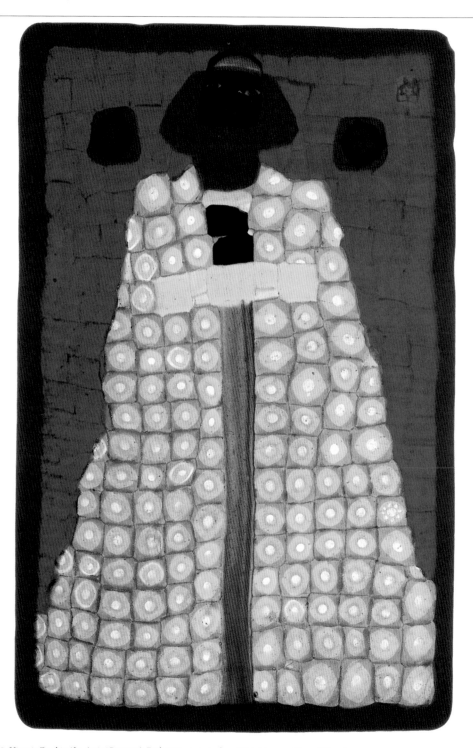

119. *Vittorio Zecchin (for Artisti Barovier),* Barbarian, *mosaic glass, 1914. Murano, Museo Vetrario*

lustrated by the *Fairyland Lustre Ginger Jar*, designed by Daisy Makeig-Jones, or more explicitly → deco, as in the *Millicent Taplin Cane Ware Vase* of 1928. However the manufactory also updated with openly abstract models and decorative themes featuring optical effects, as in the *Unique Ware Vase* (ca. 1930) with alternating black and white vertical stripes, imitating the contemporary inventions in the field of art glass, and with vases and amphoras with ribbings and sculptures with small black pottery animals in emulation of Etruscan *bucchero*. *(Pls 107 and 109)*

Weller Pottery. United States pottery active at Zanesville (Ohio) from 1872 to 1948, engaged in the

Wedgwood, Unique Ware Vase, *ca. 1930*

production of hand-crafted pottery (become fashionable owing to the products turned out by the → Rookwood and Newcomb factories) and using skillful masters like Albert Haubrich and the French decorator J. Sicar, who introduced a production, as of 1900, of → iridescent glass similar to → Tiffany's. *(Pl. 103)*

Wemyss ware. Definition of a particular English pottery production characterised by a rustic taste and bright colours, flowers, farm animals, fruit and birds being its major themes. Introduced by the Fife

manufactory in 1790 but mostly in the years 1883–1930, coinciding with the presence in the factory of the Austrian decorator Karl Nekola, production turned mainly to pitchers and large basins, tableware, jam jars, large doorstops shaped like pigs and decorations inspired by country life.

Whitefriars. English glassworks founded in London toward the end of the eighteenth century, it began to expand commercially around 1835 when it was taken over by James Powell, who wagered on the revival of the English tradition of hand-crafted blown-glass and on the reproduction of period models: including Roman and Venetian glass, medieval English glass and more typically eighteenth-century items. Along with a production of cut glass, in the 1850–60 decade the manufactory introduced coloured glass and stained-glass windows on pre-Raphaelite designs, and in 1859 executed austere, distinguished glass for William → Morris, probably conceived by → Webb. In 1922 the factory was transferred to Middlesex where it is still active in the production of tableware and large vases with floral or abstract designs rendered with unsmoothed etchings.

Whitehaven. English potteries active from 1740 to 1915, whose most well-known products date from the second half of the nineteenth century: these are mostly kitchen and tableware with printed decorations.

White washing. Pottery technique entailing soaking the earthenware in a solution of diluted white clay. After the first firing the piece appears coated with a white plaster; sometimes this sort of slip is obtained through the air-drying of the earthenware. The process allows to spare the stanniferous enamel that is used only on the parts to be decorated. Pieces processed by this technique are also called semi-majolica.

Wiener Werkstätte. Austrian decorative arts laboratories, founded in Vienna in 1903 by Josef → Hoffmann and Koloman → Moser, formerly teachers at the Kunstgewerbeschule (reorganised toward 1900) and in emulation of the English art schools of London and Glasgow. The first Viennese exhibition of 1905, which they attended with elegant book bindings, was followed as of 1906 by participations in important international fairs and the opening of new divisions, like for pottery directed by Michael → Powolny, and for metalwork, bookbinding, leather work, jewellery and furnishings. The laboratories were capable of satisfying the social and artistic requisites theorised by the English tradition, but concurrently were receptive to modernism, introducing machines in the productive cycle, adopting a logo for their production and creating a specific identity for each one of the productive sectors by the use of identifying colours. Among the countless materials used, comprising textiles and modelled concrete, metals were of particular importance: unlike pottery and glass, produced elsewhere, the works in silver and metal were entirely executed within the structure, in keeping with the rigorous simplicity and geometric elegance of form that characterised every product of the manufactory. In 1907 the production of illustrated postcards was introduced and sales centres were

Wilson, Henry (1864–1934). English designer, after training as an architect, in 1895 he engaged in designing metal-wrought articles and jewellery, with diversely-processed precious stones mounted in ornate gold settings, according to the expressive vein of → art nouveau. In 1901 he began teaching metal processing at the Royal College of London.

Wilton. English manufactory of combed wool rugs, produced on *jacquard* looms until 1860, then mechanical looms, similar to the so-called "Brussels rug" models, but featuring a greater number of threads, whose cut knots form a rich velvety texture. Sometimes they are called "Tournai rugs".

Wolfers, Philippe (1858–1929). Belgian goldsmith, after beginning in the elaborate neo-rococo

Josef Hoffmann (for Wiener Werkstätte), bracelet, gold, ivory and brilliants, 1914

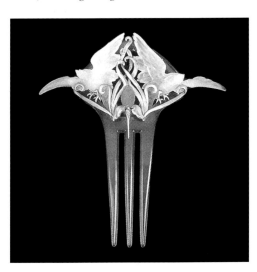

Philippe Wolfers, comb, horn, glass, gold and enamels, 1900–10

opened, and in 1910, under the direction of Eduard Wimmer, a division devoted to fashion design was opened; yet in 1914 it was dissolved and its creative period came to an end. Refounded under the name Kunstlerwerkstätten, the Vienna laboratories were active up to 1926; then they were dissolved once again and, after a last attempt to revive them, were permanently closed down after a final exhibition in 1932. *(Pls 87 and 113)*

Willets Manufactory Company. United States porcelain manufactory active in New Jersey that, between 1880 and 1900, produced imitations of the Irish pottery executed by the → Belleek factory.

style and a brief period influenced by Japanese traditional naturalism, beginning in 1892 he vigorously adopted → art nouveau stylistic principles and themes, representing insects and flower patterns with a large use of ivory, enamels and semi-precious stones (including opals, amethysts, aquamarines); in 1897 he presented in Brussels important ivory articles, and between 1897 and 1900 executed a complete series of 109 jewels that would be shown in all the international exhibitions of the period. Toward 1900 he opened branches in Liege, Antwerp, London, Dusseldorf, Ghent, Budapest and Paris. After 1910 his style became more simplified: in the early 1910s he decisively turned to abstract, strictly symmetrical forms that already anticipated the → deco manner, entirely explicited at the Paris 1925 fair for which Wolfers executed furniture, interior decorations, drapes, rugs and porcelain, soon approaching his decline. Along with jewellery he produced designs for glass items, especially for the Belgian glassworks of → Val Saint-Lambert, and after 1908 he displayed a special predilection for bronze and iron sculpture.

Woodall, Thomas (1849–1926) and George (1850–1925). English glass etchers and, after training at the Northwood manufactory, in 1874 they joined → Webb's, where they etched ornamentation on crystalline glass, and where as of 1880–1890 they executed etchings on cameo glass exhibited in the leading international events. The typologies of their products went from inkstands to glass plates for doors, candle-sticks to perfume bottles, with decorations featuring classical themes along with Chinese and Islamic ornamental motifs. Their most renowned creations however were vases and plates executed in the most explicit Victorian style.

Woollams & Company. English wallpaper manufactory known for the quality of its products, executed either by hand or machine as of 1907. The manufactory being taken over in 1876, the new owner, Frederic Aumonier, patented a process for the production of embossed wallpaper (sold after 1877) using pigments without arsenic, which had been the common use. The firm was wound down in 1900.

Worcester. English porcelain manufactory active uninterruptedly since 1751 with a high quality production. In 1862 the factory took the name Royal Worcester Porcelain Company, introducing a production in a particularly rich Victorian style, very ornate and painted (at times with as much care as for jewellery): trays, dishes, soup tureens in → *parian ware* adorned with neo-Renaissance motifs were accompanied by *Limoges ware* porcelain, one of the factory's specialties, decorated in white enamel on a navy ground (usually painted by Thomas → Bott); furthermore ivory-hued statuettes, at times glazed (after 1865) and groups of children comparable to Kate Greenaway's creations. The 1870–1880 production was influenced by Japanese tradition, even though throughout the century and in the early twentieth century series of porcelain continued to be created with flower decorations on a crème or pale green ground. Between 1912 and 1953, under the direction of Charles William Dyson Perrins, the

manufactory continued to develop: particularly famous was the series of birds of the American continent modelled in 1935 by Dorothy Doughty, followed by a series devoted to English birds. The company is still producing excellent-quality porcelains today.

Wright, Frank Lloyd (1867–1959). United States architect and designer, very famous designer and innovator in the field of architecture and the conception of new housing modes inspired from Japanese culture and models of international modernism. His furniture, already based by the end of the nineteenth century on the intersection of surfaces of geometric volumes, always displayed an absolute idea of modernism that arose from the combination between respect for materials and their function and the organic bond with the architectural surroundings where they were placed: memorable in this regard were his dining-room chairs, with their high, straight backs intended as visual screens outlining within a space an area with specific functions. Beyond the furnishings, also the textiles and stained-glass windows designed by Wright responded to this quest for an essential organic quality, selecting rigorously geometric themes in line with the 1920s' proneness to abstraction. *(Pl. 115)*

Württembergische Metallwarenfabrik. German metal, pottery and glass manufactory active since 1853 at Geislingen for the production of household utensils in silvered copper; after merging with the A.Ritter & Sohn silverwork plant it became the joint-stock company W.M.F. The division for glass production, opened in 1883, began in 1889 producing also silverplate cutlery, followed in 1894 by series of small bronze furnishing sculptures. Although maintaining a production bound to the historicist → eclectic taste, toward 1907, urged by Albert Mayer, the firm inclined toward exquisitely → art nouveau themes and motifs, especially emulating the plant world. The trademark of the factory, still in business, displayed a stylised church façade with the belltower in the middle, surrounded by a circle and topping the initials of the firm forming a triangle.

Z

Zaccagnini, Ugo (1868–1937). Italian potter, active for many years at Ginori in Sesto Fiorentino, at the end of the century he founded his own studio in Florence, assisted by his children Pietro, Prisco, Adele, Enrichetta and, mainly, Urbano who created the famous glazed terra-cotta vases bound in ropes. The firm first named Ugo Zaccagnini e Figli, in 1936 became Ceramiche Zaccagnini S.A., extending and even exporting to the American market; in the 1940s Walt Disney granted it the monopoly for the pottery reproduction of cartoons. One of the most characteristic items of the manufactory, alongside useful and furnishing ware, were animals, modelled and glazed in most cases by Fosco Martini in the 1930s and 1940s. The trademark consists of the full name etched and followed by a Z. *(Pl. 110)*

Zaccari, Ettore (1877–1922). Italian cabinet-maker, specialising at Milan in artistic carving and highly appreciated by the art dealer and painter Grubicy de Dragon, during the 1910s he produced polished black woods, or else gilt or silvered, with a luxuriant decoration inspired by the Ravenna-Byzantine style, in particular for picture frames and sculpture bases. Having become an interior decorator, he designed, along with furniture, equally tapestries and mural decorations. During the 1920s, and even after his death, the firm he had founded went on producing furniture and furnishings in a redundant → deco manner.

Zach, Bruno. Austrian sculptor, known for a group of small bronzes, usually mounted on bases of precious stones and marble, having as subject female figures in fashionable attire, in suggestive poses, with very long, tapering legs, often wearing typical 1930s slips and lingerie. Although the artist used the chryselephantine technique, he preferred patinated gilding and, occasionally, patinated bronze.

Zecchin, Vittorio (1878–1947). Italian glassmaker, born in a family of glassmakers, he first engaged in painting, in 1922 becoming draughtsman and

Ettore Zaccari, armchair, carved walnut with gildings, 1920. Genoa, Wolfsonian Foundation

technical director of the firm → Cappellin, → Venini & C., for which he produced the famous *Veronese* vases (drawn from Venetian Renaissance painting) and *Libellula*, with explicit → art nouveau references. In 1930 he collaborated with the → S.A.I.A.R. Ferro-Toso firm, in 1932 with the A.V.E.M. factory, from 1932 to 1938 with → S.A.L.I.R. and → Seguso Vetri d'Arte, and after 1938 with Fratelli → Toso. *(Pls 112 and 119)*

Zecchin-Martinuzzi. Italian glassworks founded in 1932 by Francesco → Zecchin and Napoleone → Martinuzzi after Paolo → Venini left the business. Production, marked by Martinuzzi's Novecento taste, was characterised by the use of → *pulegoso* glass, clear glass and opaque glass for the execution of large vases (for the most part modelled by Gio-

Vittorio Zecchin (for M.V.M. Cappellin & C.), vase, fumé clear glass and glass paste, 1921–25

vanni Guerrini) and jars, solid glass sculptures with animals (most of them wrought by Mario Romero), nude female figures and cacti. In 1936 Martinuzzi withdrew from the firm and in 1938 Zecchin dissolved it.

Zen. Family of Italian cabinet-makers. Carlo (1851–1918), former director of the Zara & Zen firm (active in the last decades of the nineteenth century in Milan and engaged in making → eclectic furniture for a middle-class clientele), and director by 1880 of the leading Milanese furniture-maker in → liberty style, was first and foremost a businessman, able to grasp the demands of a large share of the market; in 1898 he began a partnership with the Viennese firm of Haas and in 1902 counted as one of his collaborators Otto → Eckmann. His son Piero (1879–1950) joined the company in 1906, guiding production toward highly simplified, rational furniture.

Zipirovich, David (1885–1946). Majolica decorator born in Russia, moved to Italy after the Bolshevic revolution, he was very active at the → Deruta pottery from 1922 to 1927, a period in which

he executed a very rich group of decorative dishes, amphoras with handles and panels made of tiles, all pieces reproducing masterpieces of Italian painting from the fifteenth to the seventeenth centuries in the spirit of the return to → eclectism typical of the 1920s in Italy. *(Pl. 108)*

Zitzmann, Friedrich (1840–1906). German glassmaker, trained and then employed at Muranese glassworks, toward 1890 he won a certain celebrity exhibiting at the Bayerischer Kunstgewerbeverein in Munich some stained-glass windows in the historicist taste. Updating to → art nouveau style and taste during his collaboration with Karl → Köpping in Berlin between 1895 and 1896, he produced and sold graceful vases featuring stylised plant forms; in 1897 he exhibited → iridescent glass at the Glaspalast in Munich, where he also began teaching the technique of blown glass.

Zoli, Paolo. Italian potter, active at Faenza and trained at the studio of the → Minardi brothers, toward 1920 he formed a company with Dino Fabbri and Amerigo Masotti for the management of the La Faïence furnace, where he produced furnishing articles in keeping with the Faventine tradition, although updated in → deco style. The firm, where Francesco → Nonni also worked, closed down after a decade. The trademark is a Z inscribed in a circle with a group of three dashes on each side and in capital letters "Faenza".

Zovetti, Ugo (1879–1974). Italian designer, trained at Vienna with Rudolf von Larisch and Koloman →

Frans Zwollo, fruit bowl, gilt silver with sapphires, 1903–24. The Hague, Haags Gemeentemuseum

Moser, whose collaborator he became, he fully embraced the secessionist manner of the → Wiener Werkstätte. Arriving in Italy in 1919, he began teaching at the I.S.I.A. in Monza, and by 1922 held the chair of decoration there. He executed Indian ink drawings on vellum for textiles, pencil drawings, starched paper, marbled paper and new graphic techniques that brought him fame at the Monza Biennales and the Milan Triennales.

Zsolnay. Hungarian pottery erected in 1865 by Vilmos Zsolnay (1828–1900) after taking over the firm opened at Pécs in 1862 by his brother Ignaz, where new techniques were researched for producing iridescent, glossy surfaces, in particular with metal reflections in all shades of colour. One of the manufactory's most well-known productions was the large

vases decorated with scenes drawn from the Grimm brothers fairy tales. After Vilmos died, his son Miklos (1857–1922) successfully continued the traditional ware of the manufactory, that was nationalised in 1949 and renamed Porzelàngyàr Pécs. *(Pls 111 and 116)*

Zwollo, Frans (1872–1945). Dutch gold- and silversmith, trained in Paris and Brussels, in 1897 he began his goldsmith career at Amsterdam, designing articles in "Louis-Quatorze" style for the Bonnebaker firm, but he soon adopted the → art nouveau manner, designing jewellery, lamps and items featuring floral decorations. In 1910 he began introducing in his style strictly geometric, linear elements, that were to remain in his production up to the Second World War.

Carlo Zen, writing-desk, inlaid wood and mother-of-pearl, 1902

Trademarks and initials of designers, glassworks, jewellers and metalworks, arranged in alphabetical order, eventually indicating time and place of activity

Friedrich Adler

GARGY-ROUSSEAU

Gabriel Argy-Rousseau

Charles Robert Ashbee

Baccarat

Guido Balsamo Stella

G ☆ B

Guido Balsamo Stella

Barmin Brothers for Fryazino, 1820–50

Karl Johann Bauer

Hermann Bauer

L. BECKER

Edmond-Henri Becker

B T

Beckh & Turba

Peter Behrens

Benckiser & Co.

W|B

Wilhelm Binder

Bohnenberger, Böhmler & Co.

Rudolf Bosselt

B

Maison Boucheron

E BRANDT

Edgar Brandt

Bremer Silberwarenfabrik (B.S.F.)

Antoine Bricteux

Peter Bruckmann & Söhne, Vive

Paul Bürck

Michael Cardew

Henri Chaumeil, Paris, 1877–1944

Paul Chaumeil, 1902

MCP

Mary Chose Perry, Detroit (USA), after 1900

Christofle

CISSARZ

Johann Vincenz Cissarz

Clarice Cliff

Susie Cooper

Andreas Daub

•D•

Nelson Dawson

T-D

Théodore Deck

DESCOMPS

Emmanuel-Jules Descomps

OD

Oskar Dietrich, Vienna

EC, Strasbourg

Jan Eisenlöffel

Jan Eisenlöffel

ФАБЕРЖЕ

Peter Carl Fabergé

209

Fachschule Gablonz

Theodor Fahrner

Wilhelm Feucht

Eugène Feuillâtre

Louis Fiessler & Co.

Alexander Fisher

Maison Fouquet

Friedländer, Berlin

JFN
J. Friedmann's Vive, Frankfurt

FROMENT MEURICE
Emile Froment-Meurice

Wilhelm Fühner

Lucien Gaillard

L.GAILLARD
Lucien Gaillard

Lucien Gaillard

G A JG
Arthur Joseph Gaskin

Lucien Gautrait

Goldsmiths & Silversmiths Company

Theodor von Gosen

M.G. Großbaum, Vienna

Guild and School of Handicraft

Ludwig Habich

Hagener Silber-schmiede

Hagener Silber-schmiede

W.H. Haseler & Co.

Gustav Hauber

Theodor Heiden

Carl Hermann

HzL
Hermann Hirzel

Joseph Hodel

Josef Hoffmann

Charles Horner

Patriz Huber

Georg Jensen

Georg Jensen

Georg Jensen

Ⱦ
Georg Jensen

Gi
Georg Jensen

Georg Jensen

Georg Jensen

K. & K.
Kirchgäßner & Kraft

Kollmar & Jourdan

Robert Kraft

ℒ 𝔊
Louis Kuppenheim

René Lalique

LALIQUE
René Lalique

R. LALIQUE
René Lalique

R.L.

René Lalique

Heinrich Levinger

London 1898–1901

Liberty & Co.

Birmingham 1899–1927

Liberty & Co.

Birmingham 1893–1894
Liberty & Co. (Cymric) Ltd.

Liberty & Co.

Berthold Löffler

Lutz & Weiß

Margaret Macdonald
Mackintosh

Arthur Mackmurdo

Erik Magnussen

F. Mahla

Maison de l'Art Nouveau
(Samuel Bing), Paris

F. Manka

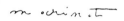

Maurice Marinot

Masriera

Martin Mayer, Mainz

Victor Mayer, Pforzheim

Adolf Mayrhofer

J.HERBERT McNAIR

J. Herbert McNair

William Moorcroft

BERNARD MOORE

Bernard Moore

Koloman Moser

Albin Müller

C.W. Müller

Theodor Müller

Keith Murray
for BRIERLEY

Keith Murray, for Brierley

Keith Murray, for Wedgwood

Murrle, Bennett
& Co

Murrle, Bennett & Co.

Murrle, Bennett & Co.

Neresheimer & Söhne,
Hanau

Evald Nielsen

Evald Nielsen

H N

Harald Nielsen

A.N.

August Nowodny

GESCHÜTZT
800

A. Odenwald, Pforzheim

Joseph Maria Olbrich

Orrefors Glasbruk

Ivos

Ivos Pacetti, Albisola

Eugen Pflaumer

Piel Frères

Otto Prutscher

Omar Ramsden

Ernst Riegel

Charles-Magloire Rivaud

R.&W

Rodi & Wienenberger

Johan Rohde

Rozet & Fischmeister

M.J. Rückert

Georg Anton Scheid, Vienna

Schmerzer & Gerike

Schöpflich Eduard
(formerly N. Thallmayr)

**Siegele & Bennett
Pforzheim**

Siegele & Bennett,
Pforzheim

Siess Joseph, Vienna

Hans Söllner, Pforzheim

Friedrich Speidel, Pforzheim

William Staite Murray

Steuben Glass Works

Turnau Fachschule

**Turriet &
Bardach**

Turriet & Bardach, Vienna

RU

Richard Unverferth

Henry van de Velde

Vereinigte Werkstätte
für Kunst im Handwerk,
Munich

VEVER PARIS

Maison Vever

Maison Vever

VEVER

Maison Vever

Alméric Walter

J.H. WERNER

J.H. Werner

O.M.WERNER

O. Max Werner

**Wiener Werk-
stätte**

Wiener Werkstätte

Wiener Werkstätte

Wiener Werkstätte

WIENER
WERK
STÄTTE

Wiener Werkstätte

Wiener Werkstätte

WW

Wiener Werkstätte

Wiener Werkstätte

M.H. Wilkens & Söhne,
Hemelingen

Henry Wilson

Eduard Wimmer

Philippe Wolfers

Württembergische
Metallwarenfabrik

**Zahn, Paul
Pforzheim**

Paul Zahn, Pforzheim

M. Zdekauer

P. Zerrenner

Frans Zwollo

F. ZWOLLO

Frans Zwollo

Trademarks, initials and signatures of European and United States pottery, majolica and china manufactories and of several master decorators, indicating place and time of activity

Altröhlau, A. Nowotny, 1838–84

Altröhlau, M. Zdekauer, 1884–1920

Aluminia, XIX century, Copenhagen (Denmark)

William Adams & Sons, 1769–1966 (Great Britain)

Adderley, 1906–47 (Great Britain)

ALBA - DOCILIA .
ALBISOLA-MARE

Alba Docilia, since 1919, Albisola (Italy)

A/D

Alba Docilia, since 1919, Albisola (Italy)

Alcora, beginning of XIX century, Valencia (Spain)

Altenburg, XIX century (Germany)

Alt-Röhlau (Stará Role) B. Hasslacher, 1813–84 (Bohemia)

Amberg, 1850–1910 (Germany)

Amstelhoek, 1897–1910, Amsterdam (Holland)

Anonima Siciliana Ceramiche, XX century, Palermo (Italy)

A

Ansbach, since 1765 (Germany)

Ansbach, since 1765 (Germany)

Ansbach, since 1765 (Germany)

Ansbach, since 1765 (Germany)

B.APÁTFALVA

Apátfalva, 1836–1928 (Hungary)

Apátfalva, 1836–1928 (Hungary)

Aprey, 1832–78, Giraud, Haute Marne (France)

Arabia, after 1874 (Finland)

Arabia, 1874–1917 (Finland)

ARTĚL

Artel, 1908–20, Prague (Bohemia)

Arzberg, affiliate of Kahl porcelain manufactory, 1890 (Germany)

Ashby Potter's Guild, 1909–22 (Great Britain)

Ashtead Potters, 1923–1935 (Great Britain)

G.L. Ashworth & Brothers, 1862–1973 (Great Britain)

Ault Faïence / Ault Potteries, 1887–1974 (Great Britain)

Auwärter & Hepke, prima metà del XX century (Germany)

Avon Art Pottery, 1930–60 (Great Britain)

John Aynsley & Sons, 1864–1997 (Great Britain)

Baranowka

Baranowka, 1801–1900 (Poland)

Barker Bros, 1876–1981 (Great Britain)

Barlows, 1920–52
(Great Britain)

J.A. Bauer Pottery
Company, 1909–62 (USA)

Bayeux, XX century (France)

J. & M.P. Bell & Co.,
1842–1928 (Great Britain)

Belleek Pottery, dal 1863
(Great Britain)

The Edwin Bennett
Pottery Co., founded in 1846,
Baltimore (USA)

Berlin, Königliche
Porzellan-Manufaktur,
1780–1880 (Germany)

Berlin, Königliche
Porzellan-Manufaktur,
1847–49 (Germany)

Berlin, Königliche
Porzellan-Manufaktur,
1849–70 (Germany)

Berlin, Königliche
Porzellan-Manufaktur,
1857 (Germany)

Berlin, Königliche
Porzellan-Manufaktur,
1875–1944 (Germany)

Berliner Kunstkeramik,
since 1945

Beswick, 1894–1969
(Great Britain)

Biot, XX century (France)

Birks, Rawlins & Co.,
1900–33 (Great Britain)

BGH

Birmingham Guild
of Handicraft

Birmingham Guild
of Handicraft

Boch Frères, since 1841,
Tournai (Belgium)

Boch Frères, since 1841,
Tournai (Belgium)

BOLERAS

Bolerás, XIX century,
Bélaház (Bohemia)

Bolerás, XIX century,
Bélaház (Bohemia)

Bolerás, trademark of the master
and the manufactory, XIX
century, Bélaház (Bohemia)

Boleslaw, Bunzlauer
Tonwarenfabrik, trademark
of Eduard Küttner,
XX century, Bunzlau (Poland)

C.H. Brannam, since 1879
(Great Britain)

Bretby Art Pottery,
1883–1997 (Great Britain)

Bristol, Putney & Co.,
dal 1852 (Great Britain)

Britannia Pottery Co.,
1920–35 (Great Britain)

Bruxelles, Etterbeek,
L. Demeuldre-Coche,
1920–30 (Belgium)

Bruxelles, Etterbeek,
L. Demeuldre-Coche,
1920–41 (Belgium)

Bucci, since ca. 1920,
Faenza (Italy)

Buffalo Pottery Company,
since 1901 (USA)

Bystrice Pod Hostynem,
1790–1858, Bistritz
(Bohemia)

Cacciapuoti, since 1927,
Milan (Italy)

Duilio Cambellotti,
1907–60, Rome (Italy)

Cantagalli, 1872–1930,
Florence (Italy)

Cantagalli, after 1930,
Florence (Italy)

Carlton Ware, 1890–1987
(Great Britain)

Cauldon Potteries,
1904–85 (Great Britain)

Rodolfo Ceccaroni,
ca. 1920, Pesaro (Italy)

Chesapeake Pottery Co.,
founded in 1880, Baltimore
(USA)

Galileo Chini, Fornaci
di San Lorenzo, 1919–39,
Florence (Italy)

Chodziez, after 1882

C.I.MA
PERUGIA
ITALY

C.I.M.A., Consorzio
Italiano Maioliche Artistiche,
since 1920, Perugia (Italy)

Clifton Art Pottery,
1905–14 (USA)

CMIELOW

Cmielòv, 1796–1882
(Poland)

Cmielòv, 1796–1882
(Poland)

Colclough & Co.,
1887–1931 (Great Britain)

Colombian Art Pottery,
XIX century, Trenton,
New Jersey (USA)

W.T. Copeland & Sons,
XX century, Stoke-on-Trent
(Great Britain)

Copenhagen, Royal Porcelain
Factory, XIX century
(Denmark)

Copenhagen, Royal
Porcelain Factory, 1889
(Denmark)

Copenhagen, Royal
Porcelain Factory, 1905
(Denmark)

Copenhagen, Royal
Porcelain Factory, 1905
(Denmark)

Copenhagen, Royal Porcelain
Factory, since 1929
(Denmark)

Copenhagen, author:
Dahl-Jensen, after 1925

Cowan Pottery,
1912–31 (USA)

Dalwitz, Frank Fischer,
since 1850

Dalwitz, since 1832
(Bohemia)

Dedham Pottery,
1895–1943 (USA)

Delft, XIX century (Holland)

Denby Pottery, since 1809
(Great Britain)

Derby, Royal Crown
Porcelain Co., since 1876
(Great Britain)

Deruta, since XV century
(Italy)

Dresden, XIX century
(Germany)

Dresden, XIX century
(Germany)

Eisenberg, after 1900
(Germany)

EPERIES

Eperies, XIX century
(Hungary)

Fabris, 1917–42,
Milan (Italy)

Fantoni, since 1936,
Florence (Italy)

Fenice, 1922–36,
Albisola (Italy)

Fenton, Crown
Staffordshire China, after
1801 (Great Britain)

Fenton, XIX century
(Great Britain)

S. Fielding & Co.,
1879–1982 (Great Britain)

Andrea Fontebasso Società
Ceramica (S.S.A.F.T.),
XX century, Treviso (Italy)

Fulham Pottery, 1864
(Great Britain)

Fulper Pottery Company,
1860–1935 (Great Britain)

Furga, after 1872, Mantova -
Canetto sull'Oglio (Italy)

Galvani, since 1855,
Pordenone (Italy)

Galvani, since 1855,
Pordenone (Italy)

W.S. George Pottery
Company, 1904–60 (USA)

Ginori, Doccia, 1884–88
(Italy)

Ginori, Doccia, 1884–1901
(Italy)

Ginori, Doccia, moulds
from Capodimonte models,
1850–1903 (Italy)

Gladding - McBean
Company, since 1875 (USA)

The Goodwin Pottery Co.,
founded in 1844,
East Liverpool (USA)

W. H. Goss, 1858–1972
(Great Britain)

A.E. Gray & Co., 1912–61
(Great Britain)

T.G. Green & Co., since 1888
(Great Britain)

Griffin, Smith & Hill,
founded in 1879,
Phoenixville (USA)

Grimwade Bros, 1886–1979
(Great Britain)

Gustavsberg, 1910–40

Hall China Company,
since 1903 (USA)

Hampshire Pottery,
1871–1923 (USA)

Sampson Hancock & Sons,
1858–1937 (Great Britain)

Neale & Palmer

Hanley, Church Works,
XIX century (Great Britain)

Harker Pottery Company,
1889–1975 (USA)

Herend, ca. 1850
(Hungary)

Herend, 1900–34
(Hungary)

Herend, 1897–1938
(Hungary)

I.
C.
S.

I.C.S., Industria Ceramica
Salernitana, first half of
XX century (Italy)

ILCA NERVI

I.L.C.A., Nervi (Italy)

.ILSA..

I.L.S.A., Albisola (Italy)

IROQUOIS
CASUAL
CHINA
Russel
Wright

Iroquois China Company,
1905–69 (USA)

The Jersey City Pottery,
founded in 1829, Jersey City,
New Jersey (USA)

Jugtown Pottery,
dal 1921 (USA)

Kahla, after 1844
(Germany)

Tonwerke Kandern A.G.,
XX century, Kandern
(Germany)

Karlsruhe, Staatliche
Majolika-Manufaktur,
XX century (Germany)

Keramis-Boch, founded in
1850, La Louvière (Belgio)

Kosolná, XIX century
(Bohemia)

Kostelec nad Cernymi Lesy,
XX century (Bohemia)

Kremnica (Körmöcbánya),
XIX century (Bohemia)

Kudinov, XIX century,
Moscow (Russia)

KERA**LVZ**

Kunstkeramik, Loder-Schenk,
XX century, Lucerne
(Switzerland)

. LA FIAMMA "
ALBISOLA

La Fiamma, Albisola (Italy)

LA FIAMMA
ROMA

La Fiamma, Rome (Italy)

LA
SALAMANDRA
PERUGIA
ITALY

La Salamandra, Perugia
(Italy)

Laveno, since 1856 (Italy)

SOCIETA'
CERAMICA ITALIANA

Laveno, since 1856 (Italy)

Laveno, since 1856 (Italy)

Laveno, since 1856 (Italy)

Laveno, since 1856 (Italy)

Leeds, XIX century
(Great Britain)

Lenci
MADE IN ITALY TORINO

Lenci, since 1921, Turin
(Italy)

LENOX

Lenox, since 1889 (USA)

Limoges, XX century
(France)

Limoges, after 1908
(France)

M.V. Lomonosov, 1917,
Leningrad (Russia)

M.V. Lomonosov, 1917,
Leningrad (Russia)

James Macintyre & Co.,
1852–1913 (Great Britain)

B.T. Maling & Sons,
1857–1963 (Great Britain)

M G
A

Mazzotti, Albisola (Italy)

Nelson McCoy Pottery
Company, 1910–90 (USA)

Medalta Potteries, 1916–55
(Canada)

Meissen, since 1725
(Germany)

Melandri, 1919–22,
Faenza (Italy)

Melandri with Zoli,
1920–21, Faenza (Italy)

Melandri with Focaccia,
1922–31, Faenza (Italy)

Melandri, 1932–43,
Faenza (Italy)

S.C.L.C
CAGLIARI
SARDEGNA
MELIS

Melchiorre Melis, since 1925,
Cagliari (Italy)

Merrimac Ceramic Co.,
founded in 1897,
Newburyport (USA)

W.R. Midwinter, 1910–87
(Great Britain)

Minghetti, Bologna
(Italy)

Minton, 1793–1968
(Great Britain)

Modra, main trademark,
XIX century, Modor (Bohemia)

Modra, XIX–XX century,
Modor (Bohemia)

Moravian Pottery and Tile
Works, XIX century,
Doylestown (USA)

Münchner Majolika
Werkstätte, XX century,
Mering (Germany)

Murán, XIX century,
Murány (Bohemia)

Nestved, author: H. Kähler,
XIX century (Denmark)

New Chelsea Porcelain Co.,
1910–51 (Great Britain)

New England Pottery & Co.,
founded in 1866,
East Boston (USA)

Newcomb College,
founded in 1896,
New Orleans (USA)

Newport Pottery Co.,
1920–64 (Great Britain)

Niéborov, 1880–92
(Poland)

Norton Pottery Co.,
founded in 1793,
Bennington (USA)

Nymphenburg, since 1747,
Munich (Germany)

Omega Workshops, 1913–20
(Great Britain)

Onondaga Pottery Co.,
since 1871 (USA)

Österreichischer
Werkbund e GmbH,
XX century, Vienna (Austria)

Ott & Brewer Company,
ca. 1900, Trenton,
New Jersey (USA)

Paden City, 1914–63
(USA)

Papa, XIX century
(Hungary)

Paragon China Co.,
1899–1968 (Great Britain)

Passau, second half of XIX
century (Germany)

Pécs, Zsolnay, since 1855
(Hungary)

Pécs, Zsolnay, since 1855
(Hungary)

Pennsylvania Museum and
School of Industrial Art,
founded in 1903
Philadelphia (USA)

Peters & Reed Pottery,
1898–1957 (USA)

Pfaltzgraff Pottery,
since 1894 (USA)

Pickard China Company,
since 1894 (USA)

Pilkington's Tile &
Pottery Co., 1899–1975
(Great Britain)

Piombati, Florence (Italy)

Poole Pottery, 1873–1992
(Great Britain)

Samuel Radford, 1879–1957
(Great Britain)

Red Wing Potteries,
1877–1967 (USA)

Richard, 1840–96,
Milan (Italy)

Richard-Ginori, Doccia, since
1896, Sesto Fiorentino (Italy)

Richard-Ginori, Mondovì
(Italy)

Richard-Ginori, San
Cristoforo, Milan (Italy)

Richard-Ginori, Serpentina,
1903, Milan (Italy)

A.G. Richardson,
1915–74 (Great Britain)

Robinson-Ransbottom,
since 1901 (USA)

Roblin, founded in 1899,
San Francisco (USA)

Rometti, since 1927,
Umbertide (Italy)

Rookwood Pottery
Company, 1880–1967 (USA)

Rörstrand, since 1725
(Sweden)

Roseville Pottery,
1890–1954 (USA)

Rosenthal A.G., after 1877,
Selb (Germany)

Rosenthal A.G., after 1908,
Selb (Germany)

Rosenthal A.G., 1933–53,
Selb (Germany)

Royal Crown Derby,
1877–1973 (Great Britain)

Royal Doulton, 1815–1968
(Great Britain)

Rozenburg, 1885–1905
(Holland)

Ruskin Pottery, 1898–1933
(Great Britain)

Salamander Works,
founded in 1848, New York
(USA)

San Pietroburgo,
Imperial Manufactory,
1891–1917 (Russia)

Santa Lucia, Siena (Italy)

Sèvres, since 1738 (France)

Sèvres, since 1738 (France)

Sèvres, Second Empire period
(France)

Shawnee Pottery Company,
1894–1982 (Great Britain)

Shelley Potteries, 1853–1972
(Great Britain)

Shelton, XX century
(Great Britain)

Signa, Società Industriale,
XX century, Florence (Italy)

Sipla, Rome (Italy)

Società Ceramica
Lombarda, end of XIX
and XX century, Milan (Italy)

Società Industria
Maioliche Abruzzese,
XX century, Castelli (Italy)

Soho Pottery Ltd.,
XIX–XX century, Cobridge
(Great Britain)

S.P.I.C.A., Rome (Italy)

The Stockton Art
Pottery Co., founded in the
second half of XIX century,
Stockton (USA)

Tosin, since 1922, Vicenza
(Italy)

Villeroy & Boch Keramische
Werke A.G., XX century,
Dresden (Germany)

Wedgwood & Co.,
XX century, Tunstall,
Staffordshire (Great Britain)

Wheeling Pottery Co.,
founded in 1879, Wheeling
(USA)

Wien Augarten, after 1922
(Austria)

Wiener Kunstkeramik
und Porzellanmanufakturen
Keramos, XX century,
Vienna (Austria)

Worcester, since 1862
(Great Britain)

Wroclaw, XX century,
Breslau (Poland)

Zaccagnini, since 1936,
Florence (Italy)

Zama, since 1929, Faenza
(Italy)

Suggested Bibliography

Suggested Bibliography

General reference books and dictionaries

Among the most exhaustive dictionaries are J. Fleming, H. Honour, *Dizionario delle arti minori e decorative*, Milan 1980; Pepe, *Dizionario dell'Antiquariato*, Torino; *Storia e tecniche delle arti decorative*, Novara 1988; especially on glasses: H. Newman, *Dizionario del vetro*, Milan 1993.

For a general orientation in modern decorative arts: *Guida all'antiquariato*, ed. by J. and M. Miller, Novara 1991; P. De Vecchi, *Guida al Modernariato e agli oggetti del '900*, Milan 1992; I. de Guttry, M.P. Maino, M. Quesada, *Le arti minori d'autore in Italia dal 1900 al 1930*, Rome-Bari 1985, and *Le arti decorative in Lombardia nell'età moderna 1780-1940*, ed. by V. Terraroli, Milan 1999.

Trademarks

On European ceramics: J. Kybalòva, *I marchi delle ceramiche*, Prague 1981; on European porcelain: E. Poche, *I marchi delle porcellane*, Prague 1991; and also J. Fleming, H. Honour, *op. cit.*; on Italian ceramics: *Mostra della ceramica italiana 1920-1940*, Turin 1982; on English and United States ceramics: P. Atterbury, E.P. Denker, M. Batkin, *Twentieth-Century Ceramics*, London 1999; D. Zuehlsdorff, *Ceramic Marks Encyclopedia 1885-1935*, New York 1999; on European silver: *Jugendstil schmuck. Die*

europäischen Zentren von 1895 bis 1915, ed. by U. von Hase-Schmudt, Munich 1998, appendix; J. Culme, *The Dictionary of Gold and Silversmiths, Jewellers and Allied Traders 1838-1914*, New York 1999; on English silver: *English Silver Hall-Marks*, ed. by J. Banister, London 1970; on glass: C. Hartmann, *Glass Marks Encyclopedia 1600-1945*, New York 1999.

Fairs and exhibitions

Fundamental reference books on the birth of modern decorative arts are *Le arti decorative alle grandi esposizioni universali 1851-1900*, ed. by D. Alcouffe, M. Bascou, A. Dion-Tenenbaum, Ph.Thiébaut, Milan 1988; L. Aimone, C. Olmo, *Le esposizioni universali 1851-1900. Il progresso in scena*, Turin 1990. More specifically, on 1902 Turin exhibition: *Torino 1902. Le arti decorative internazionali del nuovo secolo*, exhibition catalogue, ed. by R. Bossaglia, E. Godoli, M. Rosci, Turin 1994; on Monza Biennales: besides historical catalogues, V. Terraroli, *Le arti decorative in Lombardia tra Ottocento e Novecento nel dibattito tra artigianato e industria*, in *Le arti decorative... cit.*, and *L'ISIA a Monza. Una scuola d'arte europea*, ed. by R. Bossaglia, Monza 1986; on 1925 Paris exhibition: G. D'Amato, *Fortuna e immagini dell'Arte Déco. Parigi 1925*, Rome-Bari 1991;

on 1942 Rome exhibition: *E42. Utopia e scenario del regime*, ed. by M. Calvesi, E. Guidoni, S. Lux, Venice 1987.

Biedermeier and late-romantic period

Biedermeier. Arte e cultura nella Mitteleuropa 1815-1848, exhibition catalogue, Milan 2000; on furnishings: *Il mobile dell'Ottocento*, ed. by A. Boidi Sasone, E. Cozzi, M. Griffo, A. Ponte, G.C. Sciolla, Novara 1997.

Art nouveau

G. Fahr-Becker, *Art Nouveau*, Cologne 1997; *Art Nouveau 1890-1914*, exhibition catalogue, ed. by P. Greenhaulgh, London 2000; Austria: *Le arti a Vienna. Dalla Secession alla caduta dell'impero asburgico*, Milan 1984; W. Neuwirth, *Wiener Werkstätte. Avantgarde, Art Déco, Industrial design*, Vienna 1984; *Dagobert Peche und die Wiener Werkstätte*, exhibition catalogue, ed. by P. Noever, Vienna 1998; *Jugendstil schmuck. Die europäischen Zentren von 1895 bis 1915*, 1998; *Wiener Werkstätte. L'artigianato diventa arte 1903-1913*, Milan 1990; *MAC, Museo Austriaco di Arti Applicate di Vienna*, ed. by P. Noever, Vienna 1995; France: *Musée d'Orsay. Catalogue sommaire illustré des arts décoratifs*; N.Y. Troy, *Modernism and the Decorative Arts in France. Art Nouveau to Le Courbusier*, New York 1991; M. Draguet,

L'Art Nouveau retrouvé à travers les collections Anne-Marie Gillion Crowet, Milano 1999; Germany: *Jugendstil. Kunst im 1900*, Darmstadt 1982; K.J. Sembach, *Jugendstil. L'utopia dell'armonia*, Cologne 1991; *Jugendstil in Dresden. Aufbruch in die Moderne*, exhibition catalogue, Dresden 1999; Italy: R. Bossaglia, *Il Liberty in Italia*, I ed. 1968, repr. Milan 1997; I. de Guttry, M.P. Maino, *Il mobile liberty italiano*, Milan-Rome 1994; *Torino 1902... cit.*; *Arte a Milano 1906-1929*, exhibition catalogue, Milan 1995; *Aemilia Ars. Arts & Crafts a Bologna 1898-1903*, exhibition catalogue, ed. by C. Bernardini, D. Davanzo Poli, O. Ghetti Baldi, Bologna 2001; *Il Liberty in Italia*, exhibition catalogue, ed. by F. Benzi, Rome 2001.

Art deco

Y. Brunhammer, *Lo stile 1925*, Milan 1966; A. Duncan, *Art Déco*, Milan 1989; D. Klein, N.A. McClelland, M. Haslam, *L'esprit Art déco*, Paris 1991; B. Hillier, S. Escritt, *Art Déco*, 1997; guides: *L'Art Déco*, Milan 1989; *Art Déco*, ed. by E. Knowles, Miller's Antiques Checklist, London 1991; on European deco: *L'Art Déco en Europe. Tendances décoratives dans les arts appliqués vers 1925*, exhibition catalogue, Bruxelles 1989; *Designing Modernity. The Arts of Reform and Persuasion 1885-1945*, exhibition catalogue, ed. by W. Kaplan, Miami 1995; *Art Déco. Boemia 1918-1938*, exhibition catalogue, Milan 1996; on Italian deco: R. Bossaglia, *Il "Déco" italiano. Fisionomia dello stile 1925 in Italia*, Milan 1975; I. de Guttry, M.P. Maino, *Il mobile déco italiano*, Rome-Bari 1988; L. Licitra Ponti, *Gio Ponti. L'opera*, Milan 1990; R. Bossaglia, V. Terraroli, *Milano déco. La fisionomia della città negli anni Venti*, Milan 1999; *La visione del prisma. La collezione Wolfson*, exhibition catalogue, ed. by S. Barisione, M. Fochessati, G. Frantone, Milan 1999.

Furnishings

Il mobile dell'Ottocento, ed. by A. Boidi Sasone, E. Cozzi, M. Griffo, A. Ponte, G.C. Sciolla, Novara 1997; *Il mobile del Novecento*, ed. by R. De Grada, F. Gualdoni, M. Marsich, P. Scarzella, O. Selvafolta, Novara 1996, and in particular the already mentioned books of De Guttry and Maino on Italian furniture (1988 and 1994). Particularly interesting is A. Duncan, *Art Déco Furniture*, London 1984; F. Camond, *Ruhlmann. Master of Art Déco*, New York 1991; *Osvaldo Borsani*, ed. by G. Gramigna, F. Irace, Milan 1992.

Ceramics

Austria: *Michael Powolny. Keramik und Glas aus Wien 1900 und 1950*, ed. by E. Frottier, Vienna

1990; France: E. Pelichet, *La céramique art nouveau*, Lausanne 1976; A. Lajoix, *La cèramique en France 1925-1947*, Paris 1983; V. Brega, *Robj Paris. Le ceramiche 1921-1931*, Milan 1995; *French Art Nouveau Ceramics: Adrien Dalpayrat (1844-1910)*, New York 1999; Germany: *Porzellan. Kunst und Design 1889 bis 1939 vom Jugendstil zum Funktionalismus*, 2 vols, Bröhan-Museum catalogue, Berlin 1993; Great Britain: G. Clark, *The Potter's Art. A Complete History of Pottery in Britain*, Hong Kong 1995; M. Gibson, *19th Century Lustreware*, London 1999; G. Lewis, *A Collector's History of English Pottery*, London 1999; M. Messenger, *Coalport 1795-1926*, London 1999; R. Reilly, *Wedgwood*, London 1999; J. Twitchett, *Derby Porcelain*, London 1999; Italy: F.M. Rosso, *Per virtù del fuoco. Uomini e ceramiche del Novecento italiano*, Aosta 1983; *Manifatture e ceramisti italiani 1900-1960. 36 incontri*, Milano 1989; see also *La ceramica futurista da Balla a Tullio d'Albisola*, ed. by E. Crispolti, Firenze 1982; *Gio Ponti. Ceramiche 1923-1930. Le opere del Museo Ginori di Doccia*, exhibition catalogue, Florence 1983; *Riccardo Gatti (1886-1972) ceramiche*, ed. by G.C. Bojani, Faenza 1987; *Pietro Melandri 1885-1976*, ed. by L. Stefanelli Torossi, Rome 1987; *Duilio Cambellotti e la ceramica a Roma dal 1900 al 1935*, ed. by

M. Quesada, Florence 1988; *La manifattura Richard-Ginori di Doccia*, ed. by R. Monti, Milan-Rome 1988; *La manifattura Chini*, ed. by R. Monti, Rome 1989; G. Conti, G. Cefariello Grosso, *La maiolica Cantagalli e le manifatture ceramiche fiorentine*, Rome 1990; M. Munari, *Guido Andlovitz. Ceramiche di Laveno 1923-1942*, Rome 1990; *Angelo Biancini tra Faenza e Laveno. Ceramiche 1937-1940*, ed. by G.C. Bojani, F. Bertoni, Florence 1992; M. Quesada, *Forme e colori. Ceramica a Roma 1912-1932*, Rome 1992; C. Chilosi, L. Ughetto, *La ceramica del Novecento in Liguria*, Genoa 1995; L. Manna, *Gio Ponti. Le maioliche*, Milan 2000; Hungary: *La ceramica ungherese della Szeceszió*, exhibition catalogue, Florence 1985.

Metals, plastics, enamels and jewels

Carlo Rizzarda e l'arte del ferro battuto in Italia, ed. by A.P. Zugni Tauro, Feltre 1987; *Dagobert Peche und die Wiener Werkstätte*, exhibition catalogue, ed. by P. Noever, Vienna 1998; *Bijoux di un'epoca: bachelite & C.*, ed. by C. Aster Davidov and G. Rendington Dawes, Milan 1989; *Dictionary of Enamelling*, ed. by E. Speel, Plymouth 1998; *I gioielli degli anni '20-'40. Cartier e i grandi del Déco*, exhibition catalogue, Milan 1986; A. Duncan, *The Paris Salons 1895-1914. Jewelry*,

New York 1999; M. Goudly Fales, *Jewelry in America 1600-1900*, New York 1999; *L'arte del gioiello e il gioiello d'artista dal '900 ad oggi*, exhibition catalogue, Florence 2001.

Glasses

Glass 1905-1925. Vom Jugendstil zum Art Déco, Vienna 1985; R. Barovier Mentasti, *Il vetro veneziano 1890-1990*, Venice 1990; M. Barovier, *Carlo Scarpa. I vetri di Murano 1927-1947*, Venice 1991; *Lyricism of Modern Design Swedish Glass 1900-1970*, Tokyo 1992; M. Barovier, *L'arte dei Barovier vetrai di Murano 1866-1972*, Venice 1993; M. Heiremans, *Art Glass from Murano 1910-1970*, Stuttgart 1993 (with an appendix devoted to trademarks of manufactories and laboratories); F. Le Tacon, *L'Oeuvre de verre d'Emile Gallé*, Paris 1998; *Fontana Arte*, ed. by L. Falconi, Milan 1998; R. Barovier Mentasti, *Napoleone Martinuzzi vetraio del Novecento*, Venice 1992; J. Zapata, *Tiffany*, London 1993; *Orrefors Glass*, ed. by A. Duncan, London 1999; *Venini. Catalogo ragionato 1921-1986*, ed. by A. Venini Diaz de Santillana, Milan 2000; *Sklarna Lötz 1880-1940*, Prague n.d.